Confucianism and Family Rituals
in Imperial China

Confucianism and Family Rituals in Imperial China

A SOCIAL HISTORY OF WRITING ABOUT RITES

Patricia Buckley Ebrey

PRINCETON UNIVERSITY PRESS

PRINCETON, NEW JERSEY

Copyright © 1991 by Princeton University Press
Published by Princeton University Press, 41 William Street,
Princeton, New Jersey 08540
In the United Kingdom: Princeton University Press, Chichester, West Sussex

Library of Congress Cataloging-in-Publication Data

Ebrey, Patricia Buckley, 1947–
Confucianism and family rituals in imperial China : a social
history of writing about rites / Patricia Buckley Ebrey.
p. cm.
Includes bibliographical references and index.
1. China—Social life and customs. 2. Confucianism—
China—Rituals. I. Title.
DS721.E336   1991   951—dc20   91-7488

ISBN 0-691-03150-9

The preparation of this volume was aided by a grant from the National
Endowment for the Humanities, an independent federal agency

We are grateful to the Chiang Ching-kuo Foundation for International
Scholarly Exchange for its support. We also wish to thank the Research Board,
University of Illinois at Urbana-Champaign, for a publication subvention

This book has been composed in Linotron Times Roman

Princeton University Press books are printed on acid-free paper
and meet the guidelines for permanence and durability of the
Committee on Production Guidelines for Book Longevity of the
Council on Library Resources

Printed in the United States of America

3   5   7   9   10   8   6   4   2

For my parents

Miriam and John Buckley

CONTENTS

PREFACE

CONFUCIAN scholars wrote books about ritual. Funerals, weddings, and ancestral rites were prominent features of family life in China, giving drama to transitions in people's lives. In this book I try to link these texts to these rituals. I trace the multistranded connections between Chinese family rituals, the Confucian texts that specified how to perform these rites, and the society in which rituals were performed and books written. I try to show the complex interaction of authors' experiences, the ideas they articulated, the common ideas diffused throughout society, the intended and unintended effects of the efforts of the state and other privileged groups to control ideas and practices, and the ritual behavior of people at various social levels. The subtle distinctions among different ways of thinking about ritual are important to the story of this book, but no more important than the social and cultural processes through which texts were written, circulated, interpreted, and used as guides to actions.

Since in this book I emphasize how ideas take shape in social contexts, it is only right to point out how my own have been so shaped. Over the past six years, my approach to the subject of this book has been sharpened and redirected as a result of interaction with other scholars at conferences, meetings, and colloquia. These include the conferences on Neo-Confucian Education (1984), Death Rituals (1985), Religion and Society in the T'ang and Sung (1989), and Rituals and Scriptures in Chinese Popular Religion (1990), as well as seminars and colloquia at Columbia, Harvard, Illinois, Michigan, and Princeton. Similarly the final shape of this book reflects my response to the comments of scholars who read one or another of three successive drafts. These include four colleagues at the University of Illinois: Ann Anagnost, Kai-wing Chow, Peter Gregory, and JaHyun Haboush; and seven colleagues from elsewhere—Peter Bol of Harvard University, Beverly Bossler of Connecticut College, Wing-tsit Chan of Chatham College, Robert Hymes of Columbia University, Frederic Mote of Princeton University, Kidder Smith of Bowdoin College, and Rubie Watson of the University of Pittsburgh. All of these readers made remarks that sent me back to my material and forced me to rethink inferences I was drawing from it. Even when I did not follow their advice, it shaped my next draft, as I presented more evidence, brought in new arguments, or shifted my emphasis. I am thus very much in their debt.

Material circumstances also influenced the course of my work on this book. I probably would not have translated Chu Hsi's *Family Rituals* without the released time made possible by grants from the translation program of the National Endowment for the Humanities in 1986 and 1989. And I would not have written this book had I not been forced, when translating that text, to come to grips with the social, intellectual, and political context in which it was written and used. A grant from the Committee on Scholarly Communication with the People's Republic of China for short trips to China in the summers of 1988 and 1989 made it possible for me to locate and read the Ming and Ch'ing ritual manuals central to my arguments about texts. I would not have been able to complete this book as quickly without the research assistant supported by funds from the Research Board of the University of Illinois during the final year of my work. Miss Chiu-yueh Lai kept me from sinking under the weight of endless details by cheerfully and conscientiously checking citations, comparing texts, and typing the bibliography into a Chinese word-processing system.

Need I add that my family situation was not irrelevant. As always, I have found it easier to absorb myself in the history of China because I have a husband who assumes my work is important and two good-natured sons who make sure I do not let it become too important. Moreover, the typically American ways they keep ritual to a minimum in our family served to remind me that I was studying a phenomenon relatively far from my own experience.

ABBREVIATIONS

CCSLCT	*Chih-chai shu-lu chieh-t'i*
CL	*Chu Tzu chia-li* (*Chu Tzu ch'eng-shu* ed.)
CLCS	*Chia-li chi-shuo* (1589 ed.)
CLIC	*Chia-li i-chieh* (Ch'iu Chün's)
CLHT	*Chia-li hui-t'ung* (T'ang To's)
c.s.	*chin-shih* degree
CTC	*Chang Tsai chi*
DMB	*Dictionary of Ming Biography*, ed. Goodrich and Fang
ECC	*Erh Ch'eng chi*
HLTC	*Hsing-li ta-ch'üan* (1415 ed.)
NHC	*Nan-hsüan chi*
NP	*Chu Tzu nien-p'u*
PHTCC	*Pei-hsi ta-ch'üan chi*
SKCS	*Ssu-k'u ch'üan-shu*
SMSSI	*Ssu-ma shih shu-i*
SMWCKCCC	*Ssu-ma Wen-cheng kung ch'uan-chia chi*
SS	*Sung shih*
TLC	*Tung-lai chi*
TSCC	*Ts'ung-shu chi-ch'eng*
WC	*Chu Wen-kung wen-chi*
YL	*Chu Tzu yü-lei*

Citations of the classics generally give first an indication of the chapter or section, numbered in the *Analects* and *Mencius* but romanized in the other classics. After this is given a page reference in the *Shih-san ching chu-shu* edition and where available a page reference to an English translation. These references are for convenience only; all of the translations given here are my own.

For full bibliographic information, see Sources Cited.

Confucianism and Family Rituals
in Imperial China

Chapter One

INTRODUCTION

SCHOLARS of Chinese civilization have often identified ancestor-oriented family rituals as keys to Chinese culture. In 1849 the missionary and later diplomat S. W. Williams wrote that ancestral rites had had "an influence in the formation of Chinese character, in upholding good order, promoting industry, and cultivating habits of peaceful thrift, beyond all estimation."[1] Benjamin Schwartz has described "the orientation to ancestor worship" as "central to the entire development of Chinese civilization"[2] and Francis L. K. Hsu as "an active ingredient in every aspect of Chinese society."[3] Distinctive features of Chinese family organization have been attributed to ideas about ancestors; Maurice Freedman, for instance, explained that the popular idea that "the dead are somehow dependent on the living for sustenance and support" made it "essential that men and women leave behind them offspring, borne or adopted, to serve them in their mortuary needs."[4] Most observers have judged the social effects of ancestor-oriented rites in largely positive terms. Criticisms have also sometimes been voiced, however. James Addison charged these rites with fostering extreme conservatism: "any change appears disrespectful to the departed; and the dead thus rule the living."[5] Edwin D. Harvey argued that they threatened "the welfare and standards of living of the masses" by promoting large families.[6]

Periodic offerings of food and drink to ancestors were the ancestor-oriented ritual par excellence, but ancestors were also central to the other family rituals: cappings and pinning (initiation ceremonies for men and women respectively), weddings, and funerals. Capping and pinning introduce family members to the ancestors as adults and prepare them for marriage. Marriages provide for new family members who will serve the ancestors. Funerals and burials concern the gradual transformation of the dead into ancestral spirits. The way people performed these rituals not only enhanced their understandings of an-

[1] Williams, "The Worship of Ancestors among the Chinese," p. 30. Cf. Johnston, *Lion and Dragon in Northern China*, p. 349.

[2] Schwartz, *The World of Thought in Ancient China*, pp. 20–21. Cf. Bodde, *Essays on Chinese Civilization*, p. 133.

[3] Hsu, *Americans and Chinese*, pp. 230–31.

[4] Freedman, *Lineage Organization in Southeastern China*, p. 88. Cf. Yang, *Religion in Chinese Society*, p. 296.

[5] Addison, *Chinese Ancestor Worship*, p. 56.

[6] Harvey, *The Mind of China*, p. 230.

cestors, but also contributed to the relatively high degree of social integration in late imperial China. James Watson and Evelyn Rawski have asserted that "the rituals performed at marriage and at death were central to definitions of Chinese cultural identity."[7]

The importance of family rituals in Chinese society and culture is not surprising in comparative terms. Anthropologists studying a wide variety of societies have repeatedly shown how rituals create and convey basic cultural premises.[8] Through the performance of rituals people act out many of the most fundamental structures of meaning in their society, the sets of ideas and discriminations that help them interpret themselves and their relations to others. Ritual action, thus, helps reproduce culture, especially the realm of culture that seldom enters into conscious choice, the realm taken for granted, left outside the limits of debate. The principles conveyed in this way frequently serve to legitimate the social and political structure, making social distinctions part of what is taken to be in the nature of things. Participation in rituals is a public and bodily way to acknowledge these social and cosmic orders. Yet rituals do not simply express distinctions. Through a symbolic logic special to rituals, distinctions can be both expressed and denied; a single ritual or ritual sequence can both confirm distinctions and overcome them, creating sentiments of solidarity and unity. Rituals, thus, do not simply reinforce the principles of a society that exists for other reasons; they are implicated in the creation of the distinctions on which the society is based and the dynamics of resolving conflicts.[9] In the Chinese case, it has long been recognized that notions of patrilineality and assumptions about the mutual dependence of the living and the dead—ideas that structured Chinese kinship organization—were conveyed through family rituals. Conceptions of gender inequalities and social hierarchies that were basic to social relations beyond kinship—how to serve and be served, the ambiguities of dependence and deference—were also re-

---

[7] Watson and Rawski, eds., *Death Ritual in Late Imperial and Modern China*, p. ix.

[8] For the purposes used here, *ritual* may be defined as culturally constructed, patterned sequences of acts. Although anthropologists offer a wide variety of definitions of ritual, few are so narrow as to exclude the consciously staged, special-occasion rituals discussed in this book. Anthropologists often phrase their topic in terms of ritual rather than religion to avoid having to distinguish religion from the sorts of activities generally considered magic, superstition, or dabbling in the occult and also to bring out the structural similarities of religious and secular rituals.

Focus on ritual also works well in the Chinese case, as the religious dimensions of family rituals not only varied from ritual to ritual (weddings were less involved with the realm of ancestors than funerals were), but from person to person as understandings of ancestors were highly variable. Ritual as a conceptual focus also works well because there are broad similarities between modern ways of thinking about ritual and Chinese conceptions of *li*. For a discussion of these similarities, see Wechsler, *Offerings of Jade and Silk*, pp. 20–30.

[9] For a variety of good discussions of anthropological approaches to ritual, see Geertz, *Local Knowledge*, pp. 19–35; Bloch, *From Blessing to Violence*, esp. pp. 1–11; Tambiah, *Culture, Thought, and Social Action*, pp. 123–66; Moore and Myerhoff, eds., "Introduction," in *Secular Ritual*.

produced through the performance of weddings, funerals, and ancestral rites.[10]

What does make the Chinese case unusual is the longevity of much of the symbolic content of these family rituals. Many steps described in the early classics as aristocratic practice continued to be performed two thousand years later by common people, despite great changes in social structure and the introduction of radically different cosmological conceptions with Buddhism. In the nineteenth and early twentieth centuries, nearly every home had an ancestral altar where offerings were made at regular intervals. For major rites all the members of the family would assemble and show obeisance.[11] Betrothals were negotiated between family heads with the help of go-betweens and confirmed with the exchange of gifts. Grooms fetched their brides to their own homes, where the major festivities took place.[12] Funerals regularly involved wailing, placing food and drink before a symbol of the deceased, mourning garments, notification of friends and relatives, and visits of condolence. Bodies were laid out in clothes, wrapped in shrouds, and placed in thick coffins. The procession to the graveyard was a major public ceremony, and post-burial rites of various sorts were commonly performed.[13] If rituals convey basic cosmic principles legitimating the social order, how could the same principles legitimate markedly different social formations? If family rituals validate the social distinctions underlying family organization, how could they work as well in different types of families? Historical investigation can provide insight into these questions because it allows one to see the effects of change and thus to distinguish correspondences and co-occurrences from causes and effects.[14]

[10] Despite general recognition of these relationships, there have been relatively few detailed analyses of the meanings conveyed by Chinese family rituals. But see Thompson, "Death, Food, and Fertility," for an analysis of the "semantics" of food in funerary rituals in modern Taiwan; Martin, "Gender and Ideological Differences in Representations of Life and Death," also on funeral rituals; and Zito, "City Gods, Filiality, and Hegemony in Late Imperial China," on imperial ancestral rites. See also, for a more general account, Freedman, "Ritual Aspects of Chinese Kinship and Marriage."

[11] Descriptions of how people performed ancestral rites are found in Doolittle, *Social Life of the Chinese* 1:217–35; Gray, *China*, pp. 84–85, 320–22; Johnston, *Lion and Dragon*, pp. 276–81; Duara, *Culture, Power, and the State*, pp. 96–100; Hsu, *Under the Ancestors' Shadow*, pp. 50–52, 183–92; Jordan, *Gods, Ghosts, and Ancestors*, pp. 93–102; Ahern, *Cult of the Dead*, pp. 91–174; Harrell, *Ploughshare Village*, pp. 194–206; Weller, *Unities and Diversities*, pp. 24–28.

[12] For descriptions of weddings, see Doolittle, *Social Life*, 1:65–98; Gray, *China*, pp. 189–212; Fielde, *Corner of Cathay*, pp. 35–44; Doré, *Researches into Chinese Superstitions* 1:29–39; Freedman, *Study of Chinese Society*, pp. 235–72; Cohen, *House United, House Divided*, pp. 149–91; Rubie Watson, "Class Differences and Affinal Relations in South China."

[13] The fullest description of mortuary rites is de Groot, *Religious System of China*, but see also Doolittle, *Social Life* 1:168–216; Gray, *China*, pp. 278–328; Fielde, *Corner of Cathay*, pp. 49–70; Doré, *Researches* 1:41–68; Walshe, "Some Chinese Funeral Customs."

[14] Anthropologists are coming to recognize the importance of historical investigations into questions of this sort. Bloch, in *From Blessing to Violence*, p. 9, argues that only by studying "the reality of the historical process" can one account for "the complexity and the many facets

In order to explore the historical relationship between Chinese family rituals and Chinese society, in this book I focus on the mediating role of texts. In the case of a highly literate, stratified society like China, it is too simplistic to talk simply of rituals and social organization. The production, interpretation, certification, circulation, and use of texts all played major roles in perpetuating and redesigning ritual forms.[15] The most relevant texts were ones tied to the Confucian intellectual tradition. One of the early Confucian classics, the *I-li* [Etiquette and ritual], provided step-by-step instructions on how *shih* (lower officers, gentlemen) should perform family rituals. Another of the classics, the *Li-chi* [Record of ritual], provided interpretations of these and other rituals. From Han times (202 B.C.–A.D. 220) on, these texts set many of the parameters of debate within Confucianism about how family rituals should be performed. Nevertheless the imperial governments regularly issued detailed liturgies for the emperor, his relatives, and officials, and some scholars wrote unofficial guides to proper official performance. From the Sung dynasty (960–1279) on, liturgies were available for people in general, not divided by political rank, most notably the *Family Rituals* compiled by the great Neo-Confucian philosopher Chu Hsi (1130–1200), using an earlier manual by the statesman Ssu-ma Kuang (1019–1086) and the ideas of the philosopher Ch'eng I (1033–1107).[16] After the publication of Chu Hsi's *Family Rituals* in the early thirteenth century, it quickly became the standard reference work on the proper way to perform these family rituals. In less than a century two commentaries had been written for it, and a set of illustrations had been prepared that commonly came to be published with it. In Ming (1368–1644) and Ch'ing (1644–1911) times, dozens of expanded, revised, and simplified versions of it were published, the best known of which was by Ch'iu Chün (1421–1495). These Confucian liturgies were among the most common books in circulation in late imperial China. Familiarity with them shaped how people approached the performance of rites: they saw family rituals not simply as sets of gestures and words, but gestures and words for which there were written sources of authority. Those who had power over the production of these texts had influence over the ritual behavior of both the educated and uneducated and through

---

of rituals'' and thus avoid the reductionism that implies that rituals were created to communicate cosmological schemes or to give solidarity to groups. For the efforts of both historians and anthropologists to explore the historical creation of rituals, see Hobsbawm and Ranger, eds., *The Invention of Tradition*. Quite a few historians of Europe have recently written sophisticated studies of ritual in historical context. A few that concern rituals analogous to Chinese family rituals include Klapisch-Zuber, *Women, Family, and Ritual in Renaissance Italy*, esp. pp. 178–260; Brown, ''Death and the Human Body in the Later Middle Ages''; and Davis, ''Ghosts, Kin, and Progeny.''

[15] For analyses of the ways the existence of texts changes many basic social and cultural processes, see Stock, *The Implications of Literacy*, and Goody, *The Logic of Writing and the Organization of Society*.

[16] I have translated and annotated this book; see Ebrey, trans., *Chu Hsi's Family Rituals*.

that the creation of some of their most deeply held mental, moral, and emotional constructs.

In other societies besides China, texts have played significant roles in mediating the relationship between ritual and society. In both Christian and Islamic societies there were liturgical texts that described how rituals should be performed and experts who claimed special knowledge in the interpretation of these texts. China's experts, however, were not clerics, invested with special powers beyond literacy. In China there was no institutional structure comparable to the ecclesiastical establishments of the West or the Islamic world able to rule on the interpretation of canonical texts, to enforce adherence to Confucian liturgical schedules, or to provide trained experts to officiate. In China the *Family Rituals* may have become orthodox, but interpretation of it remained elastic and adherence to it remained voluntary. Not only did the church in the West regularly issue rules on key family ceremonies (baptism, confirmation, weddings, last rites, funerals, masses for the dead), but it had ways to discipline both church members and clergy in case of deviations.[17] The Chinese state did regularly issue guidelines for the performance of these rites, and made considerable efforts to publicize them. Yet it provided very little in the way of discipline for either ordinary people or the experts they employed. Moreover, the state did not deny support for Buddhism, even though Buddhist practices were invariably rejected in Confucian liturgies. Thus Confucian texts influenced ritual performance through social and political processes rather different from those in the premodern West. Understanding these distinctively Chinese mechanisms for achieving social and cultural cohesion is a major goal of this book.

In Confucian theory, ritual was seen as an alternative to force. People who routinely performed proper rituals were expected to recognize their social and ethical obligations and act on them. Yet power clearly entered into the relationships of rituals, texts, and society. Power is an intrinsic aspect of ritual itself. Those participating in a ritual are constrained to act in highly invariant ways.[18] Ideas, including ideas about how to perform rituals, also have power, a power that can be enhanced through publication, certification, and promotion. The state frequently asserted its supremacy in the realm of instituting rites. When private scholars wrote or edited liturgies, they were intruding on this role, attempting to redefine and reformulate the standards of ritualized behavior and often to appropriate to themselves established traditions that in the process they subtly altered.[19]

The ways texts mediated between ritual and society can be roughly divided

---

[17] See Duby, *The Knight, the Lady and the Priest*, on making marriage into a sacrament, and Aries, *The Hour of Our Death*, pp. 140–201, on the "clericalization" of death rituals.

[18] Cf. Bloch, *Ritual, History and Power*, pp. 19–45.

[19] On the power that comes from being able to establish the general symbolic framework of a society, see Lears, "The Concept of Cultural Hegemony."

into three processes: authorship, certification and circulation, and influence on performance. Each of these processes was complex in its own right. Authors were never passive vehicles for generating the rituals appropriate to a given society. Authors' mentalities were shaped in diverse ways by the social world around them. They had personal experience of the performance of family rituals and these experiences informed what they considered true and desirable. They had ideas not directly tied to ritual but that impinged on their thinking about how rituals should be performed, such as ideas about death and souls, the differences between men and women, and the sanctity and authority of the classics. Moreover when they wrote a book, they were not merely expressing ideas; they were performing an act that had social and political implications.

After texts were written, they needed to circulate to have much influence on how rituals were performed. Scholars, officials, and readers all took part in the process of certifying and circulating texts on ritual. Scholars attempted to establish the validity or invalidity of each others' texts in intellectual debate. The government, through its officials, encouraged adherence to particular texts. The readers of texts participated in granting them authority by buying the ones they found most useful. Those who wished to promote the use of particular liturgies were thus constrained by a partially free market: a book would not be widely purchased if it specified ritual forms most people found impossible to follow.

The circulation of liturgical texts could have shaped ritual behavior even of illiterates who had never seen a copy of any text. Knowing that such books existed, they would have assumed that there was a textual explanation for any step in a rite, much as we assume there is a physical explanation for the weather without being able to state it; this assumption would affect in subtle ways their notions of what they were doing and their willingness to improvise. But texts can also be consulted to decide what to do in a rite. Consulting a text is an act of interpretation. Even highly educated scholars disagreed on how to consult the *Family Rituals*. Did one take a free interpretation, seeking to distinguish essential principles from trivial, amendable details? Or did one take a literal interpretation, attempting to enact all of the steps and procedures described? In China there was no clerical hierarchy to rule on the validity of conflicting interpretations, so differences of opinion were accepted as inevitable.

Influence in the Chinese case was also made more problematic because Confucianism was not the only set of ideas present in Chinese society. The Confucian discourse tended to dominate discussion of family rituals, but it never succeeded in excluding all rivals. Temple-based worship of gods communicated ideas about the ways spirits were most efficaciously served. Buddhist and Taoist priests professed expertise in performing ceremonies that would aid the salvation of the dead. Astrologers and geomancers claimed special knowledge about how to select spouses and grave sites and decide on the best timing of each step in funerals and weddings. It was not enough for Confucian prescriptions to be widely known: they also had to be as compelling as alternatives or reconcilable with them.

The historical sources I have been able to draw on to study these processes are inevitably uneven. Confucian writings are best suited to presenting an internal view of the Confucian discourse on family rituals, of showing how authors interpreted earlier texts, analyzed contradictions among them, and shifted the issues of debate. To examine as well the ways external social, political, and cultural circumstances shaped their interpretations, I have tried to draw attention to the historical context in which writers lived. Scholars like Ssu-ma Kuang, Ch'eng I, Chu Hsi, and Ch'iu Chün negotiated between two complicated worlds. One was the world of the people they knew, a world that included people who sang at weddings, made offerings to their ancestors on Buddhist holidays, and who consulted experts to select burial sites. This world of people and their ritual practices was confusing and inconsistent. People admitted to contradictory beliefs; their practices derived from divergent traditions; and those in one place did things differently than those in another. We often stress the more regular features of this world and label them society or social structure. But to the individual author the particularity of his own experience—what he saw and did—was as powerful as more general patterns, even ones he could explain.

The other world these scholars lived in was the world of books and theories. Books included above all the classics, but also the histories, poetry, essays, and other works that were commonly known to well-educated men. Writers were often deeply influenced by philosophical currents of their time, especially perhaps the ideas they learned from their own teachers. From books and intellectual discussion, scholars acquired visions of society more systematic than the world of living practice they found around them. But certainly this world was also not without its inconsistencies, confusions, and tensions. Even the most educated men grasped ideas in ways that reflected their experiences. In the case of family rites, these experiences included what their own family did, what they had seen those ranked socially higher or lower than them do, and what they had learned of the practices of people in other parts of the country or world. They read the classics with perceptions and feelings deriving from their social experiences and they interpreted their experiences in terms of ideas that came in part from books.

Modern scholars of Confucianism recognize the centrality of *li* (ritual, manners, propriety) in Confucian thought and have analyzed the relationship of *li* to other Confucian ethical and metaphysical concepts.[20] My focus differs in

[20] See, for instance, Tu, "*Li* as a Process of Humanization"; de Bary, "Human Rites: An Essay on Confucianism and Human Rights"; Hall and Ames, *Thinking Through Confucius*, pp. 83–110; and Kao, *Li-hsüeh hsin-t'an*.

two major ways. I look at ritual not from within the Confucian tradition, where *li* is seen as a virtue, an undeniably positive force, but from a contemporary Western viewpoint in which the role of ritual in society is not analyzed in moral terms. Second, I pay less attention to Confucian scholars' most general statements about ritual and more to their concrete ideas about what to do, such as when a bride should be introduced to her husband's ancestors or whether one can make offerings to a deceased grandfather if one's father was a younger son. These topics were not considered trivial or derivative by Confucians of the past, who wrote on them extensively. Lower-order ideas of this sort are the ones most directly tied to social practice; they grew from it, represented it, and generated it. To analyze how texts mediated the performance of rituals, attention must be given to what texts said at this level. This level of ideas is also important because it linked Chinese of all degrees of education; all adults had some understanding of how to act in these ritual situations, and the influence of their understandings constantly crossed class lines. Sometimes ideas of what to do may have changed because of major restructuring of Confucian theoretical orientations at the highest levels of abstraction. At least as often, however, theory was stretched to accommodate or encompass changes in what people, both educated and illiterate, had come to think most fitting to do.

A major advantage of focusing on lower-order ideas is that their concreteness makes them less susceptible to misinterpretation. To understand general claims about ritual (such as "In ritual time is of great importance," or "Ritual is moral principle"), we need to know how those who repeated these claims extended them. How did believing ritual was identical to moral principle affect how a person performed any particular ritual, or which ones he performed, or which ones he told other people to perform? Inferring answers to these questions is risky because it assumes that an author's most general statements adequately sum up his thinking. Men like Ch'eng I and Chu Hsi had participated in weddings, funerals, and ancestral rites long before their philosophical positions became fixed. Their reactions to their experiences played a part in forming their views on what should be done in particular circumstances, even when they cited philosophical premises. This is not to deny that there was coherence in much of what these men thought or wrote, but it is to doubt that their own philosophical generalizations are a fully adequate guide to this coherence.

Texts, of course, are produced by members of an educated elite. In focusing on their mediating role I inevitably give considerable weight to the ways the intellectual elite shaped culture. Undoubtedly there were oral traditions concerning how to bedeck a bride, dress a corpse, and locate a grave. The intellectual elite did not simply impose its interpretations on the rest of society. As I try to show, the creation and certification of texts were dynamic, two-way processes, involving negotiation and conscious and unconscious influence and adaptation. In China as elsewhere the high culture of intellectuals was in continual dialogue with the official culture of the state and the common culture of everyday work, family, and gender relations.[21] Scholars regularly made a distinction between *li*, and *su*. *Li* were authentic rituals, universally valid patterns of acts that had clear relationships to textual sources and could bring about the moral transformation of those performing them. *Su* were customs, the vulgar, familiar traditions that developed in particular times and places, which ordinary people generally followed out of habit and which even the educated might find themselves adopting if they were not on their guard. The elite view of the differences between themselves and ordinary people is certainly not the whole story of their interaction, but given the various sorts of power the intellectual elite possessed, it is an important part of it.[22]

The ways texts mediated between rituals and society is best seen over long periods of time: key texts had effects many centuries after they were written. To allow me to trace some of these effects I have chosen to cover in at least cursory fashion much of Chinese history. The drawback to this approach is, of course, that I have not been able to analyze all facets of my topic in equal depth in each period. I have had to balance the goal of highlighting major changes (a goal requiring some consistency in treatment from one period to the next) with the goal of exploring the complexities of the creation, certification, and use of texts (a goal requiring close attention to selected incidents). The compromise I settled on was to structure the book as a series of case studies linked through time by their association with a key text, Chu Hsi's *Family Rituals*.

In Chapter Two I provide a broad sketch of the ideas expressed in early Confucian texts concerning family rituals. Later scholars' understandings of ritual were shaped not simply by the *I-li* and *Li-chi*, but also by other important early texts that dealt with ritual, including the *Analects*, the commentaries to the *Ch'un-ch'iu*, and the works of Mencius and Hsün Tzu. These texts express a wide range of views on what ritual does, how it is constituted, and how it can be used. This classical discourse assumed a society with kings, feudal lords, ministers, high and low officers, and common people, all of whom passed on their rank and distinct ritual traditions from one generation to the next. After this system was abolished, both the government and private scholars took to writing new manuals more suited to enhancing their authority and standing. These texts preserved much of the classical vocabulary despite the competition of ideas about death, souls, and bodies from outside the Confucian tradition, especially from Buddhism, religious Taoism, and geomancy.

Of all the family rituals, ancestral rites were the most closely tied to rank in Confucian theory, undoubtedly reflecting ancient ideas of ancestors as a

---

[21] For a discussion of how recognition of these processes has influenced the work of intellectual historians of Europe, see Toews, ''Intellectual History after the Linguistic Turn.''

[22] For a good discussion of recent studies on Chinese elite and popular culture, see Bell, ''Religion and Chinese Culture.''

source of power and legitimacy. Canonical rules for the performance of ancestral rites were largely concerned with setting limitations by political rank
on how many ancestors could be served, how often, and with what kinds of
offerings. By the Sung period the discrepancies between these specifications
and both common practice and the actual social hierarchy were too acute for
Confucian scholars to ignore. In Chapter Three I examine the efforts of eleventh-century Neo-Confucians to design a form of ancestral rites that would be
appropriate to their class. I devote a chapter to this one issue because it highlights a central theme of the book: the complex and ambiguous relationship
between class and ritual.

A key element in the later Confucian discourse on family rituals was the
contention that the educated elite and the state should attempt to change the
customary practices of ordinary people as part of their efforts to eliminate
heterodoxy. To understand why eleventh-century scholars saw deviate practices as dangerous, in Chapter Four I describe how the performance of weddings and funerals impinged on the lives of key figures, especially Ssu-ma
Kuang and Ch'eng I.

Chapter Five is devoted to Chu Hsi's work on family rituals, not simply
because he was the author of the *Family Rituals*, but also because he left so
much evidence of what he thought and how he arrived at his ideas, thus allowing a close analysis of what his experiences had to do with what he wrote about
ritual. This chapter, then, is the one in which authorship is most fully explored. I try to explicate not merely why Chu Hsi took the stands he did on
the issues raised by his predecessors, but why he wrote for a broader audience
than any of them had. Close examination of Chu Hsi's letters and discussions
also reveals the social processes through which issues were debated and the
influence that existing liturgies, such as Ssu-ma Kuang's *Shu-i* and the Sung
government's *Cheng-ho wu-li hsin-i*, had on the behavior of well-educated
scholars like Chu Hsi and his students in the twelfth century.

The dimension of power is more fully explored in the next two chapters on
the orthodoxy granted Chu Hsi's *Family Rituals* and on scholars' efforts to
revise its content. The imperial state recurrently asserted its authority in all
matters of defining or establishing correct rituals, an authority scholars would
sometimes dispute. Moreover, the state made sporadic attempts to outlaw undesirable ritual practices and to teach correct ones. But power entered into
shaping the discourse in other ways as well. The proliferation of books that
"revised" the *Family Rituals* can be seen as part of an attempt to control or
appropriate the discourse about correct ritual forms. Chapter Six also provides
a case study of one of the clearest cases of a dynamic relationship between
rituals, ideas about rituals, and social organization: the adaptation of ideas
about ancestral rites to emerging forms of descent-group organization.

To see how liturgical texts structured the way people performed rites, it is
also necessary to examine what the liturgical texts they used actually specified.

Toward this end, in Chapter Seven I examine the content of a dozen revised versions written in the Ming. The adjustments made by these authors were the ones they found necessary to make in practice. Moreover, the influence of Chu Hsi's ideas on common practice was largely filtered through these books, which circulated in larger numbers than Chu Hsi's *Family Rituals* itself.

The story of Confucian liturgies for family rituals roughly parallels the overall intellectual history of the Ming–Ch'ing periods. If the only sources available for reconstructing Chinese intellectual history were the revised versions of the *Family Rituals*, one could still infer that people deferred to Chu Hsi's teachings and state proclamations in the first century of Ming rule but that a major change had occurred by the mid-sixteenth century, probably associated with Wang Yang-ming (1472–1529) and an expansion of printing activity, when short versions of the *Family Rituals*, highly accommodating to popular customs, began to appear in large numbers. Yet it would be difficult to discern any major effects of the philosophical positions argued in leading intellectual circles in the seventeenth and eighteenth centuries. Intellectuals' reassertion of the importance of rooting ritual behavior directly in the classics led them to question the validity of using the *Family Rituals*, but as discussed in Chapter Eight, their qualms did not undermine the broader popularity of the *Family Rituals* in its various versions.

In Chapter Nine I evaluate the influence of the Confucian discourse on what people of all social classes routinely did for domestic family rituals. I argue that Confucian liturgies were particularly influential in establishing a common core of ritual practices. At the same time, liturgies facilitated the elaboration of ritually significant variations by leaving descriptions of many key steps sketchy. To explain why many Confucian injunctions were ignored, I consider the social and emotional context in which rituals were performed and the messages people received from other sources—Buddhist and Taoist clergy, the examples of the rich and powerful, the laws on property transfer, and so on—all of which might pull them in different directions. I also discuss at some length what class had to do with both the performance of rituals and discussions of them.

In the brief concluding chapter I review what has been learned about the role of texts in the creation of ritual forms in China, looking separately at the processes of authorship, certification and circulation, and influence on performances. I then consider the implications of the history of writings about family rituals for our understanding of the history of Chinese society.

Chapter Two

THE EARLY CONFUCIAN DISCOURSE ON FAMILY RITES

When the rituals of funerals and sacrifices are made clear,
the common people will be filial.
—*Ta Tai li-chi*[1]

THE OLDEST of the texts that mediated the performance of family rituals in imperial China were written during the Chou and early Han. These texts reflected and helped create early Chinese society and culture. In the early Chou ancestral rites were central features of political rule. In the late Chou critics of Confucians charged them with performing rituals in an exaggeratedly grave or bookish manner to gain attention. In the Han reputations for filial piety were often based on nearly suicidal mortification during mourning for parents. Family rituals clearly tapped into deeply felt emotions connected with life, death, and the survivors' relations with the dead, and were often used for ends beyond the immediate ones of bringing in brides and disposing of or honoring the dead.

Yet the early Confucian discourse on family rituals cannot be understood solely in terms of the social and emotional realities of ritual. The discourse was powerfully conditioned by the basic philosophical premises of Confucianism. Ritual (*li*) became a central concept in Confucian thinking about human nature, ethics, social harmony, cultural identity, and the relationships between the human world and the sphere labeled heaven. The *Li-chi* [Records of ritual] asserts that all moral and social order is attained through ritual, that without ritual no virtues can be perfected, that observing ritual keeps the powerful from arrogance and the humble from exceeding their station, and that a society in which rituals are observed will be a secure and tranquil one.[2] In passages of these sorts the term *li* was used to encompass the observable actions that constitute rites, ceremonies, manners, and deportment—actions that bind men to each other and link them to numinous realms. *Li* was also culture; Chinese *li* distinguished Chinese from other ethnic groups, each of which had its own *li*.

---

[1] "Sheng-te," 66:279.

[2] Outside the Confucian discourse these claims were not always accepted. Within Taoist philosophy in particular there was a strong distrust for ritual as well as for the imposition of conventional social roles and restraints on behavior in general.

The great bulk of early Confucian writing on ritual concerns the rituals of the ruler and those closest to him, his family, nobles, and highest officials. Domestic family rituals of ordinary people or even officials were, by contrast, treated as relatively marginal in early theorizing on ritual. Yet classical Confucian texts provided many basic premises for Confucian discussions of family rituals over the next two thousand years. This chapter, accordingly, concentrates on the formulation of these basic premises.

ANCESTORS

In ancient China, ancestors were central to the religious imagination, to understandings of spiritual realms and of the place of man in the cosmos. Rituals brought the living into communication with their ancestors; they integrated the human sphere with the numinous sphere beyond. Archaeological evidence for the Shang period (ca. 1500–1050 B.C.) shows the importance of divinations addressed to ancestors and sacrifices offered to the dead, including human and animal sacrifices at burials.[3] Indeed, divinations were often performed to ask the ancestors what types and numbers of victims they would like at a sacrifice.[4] The ancestors of the royal line, the object of most of this activity, were served in great temples where offerings of wine and meat were placed in bronze vessels of awesome beauty. The worldly powers of the kings were believed to depend in no small part on their ancestors' favor; at the same time, the kings' ability to influence the ancestral spirits legitimated their political power.[5] Ancestral rites also linked kings to their kinsmen. The ruling clans had myths of origin from totemic figures, and rites to these and other ancestors were important to the clan's identity and organization.[6]

Textual sources show that these beliefs about the powers and needs of ancestors continued into the early Chou (ca. 1050–500 B.C.). Violence remained central to sacrifice; one served ancestors by killing animals, or sometimes even people.[7] One of the great heroes of early history, the Duke of Chou, is portrayed in the *Book of Documents* as having a deep belief in the power of the ancestors of the royal line to affect the welfare of their descendants and indeed the whole country. When the king was ill, the duke dramatically offered to give up his own life to serve his ancestors in the netherworld if they would spare the king.[8]

Sacrificial odes in the classic *Book of Poetry* portray ancestral rites in early Chou aristocratic circles as emotionally charged rituals of great symbolic

[3] Creel, *Birth of China*, pp. 197–216.
[4] Keightley, *Sources of Shang History*, p. 33.
[5] Keightley, "The Religious Commitment," p. 213.
[6] Chang, *Art, Myth, and Ritual*, pp. 9–16, 33–42.
[7] See Lewis, *Sanctioned Violence in Early China*, pp. 17–28.
[8] *Shang-shu*, "Chin T'eng," 13:6a–13a; Legge, *Chinese Classics* 3:351–60.

power. The ancestor was represented by a human impersonator, often a grandson, who acted as a medium so that the ancestral spirit could be present among those sacrificing to him. The impersonator was offered many glasses of wine, presented the best available food, and entertained with singing and dancing. The descendants, by joining the feast, were in communion with the ancestor present in the impersonator.[9] These odes often express the idea of reciprocity between the living and dead. One ode begins by describing the preparation and careful placement of wine, grain, and meat to be offered to the ancestors. Because the rites are performed meticulously and without mistake, the ancestors will send blessings, especially long life and many descendants.

> The spirits enjoyed their drink and food
> And will grant our lord a long life.
> With full obedience and timeliness
> He performed everything.
> Thus son's sons and grandson's grandsons
> Will continue his line without interruption.[10]

CONFUCIUS AND THE CONCEPT OF *LI*

When later writers used the term *li*, they generally assumed that their readers understood what *li* was and what made it powerful and desirable. The *Analects* of Confucius provided much of the basis for this common ground. In the *Analects* Confucius seldom spoke of specific rituals but did repeatedly refer to the general category of *li*. Despite his great admiration for the early Chou leaders and respect for texts like the *Book of Poetry* and *Book of Documents*, Confucius did not put particular emphasis on communication with ancestors; his concerns were more with human virtue and good government. Sacrificial rituals remained important, but because proper performance of such rituals, especially by rulers, was one of the most effective means of attaining an orderly society and cultivating morality among its members. Thus for Confucius the rituals themselves brought results, rather than the ancestors.[11]

Confucius sometimes tended toward a cosmic view of ritual, attributing great power, even "magic" in Fingarette's sense, to proper performance of *li*.[12] When the disciple Yen Hui asked about true goodness (*jen*), Confucius replied,

---

[9] On early Chou royal ancestral rites, see also Bilsky, *The State Religion of Ancient China*, pp. 31–102.

[10] *Shih-ching*, poem 209, 13B:16a; Waley, *Book of Songs*, p. 211.

[11] Schwartz, *World of Thought*, pp. 49–50, suggests that this attitude may already have been present in the early Chou before Confucius. Bilsky, *State Religion*, pp. 124–30, 162–82, attributes the decline in the importance of ancestral rites to the weakness of the royal court and the rising importance of rites to territorial deities as the religious basis of rule.

[12] Fingarette, *Confucius—the Secular as Sacred*, pp. 1–17.

"Restraining oneself and returning to *li* is true goodness. The whole world would respond to the true goodness of one who could for one day restrain himself and return to *li*." . . . Yen Hui said, "I beg to ask the detailed steps of how to do this." The Master said, "Look at nothing that is contrary to *li*; listen to nothing that is contrary to *li*; speak of nothing that is contrary to *li*; make no movement that is contrary to *li*."[13]

In the first part of this exchange, *li* could be taken to mean propriety or correct behavior in a moral sense, and its power is described as so great that even one day's mastery of it would produce remarkable results. The second part of this exchange shows that *li* was at the same time seen as conformity to an established or external code of behavior regulating every movement, glance, and word.[14]

Confucius validated the idea that preserving a traditional feature of a rite was good in itself, even if it seemed to have no clear moral meaning. When his disciple Tzu-kung wanted to alter the established use of a sacrificial sheep in monthly ceremonies of the Duke of Lu, Confucius disagreed; he said Tzu Kung loved the sheep and therefore wanted to spare it, whereas he had similar feelings toward the rite itself.[15] The aesthetic dimensions of *li* also appealed to Confucius. He was moved by the beauty of well-choreographed ceremonies combining instrumental music, song, and dance. He once described a court dance as at once perfect beauty and perfect goodness.[16]

Although Confucius spoke of conformity to *li*, he expected it to be tempered by reason and custom. Not every detail had to be exactly as in the prescriptions: "The Master said, 'The hemp cap is the *li*, but now a silk one is worn, which is economical, so I follow the common practice. Bowing at the base of the steps is the *li*, but now it is the practice to bow after ascending the steps, which is arrogant. Even though I am opposing the common practice, I follow bowing at the base.' "[17] Confucius also argued that true emotion must lie behind ritual performance, providing ample textual authority for an inner-oriented approach to ritual: "*Li* performed without reverence, the forms of mourning observed without grief, how can I bear to look on these things."[18]

Inward virtues were not all that mattered, however; they needed the discipline of conformity to *li* to be truly effective: "Respect without *li* is tiresome;

[13] *Lun-yü* 12.1, 12:1a; Waley, *Analects*, p. 162.

[14] Chapter 10 of the *Analects* gives many examples of *li* treated as an external or objective code of behavior. The man who has mastered *li*, for instance, "When saluting his colleagues he moves his hands to the right or left as needed, while keeping his robe even in front and behind. He quickly advances with dignity" (*Lun-yü* 10.3, 10:1b; Waley, *Analects*, p. 146).

[15] *Lun-yü* 3.17, 3:10a; Waley, *Analects*, p. 98.

[16] *Lun-yü* 3.25; 3:15b; Waley, *Analects*, p. 99. On the aesthetics of ritual see Eno, "Masters of the Dance," esp. pp. 144–46, 150–51.

[17] *Lun-yü* 9.3, 9:1b; Waley, *Analects*, p. 138.

[18] *Lun-yü* 3.26, 3:15b; Waley, *Analects*, p. 101.

caution without *li* is timidity; boldness without *li* is insubordination; straightforwardness without *li* is rudeness.''[19] Likewise filial piety was not merely an attitude but a pattern of behavior. It required that ''when alive parents should be served according to *li* and when dead they should be buried according to *li* and sacrificed to according to *li*.''[20] Confucius, however, does not seem to have fully explored the implications of seeing moral feelings as deeper than ritual. He did not tell his disciples to scrutinize any discrepancies between their feelings and conventional forms, apparently expecting true inner feelings to be largely congruent with the established forms of ritual behavior.

Confucius saw ritual not only in terms of the personal actions of the ruler but also as part of the way the ruler dealt with his subjects. ''If the people are led by virtue and regulated by *li*, they will have a sense of shame and behave properly.''[21] From other passages in the *Analects* it seems Confucius thought that rulers could rule through ritual by the power of their example and the forms of interaction they initiated.[22] The *Analects* does not discuss teaching the common people ritual.

Confucius's ideas about *li* were inseparable from his ideas about human nature, ethics, and the ideal social order. *Li* was desirable because it brought people to recognize and fulfill their responsibilities toward others. Confucius assumed that everyone recognized the universal necessity of loyalty to lords, filial piety to parents, and love and compassion for children and subordinates. He also assumed that all would share his joy and awe at the prospect of a society in which friction was absent because everyone had a role to serve and served it well, that is, where hierarchical differentiation resulted in harmonious coordination. To a very large extent Confucians in later generations did make these assumptions. Nevertheless, Confucius's references to *li* are brief, and possible contradictions are not explored. Later scholars could not turn to the *Analects* to discover unambiguous answers to such questions as who had the authority to decide what constituted *li* or how to govern through *li*.

THE RITUAL CLASSICS

A key element in the Confucian discourse on ritual was a focus on texts as the repository of correct knowledge about rituals. How to perform a ritual and what each step meant were not secrets known only to gods or priests, but a part of human culture accessible to those who studied the texts of the sages. During the Han period, surviving texts on ritual came to be transmitted as three separate classics, the *Chou-li* [Ritual of Chou], *Li-chi* [Records of rit-

---

[19] *Lun-yü* 8.2, 8:1b; Waley, *Analects*, p. 132.

[20] *Lun-yü* 2.5, 2:2b; Waley, *Analects*, p. 89.

[21] *Lun-yü* 2.3, 2:1b; Waley, *Analects*, p. 88.

[22] E.g., *Lun-yü* 2.20, 2:6b–7a; 8.2, 8:1b; 11.25, 11:10a–11a; 12.2, 12:1b; 13.4, 13:3a; Waley, *Analects*, pp. 92, 132, 159–61, 162, 172.

ual], and *I-li* [Etiquette and ritual]. The *Chou-li* has little to do with family rites, dealing rather with the administrative structure said to characterize the early Chou government. The other two texts, however, became the most authoritative written sources on cappings, weddings, funerals, and ancestral rites. In later centuries scholars who wished to analyze or formulate these domestic ancestor-oriented rites invariably drew from these texts, directly or indirectly.

The *I-li* as it survives today preserves fragments of late Chou liturgies. For capping, marriage, and funeral rites, only the versions for ordinary officers (*shih*) survive. For sacrifices there is also a version for ministers and great officers (*ch'ing-ta-fu*). From other early references it is clear that in Chou times there were liturgies for at least four grades: the king, feudal lords, ministers and great officers, and ordinary officers. There do not seem to have been any Chou texts that prescribed family rites for commoners.[23]

In Han times there were two versions of what is now the *I-li*, the "new text" and "old text." The "new text" was reconstructed from the oral recitation of Kao T'ang during the major effort to recover the classics after the destruction of them during Ch'in times (256–206 B.C.). The "old text" of the *I-li* was a version discovered in the second century B.C. in ancient (seal) script and divided into fifty-six sections. After this discovery ritual scholars continued to teach the "new text" version (two of them, Tai Te and Tai Sheng, arranging the text in different order). In the Later Han, Cheng Hsüan (127–200), the greatest classical scholar of the Han, compared the new and old text versions of the *I-li* and produced a version based on the seventeen-section "new text" but drawing on the "old text" for notes.[24]

This *I-li* as arranged and annotated by Cheng Hsüan became the canonical liturgy for family rituals and the basis for all later imperial or private liturgies. The proper sequence of the steps to be followed and the names of each step were thus largely set by the end of the Han. For the four family rites, these steps were as follows:

Capping

Divining for the day
Inviting guests
Selecting a sponsor by divination and inviting him
Informing those concerned of the hour of the ceremony
Welcoming the sponsor

---

[23] The *Li-chi* contains the famous statement that "The rites do not go down to the commoners," but in context this statement meant that the daily behavior of commoners was not regulated by the same code as that of the nobility and officers. It did not mean that commoners had no rituals or did not perform weddings and funerals. See *Li-chi*, "Ch'ü-li A," 3:6a; Legge, *Rites*, 1:90.

[24] *Shih-chi* 121:3126; *Han-shu* 30:1710; Steele, *The I-li*, pp. xvi–xvii; *Ssu-k'u ch'üan-shu tsung-mu* 20:158–59.

The first capping
The second capping
The third capping
Pledging the initiate
Presenting him to his mother
Conferring an adult name on him
Entertaining the sponsor
Presenting the initiant to the relatives
Presenting him to social and political superiors
Rewarding the sponsor and assistants

Weddings

Sending the betrothal gifts
Asking the girl's name
Sending news of the favorable divination
Sending the wedding gifts
Asking the time of the ceremony
Escorting the bride in person
The shared meal and wine
The bride and groom left alone in the chamber
The bride meeting her parents-in-law the next day

Funerals

Calling back the soul
Plugging the teeth open and propping the feet
Curtaining off the hall
Sending announcements of the death
Taking up places for wailing
Receiving condolences and contributions of grave clothes
Washing the body
Putting food and valuables into the mouth
Putting on grave clothes
Setting up the libation stand and inscribed banner
The preliminary laying out
Receiving gifts
The final laying out
The encoffining
Putting on mourning garments on the third day
Wailing in the morning and evening
Divining for the grave site
Divining for the date of the burial
Taking the coffin out of the hole and presenting it to the ancestors
The farewell libation

Reading the list of contributions and gifts
The procession
The burial
Returning to wail
The sacrifice of repose
Placing the tablet in the ancestral hall
The first sacrifice of good fortune after one year
The second sacrifice of good fortune after two years

Sacrifices

Divining for the day
Divining for the impersonator of the dead
Informing the impersonator and the guests
Inspecting the animals and utensils
Preparing and arranging the food
The impersonator enters and eats
The presiding man exchanges toasts with the impersonator, then offers wine to
the liturgist and assistant
The presiding woman does the same
The presiding woman gives the presiding man a cup of wine, and he does the
same for her
Further exchanging of cups of wine with guests, relatives, and the principal heir
General drinking
The impersonator leaves
The feast

As a liturgy, the *I-li* describes what people are to do, not why they do it or
what each step means. Like any liturgical text, it presents rituals in a funda-
mentally textlike manner. Texts are linear; one word follows another in a single sequence. In actual rituals all senses receive stimuli simultaneously: color,
motion, music, words, the smells of food and fire—all are perceived at once.
In texts each step is named, which thins out the ritual by abstracting certain
features from complex, confusing, and ambiguous social situations and specifying them as the true and essential ones.

The *Li-chi* is a different kind of book than the *I-li*, and its history is more
problematic. The current edition of the *Li-chi* is a selection from a collection
of Confucian texts assembled in the early Han.[25] A few of its chapters, such

[25] Liu Te, King Hsien of Ho-chien (d. 131 B.C.), reportedly collected 131 pieces. Tai Te and
Tai Sheng made compilations from these and other texts, perhaps including some written in Han
times. Liu Hsiang is also said to have had a role in editing the text from the materials he found in
the imperial library, and Ma Jung (79–166) is said to have made some final additions (*Sui shu*
32:925). Modern scholarly opinion, however, holds that the current text is close if not identical
to that of Tai Sheng (Kao, *Li-hsüeh hsin-t'an*, pp. 24–31). Parts of Tai Te's book have also been
preserved as the *Ta Tai li-chi*, but this work was never as influential as the *Li-chi* of the younger

as "Hurrying to a Funeral," resemble the liturgies in the *I-li* in that they pre-
scribe the series of actions to be performed in a ritual. Some others, such as
"The Meaning of the Capping Ceremony" and "The Meaning of the Wedding
Ceremony," seem to be essays written to interpret the relevant chapters in the
I-li. The bulk of the book, however, consists of the writings of late Chou and
early Han Confucians. Some chapters report questions and answers on ritual
matters, with either Confucius or one of his disciples supplying the answers.
Others are philosophical essays on matters of ritual, morality, or govern-
ment.[26]

The family rituals described in the *I-li* and *Li-chi* assume a cosmos in which
ancestors depended on their descendants for food and the living could benefit
from the blessings of their ancestors. The living communicated with their ancestors through solemn divination, reports, prayers, and offerings of wine and
food. Those in charge of states, fiefs, and families were privileged and obliged
to officiate at rites; those not so privileged were expected to assist in whatever
capacity was appropriate to them. The chief sacrificer had to purify himself in
advance through abstinence of varying duration. At the appointed time, he
would enter the consecrated ancestral shrine, bow, prostrate himself, and
make offerings of food and wine. He was assisted by a variety of attendants,
including those who prepared the food, took charge of the utensils, performed
divinations, and pronounced prayers. During major sacrifices, one boy or
man, preferably a son of the chief sacrificer, would act as a vessel for the spirit
of the ancestors. This impersonator also needed to undergo purification before
the rite. During the rite he would drink the wine offered to the ancestors and
in trancelike fashion passively allow the spirits to animate him. A ritual expert
would interpret the ancestors' wishes, which in the standard liturgy of the *I-li*
was to convey blessings.

Cappings and weddings are presented in the ritual classics as concerned
primarily with assuring continuation of ancestral rites. Through the act of
dressing him in adult clothing, performed in the ancestral shrine, a boy was
transformed into a man capable of serving the ancestors. Weddings, states the
Li-chi chapter "The Meaning of Marriage," were "for the good of the two
surnames that are joined. Looking towards the past, they provide for service
to the ancestral temple; looking towards the future, they provide for the continuation of descendants."[27] Each step involved in arranging a marriage had
to be reported to the ancestors. The wedding culminated in the introduction of
the bride herself to her husband's ancestors in their shrine three months after
the wedding day. At the same time, marriage rites involved establishing ties

---

Tai and is rarely cited with regard to family rites. In the Later Han several major scholars studied
the *Li-chi*, and Cheng Hsüan wrote a commentary to it which became standard.

[26] See Kao, *Li-hsüeh hsin-t'an*, pp. 18–21; Fung, *A History of Chinese Philosophy* 1:337.

[27] *Li-chi*, "Hun-i," 20:2a; cf. Legge, *Rites* 2:428.

of affinity, and five of the six rites concerned the exchange of gifts, courtesies, and information that constituted the betrothal process.

In the ritual classics, death and ancestors were opposed categories. Those bereaved by a death could not be purified in order to communicate with their ancestors. Once the death occurred, they had to wail and alter their appearance. For the next two days the children of the deceased were expected to be too distraught to eat, and would devote their time to wailing and to preparing the equipment needed for encoffining. The encoffining, to be performed on the third day, was a major ceremony that close relatives and political subordinates should attend. Bodies had to be carefully wrapped in dozens of pieces of cloth. After the coffin was sealed, relatives of the dead changed into highly distinctive mourning garb, indicating their degree of kinship. Other austerities mourners accepted were restricted diets and abstinence from such comforts as well-padded beds. While tending to the physical remains of the dead, the mourners had to begin caring for the soul, giving it regular meals. Those who came to condole would address the dead as well as the survivors.

The classics assumed underground burial in coffins as the way to dispose of the dead. Not only was the body protected by shrouds within the coffin, but it was placed in a protective vault supplied with containers of food and drink and models of other useful objects, such as servants. Once the dead were buried, they gradually came to be treated more as ancestors than as dead people, this transition marked by the gradual incorporation of a symbol representing the dead person into the regular ancestral cult. The ceremonies that brought about this shift were a series of sacrifices, the first performed once the mourners had returned from the burial and bathed, followed by several more during the next few days, then one each near the first and second anniversaries of the death, followed by the last a few weeks later. Those in deepest mourning were to restrict their activities until the last of these sacrifices in the third year.

Besides conveying conceptions of the relationships of the living and the dead, the family rituals described in the classics clearly expressed principles of hierarchy and organization among the living. People of unequal rank did not perform rites the same way. For instance, the size of a coffin, the numbers and quality of the objects buried with it, even the date of burial varied according to the political rank of the deceased from the ruler, to nobles, to high officials, to low officials, and to commoners. The number of generations of ancestors a man could worship, the number of times a year he would perform sacrifices, and the types of foods he could offer similarly varied by rank. Kinship position also mattered. Sons of wives outranked sons of concubines, and the first son of the wife would be his father's chief mourner and later preside at sacrifices to him. It was assumed that political headship also passed to eldest sons, and the classics do not portray lords attending ancestral rites presided over by their uncles or elder brothers. Beyond these clearly specified principles of differentiation were others implicit in the structure of the rites. Only men, for instance, addressed the ancestors and ancestresses, though women could offer them food.

Most Confucian scholars from late Chou times on accepted the validity of the general scheme for the performance of rites presented in the ritual classics, not questioning, for instance, the propriety of wearing mourning garments or offering food to ancestors. This common ground, however, still left them ample room to disagree on such issues as the meaning of details of rites, the importance of adhering to details, the basis on which alterations could be made, and the uses to which rituals could be put. These difference in interpretation are apparent in late Chou texts and the *Li-chi* itself.

LATE CHOU THEORETICAL APPROACHES TO RITUAL

Three major directions in late Chou theorizing on ritual were to treat ritual rules as traditions to be punctiliously preserved, to be manipulated toward political ends, or to be rationalized and secularized.

Many of the followers of Confucius were ritualists devoted to preserving and refining the rules for ritualized conduct. What had been handed down was to be cherished and honored. These scholars stressed the value of conforming one's actions to external standards and wished to elaborate the rules to make them explicit for as many situations as possible. This punctilious strand of Confucian learning on ritual is especially well documented in the late Chou commentaries to the canonical chronicle, the *Ch'un-ch'iu* [Spring and Autumn annals]. Repeatedly the authors of the *Kung-yang*, *Ku-liang*, and *Tso* commentaries criticized an action because it violated some stricture of *li*. For instance, it was not proper for one to present marriage gifts in person, or to reverse the proper order of the tablets for a father and grandfather at the ancestral temple, or to delay a burial because of rain once the day had been chosen by divination.[28]

For the development of family rituals, one of the most crucial elements provided by these punctilious ritualists was elaboration of the theory of male-female differentiation and segregation.[29] Commenting on an instance in which a woman presented a gift of the same sort normally presented by men, the *Tso-chuan* stated: "Now for men and women to use the same sorts of gifts is to have no distinction between them. Distinction between men and women is the great restrainer of the country. If it is brought into disorder by a woman, is

[28] *Kung-yang chuan*, "Chuang 22," 8:6b; *Ku-liang chuan*, "Wen 2," 10:4a–b; "Hsüan 8," 12:9a–b.

[29] Relatively rigid ideas on these issues were apparently not uncommon in the time of Mo Tzu and Mencius. See *Mo Tzu*, "Tz'u kuo" 1.18; *Meng tzu* 4A.17, 7B:6b; Legge, *Chinese Classics* 2:307.

there any limit on what might happen?"[30] The *Li-chi*, reflecting these attitudes, specified numerous rules for male-female differentiation, prohibiting such practices as sitting on the same mat as one's married daughter when she returned for a visit.[31]

The late Chou ritualists should probably also be credited with the extraordinary emphasis that came to be placed on mourning practices. This tendency was already apparent by the time of Mo Tzu (ca. 420 B.C.), who ridiculed the austerities demanded by Confucian ritualists. Mourners had to wail without restraint, wear sackcloth tied with hemp bands, dwell in a hut, sleep on a straw mat with a clod for a pillow, and fast to the point of starvation. And all this was to last three years.[32] As presented in the *Li-chi*, Confucian prescriptions for mourning were indeed highly complex, with elaborate qualifications, exceptions, and distinctions for cases where circumstances were not entirely standard. For instance, the *Li-chi* prescribes what to do if, after the guests have assembled for a capping, news arrives of the death of a relative, or if, while mourning a ruler, one's father dies.[33] And it explains how a son's mourning for his mother changed depending on whether she was divorced and whether he was his father's principal heir.[34] The complexity of these rules created a demand for ritual experts to orchestrate funeral ceremonies, a role Confucian ritualists were qualified to fill.[35]

What I have termed here the punctilious approach to ritual often seems to modern sensibilities pedantic. Many Chinese over the centuries also found its

---

[30] *Tso-chuan*, "Chuang 24," 10:5b; Legge, *Chinese Classics* 5:108. See also *Kuo-yü*, "Lu yü A" 4:156, and "Lu yü B" 5:210–212, for expressions of similar ideas.

[31] *Li-chi*, "Fang-chi," 51:27a; Legge, *Rites* 2:299.

[32] *Mo tzu*, "Chieh sang B" 6, p. 107; Burton Watson, *Basic Writings*, pp. 67–68. Mencius provided further evidence that Confucian scholars encountered resistance in advocating the three-year mourning. When the Duke of T'eng sent an inquiry to Mencius asking how he should mourn his father, Mencius replied that three years of mourning wearing coarse clothes and eating gruel had been the practice of the three ancient dynasties for everyone from the Son of Heaven to commoners. Yet when the duke told his officials that he had decided to follow the three-year mourning, they objected that none of the former rulers of Lu had practiced it, nor any of their own state, and in matters of funerals and sacrifices one should follow one's ancestors (*Meng tzu* 3A.2, 5A:3b–4a; Legge, *Chinese Classics* 2:236–37).

[33] *Li-chi*, "Tseng Tzu wen," 18:9b, and 19:4a–6a; Legge, *Rites* 1:316, 331–33.

[34] *Li-chi*, "Sang-fu hsiao-chi," 33:15b; Legge, *Rites* 2:57. Funerals and mourning were not the only rites that Confucian ritualists elaborated. Mo Tzu also ridiculed Confucian wedding ceremonies: "When a man takes a wife, he has to escort her in person. In a formal robe, he acts as his own driver, holding the reins and handing her the strap, as if he were waiting on a stern parent. The marriage ceremony is as dignified as a sacrifice. It reverses high and low and shows disrespect to parents. They are brought down to the level of the wife, whose elevation interferes with service to them. Can this be called filial?" (*Mo tzu*, "Fei Ju B," 9:179; Watson, *Basic Writings*, pp. 125–26). Indeed, all of the role reversals Mo Tzu condemned are prescribed in the classics. (Cf. *Li-chi*, "Hun-i," 61:5a–b; Legge, *Rites* 2:429. Also, *I-li*, "Shih hun-li," 5:3b–14b; Steele 1:22–31.)

[35] Cf. Eno, "Masters of the Dance," pp. 192–95.

strictures overly rigid. Yet a large majority of the scholars who concerned themselves with ritual were working in this tradition. These men were intellectualist in the sense that they sought truth in books. They were also traditionalist in that they sought to preserve practices precisely because they were done in the past. They could point to Confucius's "love of the rite" to justify their stance. By and large they were less concerned with the emotion or symbolism behind a ritual act than with the act itself; they wanted to see acts preserved because they were part of the tradition, part of the culture that gave Chinese identity, even when others saw their performance as hollow.[36] Their defense of established rules and distinctions also had social and political dimensions, for the more complex the rules, the greater the need for scholars knowledgeable in the texts and their interpretations. In other words, punctilious ritualists were making themselves essential. Rituals were crucial to establishing and reproducing cosmic, political, and social relations; only men with their sorts of educations could ensure that the rites were done properly.

The social and political implications of ritual could also be explicitly addressed. Confucius had urged governing through ritual, and his followers often explained how this could be accomplished. In the *Kuo-yü* [Discourses of the states] and the *Tso-chuan*, advisers often made general statements about *li* and the state, ones that may well have been proverbial by then: "*Li* is the means by which to correct the people." "*Li* is the main support of a state." "One pacifies a state through *li*." "*Li* is the regulator of a state."[37] From the context in which such statements were made, what made *li* politically valuable was its capacity to create and preserve the distinctions between classes, ranks, and orders of society and to apportion material goods and responsibility among them.[38]

Hsün Tzu (ca. 310–220 B.C.) provided a theoretical elaboration of this view. He contended that the ancient sage kings had set up ritual regulations with distinctions according to rank, seniority, and role to keep people from competing for things they all desire. Thus rituals should set standards for the amount of material goods people in each rank may use. In the case of sacrifices to ancestors, ritual governs how many ancestors could be offered food and wine.

He who rules the whole realm serves seven generations of ancestors; he who rules a state serves five generations; he who rules a territory of five chariots serves three generations; he who rules a territory of three chariots serves two generations. He

---

[36] From a modern, anthropological perspective one could even argue that these ritualists were on the mark in recognizing that the key question about a rite is what is done, not what one thinks about it. On this idea, see Gilbert Lewis, *Day of Shining Red*, pp. 6–38.

[37] *Tso-chuan*, "Chuang 23," 10:2a; "Hsi 11," 13:18a; "Hsiang 30," 40:8a; "Hsüan 4," 21:18b; Legge, *Chinese Classics* 5:105, 158, 557, 296; *Kuo-yü*, "Chin-yü 4," 10:345.

[38] This mode of thinking about the political utility of *li* is also evident in the *Kuan Tzu*. See Hsiao, *A History of Chinese Political Thought* 1:347–55.

who produces his own food is not permitted to set up an ancestral hall. This is the way the accumulated merit of the ancestors is distinguished.[39]

Hsün Tzu did not think of distinctions of rank as repressive limitations, but as differentiation that allows society to function smoothly.[40]

According to Hsün Tzu, any ruler who could promote ritual would become a true king and control the whole realm.[41] The responsibilities of such a king's highest officials would be "to arbitrate rites and music, reform conduct, spread the transforming influence of education, and improve the customs of the people, taking everything into consideration and achieving uniform standards."[42] In passages of this sort, ritual is often coupled with music; just as music shapes people's emotions and creates feelings of solidarity, so ritual shapes people's understanding of duty and leads to differentiation.[43]

Some passages in the *Li-chi* go even further than Hsün Tzu in explaining how *li* serves to restrain people; *li* are compared to dikes that keep people from impulses toward lawlessness and licentiousness.[44] The people need not be involved in the rituals, or even observe them, to be influenced by them. For instance, the ancestral rites performed by the ruler in the royal ancestral temple are said to convey several messages to the people not present: the ruler's deference to the impersonator of the dead shows that everyone serves someone; the impersonator's drinking more cups of wine than the guests shows the ranking of high and low; the ruler's assembling his relatives for the ceremonies teaches kinship solidarity.[45]

Like the *Chou-li*, the *Li-chi* also gives details on another way to rule through *li*: the ruler can appoint officials to instruct the people in proper *li*. This idea is most fully developed in the chapter on the community drinking ceremony, which is explained as an occasion for demonstrating to the people the principles of social and political differentiation. Allowing those over sixty to sit "illustrates the way to honor elders." Providing progressively more dishes to those over sixty, seventy, and eighty, "illustrates the way to care for the aged." Once people have learned filial piety and fraternal duty in this way, "the state will be tranquil."[46]

Looking on ritual as a tool of government verges on the legalistic: distinctions of rank keep people in their places much the way laws and punishments do. Yet within the Confucian vision of an orderly society there was nothing

[39] *Hsün tzu*, "Li-lun," 19:234; Watson, *Basic Writings*, p. 92.

[40] Cf. Tu Wei-ming's discussion of ritual differentiation in *Centrality and Commonality*, pp. 75–99.

[41] *Hsün tzu*, "Wang-chih," 5:97; Watson, *Basic Writings*, pp. 37–38.

[42] *Hsün tzu*, "Wang-chih," 5:108; Watson, *Basic Writings*, p. 50.

[43] See DeWoskin, *A Song for One or Two*, pp. 92–98.

[44] E.g., the chapter "Fang-chi"; Legge, *Rites* 2:284–99.

[45] *Li-chi*, "Fang-chi," 51:17b–19b; Legge, *Rites* 2:291–93.

[46] *Li-chi*, "Hsiang-yin-chiu i," 61:17a–b; Legge, *Rites* 2:439–40.

more desirable than for the common people to learn proper behavior through their participation in social rituals. This molding provided a noncoercive way to achieve harmony in a society, modeled on the way children learn to behave in their families. Ritual as something to teach others thus was always double-edged: it manipulated people, but for their own good; it was condescending, but in the sense that all elementary education is condescending.

It was perhaps easier to use *li* to manipulate people when one took a secular view of it. By the late Chou, some thinkers denied any link between the performance of rites and the action of spirits. Confucius may well have had some doubts about the participation of the ancestors in sacrifices, as he was said to have made offerings to them *as though* they were present.[47] Mencius did not develop ideas about the relation of rites to unseen powers, but in his discussions of *li* tended to stress how they demonstrated respectfulness (*ching*). He argued, for instance, that following *li* is natural because it is based on reverence and respect, feelings that all people share.[48] Explicit rebuttal of the idea that spirits respond to the offerings in sacrifices is found in other late Chou texts. In a speech included in the *Tso-chuan* an adviser explained to the Marquis of Ch'u why his sacrifices did not have the effect he desired, showing that the adviser saw ancestors in an abstracted, symbolical way.

> The people are what the spirits consider important. The sage kings therefore first secured the welfare of the people and then exerted effort in serving the spirits. . . . When they presented their vessels of millet and reported them as clean and abundant, they meant that in all the three seasons no harm was done to the cause of husbandry, the people were harmonious, and the year good. When they presented their distilled and sweet liquors and announced them as admirable, strong, and good, they meant that superiors and inferiors were all of admirable virtue and their hearts not at all inclined to perversity. . . . Consequently, their people being harmonious, the spirits sent down blessings, so that every movement they undertook was successful.[49]

In this example, sacrifices lose their exchange quality and the literal meaning of the prayers is dismissed—pure offerings merely symbolize effective government. Any blessings that the spirits send are a reward for good government, not for good sacrifices.[50]

Of early thinkers, Hsün Tzu went the furthest in articulating a theory of rites based on secular principles. Sages who understood human nature and the needs of society had created the rituals. Mourning rites express love and grat-

---

[47] *Lun-yü* 3.12, 3:7a; Waley, *Analects*, p. 97.

[48] E. g., *Meng tzu* 4B.28, 8B:5a–b; 6A.6, 11A:7b; Legge, *Chinese Classics* 2:333, 402.

[49] *Tso-chuan*, "Huan 6," 6:18a–b; Legge, *Chinese Classics* 5:48–49. For other instances in the *Tso-chuan* of this sort of rationalism, see Fehl, *Rites and Propriety*, p. 118.

[50] See also *Tso-chuan*, "Chao 20," 49:10b–13b; Legge, *Chinese Classics* 5:683; *Kuo-yü*, "Chou yü 1," 1:29–32.

itude toward the dead; they have nothing to do with helping the soul find its way or propitiating supernatural forces. Failing to ornament burial of the dead was wrong, but because it was stingy, not because it was impious.[51] Hsün Tzu devoted considerable space to offering rational explanations for many of the established customs for dealing with encoffining, burial, and mourning. Thus, bodies are not buried for at least fifty days to allow time for relatives to come from afar. Bodies are washed and dressed to symbolize that one treats the dead as the living. Small models of articles like those used in real life are buried with the dead to show that one wishes to think that the dead have simply changed their residence; the models' actual uselessness shows that one indeed knows they will not be used. Mourning lasts for differing periods because the strength of grief depends on the tie to the one who has died, and the deeper the wound the slower the recovery.[52] Hsün Tzu was a rationalizer, but he was not a reformer: all of the existing practices should be continued because they could all be explained in rational ways once one understood that they were based on human nature and the patterns of heaven and earth. Hsün Tzu's concern to prove the rationality of each step of the rituals suggests that he saw his secular attitude as a potential threat to the objective, external authority of the rites. He did not want people to infer that because the rites were social creations they could be easily curtailed or ignored. He wanted established traditions preserved as much as the punctilious ritualists did.

The *Li-chi* is just as rationalistic as Hsün Tzu, not merely reflecting his ideas, but often using identical language. The *Li-chi*, in addition, goes further in the direction of rationalization by fitting separate practices into overall systems. The *tsung* (descent line or descent group) system provides a good example. There is very little early Chou evidence concerning the nature of descent groups.[53] The "Great Treatise" chapter of the *Li-chi* mentions two types of *tsung*, a lesser one that "moves" every five generations and one that does not move though a hundred generations pass. The Later Han commentator Cheng Hsüan explained this system in more detail, using much the same language employed in the *Po-hu t'ung* [Comprehensive discussions of the White Tiger Hall], a Confucian manual compiled at the direction of the court in A.D. 79.[54] Both of these sources explain that the *tsung* that continues indefinitely is a great *tsung*, headed by the eldest son of the eldest son going back to a younger son of a feudal lord who had been sent off to found his own line. The descent groups that were redefined every five generations were collateral lines

[51] *Hsün tzu*, "Li-lun," 13:239; Watson, *Basic Writings*, p. 97.

[52] *Hsün tzu*, "Li-lun," 13:239–49; Watson, *Basic Writings*, pp. 97–108.

[53] For a recent attempt to explain what *tsung* and *tsung-fa* were in the Chou, and their connection to other terms used to describe groups of kin, such as *hsing* and *shih*, see Chun, "Conceptions of Kinship and Kingship in Classical Chou China."

[54] *Li-chi*, "Ta-chuan," 34:10b; Legge, *Rites* 2:65; *Po-hu t'ung* 3B, pp. 218–19; Tjan II:574–76.

spun off from these great lines. Every time someone had two or more sons, only the eldest son would continue the sacrifices to his father and the others would be the focal ancestors of new lesser descent lines. A younger son's eldest son would make offerings to him, to be continued by the son's eldest son, and so on, for five generations. Whatever the historical accuracy of this scheme as a description of early Chou kinship practices, it does rationalize several features of early Chinese ideas about kinship and ritual. Certainly eldest sons had special responsibilities and privileges. They were the ones who would succeed to offices, and thus were expected to continue the sacrificial responsibilities associated with those offices. (Throughout the *Li-chi* ancestral temples are associated with political ranks, such as feudal lord or great officers, not with descent lines.) Moreover, the idea that kinship ties in ordinary cases last only five generations was clearly expressed in the grading of mourning obligations.

Rationalizations of ritual practice remained a common form of ritual scholarship from the Han period on. It should perhaps be pointed out that what seemed a rational explanation of a practice to such scholars need not seem the correct explanation to us. For instance, Hsün Tzu and the authors of the *Li-chi* explained variations in mourning obligations as based on variations in depths of grief. It seems never to have occurred to them that mourning gradations did not always correspond to feelings—that is, that a man might be more distraught when his mother died relatively young than when his father died in old age, or might grieve more at the death of his wife or child than at the death of either parent. Rather than allow the expression of natural feelings, such schedules for grieving provide a structure for feelings to make them correspond to the authority structure of the family.

Over time, the late Chou and early Han punctilious, political, and rationalistic approaches to ritual all worked to give weight to the moral side of ritual at the expense of the sacred or religious side. Late Chou writers used *li* to refer both to the grandest ceremonies of the ruler and the routine protocols for greeting, presenting gifts, and expressing deference. Etymologically the sacred side of *li* was prior, so that calling other kinds of formalized behavior *li* gave them a certain sanctity. In time, however, *li* as etiquette shaped notions of *li* as ritual. The deferential attitude an official adopted in approaching his lord provided the model for the way to approach ancestors rather than the other way round. Ritual came to be thought of as a marvelous means for creating moral sentiments and expressing distinctions fundamental to morality. Rituals were routinized expressions of deference.

This emphasis on morality led to a fundamental polarity in writers' understanding of ritual. In many contexts writers use *li* to refer to the rules for such details as the placement of objects during ceremonies, with no suggestion that they invested these details with great moral significance. This side of the polarity could also be expressed in Chinese with the term *i*, "form, etiquette, ceremony.'' Yet *li* was also spoken of as a virtue, and scholars like Mencius often listed it with other virtues such as humanity, filial piety, and sincerity. In such cases *li* meant the ethical attitude that leads people to treat others with respect and deference. It needs to be emphasized that this rules/ethics polarity was a *polarity*, not a duality. In common Western ways of thinking, form and content are seen as discrete, much like mind and body and reason and emotion.[55] Confucians could emphasize the form of a rite or the ethical attitude behind it, yet they did not radically separate the two: the ritual of greeting parents was filial piety and not merely its outward form.[56]

The rules/ethics polarity was related to assumptions about the locus of authority for the specifics of ritual. Many early writers treated ritual as an external, objective code of conduct, a code that would allow one to proceed without doubts toward correct behavior. Those called punctilious traditionalists here usually took this approach. Others, from Confucius on, implied that the steps of rites needed to be examined in terms of inner motivations and only followed when they accorded with the truest or most fundamental values and feelings. If carried to an extreme, such a view undermines external authority, replacing it with internal, individual authority.

Early Confucian theorists also did not all make the same assumptions about the goals for promoting the practice of ritual among the people at large. At places Mencius seemed to imply that the goal was the moral development of each person: practice in rituals would make people more filial, loyal, sincere, and good. Others like Hsün Tzu placed more stress on how rituals create and express social hierarchy and differentiation. In rituals people act out patterns of leadership and deference; moreover, even in cases where everyone performed the same rituals (such as funerals), they could reproduce and validate the principles of hierarchy by doing them in quantitatively differentiated ways.

These basic polarities remained intrinsic to the Confucian discourse on family rituals through the imperial period.

RITUAL AUSTERITIES AND INDIVIDUAL FEELINGS IN THE HAN AND POST-HAN PERIODS

Filial piety came to be exalted in the Han (202 B.C.–A.D. 220). In the *Li-chi*, Confucius's disciple Tseng Tzu asserts that true goodness, propriety, righteousness, and sincerity all lay in reverent, persistent service to parents and cautious behavior that avoided bringing shame on them. He is quoted as saying, ''Set up filial piety and it will fill the space from heaven to earth; spread it out and it will extend to the four seas; hand it down to future ages and from

---

[55] For a good discussion of the contrast between Chinese and Western thinking in these ways, see Bloom, ''On the Matter of the Mind.''

[56] See also Tu, ''*Li* as a Process of Humanization.''

morning to night it will be observed.''[57] Similar exaltations of filial piety are found in the *Classic of Filial Piety*, which reached final form in about the same period the *Li-chi* did. This text attributed to Confucius the statement that ''Filial piety is the root of all virtue and the source of all teachings.''[58]

In the Han period, mourning austerities became the most widely used measure of filial piety. Wei Piao was recommended as ''filial and incorrupt'' because when his parents died ''he wasted away from grief for three years, never leaving his hut. At the end of the mourning period, he was emaciated, his bones protruding, his appearance strange. It took several years of medical treatment before he could get up.''[59] In other cases, men were reluctant to end their mourning after the regular period was over, such as Chiang Ko who did not remove his mourning clothes for his mother until the governor of his commandery sent someone to make him.[60] Others reluctant to end mourning austerities repeated mourning for a parent who had died earlier but had not been mourned in as extreme a fashion.[61]

Severe restraints on mourners coexisted with lavish attention to the material comforts of the dead. In the Han well-to-do families built large, multichambered brick or stone tombs, filled them with precious objects, documents, and jewelry, and protected the body with several layers of clothing and coffins, apparently believing their actions would bring benefit or prevent harm, either to the earthly or heavenly soul of the deceased (*p'o* and *hun*, respectively), or to the descendants.[62] Hsün Tzu may well have thought that only commoners could believe that sacrifices affected the spirits of the dead,[63] but there seems little doubt that the bulk of the population, including the bulk of the educated, believed in the persistence of conscious spirits of the dead and the ability of their living descendants to influence them or aid them through burial practices and sacrificial rites. The Later Han skeptic Wang Ch'ung (27–ca. 97) testified that his contemporaries believed that ghosts of the dead could take human form, were aware of what was happening, and were able to harm people.[64] Perhaps anxieties about death, souls, and afterlife led both to great expendi-

---

[57] *Li-chi*, ''Chi-i,'' 48:5a–b; Legge, *Rites* 2:227.

[58] *Hsiao ching* 1, 1:2a. See also Holzman, ''Filial Piety in Ancient and Early Medieval China.''

[59] *Hou-Han shu* 26:917.

[60] *Hou-Han shu* 39:1302.

[61] E. g., *Hou-Han shu* 42:1426, 74A:2373.

[62] See Loewe, *Chinese Ideas of Life and Death*, esp. pp. 114–26, and Wang, *Han Civilization*, pp. 175–213. Powers, ''Pictorial Art and Its Public in Early Imperial China,'' suggests that part of the benefit from lavish funerary construction was for the descendants, who could gain a reputation for filial piety through such display. See also Wu Hung, ''From Temple to Tomb,'' for a discussion of this tomb and the religious attitudes underlying its construction.

[63] *Hsün tzu*, ''Li-lun,'' 13:249–50; Watson, *Basic Writings*, pp. 109–10.

[64] See *Lun-heng* 20:315–21; Forke, 1:191–201. On the ideas about spirits current in the Han, see also Bodde, *Festivals in Classical China*, pp. 49–138.

tures on coffins, tomb furnishings, and tombs, and to ascetic practices by the survivors.

The excesses to which mourning austerities were carried in the Later Han brought to the fore a fundamental tension in Confucian theories of ritual. Hsün Tzu claimed that the traditional ritual prescriptions corresponded to natural feelings and allowed for their full expression. Yet his rationalizing and secularizing turn of mind also tended to reduce the emotional force of ritual performances, to substitute reverence for awe and propriety for passion. In ordinary social life, weddings, funerals, and ancestral rites were emotionally charged occasions, and the emotions scholars felt or thought they observed in others were not always homologous with the ones specified in the *Li-chi*. From late Han times on the disjuncture between rituals and emotions became an intellectual issue. When men exceeded the specified limits on mourning austerities as a way to express their extreme distress, they were challenging the authority of inherited ritual rules. If carried to its logical extreme, such behavior would lead to people's basing the length of mourning on how distressed they felt, an implication more conservative Confucian scholars found objectionable. Ying Shao (fl. 180s), for instance, condemned such individualistic behavior on the grounds that the canonical ritual rules represent the perfect mean and cannot be improved by being exceeded.[65]

In the third and fourth centuries new approval for individual, even idiosyncratic, expression of feelings posed a major challenge to the ritual order.[66] The *Shih-shuo hsin-yü* [New versions of current tales] has many anecdotes of men who were admired for ignoring ritual conventions. Wang Jung (234–305) ignored the gradation imposed by the ritual rules and showed great grief on the death of his infant son.[67] His contemporary Juan Chi (210–263) attracted attention by eating meat and wine while in mourning for his mother.[68] Leading figures in the Neo-Taoist movement like Wang Pi (226–249) and Chi K'ang (223–262) provided philosophical justifications for following feelings.[69] Their ideas in time had an influence on Confucians, leading to a new vocabulary for discussing ritual. As T'ang Chang-ju argues, reconciliation of Neo-Taoist emphasis on natural feelings and the ritual order was in the interest of aristocrats whose status depended on the preservation of the existing social and political order.[70] This reconciliation is perhaps best seen in the debates about how mourning rites might be adapted to allow more genuine expression of feel-

[65] *Feng-su t'ung-i* 3:101. See also Miyazaki, *Ajiashi kenkyū*, pp. 116–20.

[66] Yü, "Individualism and the Neo-Taoist Movement in Wei-Chin China," esp. pp. 137–40.

[67] *Shih-shuo hsin-yü* 17:488; Mather, p. 324.

[68] *Shih-shuo hsin-yü* 23:548–49; Mather, p. 372. See also Holzman, *Poetry and Politics*, pp. 73–87.

[69] Yü, "Individualism," pp. 137–40.

[70] T'ang, *Wei-Chin Nan-pei-ch'ao shih-lun ts'ung*, p. 338.

ings.[71] Debates concentrated on exceptional cases, such as a case in which a man was separated from his wife during warfare and, assuming she had died, remarried, only to find his wife alive after the second woman had borne children. The issue then became what mourning the children of the second wife should wear for the first wife. Since neither ritual nor law allowed a man to have two wives at the same time, there was nothing in any ritual code about mourning a first mother. Should the first woman be thought of as divorced, making the second marriage fully regular and no mourning owed to the first woman? Should the second woman be considered in fact a concubine since a wife still existed, in which case the second woman's children would have to treat the first wife with more honor than their actual mother? Scholars of the time came to a wide variety of conclusions, some trying to argue strictly from the classics, some saying ritual was designed for usual events, not extraordinary ones like these, some saying it was as important to satisfy feelings as the letter of the ritual.[72] Such arguments, of course, were only possible because ritual obligations had been codified—and thereby decontextualized—in the canonical texts, and these texts carried great weight in the Confucian community. The government provided a forum for these debates but did not issue definitive rulings; it remained politically and intellectually respectable to offer yet another view.

IMPERIAL RITUAL CODES

During the centuries when the ritual classics were written and edited, China's social and political structure underwent a massive transformation. After the Ch'in succeeded in defeating the last of its rivals in 221 B.C., unified bureaucratic rule under a single emperor was extended to the entire country. The Han dynasty maintained centralized rule, combining it with promotion of Confucianism and patronage of Confucian scholars, and thus set the basic patterns of imperial governance in China. As a consequence, by the time the *Li-chi* and *I-li* were available for scholars to read, they were anachronistic reminders of a long-gone society of hereditary lords, ruling over large and small states, fiefs, and cities. Scholars studied these texts, wrote commentaries to them, and debated how to interpret them, but they also participated in designing ritual codes more suited to their own times.

The new imperial form of government required new forms of political rituals. Because the ritual classics contained no liturgies for royal, much less imperial rituals, from early in the Han dynasty emperors turned to Confucian scholars to devise appropriate court rituals, which they generally did by scaling up items found in the canonical texts. Court scholars were often attracted

[71] Yü, "Individualism," p. 142. See also Yü, *Chung-kuo chih-shih chieh-ts'eng shih lun*, pp. 350–72.

[72] *Chin shu* 20:635–40. For examples of other such debates, see *T'ung-tien*, ch. 45–59.

to comprehensive schemes that linked the rituals performed by every segment of society, inspired by the "Monthly Ordinances" chapter of the *Li-chi*, which specifies exactly which rituals and ceremonies the ruler should perform and which he should command others to perform, down to ordinary people's sacrifices to the local god of the soil.[73] The *Li-chi* provided ample canonical authority for the idea that kings could institute rituals, but scholars presented themselves as necessary advisers. The creation, critique, and editing of liturgical texts, and the scrutiny of imperial performance, became a major political activity of scholarly officials. Indeed, one of the most effective ways for scholars to influence state policies was to couch their discussions in terms of the rituals surrounding the emperor, the area of their undisputed expertise.[74]

A significant side effect of the long tradition of scholarship on state rituals was the elaboration of views of ritual that stressed the importance of considering change over time and of making adaptations to meet varied circumstances. Emperors naturally required more grandiose ceremonies than commoners, but political rank was not the only circumstance to be taken into account. Imperial mourning was routinely curtailed, substituting days for months in the canonical formulation, because the emperor also had a duty to sacrifice to heaven and various deities, a duty he could not perform while in mourning. Thus decisions on ritual had to involve careful assessment of all the relevant factors, and should be based on balancing considerations (*che-chung*). Single-minded insistence on absolute principles was seldom appropriate. Ritual was subject to change over time much like government institutions more generally. This view of ritual is well summed up in the one hundred *chüan* devoted to describing the evolution of key rites in Tu Yu's (735–812) early ninth-century encyclopedia, the *T'ung-tien* [Comprehensive institutes].

Successive imperial governments did not pay attention solely to court rituals. In A.D. 87, Ts'ao Pao compiled under imperial order a new ritual code that included "the regulations for cappings, weddings, and the auspicious and ill-omened endings and beginnings of life, graded from the Son of Heaven down to commoners."[75] Punctilious scholars who did not approve altering the rituals in the classics in any way objected strenuously to his new manual, so it was never circulated. Most of the subsequent dynasties did issue ritual codes.[76] Governments also issued a variety of other rules concerning family rituals, especially as they affected officials. During the reign of Emperor An (r. 107–125), officials were ordered not to retire from office to mourn relatives other than parents, and in 122 high officials were ordered not to retire to mourn

---

[73] Bodde, *Festivals*, p. 16.

[74] On the politics of court ritual, see (for the Han) Bilsky, *State Religion*, pp. 287–330, and Loewe, *Crisis and Conflict in Han China*, pp. 164–92; and (for the T'ang) Wechsler, *Offerings*, and McMullen, *State and Scholars in T'ang China*, pp. 113–58.

[75] *Hou-Han shu* 35:1203.

[76] *Sui shu* 33:969–71.

anyone, a rule later reversed several times.[77] Burial procedures were also the subject of status laws. For instance, a Northern Ch'i (550–557) law specified the sorts of shamanlike figures princes, princesses, and the very highest officials could have to lead funeral processions and drive away noxious influences.[78] In the Sui (581–618), regulations covered even more items, such as the clothes the corpse could be dressed in, the number of jewels to be put in the coffin, the decoration of the catafalque, the number of bearers, the size and shape of the grave marker, and so on.[79] T'ang rules on such matters went down to commoners.[80] Wedding rites were also sometimes regulated. The Northern Ch'i set maximum amounts of various objects that officials could present as betrothal gifts, with commoners allowed to give half as much as officials.[81] Sumptuary legislation of this sort was fully in accord with the view of ritual as above all a means of expressing and creating social and political hierarchy. By claiming to orchestrate how each level of society would perform family rituals, the rulers were publicizing their model of the structure of society. What might have been thought of as purely private and family matters—the relations of men with their ancestors—were made into political matters and tied to allegiance to the ruler and the state.[82] There is no evidence, however, that the government ever made efforts to monitor what people did. Enforcing rules was not as crucial as having rules.

The only imperial ritual guide to survive from the T'ang (618–907) or earlier is the *Ta-T'ang K'ai-yüan li* [Ritual of the K'ai-yüan period of the Great T'ang], issued in 732 in 150 *chüan*.[83] Besides describing the rituals performed by the emperor and other members of the imperial family, this manual specified the steps in family rituals high, middling, and low officials should perform at home, based closely on the *I-li*. Perhaps reflecting the view that rituals change over time and should accord with circumstances, the *K'ai-yüan li* accepted several common customs not of canonical origins, including ancestral rites to be held at graves and worship of the spirit of the earth before excavating a grave.[84] Yet no elements of Buddhist or Taoist origin were included. Both religions were generously patronized by the T'ang court, but the *K'ai-yüan li* presents an exclusively Confucian program for ritual performance; it did not mention, for instance, the popular Buddhist ghost festival.[85] At the

[77] *Sung shu* 15:387–93.

[78] *Sui shu* 8:155.

[79] *Sui shu* 8:156–57.

[80] *T'ang hui-yao* 38:691–98. See also rules on ancestral temples in *T'ang hui-yao* 19:387–92.

[81] *Sui shu* 9:179.

[82] Cf. Bloch's interpretation of somewhat similar schemes in Madagascar in *From Blessing to Violence*, pp. 118–19.

[83] On this code, see McMullen, "Bureaucrats and Cosmology."

[84] *Ta-T'ang K'ai-yüan li* 78:6a–7a, 147:10a–b.

[85] On patronage, see Weinstein, *Buddhism Under the T'ang*; on the ghost festival, see Teiser, *The Ghost Festival in Medieval China*.

state level, at least, ritual remained the preserve of Confucian scholars; trained in the ritual classics and dynastic ritual codes, they served as the experts able to debate the propriety of each item and step.

During the long early imperial period, governments rarely showed much concern with the rituals that common people performed. Some local officials tried to eradicate wedding or funeral practices so deviant that they marked the performers as ethnically non-Han, such as marrying a brother's widow (levirate) or failing to wear mourning clothes. Some would work to eliminate offensive local religious practices, but they were generally too busy dealing with demon worship, insubordinate local gods, and cults involving human sacrifice to worry about minor deviations in ancestral rites or other family rituals.[86]

STATUS IMPLICATIONS OF RITUAL BEHAVIOR AND PRIVATE RITUAL GUIDES

With the establishment of imperial bureaucratic rule, only the imperial family and a small number of nobles inherited privileged status; everyone else was legally a commoner by birth. As a consequence, the gradations in ritual performance by rank so stressed in the *Li-chi* no longer matched society. It became common to convert the canonical distinctions into bureaucratic equivalents (the very highest officials equaled *ch'ing*, the next *ta-fu*, the lowest *shih*), but these offices were not hereditary and so such systems were schematic representations of political hierarchy, not well matched to social distinctions. Among the people at large the link between social status and ritual performance often took a different form. Ritual rules did not keep people from usurping the privileges of their superiors. Rather, fulfilling ritual norms became a good way to assert elite status. The Han histories describe numerous men who gained respect because they modeled their every movement and gesture on the ritual classics.[87]

After the Han dynasty fell, the links between status and ritual behavior became even stronger. In this period of disunion, short dynasties, and alien rulers, family background became a major basis for judging people's social worth and suitability for office.[88] The most aristocratic families in the South in the fourth, fifth, and sixth centuries and their counterparts in the North in the late fifth and sixth centuries readily condemned social upstarts because of their crude manners and ignorance of fine points of ritual. In turn they justified their own privileges by pointing to their preservation and refinement of traditional—and distinctly Chinese—mores. Also contributing to emphasis on con-

---

[86] See Miyakawa, "The Confucianization of South China"; Stein, "Religious Taoism and Popular Religion from the Second to the Seventh Centuries"; and Levi, "Les Fonctionnaires et le Divin."

[87] E.g., *Hou-Han shu* 43:1457, 53:1743, 79:2573.

[88] See Ebrey, *Aristocratic Families of Early Imperial China*, pp. 15–33.

formity to fixed patterns of behavior was the political disorderliness of the age; people seem to have craved predictability and order in the spheres they could control, family life and social interaction.[89]

Yen Chih-t'ui (531–591) is a good example of an aristocrat who valued adherence to inherited forms. He wrote his *Yen-shih chia-hsün* [Family instructions of Mr. Yen] for his sons who had grown up in the North and had never known the orderly aristocratic society of the South that he remembered. Yen noted the inadequacies of the ritual classics as guides to behavior and the penchant of aristocrats for criticizing each other's deportment.[90] To aid his sons he had written down some of the unspoken rules of refined behavior that he learned in his youth in the South, such as the taboos on the names of deceased parents and grandparents and the proper use of various kinship terms and honorifics.[91] He outlined regional differences in wailing (Southerners would appeal to the dead in words while wailing) and condoling (Southerners would visit within three days or risk their friendship) and pointed out that in the South men sometimes were dismissed from their posts if they did not look grief-stricken when they returned from mourning.[92] To illustrate how embarrassing it could be not to know what to say, he pointed to the example of a Southern Ch'i emperor who was unquestionably filial toward his mother yet when he realized that he would die before her expressed regret that he would not be able to arrange her funeral and burial. "For someone whose inborn nature was so filial not to know the taboos in a case like this resulted from lack of study."[93]

During the T'ang, when men from "old families" had fewer political advantages than they had in the Northern and Southern Dynasties, the superiority of their deportment and mastery of ritual forms were given even greater weight in justifications for their social eminence. Men were criticized or praised according to how they acted while in mourning, the efforts they took to bring their relatives' bodies back for burial in family graveyards, and the solemnity with which they performed ancestral rites.[94] Through the T'ang, emperors expressed anger or chagrin at the claims of the aristocratic families to have superior family traditions and deportment. Even as late as 848, Emperor Hsüan-tsung was embarrassed to discover that the daughter he had married into the aristocratic Cheng family had gone out to amuse herself while her husband's

---

[89] Ch'ien, "Lüeh lun Wei-Chin Nan-pei-ch'ao hsüeh-shu wen-hua yü tang-shih men-ti chih kuan-hsi," pp. 42, 44.

[90] *Yen-shih chia-hsün* 2:69; Teng, p. 22.

[91] *Yen-shih chia-hsün* 2:69–85; Teng, pp. 23–29.

[92] *Yen-shih chia-hsün* 2:101–108; Teng, pp. 34–37.

[93] *Yen-shih chia-hsün* 3:187; Teng, pp. 70–71.

[94] E.g., *Chiu T'ang shu* 136:3755, 188:4928, 119:3437. See also Ebrey, *Aristocratic Families*, pp. 96–100; Takeda, "Tōdai shizoku no kahō ni tsuite."

younger brother was ill.[95] Not only were women to stay at home performing their proper duties, but they were to give special attention to ancestral rites. Funerary inscriptions for high-ranking women commonly praise them for the seriousness with which they carried out these ceremonies.[96]

The emphasis on deportment common in the Northern and Southern Dynasties and the T'ang led many authors to compile private ritual guides. As early as the Later Han, Cheng Chung (d. 114) wrote a *Hun-li* [Marriage rituals] that discussed the symbolism in the great plethora of objects that had come to be used as betrothal gifts.[97] Lu Ch'en's (274–340) *Tsa-chi fa* [Miscellaneous rules on sacrifices] gave a long list of the food that could appropriately be offered in sacrifices in each of the seasons.[98] Other books were clearly liturgies. Ssu-ma Kuang (1019–1086) in the Sung cited the T'ang official Meng Hsien as an authority for using the solstices and equinoxes for the seasonal sacrifices rather than choosing days by divination as in the *I-li*.[99]

In the fifth century guides to the verbal forms to be used in rituals and ritualized activities appeared. Called *shu-i* [letters and etiquette], these books provided the written language to be used in engagement and condolence letters as well as the oral formulas to be pronounced in rites. Wang Hung (379–432), of the aristocratic Lang-yeh Wang family in the South, wrote a ten-*chüan shu-i*, and others followed in rapid succession.[100] Substantial parts of those written in the T'ang survived at Tunhuang.[101] Tu Yu-chin, in his early eighth century *Shu-i ching* [Mirror of *Shu-i*], argued that a new *shu-i* was needed because the fifth-century *Shu-i* by Wang Chien was outdated in such matters as the terms used to refer to relatives. The first chapter of his text is devoted to auspicious matters, including weddings, the second chapter to ill-omened matters, primarily funerals. After diagrams of the mourning grades and the principles for writing ill-omened letters, it gives forms for letters announcing deaths, condolence letters, and letters for "ghost marriages" between those who died unmarried. It also provides texts to be read at the sacrifices at successive stages of the funeral and phrases for oral condolences, including ones women would use.[102] Cheng Yü-ch'ing (748–820), a high official who rose to chief minis-

---

[95] *Tzu-chih t'ung-chien* 248:8036. See also Ch'en, *T'ang-tai cheng-chih shih shu-lun kao*, pp. 53–69; Twitchett, "Composition of the T'ang Ruling Class."

[96] See *Ch'üan T'ang wen* 590:18b, 22b, and 591:1b for examples from the writings of Liu Tsung-yüan.

[97] *Yü-han shan-fang chi i-shu, i-li lei*, p. 805.

[98] Ibid., p. 1,083.

[99] SMSSI 10:113. For other guides to sacrificial rites written in the T'ang, see *Chiu T'ang shu* 191:51101–2; *Ch'ung-wen tsung-mu* 2:79; *Hsin T'ang shu* 58:1492; CCSLCT 6:179–80.

[100] *Sui shu* 33:971; *Chiu T'ang shu* 46:2008–9. These sources also list six other pre-T'ang *shu-i*.

[101] See Ebrey, "T'ang Guides to Verbal Etiquette," and Chou, "Tun-huang hsieh-pen shu-i chung so-chien ti T'ang-tai hun-sang li-su."

[102] Pelliot number 3637 and 3849.

ter,[103] noted in the preface to his *shu-i* that families of *shih-ta-fu* (the educated elite) had to know the forms of rituals but "the ritual classics are confusingly arranged, making them difficult to consult. Therefore, able scholars have selected and arranged the essentials of the auspicious and ill-omened rites and labelled them *shu-i* to transmit to the age."[104] A *shu-i* written by a local Tunhuang official described wedding rituals, including the ceremony for delivering the documents, the announcements to the ancestral spirits during the wedding, and several steps in the wedding itself, such as the words a boy uses when he tosses coins and fruit on the nuptial bed.[105] Very little in these descriptions is based on the *I-li*; rather they are based on popular practices, several of which survived into the Sung period.

Why would etiquette books include uncanonical practices like "ghost marriages" and tossing seeds and coins on the bed in the nuptial chamber? I suspect the reason is that whether a practice was canonical in origin had little to do with the social implications of its practice in this period. Ritual was certainly thought of as distinct from vulgar custom, but ritual did not have to be identical with the classics. In this age before printing, not even every scholar would have personal copies of the classics; the government ritual codes were probably rarely found anywhere outside government offices. Scholars trained in the Confucian tradition would have had general understandings of the content of the classics, and could probably locate copies to consult if need be. When they conformed their behavior to canonical specifications, their examples could be powerful: filial sons who spent the mourning period in huts by the sides of their parents' graves clearly impressed their neighbors. Yet, right and proper rites were seen not simply as the ones in the classics, but rather as the ones that had been preserved by the best families. Such traditions, by creating cultural identity, were a repository of value, much the way the classics were.[106] This approach challenged the view of the punctilious traditionalists who saw preserving the forms expressed or implied in the classics as essential. Yet notice that educated men who were willing to include practices with no basis in the classics were still oriented toward texts: basing behavior on orally transmitted customs was not satisfactory. If the old genres of commentaries on the classics and government ritual codes were inadequate to their needs, new genres had to be created. Educated men had to have texts both for their convenience as reference works and for the validity they conferred on what they described.

[103] *Chiu T'ang shu* 158:4165–66.

[104] *Tun-huang pao-tsang* 48:195.

[105] *Tun-huang to-so* 74:293–98.

[106] Cf. Bol, *This Culture of Ours*, on the importance of *wen*, the accumulated literary traditions, as a source of value during the T'ang.

RELIGIOUS CHANGES AND
INTELLECTUAL COMPARTMENTALIZATION

Throughout the early imperial period, the community of Confucian scholars turned to texts, especially the *I-li*, *Li-chi*, and the commentaries that came to be incorporated in them, as sources of authority for the performance of family rituals. Supported in their work by the government, they devoted enormous efforts to establishing correct versions of these texts and determining what each word and phrase in them meant. In the T'ang, K'ung Ying-ta (574–648) wrote a subcommentary to the *Li-chi* and Chia Kung-yen (fl. 650s) wrote one for the *I-li*. Through state commissions Confucian scholars prepared liturgical manuals for the court and all of its officials. Scholars also wrote many private manuals for the performance of family rituals.

As this work progressed, the Confucian discourse on family rituals seems to have diverged further and further from the performance of them. By the time of Hsün Tzu the original cosmological assumptions underlying traditional funeral and sacrificial rites were no longer universally held by the most highly educated. From Han times on there is increasingly abundant evidence that the views of ordinary, uneducated Chinese, while still strongly religious in the sense that they recognized all sorts of spirits and unseen powers, diverged from ancient ideas in ways that weakened the fit of canonical rituals.

Already by late Han times conceptions of the fate of the dead included judgment by underworld bureaucrats and a sorting of the dead for different fates.[107] With the progressive spread of Buddhism from the second century on and the emergence of Taoist religion in approximately the same period, Chinese conceptions of afterlife were greatly enriched. Traditional canonical funeral and burial practices were based on the assumption that the dead need material goods, especially food and drink, but did not take into account any idea that they might need to have their sins expiated, or that the actions of the survivors could have an effect on where the souls of the dead would go. Buddhist notions of karma and transmigration introduced a radically new way of thinking about the connection of the physical remains of the body to the afterlife. One was to be reborn in another body; the way the old body was handled had nothing to do with rebirth. These ideas undermined the ancient notion that the dead can be made physically comfortable by the way they are buried.

The Buddhist and Taoist churches also introduced to the general populace a different kind of religious expert, the monk or priest educated in textual traditions. In the classics, a male family member is the primary officiant in family rituals; he can be assisted by a variety of specialists, but cannot dele-

---

[107] See Yü, "O Soul, Come Back," and Seidel, "Traces of Han Religion in Funeral Texts Found in Tombs."

gate to them the primary tasks. In actual practice, common people had long been able to call on shamans or mediums to help them deal with gods and ghosts. But Buddhist and Taoist clergy claimed more specialized knowledge of how to deal with sacred forces, and claimed that the ceremonies they performed were especially efficacious. Buddhism also brought familiarity with modes of communicating with gods and spirits through burning incense, prayer, and meatless offerings. As these newer ideas gained hold, new mortuary rituals came to be developed and widely practiced, such as the ghost festival in the seventh month.[108]

The gradual proliferation of ideas about grave geomancy constituted another significant cultural change. The underlying presuppositions of geomancy go back to the ancient idea that the living benefit when their ancestors are comfortable, but the elaboration of theories about the forces of the earth and their effect on the living seems to have begun in the Han and grown considerably in the post-Han period. These theories drew from several strains of cosmological thought, including yin-yang, five phases, and *I-ching* traditions, as well as less philosophically based divinatory traditions. By the early T'ang, geomancy was already playing a major role in decisions about where to bury, leading to criticism that people would scatter graves and delay burials in the belief that they might gain longer life, high rank, or riches.[109]

The diversification of religious ideas from Han through T'ang times transformed the way family rituals were performed. Buddhist clergy came to play major roles in funeral services and geomancers in matters related to burials. Buddhist monks also sometimes took over partial responsibility for ancestral rites. At the level of the government and official elite, the development of these new forms and new ceremonies led to an intellectual compartmentalization that avoided conflicts. Although the T'ang government generously patronized Buddhism and Taoism, it did not issue a liturgy that incorporated ceremonies of diverse origin. Among those whose social standing required that they perform Confucian rites, Buddhist or Taoist rites could not be haphazardly substituted, but there seems to have been little objection to performing them in addition to the canonical Confucian rites. Confucian thinking about ritual remained confined to the established genre of commentaries on the ritual classics, discussions of points concerning court ritual, and disputations on what constituted the correct ritual practice according to either the text or the basic meaning of the classics. Ritual (*li*) meant Confucian ritual, and thus had nothing to do with Buddhist or Taoist ceremonies. This tendency to compartmentalize fields of knowledge was widespread in T'ang Confucianism. As McMullen has pointed out, state patronage of Confucian scholars and Confucian rituals coexisted effectively with state patronage of Buddhism and Taoism

---

[108] See Teiser, *Ghost Festival*.
[109] *Chiu T'ang shu* 79:2723–26.

and private commitment to either religion on the part of many Confucian officials. Neither the state nor the scholarly community felt compelled to sustain exclusive positions or demarcate the limits of what was admissible.[110]

Everywhere, perhaps, rituals tend to ossify, to tend toward empty formalism. According to Tambiah, "All the substantive features which nourish the formalism of ritual also conspire to empty it of meaning over time. Cosmological ideas, because they reflect the epistemological and ontological understandings of a particular age in which they originated, and because they are subject to the constraints of remaining accurate and invariant, are condemned to become dated over time and increasingly unable to speak to the minds and hearts of succeeding generations facing change and upheaval."[111] In these circumstances, old rituals may still be followed, but to express social and political differentiation more than to communicate fundamental, deeply held cosmological truths.

In the Chinese case, ossification coexisted with abandonment and hybridization. Many specific steps and procedures described in the classics (such as divining with stalks for the timing of many rites) fell out of common practice, even among those who read the classics. In other cases ritual procedures of noncanonical origins—ones more closely tied to newer cosmological conceptions and social realities—were fitted into the syntax of the Confucian ritual sequence, much as dialectical words can be absorbed into a basic language structure. Thus Buddhist monks could lead funeral processions, geomancers choose the time to bury, and brides' families act out symbolic resistance to her departure.[112] In other words, even if the discourse on family rituals was compartmentalized, practice was not.

Chinese family rituals were comprised of many specific ritual acts, and a large share of these specific acts remained close to the descriptions in the classics. Some of these steps had undoubtedly ossified by T'ang times. The rituals associated with ancestral rites, in particular, seem often to have come to carry more meaning about intellectual and political allegiances of those performing them than about how they conceived of death and afterlife. The Confucian discourse, by intellectualizing rituals and elaborating political models of ritual differentiation, inadvertently fostered these trends. Nevertheless, not all of the rites that remained close to classical forms seem to have ossified. From my reading of the admittedly limited sources, people did not wail or dishevel their hair at funerals primarily to assert their social and political standing, but because these ritual forms were the best ways they knew to handle difficult and possibly dangerous circumstances.

---

[110] McMullen, *State and Scholars*, p. 259.

[111] Tambiah, *Culture, Thought, and Social Action*, p. 165.

[112] These sorts of adaptions are discussed in some detail in Chapters Three and Four.

CONCLUSIONS

Covering as it has an extremely long span of time, this chapter has touched on many of the ways Confucian texts helped shape the performance of rituals. Even before the invention of printing, the texts of the classics and the writings of revered scholars were in wide enough circulation to influence, at least indirectly, the ways people thought about these rituals and also how they acted. The *I-li* and *Li-chi*, as edited and interpreted by later scholars, were undoubtedly the most influential texts in establishing the names and sequences of the steps that constituted Confucian family rituals. But such rules could never be mechanically put into practice. They were read in the light of the moral, social, and political theories articulated by Confucius, Mencius, Hsün Tzu, more anonymous authors of the commentaries to the *Ch'un-ch'iu* and the discursive essays in the *Li-chi*, and later thinkers like Wang Pi, Yen Chih-t'ui, and Tu Yu. They were acted on in complex social situations in which ritual performance had multiple social and political implications. Scholars' commitment to the sanctity of the canonical texts meant that they did not purposely rewrite them to reflect new social, political, or religious realities. Rather men wrote new texts to supplement them, most notably imperial ritual codes and private etiquette books. Those who chose to turn to Confucian texts could turn to more than one text and choose among alternative wordings.

Those who did consult these texts could not help being affected by them. Theorists had made rites into an intellectual object: rituals were something to be analyzed in words, specified in books, and manipulated by those who could base arguments on books. Just as liturgies made rituals more textlike, so discursive writings on ritual made the emotional response to participation in rituals more intellectual. In such a cultural environment, rituals could not undergo anything approximating a "natural" evolution, in which the forms of rites and social forms continually changed to reflect changes in the other. For Confucians, family rituals were occasions to act out certain intellectual allegiances as much as transform strangers into brides, children into adults, or dead bodies into ancestors.

Those unable to read were less constrained by the existence of these texts. It was easier for them to adopt ritual practices recommended by Buddhists, Taoists, geomancers, and other ritual experts who drew on texts and traditions outside of or at odds with the Confucian texts. At times the illiterate may have been influenced by Confucian texts anyway, as they imitated the behavior of higher-ranking people. And when they were not imitating such behavior they were still participating in a ritual system in which Confucian texts played a role as the educated could label them vulgar on the basis of their ignorance of rules encoded in texts.

Chapter Three

REDESIGNING ANCESTRAL RITES FOR A NEW ELITE IN
THE ELEVENTH CENTURY

The ritual texts record the affairs of only one time. The
enlightened way is to expand them so that they can
influence later ages.
—Ch'eng I (1033–1107)[1]

THE ELEVENTH century was a time of dramatic advance in many facets of
culture. The Sung state, founded in 960, was secure within restricted boundaries. The invention of printing had sparked growth in the supply of books,
making education more widely available. The government was as favorably
disposed toward scholars as any in Chinese history. The examination system
for recruitment to office was greatly expanded; in time about half of those
holding government posts had first entered the bureaucracy through success in
highly competitive examinations. Technical advances in industry and agricul-
ture contributed to expansion of the economy and the population. The capital,
K'ai-feng, in the center of North China, became a major metropolis, housing
close to a million people, and there were three or four other cities of comparable size. By the close of the century the total population of the country
reached about one hundred million.

During the early Northern Sung (960–1126), a new type of social and political elite came to the fore, the *shih-ta-fu* or educated class. The T'ang dynasty
had been brought to power by a small circle of families that considered themselves aristocrats, and until nearly the end of the dynasty a restricted circle of
aristocratic families very visibly held onto dominant places in social life and
the higher ranks of the bureaucracy. During this period, the pedigrees and
relative eminence of these families were much discussed among officials and
the educated more generally. In the Sung, by contrast, neither the bureaucracy
nor social life was in any comparable way the special preserve of a clearly
identifiable group. Relatively few families eminent in the T'ang survived the
century of warlord domination to retain their eminence into the Sung. In the
early Sung a socially diverse group was able to gain office and attempt to pave
the way for their descendants.

The early Sung rulers tried to bolster the standing of official families as a

---

[1] ECC i-shu 15:146.

counterweight to the warlords. They were extraordinarily generous in granting the *yin* ("protection") privilege to officials, going far beyond T'ang precedent. Throughout the eleventh century higher officials were granted the right to nominate sons, grandsons, brothers, brothers' sons, sisters' sons, and other relatives to office on successive occasions, including emperors' birthdays, imperial suburban sacrifices, their own retirement, or at their deaths according to their testamentary requests.[2] They also expanded the government school system, the use of sponsorship for promotion through the bureaucracy, and the total size of the bureaucracy.[3] Gradually more and more men were attempting to enter office through the examinations for the *chin-shih* (presented scholar) degree. Only 20,000 to 30,000 candidates were taking the prefectural qualifying examinations in the early eleventh century, but by the end of the century this number had risen to 79,000.[4]

Once one member of a family reached the middle regions of the bureaucracy it was often possible for the family to produce officials generation after generation.[5] A rather extreme case is given in an epitaph for Li Yen-chen (d. 1214). Six generations of his ancestors back to the famous chief councilor Li Fang (925–996) are given, and all held official posts.[6] Moreover, families might have many officials at the same time. When Han I (972–1044) died at seventy three, six sons and three grandsons already held official rank.[7] Ssu-ma Kuang (1019–1086) once mentioned that twenty-three of his Ssu-ma relatives were holding office.[8]

When the Northern Sung *shih-ta-fu* families are compared to educated families of the Ming and Ch'ing periods, their success in placing members in office is remarkable. But eleventh-century scholars and officials could not make that comparison. Because their standard was the aristocratic families of the T'ang, they were often troubled by a sense that their roots were shallow and their family's standing insecure. Prominent men like Wang Tan (957–1017), Lü I-chien (978–1043), Han Ch'i (1008–1075), and Ch'eng I (1033–1107) came from families that had relocated between late T'ang and early Sung, giving them weak local roots. Many writers expressed regret that they did not have genealogical sources that would allow them to trace their ancestry

[2] See Umehara, *Sōdai kanryō seido kenkyū*, pp. 423–500. For a discussion of his evidence in English, see Ebrey, "Dynamics of Elite Domination," pp. 502–5.

[3] See Lee, *Government Education and Examinations in Sung China*, and Lo, *An Introduction to the Civil Service of Sung China*.

[4] Chaffee, *The Thorny Gates of Learning in Sung China*, p. 35.

[5] See Hartwell, "Demographic, Political, and Social Transformations of China, 750–1550," and Hymes, *Statesmen and Gentlemen*, pp. 29–38. The ability to keep producing officials seems to have stemmed in part from the advantages the children of officeholders had in the examinations. See Chaffee, *Thorny Gates*, esp. pp. 61–65.

[6] *Ho-shan chi* 71:14a–b.

[7] *Su Hsün-ch'in chi* 16:208.

[8] SMWCKCCC 65:810–11.

back to the T'ang and earlier.[9] Ou-yang Hsiu (1007–1072) and Sung Ch'i (998–1061), in their new version of the history of the T'ang (*Hsin T'ang shu*), added an innovative feature—genealogies of the families of the chief ministers. The preface explained:

> Just as the T'ang dynasty endured for many generations, its officials cultivated their family traditions and worked to make their houses eminent. Their talented sons and worthy grandsons preserved their hereditary virtue. Sometimes fathers were succeeded by their sons in office; sometimes everyone was prominent for several successive generations; sometimes [these traditions] lasted without break to the end of the T'ang. Were they not magnificent![10]

Scholars' sense that they did not measure up to the T'ang example probably became worse as competition for office increased in the mid-eleventh century. Even with all the advantages officeholders had, perpetuating unbroken lines of mid-rank officials was not easy. Not only did some men have no sons, or sons who died early, but some sons were undoubtedly insufficiently talented to gain posts, even with every possible advantage. By midcentury, as the sons, nephews, and grandsons of high and mid-rank officials took their places in the lower ranks of the bureaucracy, there was less room for the sons of lower-rank officials, not to mention men from other families.

It was in this social context that leading scholars and thinkers of the eleventh century began to discuss strengthening and redesigning ancestral rites. Of all the family rituals, ancestral rites had always had the closest connection to social and political rank. In the classics rulers, nobles, great officers, and ordinary officers were all to perform ancestral rights differently. They were to express the gradations of their ranks through the frequency with which they performed sacrifices, the kinds and quantities of offerings they made, and the number of generations of ancestors they served. Detailed schedules incorporating these principles were provided by the T'ang government in its ritual code, the *K'ai-yüan li*. In neither the classics nor the *K'ai-yüan li* were there schedules for ancestral rites for those without office, even well-educated ones who would consider themselves *shih*. To establish how the educated elite in Sung times should sacrifice to their ancestors would serve symbolically to establish their position in Sung society.

Revitalizing ancestral rites was also attractive because ancestral rites were thought to enhance kinship solidarity and the sense of connection to others. In the *Li-chi* cappings were said to teach adult responsibilities and weddings the differentiation of male and female.[11] Yet Sung scholars seem rarely to have been convinced that the best way to get men to act less childish was to perform

---

[9] See Johnson, "Last Years of a Great Clan," pp. 75–102; Ebrey, "Early Stages of Descent Group Organization," pp. 24–26.

[10] *Hsin T'ang shu* 70A:2179.

[11] *Li-chi* "Kuan-i" 61:2a–b, "Hun-i" 61:6b; Legge, *Rites* 2:426–27, 430.

the capping ceremony when they were twenty or that the best way to get wives to act more feminine was to be sure that no music was played at their weddings. But scholars do seem to have believed that joint rites to common ancestors would lead to greater mutual affection and greater social solidarity among the descendants. They saw nothing exaggerated in the assertions to this effect in the "Great Treatise" chapter of the *Li-chi*.

RITUAL IN NEO-CONFUCIAN THINKING

In rethinking ancestral rites, eleventh-century men were participating in a major revitalization of Confucianism generally called Neo-Confucianism. The Neo-Confucian movement had roots going back to the second half of the T'ang dynasty when a series of leading intellectuals, troubled above all by the political disarray around them, called for reviving the "way of the sages" and thus re-creating a society as great as the "antiquity" portrayed in the classics.[12] This movement gained greater momentum during the eleventh century when the desire to reestablish the greatness of antiquity invigorated all of the arts of the literati—poetry, painting, calligraphy, history, philosophy, and classical studies. Scholar-statesmen like Fan Chung-yen, Ou-yang Hsiu, Han Ch'i, Fu Pi, Wen Yen-po, Ssu-ma Kuang, Wang An-shih, and Su Shih were active in the broad revival of Confucianism going on in the intellectual circles of their day, sharing its leadership with great teachers and writers, such as Sun Fu, Hsü Chi, Hu Yüan, Shih Chieh, Li Kou, Chang Tsai, Ch'eng Hao, and Ch'eng I. Great teachers could attract several thousand students, most of whom intended to attempt the civil service examinations. Yet their students did not learn only the subjects that would be tested by the state examiners. They discussed with their teachers more abstract subjects such as the nature of sages and the way to restore government by sages. Almost all topics that had formed a part of the traditional body of Confucian learning were reexamined, family rituals among them.[13]

During the eleventh century the Neo-Confucian movement encompassed a wide spectrum of approaches to scholarly issues. The great scholar-statesmen were generally committed to reviving all facets of learning and service broadly associated with Confucianism and the literati. As the bearers of culture, *shih* should regulate their lives by the rules of the inherited culture, a principal element of which was ritual in all its meanings. But rituals were also important

[12] On the differences between the Confucianism of early and late T'ang, see McMullen, *State and Scholars*. For the new currents of the late eighth and early ninth centuries, see Pulleyblank, "Neo-Confucianism and Neo-Legalism in T'ang Intellectual Life, 755–805," and Hartman, *Han Yü and the T'ang Search for Unity*.

[13] On eleventh-century Neo-Confucianism and its relationship to broad cultural trends, see Bol, *This Culture of Ours*. A brief overview, still useful after several decades, is de Bary, "A Reappraisal of Neo-Confucianism."

to achieving an orderly society. In general these men were comfortable with relatively secular, demystified views of ritual, and tended to keep in mind all the social and political benefits of everyone adhering to ritual.

Scholar-statesmen like Ssu-ma Kuang, Han Ch'i, Ou-yang Hsiu, Sung Ch'i, and Wang An-shih often contrasted custom (*su*) with ritual (*li*), making an imprecise distinction based on the intentions of the performers and the history of the practices. Custom was generally used to mean what people in any given social group commonly did. Customs might be satisfying because familiar, but were not rooted in ethical principles or the traditions preserved in the classics. Customs were associated with ordinary, uneducated people and thus were often marred by the weaknesses to which they were prone, such as vulgar desires to show off wealth. Ritual these scholars viewed as what people should do, the refined, pious, serious effort to model performance on approved, traditional standards that would have the power to transform those participating. In the ideal state of affairs custom and ritual would be indistinguishable because authentic rituals would become habitual customs.[14]

Of the scholar-statesmen, the one to leave the most lengthy discussions of family rituals was Ssu-ma Kuang. From a well-established official family, Ssu-ma Kuang had a distinguished career in the central government until the rise of Wang An-shih (1021–1086); thereafter he was the leader of the opposition.[15] One of China's most accomplished historians, he wrote the monumental *Tzu-chih t'ung-chien* [Comprehensive mirror for aid in government], a history of China from antiquity to the founding of the Sung. He believed that accurate understanding of the success and failure of political policies over the course of history would reveal the workings of moral principles and would provide many lessons for his own day.[16] In his years as an active official, Ssu-ma Kuang often expressed belief in the importance of ritual at all levels of society. For instance, in 1062 he wrote a memorial that began with the assertion that "Whether a state is orderly or disorderly is rooted in ritual." He then proceeded through a review of history to show that dynasties were generally overthrown by rebellious officials and disloyal subjects. Promotion of Confucianism in general and ritual in particular was the way to instill proper respect for authority and ensure the security of the throne.[17]

[14] Ssu-ma Kuang's ideas and assumptions about ritual will be made clear in this chapter and even more in the next. For the views of some of his contemporaries, see Ou-yang Hsiu in *Hsin T'ang shu* 11:307–8; Sung Ch'i in *Ching-wen chi* 25:318–20; and Wang An-shih in *Wang Lin-ch'uan chi* 75:478.

[15] Ssu-ma Kuang's grandfather, father, and elder brother all held office. For Ssu-ma Kuang's accounts of his family, see SMWCKCCC 77:952–54; 79:980–83.

[16] On Ssu-ma Kuang's political thought, see Bol, "Rulership and Sagehood, Bureaucracy and Society," his *This Culture of Ours*, and Sariti, "Monarchy, Bureaucracy, and Absolutism in the Political Thought of Ssu-ma Kuang." For his historical scholarship, see Pulleyblank, "Chinese Historical Criticism," and Hartwell, "Historical Analogism, Public Policy, and Social Science in Eleventh- and Twelfth-Century China."

[17] SMWCKCCC 24:347–51. Cf. Bol, *This Culture of Ours*, ch. 7: "Ssu-ma's antiquity is of a

In his later years, Ssu-ma Kuang wrote a ten-chapter manual for the performance of rites, his *Shu-i* [Letters and etiquette]. The first chapter of the *Shu-i* gives forms for official and private letters, much as T'ang guides with the title *shu-i* had, and Ssu-ma Kuang relied heavily on these earlier guides for the wording of his letters. The other nine chapters contain liturgies for cappings, weddings, funerals, and ancestral rites.[18] Although Ssu-ma Kuang consulted T'ang *shu-i*, he did not write within the conventions of that genre. His *Shu-i* is both more scholarly and more polemical. The main text often echoes the language of the *I-li* and *K'ai-yüan li*. (No new ritual guide issued by the Sung government had replaced the *K'ai-yüan li* for these purposes.) The extensive notes discuss the canonical basis for the steps outlined. Where there was disagreement among the established authorities concerning the steps or sequence in a rite, Ssu-ma Kuang usually explained the rationale for his choice, citing various classics, commentaries, imperial regulations, and customary practices. His goal in writing the *Shu-i* was not limited to establishing an approved liturgy; he was just as concerned with convincing people to follow it, and many of his most vigorous passages are scathing attacks on contemporary customs.

Orderly performance of the rituals of respect and deference within the domestic setting clearly had great appeal to Ssu-ma Kuang. To achieve this the rules had to be clear. In this *Shu-i*, he attempted at every step to define the limits of what could be considered Confucian ritual. He was offended that the manners of the *shih-ta-fu* had been contaminated by all sorts of deviant customs. Class pride and an intuitive feeling for class survival may both have been involved. Ssu-ma Kuang was frugal by nature, and was ready to adjust established forms to make them less costly.[19] But he did not worry much that a procedure was difficult, or that doing it would make one conspicuous. In retirement he is said to have fashioned clothes according to the descriptions in the classics and worn them both at home and when out visiting.[20] He made a great many large and small adjustments to contemporary customs, but saw these as compromises or simplifications, not improvements on the classics.[21]

Of the thinker-teachers, the two whose views on ritual turned out to be most significant were Chang Tsai and Ch'eng I. Chang Tsai developed a theory of *ch'i*, the material force out of which all phenomena are formed, and Ch'eng I

---

piece with the tradition of imperial governance, in which political stability required persuading and coercing the people to accept their allotted roles. Ssu-ma's world is marked by hierarchy, boundaries, and restraints."

[18] The essay on family management is included in full in *Chu Hsi's Family Rituals*, and thus is available in my translation of that book. Most of chapter ten on ancestral rites is translated without annotation in Ebrey, *Chinese Civilization and Society*, pp. 79–83.

[19] On his ideas about frugality and its relation to family property, see especially SMWCKCCC 67:839–40.

[20] *Shao-shih wen-chien lu* 19:210.

[21] For Ssu-ma Kuang's ideas on ritual, see also Yamane, "Shiba Kō reisetsu kō."

along with his brother Ch'eng Hao developed a theory of *li*, the pattern or principle that extends everywhere and governs all things. Thus all three contributed toward developing a new Confucian metaphysics, an ontology that would support Confucian ethics. All three stressed self-cultivation, or the arduous process of learning that would overcome bad habits and inclinations and lead to the discovery of the true sagelike nature in the learner.[22]

Chang Tsai was credited by contemporaries with leading a revival of ancient ancestral and funerary rites.[23] He fully legitimated the practice of traditional rituals in terms of his ontological theories of *ch'i*. He argued that the practice of correct rituals provided excellent discipline for the student intent on self-cultivation, writing that nothing helped people progress in their studies as quickly as ritual, for when they "make their actions accord with ritual, their *ch'i* spontaneously becomes good."[24] That is, through ritual practice, one could overcome bad *ch'i*; one could free oneself from the entanglements of conventional social life and recover one's true nature. "The reason I have students first study ritual is that by studying ritual they can rid themselves of contemporary customs that through habit come to bind them. . . . Also by studying ritual one can gain fixity."[25] But Chang Tsai saw students progressing beyond mere submission to outward authority toward a selective evaluation of the rituals to follow:

> Ritual is principle [*li*]. One must exhaustively study the principles; the rituals are the means to put into practice their moral meanings. Once one understands the principles one can institute rituals. . . . The current ritual texts are incomplete, so one must first seek the intent of the ritual before evaluating it. Rituals instituted in this way are the ones of the sages, the others were added by later Confucian scholars and can be accepted or rejected.[26]

Thus, in Chang Tsai's view, those who mastered the meaning of the rituals could decide which were faulty and dispense with them and create new ones in their place that were more authentic in that they were based on true moral principles. This view radically challenged the punctilious traditionalist approach to ritual and the authority of the classics. Although scholar-officials had often designed rituals for the emperor from inferences of these sorts, they were doing so on the authority of the ruler and moreover were filling in gaps in the classics. They had generally refrained from redesigning the rituals for gentlemen that were already clearly specified in the *I-li*.

Like Ssu-ma Kuang and other scholar-statesmen, Chang Tsai saw social

[22] On the Ch'eng brothers' philosophy, see Graham, *Two Chinese Philosophers*. On Chang Tsai's philosophy, see Kassoff, *The Thought of Chang Tsai*.

[23] CTC, p. 383, ECC i-shu 2A:23. See also Yamane, "Chōshi reisetsu kō."

[24] CTC, p. 265.

[25] CTC, p. 330. Cf. Kassoff, *The Thought of Chang Tsai*, pp. 81–82.

[26] CTC, pp. 326–27.

and political benefits from the promotion of ritual. Standardized rituals would promote social unity, just as the unstandardized rites of his day led to disarray. "In ancient times rituals were discussed and then set. Thereafter, every family practiced them the same way. Today there are no established forms, so each family makes its own decisions." This deplorable situation, he said, could be called "different customs for each family."[27] Chang Tsai wrote a "Sacrificial Rituals" that does not survive.[28] His surviving treatise on the classics, however, has many comments on particular rituals, confirming both his respect for the discipline of following established forms and his willingness to alter them when he believed a different practice would be better.[29] For instance, he wished to adhere to the canonical rule of wearing only one year's mourning for a mother when the father survived, but to combine the ancient rituals with current practice he suggested that after removing the second grade mourning clothes at the end of the year the sons could wear darkened clothes till the end of the first grade (three-year) mourning period.[30]

Ch'eng I wrote a one-chapter treatise on sacrifices, a liturgy for weddings, and a few essays on particular ritual issues, only fragments of which survive.[31] His students, however, recorded many of his conversations dealing with ritual issues. They reveal that he was primarily concerned with the idea or principle behind rites, and less so with the details of what had been done in classical times or what should be done in his day.[32] He emphasized the internal pole of ritual theory and warned of the dangers of sticking too closely to ancient forms. He or his brother once said,

In practicing rituals, one must not become entirely mired in antiquity. One must recognize that as the style [or climate] of the ages are different, so where one dwells must also be different. Modern people's appearance is not the same as the ancients', and if they exclusively used ancient things, they would not match. Even though these were instituted by the sages, adjustments must be made.[33]

Like Chang Tsai, Ch'eng I frequently asserted that it was possible to create new ritual forms on the basis of moral principles (i-i ch'i-li), and he evaluated practices of his day not merely on the basis of their canonical roots, but also according to human feelings and whether or not they harmed morality. He said, for instance, that one should study ritual texts to understand the intention of the former kings; once that was done one could make changes.[34] In response

27 ECC i-shu 10:113.
28 *CCSLCT* 6:180.
29 CTC, pp. 258–65, 289–303.
30 CTC, p. 300.
31 *CCSLCT* 6:181; ECC wen 10:620–29.
32 For Ch'eng I's views on ritual, see also Yamane, "Ni-Teishi reisetsu kō."
33 ECC i-shu 2A:22.
34 ECC i-shu 2A:23. This passage could be by Ch'eng Hao, as it is unidentified. The phrase i-

to a question on whether to give credence to the ritual systems in the *I-li*, he said to believe only what made sense. On another occasion he said that "the source of rituals is people's feelings; the sages merely made them into a way."[35] In other places he argued that much of the *Li-chi* was based on the distorted theories of conventional Confucian scholars rather than sayings of the sages, and that great worthies and sages should not be constrained by ritual.[36]

FAMILY SHRINES AND STATUS AMBIGUITIES

In the mid-eleventh century, scholar-official families were often unsure how they should perform ancestral rites. Although families at all social levels performed ancestral rites of some sort, the social and intellectual changes of the time had undermined conventional understandings of what was proper. This uncertainty is revealed in an account Shih Chieh (1005–1045) wrote in 1042 when he was in retirement from office because of mourning for his father[37]:

> According to the regulations of the Chou dynasty, the Son of Heaven had seven ancestral shrines [*miao*], feudal lords five, great officers three, higher officers [*shih-shih*] one, and commoners made offerings in their chambers. According to T'ang regulations, those of rank three or higher could erect shrines, expanded in the tenth year of T'ien-pao [751] to include "pure" officials of rank four. My post now is secretary to a regional commander, in our dynasty a rank seven B post. Some commentators say that a higher officer is an upper officer and an official teacher is a middle or lower officer, and that commoners belong with lower functionaries. I am a commoner, but I previously had an appointment from the emperor, lower than higher officer. Should I be classed as an official teacher? By the Chou system I could then have one ancestral shrine, but by the T'ang system I could not have any. Now I make sacrifices in my chamber [i.e., as a commoner]. As my late father was a rank five official of the eastern palace, to honor him in the chamber is really an insult to his spirit according to the way of ghosts, but my rank is too low to set up a shrine.
>
> Because differentiation by rank should not be violated, I have sought a compromise. In the northeast of my house compound I have built a hall of three pillars for [the spirit tablets of] my father and [his five successive wives] the ladies Kuo, Ma, Liu, Yang, and the second Liu. The presentation of the new crops [in the fall] will be made only to my late father and the five ladies, but for the seasonal rites,

---

i ch'i-li had a canonical source in the *Li-chi*. It was the contexts in which Chang Tsai and Ch'eng I evoked it that was new, not the idea itself.

[35] ECC i-shu 22A:285–86; 25:327.

[36] ECC i-shu 18:211, 240.

[37] Shih Chieh is generally recognized as an important early exponent of Confucian revival. See, for instance, Ch'ien, *Sung Ming li-hsüeh kai-shu*, pp. 6–9, and de Bary, "A Reappraisal," p. 92. On Shih Chieh's family background, see also Matsui, "Hoku Sō shoki kanryō no ichi tenkei."

my grandfather and grandmother will also be seated. This is a new idea based on old rituals; it extends the way of spirits but is rooted in human feelings.[38]

Shih Chieh consulted both the classics and T'ang regulations before deciding what to do, but in the end gave considerable weight to what he saw as his particular situation and the honor he believed was due his father.

Ad hoc compromises of this sort naturally led educated men to do things differently one from another. Tu Yen (978–1057) was quoted as saying, "When people make sacrifices to their ancestors, they either are simple and negligent or they are demanding and profane. Few attain the mean."[39] Ou-yang Hsiu reported that Tu's family was the only one to have preserved the family practices of the ancient high officials through the T'ang dynasty to their own day. "Since the T'ang was destroyed, the *shih* [educated gentlemen] have lost the old rituals and simplify everything. Only the Tu family have preserved their family's ways, unaffected by contemporary customs [*shih-su*]."[40] The Tu family was said to have descended from the T'ang scholar-statesman Tu Yu (735–812), and also to have followed a distant ancestor's ritual guide (*shu-i*), making the four seasonal rites at the equinoxes and solstices, using mats instead of tables and chairs, not burning paper money, and having the younger men in the family (not the servants) serve as assistants.[41] It is worth noting that in the classics one divined for the day for the rituals rather than use solar dates, and the assistants seem to have been servants, not sons. Thus Ou-yang Hsiu found the Tu family admirable because they had preserved their family traditions and maintained a distance from custom, not because their practices were identical to those described in the classics.

Han Ch'i seems to have shared the Tu family's concern with preserving the ritual forms of T'ang high officials. In 1070 he wrote a manual for ancestral rites for his family, explaining in the preface (all that survives of it) that in his day families of officials merely followed ordinary custom (*su*) in their ancestral rites and were unable to carry out rites the way high officials had in the T'ang when ancient forms had still been practiced. Although the court nearly thirty years earlier had given permission for officials to erect family shrines, no detailed regulations had yet been issued. Ever since he had taken over the rites in his family, he had been troubled by his failure to find a balance between custom and ritual, and so compared seven manuals for rites written in the T'ang, "selecting what can be performed from earlier theories, deliberating on what is difficult to discard from contemporary custom, and deciding on

---

[38] *Tsu-lai Shih hsien-sheng wen-chi* 19:234–35.

[39] *Tao-shan ch'ing-hua*, p. 2. Tu Yen wrote a one-chapter book on the rituals for the seasonal sacrifices that has not survived. CCSLCT 6:180.

[40] *Ou-yang Hsiu ch'üan chi* Chü-shih chi 31:217. Chang Fang-p'ing also said that Tu Yen's family had ritual forms for all of the steps of the ancestral rites (*Le-ch'üan chi* 39:55a).

[41] *Ch'üeh-sao pien* 2:115.

the basis of human feelings.'' Should the court ever issue regulations, his descendants should naturally follow them instead.[42]

Despite their very high political rank, neither Tu Yen nor Han Ch'i set up a family shrine (*chia-miao*). As Han Ch'i mentioned, the Sung government had not issued workable rules. Officials of rank four or higher in the T'ang had had the privilege of erecting a family shrine where they could make offerings to three or four generations of ancestors, depending on rank. Lower officials were to make offerings only to their parents and grandparents and only in their homes.[43] Ssu-ma Kuang believed that almost all T'ang officials took advantage of these privileges to erect family shrines, citing the exception to prove the rule.[44] Whether he was right or not, by Sung times officials did not have family shrines. In 1041 Emperor Jen-tsung, disturbed that even his highest officials made offerings in their homes, encouraged the erection of family shrines according to the old (T'ang) schedule.[45] In 1050 Sung Hsiang (996–1066) wrote a memorial noting how shameful it was that nobles and officials were performing ancestral rites indistinguishable from ordinary people. He stressed the need to take new circumstances into account; as Sung officials did not have hereditary fiefs like ancient lords, it was necessary to clarify the procedures for succession to a shrine.[46] Limiting family shrines to higher officials after all excluded not only peasants and artisans but also lower officials like Shih Chieh and educated men who considered themselves *shih* or *shih-ta-fu* in the Sung sense of these terms but who did not hold office. In response to Sung Hsiang's memorial, rules were issued allowing the highest officials to set up four altars and the next highest officials to set up three. The following year Wen Yen-po (1006–1097) asked permission to erect a shrine. Not knowing how to proceed, he delayed construction until he happened to visit Ch'ang-an where he saw Tu Yu's old family shrine. Then in 1056 he built a shrine on that model.[47] Note that it was again the model of the T'ang aristocratic families, not the classics, that was sought. To Ssu-ma Kuang, nevertheless, Wen Yen-po was to be admired for the virtues of ''tracing far back to restore antiquity, practicing ritual to bring about moral transformation.''[48] Very few other Sung officials built family shrines, even after Wen Yen-po's example.[49]

If family shrines were a privilege of rank, where should other people make their offerings? Shih Chieh labeled his building a ''sacrificial hall'' (*chi-*

[42] *An-yang chi* 22:9b–10b.

[43] On the successive legislation on family shrines, see *Wen-hsien t'ung-k'ao* 104:945–48 and 105:951–54.

[44] SMWCKCCC 79:973.

[45] Ibid.

[46] *Sung hui-yao* li 12:1a–b.

[47] SMWCKCCC 79:973–74.

[48] SMWCKCCC 79:974.

[49] YL 90:2303.

t'ang). Ssu-ma Kuang reported that many people had rooms called "image halls" (*ying-t'ang*), the term "image" referring to the ancestral portraits they kept there. He considered this practice unobjectionable, even for officials qualified to build family shrines.[50] Ch'eng I also sometimes used the term image hall, once stating that it was all right for the rich and educated without office to build image halls.[51] Ch'eng I is said to have asserted that "*shih-ta-fu* all must set up family shrines [*chia-miao*],"[52] but there is no evidence that his family did so.

PRESIDING AT RITES AND THE *TSUNG* SYSTEM

There was more than one way to remedy the poor fit between classical ancestral rites and contemporary society. At the same time that the scholar-statesmen discussed above sought to revise the ritual codes to match new social realities, a few thinker-teachers proposed reviving the ancient descent-line system, the *tsung* system, thus redesigning society to match the classics better. Ancestral rites were central to their schemes.

The classics were generally interpreted to mean that the descent-line heir (*tsung-tzu*) of a particular ancestor was the only one fully qualified to manage sacrifices to him. The descent-line heir of each ancestor was his eldest son and, after the latter's death, *his* own eldest son, and so on. In the case of a great line (*ta-tsung*) descended from a younger son of a feudal lord, the line would continue indefinitely and thus each ancestor in the direct line would receive sacrifices in perpetuity. Younger sons would continually be the focus for new lesser lines (*hsiao-tsung*) that would last four generations, after which ancestral rites would cease.

The *K'ai-yüan li* did not follow the *tsung* system in its provisions for ancestral rites, instead phrasing them in terms of official rank. The implication, no where refuted in the text, is that an official could make offerings to his great-grandfather even if his grandfather was a younger brother. This approach probably reflected the realities of family organization. In ancient times, descent lines were the core of kinship groups, but since Han times, the basic kinship group at all social levels had been the coresident family (*chia*). The *tsung* system was suited to the Chou aristocratic system in which the family patrimony was an indivisible office or appanage, rather than private property that could be freely bought, sold, or mortgaged. Brothers were differentiated according to age, with the eldest son responsible for preserving the ancestral rites and the patrimony that supported them. But in the imperial period descent was not thought of in terms of a single line. Younger sons were just as much expected to marry and have children as older ones and would share equally in

50 SMSSI 10:113.

51 ECC i-shu 22A:286.

52 ECC wai-shu 1:352. Cf. ECC i-shu 18:241.

the family estate if and when it was divided. Division could rarely be delayed much beyond the death of the father as family head so that it was exceptionally rare for all of the descendants of a great-great-grandfather to live together.[53]

In the mid-eleventh century a few Neo-Confucian scholars seriously proposed reviving the descent-line heir system. In 1043 Li Kou (1009–1059) wrote a set of fifty essays on how the *Chou-li* could be used to design a better social order, one of which was devoted to the *tsung* system. He also prepared a diagram to explain how the nesting of the various *tsung* worked.[54] Li Kou was particularly concerned with giving organizational focus to distant relatives though the great-line (*ta-tsung*) system.

> The five grades of mourning are a major means of attaining order among people. But they extend back only to the great-great-grandfather and to the third collateral line. When [kinship ties] end with the great-great-grandfather, we forget those more remote. When cousinship ends with the third collateral line, we forget the more distant. Therefore when great lines are established to succeed to the ancestors, and agnatic kinsmen beyond the five generations assemble at the home of the descent-line heir in generational sequence, then the first ancestor will receive sacrifices forever and the members of the clan will remain close indefinitely.[55]

In 1055 Su Hsün (1009–1066) compiled a genealogy for the descendants of his great-great-grandfather, much as Shih Chieh had, and like him had it carved on stone and erected by the family graves. Unlike Shih Chieh, however, he explicitly related his efforts to the revival of the *tsung* system. He described how the ancient *tsung* system worked, with its division into the great line that continues indefinitely and the nesting lesser lines that break off from it every generation and are composed, respectively, of the descendants of great-great-grandfather, great-grandfather, grandfather, and father, each led in ritual by its descent-line heir.[56] Unlike Li Kou, Su Hsün was primarily concerned with the lesser descent line. He wrote that only the Son of Heaven and those who had from the beginning been of great officer rank could in his day form great lines. All others, such as his family, should look on their patrilineal relatives in terms of the lesser descent-line system.[57]

Chang Tsai also proposed reviving the *tsung* system. As he explained, the key implication of organizing ancestral rites on the descent line rather than the household basis was that a younger son, even if he lived apart from his elder brother, would not keep a tablet for his father or make offerings to him. In the

---

[53] On the relationship of property law to Sung family organization, see Ebrey, *Family and Property in Sung China*, pp. 81–155.

[54] *Li Kou chi*, pp. 114–15, 130–32. Cf. Hsieh, *Life and Thought of Li Kou*, esp. pp. 73–76, 104–12.

[55] *Li Kou chi*, p. 114.

[56] *Chia-yu chi* 13:130–31.

[57] *Chia-yu chi* 13:131.

next generation his own eldest son would make offerings to only one generation (to him), though in all cases the younger sons and descendants of younger
sons were supposed to join in as participants at the rites held before the tablets
in the possession of the descent-line heir. Chang Tsai tried to convince his
contemporaries that this system was not unfair to younger sons.

> What the ancients meant by "younger sons do not sacrifice" is just that the de-
> scent-line heir sets up the shrine and presides at it. The younger son, although he
> cannot sacrifice, is no different from the one who presides at the sacrifices in
> purifying himself and in expressing his reverence. If he can attend, he helps in
> person; if he cannot, he helps by supplying goods.[58]

Chang Tsai realized that reorganizing according to *tsung* principles would re-
quire real changes in kin behavior but thought it could be done:

> The families of great officials today could set up the descent-line heir system. For
> instance, if a man has several sons, the eldest should be made the main line and
> raised and provided for as the descent-line heir, in accordance with the family's
> wealth. Once the descent-line heir has ample resources, if he wishes it, he can
> distribute some of the assets equally to the kinsmen. . . . If the descent-line heir
> is not good, [the father] should install the next worthy one.[59]

Chang Tsai, thus, did not talk about giving up sacrifice to one's grandfather
and great-grandfather if one's father or grandfather were younger brothers.
Rather he proposed starting by making distinctions among one's sons that
would affect rites in subsequent generations.

Ch'eng I took positions very similar to Chang Tsai on ancestral rites and
undoubtedly they influenced each other.[60] On the *tsung* system, he remarked:

> If the system of the descent-line heir is not established, there will be no hereditary
> officials at court. One or two great families of officials ought to establish the
> descent-line system. Once the system is [fully] established everyone will know
> where he came from.[61]

As I have discussed elsewhere, part of the motivation for promoting the
lesser descent-line system seems to have been a desire to get educated men to
look beyond the narrow (and possibly selfish) interests of their own household
to a wider group consisting of all those descended from a common ancestor.[62]
The injunction of the *Ta-hsüeh* [Greater learning] to regulate one's family in

[58] CTC, p. 260. This same passage is attributed to Ch'eng I in ECC i-shu 15:165.

[59] CTC, p. 260.

[60] Several passages on the *tsung* in each of their collected works are word-for-word identical,
but they each have enough other passages relating to sacrifices and related topics to show that they
shared very similar views, even if some passages are misattributed.

[61] ECC i-shu 17:179.

[62] Ebrey, "Early Stages of Descent Group Organization," p. 39.

preparation for governing the world seemed more noble if taken to mean a wider group of kin. Chang Tsai and Ch'eng I both seem to have idealized life among kinsmen. It is probably significant that neither lived near his cousins. Chang Tsai's father was from Ta-liang (Shantung), but had died at a post not far west of Ch'ang-an while Chang Tsai and his younger brother were young, and they then made this their home.[63] The Ch'eng family was originally from Hopei, but Ch'eng I's great-great-grandfather about a century earlier had moved south during the wars of the Five Dynasties, first to Li-ch'uan west of Ch'ang-an, then to K'ai-feng.[64] Ch'eng I had second cousins in K'ai-feng, third cousins near Ch'ang-an, and fourth cousins in Hopei.[65]

The attraction of the *tsung* system did not lie simply in the vision of kinship solidarity it evoked. Chang Tsai associated it with families of great officials and Ch'eng I with hereditary official families. Their desire to institute descent-line principles thus may also reflect a desire to enable families of officials to maintain their standing, at least through one son, generation after generation, without having to depend entirely on the government.[66]

It should be stressed that whereas an interest in revitalizing ancestral rites appears to have been quite widespread among scholar-officials of the Northern Sung, only a few went so far as to urge a revival of the *tsung* system. Han Ch'i apparently rejected the calls for reviving the *tsung* system as he referred to himself as taking over ancestral rites for his family even though he was a

[63] CTC, p. 381.

[64] For Ch'eng I's and Ch'eng Hao's accounts of their family, see ECC wen-chi 4:495–97, 499–501, 12:645–60. On their family see also Yao Ming-ta, *Ch'eng I-ch'uan nien-p'u*, esp. pp. 1–15.

[65] Something of Ch'eng I's idealized view of the settled life among the descendants of his ancestors can be seen in his description of his visits to the old home of his great-great-grandfather near Ch'ang-an.

When the Junior Preceptor settled in Li-ch'uan, his house was modest and cramped. When I was young I once visited it; it still had titles for each room that my late father, the Palace Grand Master, had written. Ten years later I visited again, but it had already been sold by the descendants of the branch descended from Fourth Grandfather. As others were living there I could not bear to go to look at it. . . . When my late father was prefect of Feng, Fourth Grandfather asked if he would like to have the house, but he replied that whether Uncle had it or he did was the same, so long as he took good care of it. [Fourth Grandfather] also took out a small seal of the Junior Preceptor's and showed it to me, saying, "This was your ancestor's; you keep it." I said, "It is good enough if Grandfather keeps it," not accepting it to calm his suspicions. I also did not dare to ask to see the edicts from Emperor T'ai-tsung, or the portrait of the Vice Director, which still survived. Who would have thought that a few years later Fourth Grandfather would die, so that when I returned a little later to Li-ch'uan everything would be scattered! Recalling it is painful. (ECC wen-chi 12:657–58)

Twenty years later when Ch'eng I again returned he was able to find a few souvenirs of his great-great-grandfather in the possession of three different relatives.

[66] Cf. Bol, "Ch'eng Yi and the Cultural Tradition," especially his discussion of Ch'eng I's attitude toward his qualification to advise the emperor based on his descent from meritorious officials.

sixth son and his eldest brother, while long dead, had grandsons and great-grandsons.[67] Ssu-ma Kuang was also unconvinced by current talk of reviving the *tsung* system and in his liturgical manual had the male family head preside at sacrifices. He explained:

> According to the "Ch'ü-li" [chapter of the *Li-chi*], a younger son does not sacrifice. In the "Tseng Tzu wen" [chapter of the *Li-chi*], when the descent-line heir is a *shih* while a lesser son is a great officer, they sacrifice with the higher rank sacrificial meats at the home of the descent-line heir. In ancient times the agnatic kinsmen of feudal lords, ministers, and great officers all lived together in a single state; thus they could perform rites this way. Nowadays when elder and younger brothers all serve in office, they scatter in all directions. Even younger brothers think of their parents at the four seasons. How can they fail to make sacrifices![68]

Why did Ssu-ma Kuang disagree with Chang Tsai and Ch'eng I on this issue? In many ways their social and intellectual backgrounds were similar. All three were contemporaries, Ssu-ma Kuang a year older than Chang Tsai and fourteen years older than Ch'eng I. They all were ardent in their commitment to revive a true Confucianism based on the teachings of the ancient sages. All, moreover, came from well-established official families of North China. Ssu-ma Kuang's family had lived in Shen-chou, west of Lo-yang, for over seven hundred years. During the period when Wang An-shih's New Policies were being promoted (1068–1085), both Ch'eng I and Ssu-ma Kuang spent much of their time in the city of Lo-yang where they saw each other from time to time and shared many common friends.[69] Ssu-ma Kuang's lack of interest in the *tsung* system probably reflects his disinclination to discard traditions that had accumulated over centuries in order to revive practices described only in the classics. A conservative in most senses of the term, Ssu-ma Kuang always tried to maintain and strengthen the traditional sources of social order and authority. At the same time, Ssu-ma Kuang's support for having the household head preside at ancestral rites may reflect his personal experience in his large, multigeneration family. All those descended from his great-grandfather lived together.[70] In his writings on family organization and ethics in his *Chia-fan* [Models for the family] and *Chü-chia tsa-i* [Miscellaneous proprieties for managing a family] he argued for a strongly hierarchical family with the family head exercising great authority over other family members.[71] For the family head to lead all of the members, lined up in order,

[67] See *An-yang chi* 46:13a, 29b.

[68] SMSSI 10:113.

[69] A good source for literati social and cultural life in Loyang in this period is the *Shao-shih wen-chien lu*, written by Shao Yung's son Po-wen (1056–1134).

[70] Ssu-ma Kuang describes the organization of his family in several epitaphs for close relatives. See especially SMWCKCCC 77:952, 954, 79:980–82.

[71] *Chia-fan*, passim. SMSSI 4:41–46; Ebrey, *Chu Hsi's Family Rituals*, pp. 24–34.

through regular rites, would have reinforced this order. Ssu-ma Kuang did not yearn to create a new extended kin unit. Nor did he want to disturb the tradition of the family head (probably the oldest male) presiding at the rites in favor of the representative of the descent line (the eldest son of the eldest son of the eldest son, who might be a child if his father died young). Ssu-ma Kuang was himself a younger brother and by repute quite respectful to his elder brother, but he apparently conducted ancestral rites himself when he lived in Lo-yang apart from his brother.

DISCARDING STATUS LIMITATIONS

Ch'eng I's efforts to revitalize ancestral rites were not confined to promoting the *tsung* system. He also proposed a major reinterpretation of the classics to bring the rules for ancestral rites into conformity with society. Ch'eng I's best-known contribution to the Confucian discourse on family rituals was his legitimation of forms of ancestral rituals that, by both canonical standards and government rules, were highly presumptuous. Both Chang Tsai and Ssu-ma Kuang followed the common upper-class practice of making offerings to three generations of ancestors, which was certainly generous by canonical standards, as this was the level specified for ministers (*ch'ing*). Shih Chieh, as seen above, restricted himself to two generations. Neither Ssu-ma Kuang nor Chang Tsai explicitly discussed what commoners should do, as the classics had permitted them only to make offerings to their fathers and the government codes were largely silent on this issue. Ch'eng I, willing to create new ritual forms, argued that people of all ranks should be able to make sacrifices back four generations.

> There are no distinctions in the five grades of mourning garments from the Son of Heaven down to commoners: all of them wear mourning up to their great-great-grandfather. If this is the case with mourning, it should also be the case with sacrificial offerings. The details cannot be known, but the principle is this: even those with seven or five shrines only go back to their great-great-grandfather; even great officers and *shih* with three, two, or one shrine, or who make offerings in their chamber, despite their differences, may sacrifice to their great-great-grandfather without harm. If they only sacrifice to their parents, it is like the animals who only know their mothers and not their fathers. To make offerings to parents but not grandparents is not the way of humans.[72]

Elsewhere Ch'eng I went further and stated that the idea that the number of altars should vary from seven for the Son of Heaven on down was nothing but a theory of ritualists. Since ritual could be created on the basis of moral principles, it was perfectly all right for educated men without office to build image

---

[72] ECC i-shu 15:167. Cf. ECC i-shu 15:163.

halls. When one of his students asked specifically about the common practice of not sacrificing to great-great-grandfathers, he said that it was very wrong.[73] To the extent that most people exceeded the canonical limitations on generations, Ch'eng I was accommodating custom; he was bringing current practice within the sphere that could be labeled Confucian.

Ch'eng I was also ready to discard sumptuary rules with regard to the objects used to represent the ancestors in rites. He advocated general use of wooden tablets inscribed with the names and titles of the ancestors, a practice referred to in the classics as used by kings and feudal lords.[74] He drew diagrams of what ancestral tablets were to look like, explaining the symbolism of their dimensions in cosmological terms.[75] In this case Ch'eng I was not validating contemporary practice, but trying to reform it by a creative adaption of ancient forms. Some of his contemporaries may have used objects called tablets, but practice does not seem to have been standardized. Wen Yen-po was said to have used spirit boards (shen-pan), drawing on a tradition going back to the third century.[76] Ssu-ma Kuang used prayer boards (tz'u-pan) for the rites and also mentioned portraits.[77] Ch'eng I, like Chang Tsai, objected to the use of ancestral portraits, arguing that unless every hair was drawn exactly, one was not actually sacrificing to one's ancestor, but to someone else.[78] But he offered a substitute, tablets, that many people in time found satisfactory, perhaps in part because it had once been a privilege of high rank.

The limitation on performing rites only four times a year Ch'eng I also discarded. In this he seems to have been accepting what was commonly done at all social levels. Wen Yen-po made offerings five times a year, at New Year, the Clear and Bright festival in the spring, the fall equinox and the summer and winter solstices.[79] Chang Tsai described his own practice as consisting in a single offering at the beginning and midpoint of each month and at New Year, and triple offerings at the seasonal sacrifices on the solstices and equinoxes. At Clear and Bright and the Ten-one festival he made a single offering and visited the graves.[80] For death day anniversaries, Chang Tsai would take out all the tablets and offer wine and food but not burn paper money.[81]

In his schedule for rites, Ch'eng I had the four seasonal rites, as in the classics, but added two others based loosely on canonical precedents for royal

[73] ECC i-shu 22A:285–86.

[74] On one occasion Ch'eng I allowed some sumptuary differentiation, saying commoners should use placards (p'ai) instead of tablets (chu) for listing their ancestor's names (ECC i-shu 22A:286).

[75] ECC wen-chi 10:627–28.

[76] SMWCKCCC 79:975.

[77] SMSSI 10:115, 121.

[78] ECC i-shu 22A:286; CTC, p. 298.

[79] SMWCKCCC 79:975.

[80] CTC, pp. 289–90, 315, 365–66.

[81] CTC, p. 289.

sacrifices, one to first ancestors (*shih-tsu*) at the winter solstice, the other to early ancestors (*hsien-tsu*) on the lunar first day of spring.[82] He also added a third sacrifice to deceased fathers in the last month of fall, possibly based on contemporary custom as Shih Chieh also sacrificed to only one generation in the fall. Like Chang Tsai, Ch'eng I had sacrifices on death-day anniversaries, holding them in the main room of the house rather than the ancestral hall.[83] Ch'eng I did not mention New Year or Clear and Bright, perhaps not wanting to copy custom so exactly. The first day of spring and New Year were normally very close, however, and he may have seen his designation of a rite on the first day of spring as a slightly more canonical version of the popular rite.

RITES TO EARLY ANCESTORS AND RITES AT GRAVES

In the classics only great lines descended through first sons from a remote first ancestor (supposedly a younger son of a feudal lord) made sacrifices to their ancestors more than four generations back. Li Kou had wished to reestablish this system as a way of fostering kinship solidarity. In practice, many Sung families made sacrifices to distant ancestors, but as a component of sacrifices at graves rather than in halls or in household shrines. Sacrifices had been made at graves for many centuries, but the practice was not rooted in the classical *tsung* system.[84] The practice had received imperial approval in the T'ang, and if anything grew in importance in Sung times.[85] Shih Chieh, for instance, built a hall by the side of his ancestors' graves to provide cover for the stele recording the family's genealogy and room for sacrificial rites. "Each year when we visit the graves to make reports and bow, we always offer sacrifices, so we need somewhere to set up the equipment."[86] Han Ch'i wrote an account of an impressive ceremony he performed on the Clear and Bright festival at the graves of his parents and grandparents. He also wrote many poems to commemorate visits he made over the years to his family's graves.[87]

Rites at graves presented two problems to Confucian scholars—were graves an appropriate site for sacrifices, and if so, should distant ancestors receive sacrifices there as well as recent ones? Visiting tombs to make announcements to ancestors was mentioned in the classics, but sacrificing (*chi*) to them there was not. Ch'eng Hao (or Ch'eng I in his earlier years) did not seem inclined to endorse rites at graves, as he stressed that they were not a canonical ritual,

[82] The royal *ti* sacrifice was generally taken to be a sacrifice to the founder of the line and the royal *hsia* sacrifice to be to all of the early ancestors. The classics included several contradictory references to when these sacrifices would be offered.

[83] ECC i-shu 18:240; wen-chi 10:628–29.

[84] See Wu Hung, "From Temple to Tomb," for evidence that it was fostered by the practices of the Later Han imperial family.

[85] Ebrey, "Early Stages of Descent Group Organization," pp. 20–29.

[86] *Tsu-lai Shih hsien-sheng wen-chi* 19:235–36.

[87] *An-yang chi* 2:12b–13a, ch. 18–20, passim.

and that emperors in instituting them had simply followed custom.[88] Chang Tsai, however, approved of grave rites, and Ch'eng I eventually came to include them in his schedule.[89] He seems to have done this because he saw them as relatively harmless:

> Someone asked, "What is the basis for the modern rite of bowing and sweeping [at graves]?"
>
> He said, "This rite did not exist in antiquity, and simply became customary [su]. However, it does not harm moral principles [pu-hai i-li]. The ancients were straightforward and sincere. Burial is simply hiding the body and earthly soul; the spirit always returns to the shrine. Once [the body] is buried, a wooden tablet is set up, and once the mourning rites are over, the wooden tablet is settled in the shrine. Therefore the ancients simply concentrated on the offerings in the altar. Today people also use the rite of bowing and sweeping. It is just that it should be done on a simpler scale than the sacrifices for the four seasons.[90]

Elsewhere Ch'eng I endorsed sacrifices to early ancestors in quite strong language, not specifying where they should be performed: "All known ancestors, no matter how distant, must be given sacrifices. How can ancestors not be repaid? How can one complain that there are too many? One's root is there. No matter how far it is, it must be repaid."[91]

Justifying rites at graves and rites to early ancestors (which were generally performed at graves but did not have to be) was just as major a breakthrough as allowing gentlemen and commoners to sacrifice to great-great-grandparents. Above all, it allowed the movement to re-create Confucian ancestral rites to graft itself onto already well-developed sentiments and practices. Getting one's relatives to do something they had never done before was naturally more difficult than giving a different name to a rite they already performed.

CONCLUSIONS

This chapter has covered only one century and only one of the four family rituals. By narrowing its scope I have been able to explore in some detail what existing texts such as the classics and K'ai-yüan li had to do with the performance of ancestral rituals among the educated, how these men interpreted such texts and handled contradictions among them, how they used terms or ideas from books to interpret their own actions or the actions of those around them, how they drew from their own experiences to give meaning to what they read in books, and how all of these processes impinged on the writing of new

[88] ECC i-shu 1:6.
[89] ECC i-shu 1:6, 2B:51.
[90] ECC i-shu 18:241.
[91] ECC i-shu 17:180.

books, such as Chang Tsai's "Sacrificial Rituals," Ch'eng I's "Wedding Rituals," and Ssu-ma Kuang's *Shu-i*.

Through a complex set of debates on fine points of ritual, the Sung intellectual elite gradually worked out a way to perform ancestral rites that suited their needs and interests. The eleventh century was a more mobile, urbanized, and commercialized society than anything known previously in Chinese history. Men in the ruling elite were searching for ways to define their identity, responsibilities, and privileges. Troubled by the diversity and instability around them, they searched for ways to enhance their sense of connection without losing their distinct identity. Ch'eng I rejected many traditional status distinctions and sumptuary principles; Ssu-ma Kuang did not so explicitly reject them, but he tended to ignore them, discussing the forms of ritual in universalistic ways. Each worked hard not to define the boundaries of appropriate ritual behavior too narrowly along canonical grounds, each accepting many (though not the same) contemporary practices. They did this because in their social milieu there was no real social class difference between a high official and a mid-rank one, or even between the son of an official who had himself gained office and his younger brother who had not (like Ch'eng Hao and Ch'eng I). They preferred to draw a line between those who practiced ritual and those who followed custom. This was a line with which they were intellectually comfortable; it allowed them to view what we might see as social class distinctions as instead differences of ethics and intentions.

The measures proposed by eleventh-century scholars can easily be seen in ideological terms. Ancestral rites celebrate ancestry; the *tsung* system evoked images of hereditary officials. Both promoted the independence of the elite from the government. The Northern Sung government perceived no threat, however, and largely left scholars to debate the issues among themselves. And even if these proposals were intended to enhance the security of the *shih-ta-fu* stratum, they also benefited ordinary, uneducated folk by de-emphasizing political rank and thus reducing barriers to upward social mobility. The distinction between those who followed ritual and those who followed custom was not nearly as rigid as the distinction between officials and commoners or rank five officials and lower officials.

Even if there were ideological dimensions to proposals for forms of ancestral rites, people with very similar family backgrounds could argue for distinctly different positions. Ssu-ma Kuang and Ch'eng I provide the best examples. Their family status was remarkably similar; the only major difference in their backgrounds was that the Ssu-ma family had been resident in the same area for centuries, but the Ch'eng family had relocated several times in the preceding century. Yet these two men took opposing stances on most of the debated issues concerning ancestral rites. Ch'eng I was for the *tsung* system, Ssu-ma Kuang not; Ch'eng I was for allowing everyone to sacrifice to four generations of ancestors, Ssu-ma Kuang not; Ch'eng I was for performing ancestral rites on more occasions than the canonical four, Ssu-ma Kuang not; Ssu-ma Kuang tolerated ancestral portraits, Ch'eng I did not.

Philosophical commitments and larger cultural orientations provide the only satisfactory explanations for the differences between these two men. Ssu-ma Kuang, like many other scholar-statesmen of his age, saw value in a wide range of traditions, including those documented in the classics, but also those known from other written sources, including imperial ritual codes and etiquette books. Ch'eng I approached ancestral rites above all in terms of ethics. Those familiar with Ch'eng I's philosophy will have noticed many ways his comments on ancestral rituals are congruent with his larger philosophical positions. His willingness to dismiss the ritual classics as the product of Han Confucians of no distinction is not unlike his attitude toward much of the cumulative learning of Han through T'ang Confucian scholars. His attention to the inner meaning of rites is matched by concern with the inner meaning of other social and political phenomena. Ch'eng I's search for basic meanings can also be related to his philosophical emphasis on principle or pattern (li). His larger attitudes toward rites make sense in terms of his notions of human nature, as he generally saw insight as more crucial than discipline in recovering the true goodness in people's inborn nature.

Philosophical premises were important because discourse on ancestral rites was highly intellectualized. In Chapter Two I mentioned that by writing about rituals, scholars made rituals into an intellectual object, something to think about more than something to do. This process was carried the furthest for ancestral rites, perhaps because their symbolic meanings appeared transparent and closely linked to the ethics of filial piety and the hierarchical structure of society. Scholars evaluated them not on the basis of their efficacy, on their ability to bring rewards of a social, spiritual, or material sort. They did not debate what ancestors were or how they were affected by offerings of food or drink. Rather they analyzed ancestral rites in terms of their symbolism, especially the ways they symbolized the hierarchy of society.

People did, of course, also perform ancestral rites, and their performances were not unrelated to the discourse about these rites. Performance took place in real-life situations in which not all goals were readily attainable. Ch'eng I reported having tried to reform the practice of ancestral rites in his own family, which included quite a few relatives senior to him in both age and ritual seniority. Ch'eng I's father was an eldest son, but his grandfather was a second son, so that according to the *tsung* system rites to his great-grandfather were the responsibility of his grandfather's elder brother and his eldest son and senior grandson. Ch'eng I would not even have been in charge of the rites to his father, who died in 1090, for they would have been the responsibility of Ch'eng Hao's eldest son Tuan-i. Ch'eng I reported that because "many in the family liked the old customs from Ho-pei [where the family had come from a century earlier] [he] had not been able to make thorough changes; rather [he] had fostered gradual recognition of the principles.''[92] Ch'eng I or Ch'eng Hao reported that in their family for sacrifices they had the men and women in different places, but beyond that they had only tried slight changes in one or two places where the family's practice most harmed moral principles.[93]

[92] ECC i-shu 18:240.
[93] ECC i-shu 2B:51.

Chapter Four

COMBATING HETERODOXY AND VULGARITY IN
WEDDINGS AND FUNERALS

It would be no small contribution to get the common
people to abandon evil customs and participate in ritual.
—Ssu-ma Kuang (1019–1086)[1]

OF THE STANDARD set of family rituals, ancestral rites were the ones most tied
to social and political rank and yet at the same time the most private, as they
were largely performed within the confines of homes. Scholars could plausibly
propose rather radical restructuring of them. Weddings and funerals, by contrast, were performed publicly and often at great expense. They involved processions through towns and across the countryside, with some of the participants dressed in highly distinctive costumes. Heightened emotions—
excitement, joy, grief, fear, anger—were intrinsic to these rituals. Like rites
of passage in other societies, weddings and funerals in China provided structured and dramatic ways for people to work through the social tensions and
psychological uncertainties attendant on transitions from one status to another.

FOUR INCIDENTS

To provide a sense of what weddings and funerals meant in North China literati social circles in the eleventh century, I will recount four incidents, quoting
the primary sources at length.

In 1041 the teacher and scholar Shih Chieh (1005–1045) finally completed
the burial of seventy of his relatives who had died during the preceding five
generations. Shih Chieh's family came originally from Hopei, but at the end
of the T'ang his great-great-great-grandfather had moved to Feng-fu county in
Shantung. Shih Chieh's father was the first in this family to serve in office. At
twenty-six *sui*, in 1030, Shih Chieh passed the *chin-shih* in the top class (along
with Ou-yang Hsiu and Ts'ai Hsiang, discussed below). He went on to serve
in a few low local posts before resigning to mourn for his stepmother. It was

[1] SMWCKCCC 69:858.

during this mourning period that he and his father undertook the permanent burial of the coffins that had been left with only temporary protection.[2]

Burying so many relatives was undoubtedly an expensive undertaking, so Shih Chieh wrote to friends and acquaintances to request assistance. An early letter was sent to a prefect named Hu who probably knew his father. The letter began with a discussion of the importance of filial piety, then went on:

> My father is seventy-one *sui*, and yet five generations have not yet been buried. We have divined that the next *hsin-ssu* year [1041] is auspicious. The shrouds and coffins have not yet been prepared because of the inadequacy of our salaries. . . . My family has forty members to feed. Since my great-great-grandfather, it has farmed for a living, but the fields are poor and the oxen weak, so we have regularly been in straits. Every year we have maximized what we could get from the weather, the land, and our labor, plus have had my father's and my own salaries, and yet these forty have just had enough to eat. Now my salary is stopped [because I am in mourning].[3]

After that letter was sent Shih Chieh's father also died. He then wrote to his classmate Wang Kung-chen (1012–1085), who had passed first in the examination of 1030.

> When people suffer calamities, they weep, shout, and rail to seek help from others. . . . The Shih family, for over a hundred years, from the Chou and Han [of the Five Dynasties] through the eighty-one years of the Sung, has had seventy deaths, from my great-great-grandfather to his sixth-generation grandchildren, but none are yet reburied. This can truly be called a calamity. Only by weeping, shouting, and railing to seek help from others will a remedy be possible. This is why I am writing to you from several hundred *li* away, my voice and spirit broken, weeping silently. . . .
>
> My late father was working on the [burial project] for thirty years, until the eighth month of [last] year, but before his goal was achieved he died. Near his end, he was ready to face death, but took my hand and instructed me, "I will not rest if you cannot fulfill my goal." Seventeen months have passed since I accepted this order, during which I have not dared to eat well, sleep calmly, dress warmly, or amuse myself with wine. . . . I am in great fear of failing my father's instruction and being charged by everyone with the sin of unfiliality. In the light of day I will be blamed; in the dark regions my father will nurture resentment, and the *hun* souls of the seventy dead will have nowhere to go. . . . This major task will require 500,000 cash.[4]

---

[2] *Tsu-lai Shih hsien-sheng wen-chi* fu-lu 2:260–61. The coffins had probably been left above ground and covered with clay or soil as a transitional measure, a custom in North China of considerable antiquity.

[3] Ibid. 17:203–4.

[4] Ibid. 14:168–70.

An even more direct request was sent to a certain Mr. Tung who had served with his father:

> Recently I traveled to Ssu-shang and the capital to collect personally the bones of my grandmother and parents in order to bury them in the region between T'ai-shan and Tsu-lai [in Shantung]. Because we were too poor to be able to prepare the coffins and vaults, my father would look up to Heaven and weep each morning and night. . . . You sir are amply supplied with wealth and rich in moral principles. You ought to complete my father's burial. This will show how you fulfill your desire to help worthies and assist the way.[5]

Apparently some of those solicited responded, for on the eighth day of the eighth month of 1041 Shih Chieh was able to finish the burial. He reported that the graveyard was 408 by 360 feet for a total of seventeen *mu* and had 1,880 trees growing on it. In front of the graves he erected a stone stele five feet tall, inscribed with a full genealogy of his family over the one hundred fifty years since they had first moved to that area.[6] It concluded:

> Alas, the Shih family has been fed from these fields for one hundred fifty years and has buried in this spot for over ninety years. From the first ancestor to K'uei, for eight generations, we have been able to avoid losing the old fields and to make the ancestral offerings. Now we make thirty-two graves for those from the great-great-grandfather generation on down, returning them to the great graveyard. . . . As long as the descendants of the Shih family are worthy, the graveyard will be secure and the graves peaceful, the trees will flourish, and the sacrifices will be made on time. Should any be unworthy, anything might happen. Take heed![7]

The second incident can be described more briefly as it is not so fully documented. In 1046 Shih Chieh's classmate Ts'ai Hsiang (1012–1067) was appointed prefect of Fu-chou, in Fukien, just north of his hometown of Hsing-hua. While there he posted "five warnings" for the local population, parts of which concerned weddings and funerals.

> When [people's parents] die, they bankrupt themselves, selling their homes, to set out wine and food for relatives and friends and to make donations to the Buddhists to seek blessings in the netherworld. These actions are not based on feelings for their parents, but on desires to show off in front of others. . . . Marriages concern the desire for descendants, not wealth. When I observe current customs, those who choose wives do not pay attention to family status, but only seek a dowry in line with their wealth. As a consequence, relatives through marriage all

---

[5] Ibid. 16:187–88.

[6] Ibid. 19:235–36, fu-lu 1:255.

[7] Ibid. fu-lu 1:250–55. There were thirty-two graves rather than seventy because husbands and wives were regularly buried together. A grave might also include more than one wife or a child who died young.

become enemies. This can be traced back to the day of the wedding, when, having spent a great deal, they search the trousseau cases, in the morning searching one and the evening another. The mother-in-law insults the bride, the husband mal-treats his wife, each making endless demands.[8]

Sometime later Ts'ai Hsiang posted a notice entirely devoted to the problem of funeral feasts. He referred again to the ruinous expense, elaborating:

When a death occurs, no one in the family dares wail until they have arranged a sale or mortgage of land or houses. Not until the settlement has been negotiated can they lay out the body. . . . On the eve of the burial, neighbors, whether ac-quainted or not, all come to condole, eating meat and drinking wine to their fill without restraint, until the resources of the family in mourning are totally de-pleted. In such situations neighbors should be making gifts to help the family in mourning. How can they willfully eat meat and drink wine, holding a feast! These are people with no sense of ritual. The monasteries hold maigre feasts to which monks and laymen are invited, including some not acquainted [with the de-ceased's family]. If the feast is not adequate, 200 cash has to be given to each person. Any shortage leads immediately to quarreling. . . . Is this any different from begging![9]

Ts'ai Hsiang had this prohibition inscribed on a stone and erected at the gate to the city. Many years later when Ou-yang Hsiu composed Ts'ai Hsiang's epitaph, he gave considerable emphasis to Ts'ai's efforts to reform family rituals in Fu-chou.[10]

The third incident occurred in 1063. At the end of the third month, Emperor Jen-tsung died after reigning for forty-one years. A few days later the chief councilor Han Ch'i (1008–1075) was appointed to take charge of constructing a tomb for him, and 1,500,000 cash, 2,500,000 pieces of silk, and 50,000 ounces of silver were set aside for the expenses, along with instructions that economy should be followed. In less than two weeks, 46,780 soldiers were sent out to construct the tomb. Ts'ai Hsiang, then financial commissioner, urged that the tomb be modeled on the one built for the previous emperor who had died in 1022. Several other officials responded by urging that it be done on a smaller scale, in line with the instructions on economy.[11] Ssu-ma Kuang, then in charge of the remonstrance bureau, joined the pleas for economy, even suggesting that officials contribute the gifts they had recently received to help with the expenses of the tomb.[12] He also wrote a memorial discussing the siting of the tomb:

[8] *San-shan chih* 39:4b–5a.
[9] *San-shan chih* 39:5b–6a.
[10] *Ou-yang Hsiu ch'üan-chi* Chü-shih chi 35:245–47.
[11] *Sung hui-yao* li 37:9a–10a.
[12] *Hsü tzu-chih t'ung-chien ch'ang-pien* (Chung-hua ed.) 198:4797–99.

I have heard that Your Majesty wishes to have the great burial on the twenty-seventh day of the twelfth month and that the court has sent its commissioner to supervise the tomb work. I do not know if a site has yet been chosen. Some say that there are plans to search widely outside of Yung-an county [where the previous Sung imperial tombs were located] for an auspicious site. In my ignorance, I consider this to be a mistake. Books on yin-yang cause people to be constrained and fearful, and of these the most harmful concern burial. The families of literati and commoners may delay a burial for generations as they seek a site or a time for burial. I have long been deeply troubled by this custom, but have not had the time to request that the state ban these books. Now the major task of the imperial tomb should be done according to the codified rituals of the former kings. The *Book of Burials* derives from vulgar, convoluted talk. The yin-yang officers of the directorate of astronomy are all ignorant folk of the marketplace. How are these [books and people] worth consulting?[13]

Ssu-ma Kuang next argued that the classics already prescribed when and where to bury:

In ancient times, the Son of Heaven was buried after seven months, feudal lords after five months, great officers after three months, and gentlemen after a month. They were buried on the north side with their heads to the north. No one asked about the year or month or evaluated the hill or mound. Yet if one examines the luck or ill-fortune of their descendants, was it any different from today? . . .

In the *Chou-li* the tomb master took charge of the public graveyard. The first king was buried in the middle, and others were on the left and right in *chao-mu* order.[14] It is evident that the tomb master did not select according to topography. And yet Chou possessed the realm through the reigns of thirty-six kings, for 867 years. For kings receive their mandate from Heaven and their fate is based on constant principles. The rise and fall of states depends on the quality of their virtues. It is definitely not tied to the auspiciousness of the place or time of burial. Now, burial is hiding [two homonyms]. Its basic purpose is to make the forebear's body comfortable. Any land will do so long as the soil is thick, the water low, and the land is high, level, and solid. How can descendants seek blessings through [burial]?[15]

The response to this memorial has not been preserved, but it may have had some effect. The tomb for Jen-tsung was built relatively far from the earlier imperial tombs, but still within the same county.[16] Ch'eng I, however, gave

---

[13] SMWCKCCC 27:381.

[14] *Chao-mu* order was the order used for the arrangement of ancestral tablets on an ancestral altar, with odd-numbered generations on one side and even-numbered generations on the other.

[15] SMWCKCCC 27:381.

[16] For an archaeological report on these graves, see Kuo et al., "Ho-nan Kung-hsien Sung-ling tiao-ch'a."

Wen Yen-po (1006–1097) the credit for dissuading the emperor from the move by putting his arguments in terms of blessings and misfortunes.[17]

A few months after the interment took place, in the third month of 1064, Ssu-ma Kuang heard another rumor that a new temple was to be set up by the side of Jen-tsung's mausoleum. He suspected that the emperor's desire for this temple might have come from his knowledge that officials commonly set up Buddhist shrines near their ancestors' graves.[18] He therefore argued both that the analogy was poor and that the intercession of Buddhist monks was useless.

> The families of officials who do not have people to guard their graves set up temples by the side of the graves, attracting [a monk] with some small profit just so that he will look after the plants and trees. But the state protects the mausoleums, its officials taking full charge. Therefore it does not matter how close the temple is. If one says [the temple] is to make offerings to seek blessings, then I would counter that no one knows about life and death and the theories of the Buddhists are vacuous and hard to test. Should the dead be without consciousness, then the offerings are useless. If they are conscious, as the Buddhists say, then as Emperor Jen-tsung was compassionate and frugal, loved life and hated killing, and benefited the whole world and its living things through his compassion, why should we need to set up a temple and ordain a few more monks for him to be born in the heavenly paradise? Moreover, near the end of his life Emperor Jen-tsung granted plaques to over a thousand previously unrecognized temples of a hundred or more rooms. Surely this earned him enough merit for long life and unlimited blessings! And yet within a few months he died. If this is used as a test, it is clear that the Buddha is not able to grant people blessings. Your Majesty and the grand empress dowager both saw this with your own eyes.[19]

Whether this memorial had any effect is not recorded.

The fourth event to be recounted here is Ssu-ma Kuang's funeral. In 1085 Emperor Shen-tsung died and was succeeded by the nine-year-old Che-tsung. The empress dowager, acting as regent, ended the reform policies initiated by Wang An-shih (1021–1086) and recalled leading conservatives to court, the most prominent of whom was the sixty-seven *sui* Ssu-ma Kuang. In the ninth month of the following year he died. The mourning and burial ceremonies were highly political affairs. The poet, artist, and statesman Su Shih (1036–1101) reported that both the empress dowager and the emperor went in person to Ssu-ma Kuang's home to wail their grief.[20] They canceled court for three

---

[17] ECC i-shu 2B:58.

[18] On this practice, see Chikusa, *Chūgoku bukkyō shakai shi kenkyū*, pp. 136–98, and Huang, *Sung-tai fo-chiao she-hui ching-chi shih-lun chi*, pp. 241–300. Chikusa, in "Shiba Kō O Anseki yo bukkyō," p. 483, reports that Ssu-ma Kuang had a temple of this sort by his ancestors' graves.

[19] SMWCKCCC 30:412–13. In this part of the memorial, Ssu-ma Kuang uses Buddhist terms, showing his familiarity with at least the outlines of the Buddhist counterarguments.

[20] For the etiquette to be followed for an imperial condolence visit, see *SS* 124:2903.

days and gave his family funerary gifts of first-rank ritual dress, three thousand ounces of silver, four thousand pieces of silk, and camphor and mercury for the laying out. They also ordered palace officials to supervise having the body returned to Ssu-ma Kuang's home county. Su Shih also reported that "A commoner in the capital drew a portrait [of Ssu-ma Kuang], which he printed and sold. Families would set out the print and pray to it when they ate or drank. People from all directions sent to the capital to buy copies, so that the artist became rich."[21] In the inscription Su Shih wrote for Ssu-ma Kuang's funerary stele he stated further that when he died:

> The common people in the capital closed the markets to go to condole, selling their clothes to make offerings. Those who followed the procession, wailing in the streets, must have numbered ten million. . . . [When the officials sent to accompany the coffin returned] they reported that the common people cried for [Ssu-ma Kuang] just as though they were crying for their own parents. Several tens of thousands came from all directions [to Hsia] for the burial. Old men from Feng-chou in Ling-nan came one after the other to offer sacrifices and Buddhist services on his behalf. Over a hundred of these men held lit incense up to their foreheads, crying out their sorrow, to send off the burial procession.[22]

The emperor himself wrote the title for Ssu-ma Kuang's grave-side stele, "Loyal, Pure, Refined, and Virtuous," and ordered Su Shih to compose the text.[23]

Several anecdotes record that Ch'eng I took charge of managing the funeral, and that Su Shih was not happy with the way he handled it. According to Shih Tzu-chih, a follower of Ch'eng I:

> When Wen-kung died, the court ordered Master [Ch'eng] I-ch'uan to take charge of the funeral. The day that the services in the Hall of Light [for the recently deceased emperor] were completed, the two Su brothers went to wail for Wen-kung and on the way ran into Chu Kung-shan [Kuang-t'ing, 1037–1094]. In response to their inquiry, Kung-shan said, "I went to wail for Wen-kung, but Master Ch'eng said that congratulations and condolences may not be made on the same day," The Sus, annoyed, turned back, saying, "As obstinate as Shu-sun T'ung."[24]

Lü Pen-chung (1084–1145) provided a different version of this incident:

> When the venerable Ssu-ma died, after the service at the Hall of Light was over, Su Tzu-yu [Ch'e, 1039–1112], who was a remonstrance official, wanted to go to

---

[21] *Su Shih wen-chi* 16:491.

[22] *Su Shih wen-chi* 17:512–13. This scene continued to be discussed into the next century. See *Yün-ku tsa-chi* 3:10a–b.

[23] *Su Shih wen-chi* 17:514.

[24] ECC wai-shu 11:415–16. Shu-sun T'ung was a pedantic ritualist of the early Han.

condole. [Ch'eng I] Cheng-shu forcibly stopped him, saying, "You have just participated in an auspicious ritual. You may not condole for a death." Tzu-yu disagreed and said, "There is the saying, 'When he wailed he then would not sing.' Where does it say that when he sang he then would not wail?"[25]

In another anecdote preserved by Chang Tuan-i (1179–1250), Su Shih is said to have wanted to manage the funeral himself, but Ch'eng I had gotten there first. When Ch'eng I had the body laid out according to the ancient rituals, Su Shih pointed at the body and said, "One thing is missing. There should be a document saying, 'Sent to the Great King Yama.' "[26]

Thirty-eight days after Ssu-ma Kuang's death, work on his tomb began. Soldiers from four neighboring prefectures were assigned to the excavation. By the first month of 1087, they were done and the burial took place. To complete the aboveground structures, however, took seven months and sixteen thousand craftsmen. To the southeast of the tomb a two-story building forty-five feet tall was built. The stone stele inscribed with the epitaph was housed in a structure with double towers, surrounded by a covered veranda. The grave complex was, moreover, hidden and protected by a wall on all sides.[27]

Ssu-ma Kuang's only son K'ang (1050–1090) was naturally the chief mourner. Fan Tsu-yü (1041–1098) reported that he managed the funeral entirely according to the family's classically based rules. K'ang insisted on returning the 2,000 ounces of silver the court had contributed to the funeral expenses. Once the burial had taken place, he lived in a hut near the grave, eating coarse food and sleeping on the ground, as a consequence of which he got a stomach ailment from which he never recovered, dying four years after his father at age forty-one.[28]

These four incidents are only a handful of the hundreds of such events that men like Ssu-ma Kuang and Ch'eng I would have known of directly or by repute. They illustrate the public and political side of ancestor-oriented rituals and the range of concrete and abstract problems scholars had to contend with in thinking about them. Weddings, funerals, and burial were not marginal events, to be handled with as little fuss as possible. Rather they were major personal and family acts, acts that others observed and judged. Not infrequently, educated men like Shih Chieh took on reform of the way they and their kinsmen took care of the bodies of their ancestors. For instance, Ssu-ma Kuang's grand uncle Kao (968–1030) had undertaken a similar burial project for twenty-nine relatives who had long laid unburied.[29] Han Ch'i undertook a

[25] Quoted in *Hsü tzu-chih t'ung-chien ch'ang-pien* (Shih-chieh ed.) 387:5b. The allusion is to a statement about Confucius in *Lun-yü* 7.9; 7:3a–b; Waley, *Analects*, p. 124.

[26] *Kuei-erh chi* 1:11. King Yama was one of the ten kings of the underworld involved in judging the dead according to folk religion.

[27] *Ssu-ma Wen-kung nien-p'u*, pp. 301, 305.

[28] *Fan T'ai-shih chi* 41:13a–16b.

[29] *Shan-yu shih-k'o ts'ung-pien* 14:24b.

major burial of this sort in 1045, as did Ch'eng I and his father and brother in the late 1050s.[30] These projects were demanding, not only because it was often difficult to decide on the appropriate historical or canonical precedent, but also because whoever undertook them needed to gain the cooperation of his kinsmen, overcome customs at odds with the Confucian tradition, and collect funds.

Public expressions of Confucian piety were especially pronounced in mourning activities. Quite a few of Ssu-ma Kuang's contemporaries, like him, asked not to have Buddhist funeral services, and even more, like Ssu-ma K'ang, attracted attention for the seriousness with which they adhered to classical forms in mourning their parents. Sung Ch'i (998–1061), Shao Yung's (1011–1077) father Shao Ku (986–1064), and Ch'eng I's uncle Ch'eng Fan (1019–1075) all requested that their children omit all Buddhist services.[31] Many cases of rigorous mourning are recorded in the Sung history. For instance, the Confucian teacher Hsü Chi (1028–1103) was said to have spent the mourning period in a hut at the grave, sleeping on a mat with a clod of dirt for a pillow, not removing the mourning hemp bands, and wailing by the side of the grave on snowy nights.[32]

In their service as officials, educated men faced other problems. Diversity in ritual practices was widely perceived as undesirable, as it would lead to diversity in values.[33] Officials who wanted to do something about this had to decide which of the customs of commoners most needed to be reformed and how they could accomplish it. Ch'eng I described his brother's mixed success in suppressing cremation.[34] Ssu-ma Kuang reported that he and his brother tried to encourage reform of local customs in their community by making a contribution of a thousand cash to the funeral expenses of a man who abstained from wine and meat for the full mourning period.[35] Central government officials also regularly had to deal with family rituals. Besides the memorials given here, Ssu-ma Kuang wrote on the propriety of burying an empty coffin when a body could not be found, the propriety of Buddhist nuns participating in palace mourning rites, the need for the emperor to personally perform the peace sacrifice to the previous emperor, the honor the emperor (adopted by his predecessor) could properly confer on his natural father, and the placement of tablets in the imperial ancestral hall.[36] If other officials' memorials were included, the list of topics would naturally be much greater.

[30] *An-yang chi* 46:1a–7a; ECC wen-chi 12:650.

[31] See *Ching-wen chi* 48:620; *Shao-shih wen-chien lu* 20:220–21; ECC wen-chi 4:501.

[32] SS 459:13473.

[33] See the evidence in the last chapters and the sources cited there in notes 14, 16, and 17.

[34] ECC wen-chi 11:633.

[35] SMWCKCCC 69:858.

[36] SMWCKCCC 18:276–77, 28:390, 392–93, 35:467–68, 36:477–79, 37:484–85, 489–90. On the adoption issue, see also Fisher, "The Ritual Dispute of Sung Ying-tsung."

There were many ways a committed scholar could act on the imperative to purify ritual practices. He could set a good example, talk to relatives and neighbors, write persuasive essays to lead readers to give up undesirable practices, or write guidebooks specifying exactly what readers should do. If he served in a central government office he could propose reforms of national policies; in local office he could strengthen enforcement of existing policies. All of these approaches found adherents. Here I will focus not on political efforts or personal example, but on writing texts. The most influential texts turned out to be Ssu-ma Kuang's *Shu-i* and Ch'eng I's surviving writings and dialogues.

NEO-CONFUCIAN OPPOSITION TO HETERODOXY AND VULGARITY

One reason Neo-Confucian scholars wrote about the rituals for weddings and funerals was already discussed in the last chapter. Scholars were trying to define the mores appropriate to their class. To do so they had to work through the problems of their relation to people with less education, some of whom might be their own relatives. Discussion of family rituals was often framed in terms of what commoners should cease doing, but criticisms of commoners' practices could be, intentionally or not, criticism of the intrusion of popular practices into the ritual behavior of the educated and insecurity about the ability of the educated to demonstrate their cultural superiority.

An equally important motivation behind criticism of funeral practices was opposition to Buddhism. For Han Yü (768–824) in the T'ang and for even more scholars in the early Sung, reviving Confucianism required curbing or eliminating the influence of Buddhism in Chinese culture and society.[37] Han Yü had called for returning all Buddhist and Taoist clergy to lay life.[38] Sun Fu (992–1057) wrote that allowing a teaching of the barbarians to bring disorder to "the teachings of our sages" was a great humiliation to Confucian scholars. Confucians, by not maintaining the practice of their virtues and rituals, had allowed Buddhism and Taoism to deceive the people with intimidating talk of "life and death, suffering and blessings, emptiness and retribution."[39] Li Kou (1009–1059) thought Han Yü's proposal to defrock the monks and burn their books was impractical; instead he advocated an end to both ordinations and repairs of temples.[40] In about 1034 Shih Chieh wrote two essays castigating

---

[37] Complaints against Buddhism per se were not new. See Weinstein, *Buddhism*, for repeated criticisms of Buddhism through the T'ang by officials and rulers. But coupling suppression of Buddhism with revival of an "ancient" Confucianism of the sages does appear to be largely a development of the late T'ang and especially the early eleventh century.

[38] See his essay and memorial translated in part in de Bary et al., *Sources of Chinese Tradition*, pp. 427–34.

[39] *Sung-Yüan hsüeh-an* 2:92.

[40] *Li Kou chi*, pp. 140–41 (cf. pp. 218, 246, 322).

Buddhism as un-Chinese. Just as it was anomalous for mountains to fall and rivers to stop, so was it perverse for Chinese to follow foreign ways. For Chinese of all ranks "to forget their ancestors and abandon sacrifices to them, serving instead barbarian ghosts, is perverse."[41] In his essay, "On the Central Country," Shih Chieh argued that there was a solution: the barbarians should be barbarians and the Chinese Chinese, each side following its own customs, teachings, and rituals.[42] Shih Chieh was not worried only about the hold of Buddhism on the educated class; it was its pervasive influence throughout society that threatened Chinese cultural identity.

Ou-yang Hsiu argued for a more gradual approach to solving the problem of Buddhism in his two essays, "On Fundamentals," written in 1042. In the past Buddhism had gained strength after each suppression, so suppression was not the answer. Buddhism should be looked on as a disease that had taken over because of the weakness of the body, in this case the weakness of Confucian moral principles and rituals. If these could be revived, the presence of Buddhism and Taoism would not matter because they would have no hold on people. In ancient times all people were instructed in the proper rites for weddings, funerals, and sacrifices, thereby learning the principles of seniority and restraint. If instead of prohibiting Buddhism, instruction in Confucian rites were restored, people would naturally turn away from the barbarian practices to the superior Chinese ones.[43]

The hostile tenor of this anti-Buddhist rhetoric suggests that more was involved than intellectual rejection of Buddhist doctrines or worries over misspent resources. Yet there are no signs that the educated class was in fact imperiled by any new upsurge in the dominance of Buddhism. Buddhism was certainly flourishing in the eleventh century, but it had been flourishing for centuries.[44] Nor will any simple class analysis explain their hostility: these men did not come from a purely Confucian social stratum, as Confucian scholars often had close relatives who practiced Buddhism. Their image of the purely Confucian society was one they created from books, not from memories of their childhood.

Calls to combat Buddhism probably struck a receptive chord among many of the educated in the 1030s and 1040s because of their perception that social order and cultural identity were endangered.[45] The Confucian tradition attrib-

[41] *Tsu-lai Shih hsien-sheng wen-chi* 5:60.

[42] Ibid. 10:116–17.

[43] *Ou-yang Hsiu ch'üan-chi* Chü-shih chi 17:121–24; partially translated in de Bary et al., *Sources*, pp. 442–45. For a good discussion of Ou-yang Hsiu's intellectual life, see Liu, *Ou-yang Hsiu: An Eleventh-Century Neo-Confucianist*, esp. pp. 85–130, 155–72.

[44] On Buddhism in the Sung, see Huang, *Sung-tai fo-chiao*.

[45] Most studies of Confucian opposition to Buddhism concentrate on the efforts at intellectual refutations that were more characteristic of later critics like Ch'eng I and Chu Hsi, rather than the initial impetus to decry Buddhism, generally on a more emotional and less philosophical plane.

uted great power to rituals to shape people's understandings of the ideal social order and their place in it. But Buddhism was alien and, compared to Confucianism at least, egalitarian. The Buddhist idea that everyone was equally capable of attaining heaven seemed to threaten the moral and social vision embedded in classical Confucianism with its stress on a hierarchical array of interdependent roles and statuses. The troubling aspects of the social changes generated by the expansion of the economy—the lack of fixed patterns of respect and deference—could be linked to Buddhism on the grounds that Buddhism undermined the hierarchical virtues of loyalty to lords, filial piety to parents, and differentiation by gender. The foreign origins of Buddhism were undoubtedly felt more acutely because the inability of the Sung state to vanquish the Khitans fostered a desire to reassert the superiority of everything *Hua* (Chinese) over everything *hu* (barbarian).[46]

The antiheterodoxy strand of Neo-Confucianism converged with ambitious plans to remodel all of society. Officials and scholars wished to "transform through education" (*chiao-hua*) the entire populace. Criticisms of the prevalence of Buddhist rituals often made explicit reference to their hold among ordinary uneducated people. Thus it is possible that changes in social organization stimulated this essentially new concern with the ritual life of commoners. Some of these anti-Buddhist polemicists implied that if scholars did not act quickly, they would be faced with having to rule a populace so absorbed in Buddhism and Taoism that they would not respond to appeals to the Confucian values upon which, these men believed, all social order rested.[47]

Because the hold of Buddhism was especially visible in funeral rites, scholars rejected intellectual compartmentalization and hybridized rites. Confucianism and Buddhism could not occupy separate spheres. Customs of noncanonical origin had to be identified and analyzed so that they could be accepted or rejected on rational grounds. Where rituals had ossified, they had to be revitalized, re-created in ways that would carry meaning for men in the new age.

As seen in the last chapter, many scholars' views on ancestral rites had an academic flavor: they were based more on principles inferred from books than on what was actually going on in ritual practices. In the case of weddings, funerals, and burials, however, real life constantly impinged on their thinking. There is a negotiated quality to scholars' ideas about these rituals; they were

---

For the philosophical attacks on Buddhism, see Graham, *Two Chinese Philosophers*, pp. 83–91; Fu, "Chu Hsi on Buddhism"; and Ch'ien, "The Neo-Confucian Confrontation with Buddhism."

[46] On Sung China as part of a multistate system, see the essays in Rossabi, ed., *China among Equals*, especially Tao, "Barbarians or Northerners."

[47] Opposing the Buddhist intrusion into funeral practices thus was comparable to opposing local cults that seemed un-Confucian. As Johnson argues in "The City-God Cults of T'ang and Sung China," p. 425, officials, like clerical elites, saw suppression of such cults as crucial to their own claims of spiritual authority and thus their legitimacy.

built up through interaction with kinsmen, neighbors, subjects, and friends. In this chapter I examine how Ssu-ma Kuang and Ch'eng I sorted out what they saw around them in the practice of weddings and funerals.[48] When were they responding to social practices around them, when were they responding to other books? Why did they comment at length on some practices and remain silent on others? How adequate were their intellectual frameworks to understanding what was going on around them?

WEDDINGS

In eleventh-century China, as in most other places, weddings were thought of as happy occasions. The main participants were young. No dire consequences were anticipated if mistakes in the ritual performances occurred. The rituals themselves consisted of activities (such as exchanges of gifts, letters, and meals) that were familiar and intrinsically enjoyable.

The best description of how weddings were commonly performed in the Northern Sung is in the *Tung-ching meng-hua lu* [Dreams of splendor of the Eastern capital], which describes the customs in the capital, K'ai-feng.[49] Betrothal was accomplished by a long series of exchanges of goods and letters. The initial inquiry was handled by go-betweens, who usually traveled in pairs. They would present to the girl's family a "draft card" listing vital data concerning the boy in question (such as his father's, grandfather's, and great-grandfather's names and titles, if any; his mother's surname; and his date of birth). The girl's family, if interested, would return a card with similar information. If this proved satisfactory to the boy's side, "detailed cards" would be exchanged, with such information as the contents of the girl's dowry and whether the groom's parents were still living.[50] If desired, the groom's family could send a female relative or servant to inspect the bride. To signify that an agreement was being reached, the man's family would send jars of wine, carried on a red frame decorated with flowers. The bride's family would return a pair of the jars filled with water and containing three or five fish and a pair of chopsticks. The betrothal would be made fully binding when the man's family sent the betrothal gifts, which from other sources probably included silk and possibly money. The last major step in the marriage exchanges would take place a day or two before the wedding itself, when the groom's family would

---

[48] Capping is not discussed in this chapter because it was important to neither theory nor practice. Both Ssu-ma Kuang and Ch'eng I asserted the importance of these rites, and repeated the classical statement that without capping there would be no adults (ECC i-shu 15:146; SMSSI 2:19). Neither, however, devoted much attention to reviving these rituals. Ch'eng I once said that contemporary clothing should be used for the ritual, while Ssu-ma Kuang provided a rather archaic liturgy (ECC i-shu 17:180; SMSSI 2). On the capping ceremony, see Waltner, "The Moral Status of the Child in Late Imperial China."

[49] *Tung-ching meng-hua lu* 5:30–32.

[50] For sample cards see *Shih-lin kuang-chi* ch'ien-chi 10.

send items "to hasten the dowry," such as hair ornaments or cosmetics. The bride's family acknowledged this message by returning items of men's clothes. They also had to send people to "make up the room," that is, deliver the dowry. These exchanges not only involved considerable financial outlay, but also conveyed symbolic meanings, often by puns ("fish," for instance, sounds like "surplus" in Chinese). Numerous small gifts, each matched with a return gift (sometimes made up from part of the original gift), masked any sense that the bride was being traded for gifts. These gifts established indebtedness on the part of each family, setting the stage for further exchanges and further social contact after the wedding took place.

On the day of the wedding, the groom would be dressed in finery and sent off with companions, musicians, and an empty sedan chair to get the bride. The bride would be similarly decked out, her face often covered with a veil. Music would be played to get the bride to climb into the chair, and her attendants would make a show of resisting. Some of the bride's relatives would join the procession as it returned to the groom's house. On arrival there, people would clamor around the gate, asking for coins or trinkets before letting the sedan chair pass, again impeding the progress of the wedding. Once the bride was down from the chair, a diviner would toss grains, beans, and coins about the gate while reciting a prayer, and children would compete to grab them. As the bride was not supposed to step onto the ground, a green cloth or rug would be laid out for her to walk on. She would be led in by someone holding a mirror and walking backward, and would have to step over a saddle and a steelyard. She then would be seated within the bridal chamber behind curtains. The groom, meanwhile, would have to sit on a high seat in the main room, while the matchmaker and various female relatives would each drink a cup of wine to ask him to come down. Not until his mother-in-law asked him to descend would he finally come down.

The groom would then go to get the bride. One end of a long sash would be tied to the bride's hand and the other end to the groom's belt-plaque. The groom would back out, leading her to the family altar where she would bow to his ancestors. Next she would walk backward, leading him back into the bridal chamber, where they would bow to each other. At this point they would both sit on the bed. Coins and candies would be scattered over the bed amidst considerable merriment and songs.[51] Then a lock of hair from each of them would be tied together. Next they would drink wine from two cups tied together with a cord, throwing the cups to the floor when finished. One cup's landing up and the other down would be taken as an auspicious sign. Soon thereafter the couple would be left alone. The following day the bride would bow to all of her husband's senior relatives and present gifts such as embroi-

[51] Texts for these songs are given in late Sung sources, such as the reference book *Shih-lin kuang-chi* ch'ien-chi 10.

dered shoes, and the groom would pay a courtesy call to the bride's family. Within a week, both the husband and wife would go to the bride's home, where they would be feasted.

Sung wedding ceremonies as actually performed conveyed many ideas, only partly systematized, about the meaning of marriage, the importance of fertility, the complementarity and differentiation of male and female, social and cosmological hierarchies, the nature of affinity, and so on. Some of the meanings conveyed in wedding ceremonies were consistent with the classical vision. In the classics, weddings were said to promote social morality by illustrating the distinctions or differentiation between men and women. The idea here seems to be that by going through the ceremonies, which repeatedly had the man or his family take the lead, the young groom would be impressed with his authority, the young bride inspired to comply and demur. Or as Ssu-ma Kuang put it, ''the boy leads the girl, the girl follows the boy; the duty of husbands to be resolute and wives to be docile begins with this.''[52] Ssu-ma Kuang and Ch'eng I saw and approved these elements in the rites of their day. Thus both Ssu-ma Kuang and Ch'eng I approved of the bride and groom's bowing to each other and Ch'eng I also approved of veils.[53] Other sorts of symbolism they did not recognize or did not approve. They took no delight in the physical tying of the bride and groom together, either by a sash or with locks of hair. They did not see the way these acts gave physical form to the common ways of talking about marriage as a knot. Ssu-ma Kuang referred to the rite of tying locks of hair as ''ridiculous'' and Ch'eng I argued it was based on a misunderstanding of literary allusions.[54] Since weddings were supposed to teach the differentiation of male and female, Ssu-ma Kuang found the practice of putting flowers in the groom's hair unacceptable as it seemed unmasculine.[55]

Ssu-ma Kuang's liturgy for weddings is much closer to the *I-li* and *K'ai-yüan li* than to the *Tung-ching meng-hua lu*'s description of common practices. Classical wedding rites, as described in the *I-li*, took place at dusk, without any music or congratulations. No mention is made of anyone from the bride's family (other than attendants) accompanying her or joining the banquet at the groom's house. Moreover, the classics do not refer to actions or words that evoked the bride's sexuality or fertility in any obvious way. Ssu-ma Kuang wanted solemnity to surround each step of the betrothal process and repeated the classical rule that no music was to be played at weddings. He had the heads of the two families make reports to their ancestors at several stages

---

[52] SMSSI 3:35.

[53] SMSSI 3:36; ECC wen-chi 10:622.

[54] SMSSI 3:37; ECC i-shu 10:113.

[55] SMSSI 3:34. Ou-yang Hsiu made even more fun of the practice of calling the groom down from a high seat. See his *Kuei-t'ien lu* 2:34–35, translated in Ebrey, ''Education through Ritual,'' p. 284.

of the betrothal process, specifying the steps of the ceremonies and the words to be used. In the various encounters between the two families, he gave women no role, undoubtedly because of his concern to protect the authority of the senior men, a subject he elsewhere wrote on at length.[56] On the wedding day itself, he wanted as much of the common frivolity avoided as possible. People should, for instance, let the bride ride in a carriage rather than a sedan chair.[57]

The exchange side of marriages seems to have bothered Ssu-ma Kuang the most. Rather than something to exploit for its symbolic potential or manipulate to express the inherent tensions created by any marriage, he labeled it mercenary and vulgar. He wanted families to stick to the canonical gifts of a wild goose (or a wooden substitute) for the calling gift and silk and deerskins for the betrothal gift. On their marriage letters they should not indicate gifts and dowry, but only the names and offices of the family heads.[58] Emphasis on dowries seems especially to have troubled him, as it had Ts'ai Hsiang when he found people selecting brides for their dowries in Fu-chou. Ssu-ma Kuang argued that because wives played a major role in the success of families, they had to be selected according to their virtue, not the wealth or temporary honor of their families. "A bride chosen because of greediness for transient wealth and rank will seldom fail to presume upon them and treat her husband with contempt and her parents-in-law with disdain."[59] Moreover, negotiating dowries was distinctly vulgar.

> Nowadays it is the custom for covetous and vulgar people first to ask about the value of the dowry when selecting a bride and the amount of the betrothal gift when marrying a daughter. Some even draw up a contract saying "such goods, in such numbers, such goods, in such numbers," thereby treating their daughters as an item in a sales transaction. There are also cases where people go back on their agreements after the wedding is over. These are the methods used by brokers dealing in male and female bondservants. How can such a transaction be called a marriage among gentleman-officials [shih-ta-fu]?[60]

Emphasis on dowries also led the parents of daughters to have to use up too much of their wealth, so that it had become the custom "for people to be pleased when sons are born and sorry when daughters are born, so sorry that sometimes they do not raise them."[61]

---

[56] See, especially, his *Chia-fan*.

[57] SMSSI 3:34–37.

[58] SMSSI 3:31.

[59] SMSSI 3:29.

[60] SMSSI 3:33.

[61] SMSSI 3:33. Other Northern Sung writers also noticed and objected to the emphasis placed on providing daughters with dowries. Ting Chih (ca. 1060) and Chu Yü (ca. 1075–1119 +) wrote that recent recipients of the *chin-shih* degree would bargain for good dowries from official families

Elsewhere I have argued that this escalation in dowries was probably related to the great usefulness ties through marriage had gained in the Sung political arena.[62] Some local officials, including Ch'eng I's maternal uncle, tried to curb escalation of dowries by setting legal limits on their size.[63] Ssu-ma Kuang's distaste for the emphasis commonly placed on dowry was undoubtedly related to his concerns for the management of family property. In other writings he objected to allowing any property to be considered private rather than family property, whether it be sons' official salaries or daughters-in-law's dowries.[64]

Where Ssu-ma Kuang and Ch'eng I disagreed on wedding rituals was in the timing of the bride's introduction to her husband's ancestors. Ssu-ma Kuang was willing to accept the contemporary practice of introducing the bride to her husband's ancestors on the day of the wedding rather than wait the three months the *I-li* had required. Indeed, he noted that "In antiquity this rite did not exist. Today it is called, 'Bowing to the ancestral spirits.' It cannot be omitted."[65] A three-month waiting period probably did not seem feasible in the Sung as it implied a "returnability" of brides ill-suited to the creation of strong ties between intermarrying families. Ch'eng I, however, retained the three-month delay, not commenting on any difficulties people might have in adopting this practice.[66]

Ssu-ma Kuang and Ch'eng I each argued that certain departures from the classics should be rectified—in Ssu-ma Kuang's case music forbidden and congratulations disallowed, in Ch'eng I's case the bride's presentation to the ancestors delayed. Neither, however, seems to have noticed how modern wedding rites had changed the relationships of the two families. In the classics, during the betrothal process contact between the two families was, by Sung standards at least, asymmetrical. Gifts were not answered with countergifts, and a servant rather than a go-between acted as a messenger between the two families. At the wedding not only did the bride's family not attend the groom's family feasts, but there was no specified role for other affines, nor any required post-wedding visits. Thus, one of the most basic changes in the marriage rituals seems to have escaped the notice of these two scholars. As a consequence, to both Ssu-ma Kuang and Ch'eng I weddings were among the least problematic of the family rituals, marred only by mercenary concern with the

---

with marriageable daughters, some families coming close to offering bribes (*Sung wen-chien* 61:852–53; *P'ing-chou k'o-t'an* 1:16).

[62] Ebrey, "Shifts in Marriage Finance from the Sixth to the Thirteenth Centuries."

[63] ECC wen-chi 4:504. Another official, Sun Chüeh (1028–1090), while in Fu-chou (Fukien) simply issued an order that dowries were not to exceed one hundred strings of cash, which, we are told, promptly led to several hundred weddings (SS 344:10927).

[64] See Ebrey, "Conceptions of the Family in the Sung Dynasty," p. 225.

[65] SMSSI 3:36.

[66] ECC wen-chi 10:622.

property exchanged and a tendency toward frivolity, and not by the intrusion of Buddhism or by anything that could be classed as impious, unfilial, or likely to undermine the social order. Contemporaries who read what Ssu-ma Kuang and Ch'eng I had to say about weddings might well infer that preserving dignity was the most crucial issue. By not making more of an issue of the ways contemporary rites differed from classical ones, these authors, probably unintentionally, left considerable room for maneuver in actual ritual situations. Features of the rites that played important roles in working out the relationships between the two families were not made a part of the ritual core, the invariant part of the ritual that everyone must perform the same way.

FUNERALS

The funeral practices commonly performed in Sung times drew elements from divergent traditions, the most important of which were the canonical teachings of the obligations of the filial child toward his dead parents; Buddhist teachings about death, karma, and transmigration, heaven and hell, much of which had long before Sung times also been adopted by Taoists; indigenous ideas about yin-yang, auspiciousness and inauspiciousness of times, places, and activities that were vaguely associated with shamans and geomancers; and ideas about ghosts of ancient indigenous origins but modified over time by Buddhist and Taoist conceptions of the fate of the dead. Sung sources suggest that most people accepted such hybridized rites; they could wear mourning garments based on Confucian teachings, call in monks to aid the salvation of the dead one's soul, avoid dates for the encoffining deemed ill-omened, and take precautions against the return of the ghost. It apparently made sense to them to use the expert or practice most efficacious in a particular situation. They were comfortable with a compartmentalized approach.

Few Neo-Confucian scholars could accept the authenticity of hybridized rites. Ssu-ma Kuang and Ch'eng I were in full agreement that filial piety required careful attention to the complex of ritual behavior associated with funerals and burial. Ssu-ma Kuang devoted half of his *Shu-i* to discussing these rites. Ch'eng I did not discuss their details very often, but he expressed no reservations about the need to adhere to the canonical procedures. He or his brother once said, "Sending off the dead is the most important thing in the world. If a person in his heart is able to do the utmost in this one matter, he will then be able to manage the great affairs of the world."[67]

Ssu-ma Kuang, in his *Shu-i*, did not insist that everything be done exactly as specified in the classics. Yet he did want clearly specified rules and procedures. The first phase of mourning involved wailing, encoffining, putting on mourning clothes, and setting out food and drink before a symbol of the dead.

[67] ECC i-shu 6:93.

Ssu-ma Kuang identified several practices common at this stage as unacceptable. The sorts of boisterous feasting Ts'ai Hsiang found in Fu-chou were common among "ignorant rustics" in Ssu-ma Kuang's home county, and he was just as critical of them. He reported that immediately after the death relatives would bring food and wine to the house of the bereaved and all would eat and drink for several days, sometimes even playing music to "amuse the corpse," evidence to him of how benighted customs had become.[68]

Ssu-ma Kuang complained that people would select an auspicious day for encoffining based on yin-yang theories, sometimes resulting in long delays before encoffining and consequent decomposition of the body.[69] Ssu-ma Kuang was more tempered in his reactions to other deviations. Although he wanted the encoffining to be treated seriously, he did worry about the expense of various requirements. Not everyone received the government subsidies his family did when he died, though all officials were supposed to receive some expense funds.[70] Thus Ssu-ma Kuang proposed ways "poor" families could reduce costs. For instance, they need not use as many pieces of cloth for the laying out as the fifty-two pieces given in the *I-li*. It would be enough to use one piece for the preparatory stage and whatever was available from the deceased's own clothing plus gifts for the first and second dressing.[71]

Ssu-ma Kuang could also accept compromises on mourning garments. Since classical times, the Chinese had conceptualized the obligations the living owe to their dead relatives in terms of five grades of mourning, these grades governing the type of garment worn, how long it was worn, and other austerities practiced. Even though the mourning grades were of social importance, especially to officials, by Sung times the clothing actually worn seems to have deviated considerably from the classical prescriptions. Ssu-ma Kuang wrote that "recent custom is very affected by superstition and no one wears hemp except a child for parents, a wife for parents-in-law, a wife for her husband, or a concubine for her master. Anyone who tried to wear it [in other cases] would be ordered to stop by his seniors and ridiculed by others, so it cannot be insisted on."[72] Although he disapproved of the superstition underlying such behavior, his approach was concessionary. Instead of hemp, for the

[68] SMSSI 6:65; SMWCKCCC 69:857–59.

[69] CL 26b–27a; Ebrey, *Chu Hsi's Family Ritual*, p. 84. In the canonical schedule, encoffining should take place on the third day.

[70] *Sung hui-yao* li 44:1a–4a gives the schedule issued in 1074 for funerary contributions according to the rank of the official. For instance, for an administrative assistant (*p'an-kuan*, usually rank six to eight) the government would issue on his death sixty lengths of silk, six bottles of wine, and three sheep. For his parents' deaths he would get almost as much, but less for other close relatives. These funds were apparently not always forthcoming, for when Ch'eng I's father died, Wen Yen-po wrote a memorial specially asking for government assistance with the funeral expenses (*Lu-kung wen-chi* 32:4b).

[71] SMSSI 5:58.

[72] SMSSI 6:68.

lower three grades of mourning, Ssu-ma Kuang allowed people to use raw white silk.[73]

Ssu-ma Kuang showed less flexibility concerning the physical symbol for the soul of the dead, before which oblations of food would be placed. He accepted the use of a "soul cloth" even though the Sung government's regulations retained the classical wooden *chung*, arguing that the cloth was a satisfactory simplification.[74] He rejected as extremely vulgar (*pi-li*), however, the common practice of representing the deceased by setting out a full set of clothes, including a hat and shoes, on a chair. On the use of portraits he had mixed feelings. Sometimes, he said, artists would be invited in to paint the likeness of the deceased before the encoffining, especially unsuitable when the dead person was a woman.[75]

Where the classics did not provide adequately detailed procedures, Ssu-ma Kuang offered his own. For instance, he added to his liturgy the appointment of a funeral director. This post could be filled by a friend or acquaintance (as in the case of Ch'eng I managing Ssu-ma Kuang's funeral) or a competent relative who did not owe the highest degree of mourning. Ssu-ma Kuang also specified in some detail the etiquette for condolence visits, basing his descriptions on current practice and making reference to T'ang period *shu-i*, which had devoted much of their space to the appropriate language to use for condolence visits and letters.[76] Condolers, dressed in plain clothes without ornaments, would bring gifts of incense, tea, candles, wine, fruit, money, silk, or mock money. Mock money was the most common, but to Ssu-ma Kuang also totally useless, so he urged confining gifts to items of practical value to the bereaved. When a condoler entered, the mourners wailed; the condoler expressed his sympathy in formal language, then would move to the soul seat where he would make an offering of tea or wine and present an elegy (literally "sacrificial text"), which might be burnt after being read.[77] The etiquette of condolence visits was quite complex. For instance, Ssu-ma Kuang reported that a widow in mourning should meet only close friends of her sons who had previously been introduced to her, never friends of her deceased husband.[78]

Although most people seem to have performed at least a simplified version

[73] SMSSI 6:67. Probably many people put on these garments only when they visited the house of the deceased or joined the funeral procession, for Chang Tsai reported that when he first wore the lower grades of mourning he was afraid people would make fun of him (CTC, p. 291).

[74] SMSSI 5:54.

[75] SMSSI 5:54.

[76] See Ebrey, "T'ang Guides"; Chou, "Tun-huang hsieh-pen shu-i chung so-chien ti T'ang-tai hun-sang li-su."

[77] SMSSI 9:55–57. These texts survive in great quantity in the collected works of Sung authors.

[78] SMSSI 5:57. Condolers expected to be offered food and drink, adding to the expenses of the bereaved. Probably many expected wine (prohibited to the mourners), as Ch'eng I's refusal to serve wine to someone who came to condole him on his father's death was unusual enough to attract notice (*Sung ssu-tzu ch'ao-shih* Erh-Ch'eng 7:171).

of the classical set of encoffining, oblations, and mourning garments, they also had Buddhist services performed.[79] In folk Buddhist teachings, each seven days marked a new stage in the progress of the soul through seven stations of judgment on its way to rebirth on the forty-ninth day. Funeral services, scheduled for some or all of these "seven sevens," were seen as a way of helping the soul through these passages by transferring merit to it. The major activity of these services was the chanting of sutras. The monks who performed them were fed vegetarian meals, and the relatives and guests who came to observe were also fed. In K'ai-feng it was possible to hire caterers who would prepare and deliver these meals.[80] Occasionally monks might be asked to give sermons on Buddhist topics.[81]

Ssu-ma Kuang's skepticism concerning the utility of Buddhist services was already seen in his memorial on the imperial grave-side temple cited above. In his *Shu-i* he developed these arguments further.

It is the current custom to believe the falsehoods of the Buddhists. At the moment of death, at each of the seventh days until the seventh seventh day, at the hundredth day, the full year, the second full year, and the removal of mourning clothes, people feed monks and hold ceremonies. Some perform the great assembly of water and land, copy sutras, make statues, and build stupas and temples.[82] They say that they are obliterating the sins of the dead before Heaven, so that they will surely be born in paradise and receive all kinds of pleasures; and that if they do not do this for them, they will just as surely enter hell, be sliced, roasted, pounded, and ground, receiving unlimited waves of suffering. They do not realize that when a human being is filled with blood and breath he feels pain; but should he trim his nails or shave his hair and then roast or slice them, he suffers nothing. How much more true is this for the dead where the body and spirit are separated from each other! The body has entered the yellow regions where it rots and disappears with the trees and stones. On the other hand, the spirit whirls like the wind and fire, going who knows where. Even if one were to slice, roast, pound and grind the body, how would the spirit know anything more about it?[83]

In other words, although people performed Buddhist services according to a regular schedule, thinking that they were aiding their parents' salvation, in fact they are accomplishing nothing because the dead body cannot suffer pun-

---

[79] For Buddhist and Taoist funeral practices in general, see Matsumoto, "Sorei, sairei ni miru Sōdai shūkyōshi no ichi keikō."

[80] *Tung-ching meng-hua lu* 4:26.

[81] Levering, "Ta-hui and Lay Buddhists: Ch'an Sermons on Death."

[82] The water and land ceremony was a Buddhist ceremony held to aid the deceased gain a speedy rebirth, performed either for the recently deceased or for ghosts that had not settled satisfactorily.

[83] SMSSI 5:54–55. For a longer translation, see Ebrey, *Chu Hsi's Family Rituals*, pp. 79–80.

ishment. Ssu-ma Kuang went on to argue that if perchance paradise actually existed, the good would be reborn there anyway. To assume one's parents had not been good was hardly filial. Ssu-ma Kuang also made fun of the idea of transferring merit, as this implied that the Buddha could be bribed into treating sinners favorably and that the rich would fare better than the poor.[84]

Ch'eng I disapproved of Buddhist services as much as Ssu-ma Kuang did. His family is said to have been one of the few in Lo-yang that did not perform them. He noted how Buddhist services conflicted with Confucian canonical rituals, especially in the use of music and other forms of entertainment. The *Li-chi* had stated that music was not appropriate for mourning,[85] a rule generally interpreted as allowing dirge singers but not instrumental music. Ch'eng I complained that in Buddhist services cymbals and gongs were used, which he saw as originally Indian instruments, used by monks out begging to attract donors.[86]

BURIAL

In China the standard method of disposing of the dead from early times had been underground burial in coffins, accompanied with grave goods.[87] From Han times on husbands and wives were commonly buried together in the same or adjoining graves. After the Han period, the growing acceptance of Buddhist notions of death and afterlife and the gradual proliferation of ideas about grave geomancy seem to have contributed to a slow decline in the number and quality of grave goods. Typical officials' graves were, by Sung times, smaller and less ruinously expensive than they had been in the Han or even the T'ang. The one area in which Sung graves seem to have exceeded those of earlier eras was in the technical aspects of making them strong and waterproof. These technical issues were of concern to both Ssu-ma Kuang and Ch'eng I.

Ch'eng I wrote about his own studies into the best methods to delay decomposition. His great-great-grandfather Yü (913–984) had been buried near Ch'ang-an, where he had earlier buried his own father while in office there. Later some members of the family moved to K'ai-feng while others stayed in the old area. Then in the late 1050s Ch'eng I's father started a new graveyard at I-ch'uan near Lo-yang, interring Ch'eng I's long-deceased great-grandfather and grandfather, along with other family members who had died over the

[84] Ssu-ma Kuang was ignorant of or did not choose to discuss the Buddhist explanation for these practices in terms of the multiplication of merit by making gifts to the Buddhist *sangha*. On these ideas, see Teiser, *Ghost Festival*, pp. 196–213.

[85] See *Li-chi* "Ch'ü-li B," 4:9a; Legge, *Rites* 1:103.

[86] ECC i-shu 10:114.

[87] On Chinese mortuary customs in general, see Liu, *Chung-kuo tsang-su sou-ch'i*.

years (such as Ch'eng I's mother, who died in 1052). Ch'eng I described his experiences this way:

> From the time I was young, I kept planning for the burial of my great-grandfather, the forest bureau official, and his descendants. As the years went by I gave careful thought to the matter, wanting to learn what materials could affect the bones and decay. Later I heard that in the Hsien-yang plain someone had excavated a tomb from the Eastern Han period in which the cypress coffin had survived. Also when the fortifications of Prince Han-hsiu were torn down, they found old cypress logs that were as strong as new. From the proverb "pine lasts a thousand and cypress ten thousand" I knew that cypress is the most enduring [kind of wood]. But as my plans were not yet set, I glanced through miscellaneous books, finding reference to the fact that when pine resin is put in the earth, after a thousand years it becomes *fu-ling* fungus and after ten thousand years amber.[88] Suspecting that nothing lasted longer than these, I made the coffins of cypress and coated them with pine resin. . . . Over the next thirty-four years, I managed seven burials. . . . The reason one should not let soil touch the body is not that it is dirty, but that it contains worms and insects, which can attack the bones, a dreadful thought. . . . Only if the wood is strong and the seams sealed can they be kept out. For strength, cypress is best; for the seal, lacquer.[89]

Ssu-ma Kuang took similar interest in the technology of burial, adding lengthy discussions of it to his *Shu-i* not based on the *Kai-yüan li* or any classical texts. Parts of his text now lost discussed the need for the size of the coffin to be kept within limits so that the vault would not have to be too large, making it vulnerable to thieves who wanted to break it open.[90] Ch'eng I, it might be added, had personal experience with grave robbers; in 1091 he reburied several of his ancestors when he found that their tombs near Ch'ang-an had been robbed.[91]

From archaeological evidence, it is known that tomb construction varied by region and time period.[92] In North China during the Northern Sung, both dirt pits and brick vaults were used. Brick vaults could be simple, rectangular ones with flat or vaulted ceilings not much larger than the coffin, or they could be quite large with hexagonal, octagonal, or round chambers at the end of tomb paths. The most elaborate were multichambered, looking like mansions with bricks laid in ways that resembled the eaves and bracket construction techniques of temples and mansions. These tombs often had the brick walls plas-

---

[88] In *Shih-chi* 28:3226 the *fu-ling* fungus, found under thousand-year-old pine trees, was said to confer immortality on those who ingested it.

[89] ECC wen-chi 10:626.

[90] CL 23b; Ebrey, *Chu Hsi's Family Rituals*, pp. 72–73.

[91] ECC wen-chi 12:661.

[92] For an overview of the archaeological evidence for Sung tombs, see Hsü, "Sung-tai mu-tsang ho chiao-ts'ang ti fa-ch'üeh."

tered and painted with scenes of home life, entertainment of guests, guards protecting the gates, and so on.[93] Or they could have scenes constructed out of the bricks themselves.[94]

Ssu-ma Kuang discussed both vertical grave pits and horizontal cave chamber ones. He wrote that the choice of method largely depended on the local soil.

> Nowadays in regions with loose soil, people make a tomb straight down, with a base of stone or bricks, just big enough to hold the coffin, and cover it with stone. Every time they spread a foot of dirt on it, they stamp on it to make it solid. When it gets up to five feet or so, they use a pestle to make it firm, fearing that if the earth is thin [the body] stored beneath the stone will be susceptible to shaking. . . .
>
> In regions with compact soil, people first excavate a path some number of feet deep and then dig a room as the tomb at the end. Some line it with bricks, others simply have a dirt room. The entrance is closed with several layers of bricks. They then fill in the border path with dirt. The problem with these tombs is that as the years go by they inevitably collapse, as they are not as strong as vertical shaft tombs.[95]

Inside the tombs, Ssu-ma Kuang proposed placing all of the standard grave goods allowed by the government, including wooden figurines, models of furniture, baskets and jars of food and drink, and a stone slab inscribed with an epitaph.[96] He remarked that his own family dug graves thirty-three feet deep, that depth possible because the groundwater was low in their area.[97] His contemporary Sung Ch'i urged burial thirty feet down, which to him was a very simple burial.[98] Digging so deep was heavy work, so Ssu-ma Kuang explained

[93] Particularly impressive tombs of this sort were found at Pai-sha, in Honan, southwest of Kaifeng and southeast of Loyang. Three tombs were found close to each other, probably for a father, son, grandson, and their wives. The first tombs had a path 5.8 m long with steps up to the surface and pictures of three men, attendants of various sorts, on each side. Next was a large gate, like the gate to a courtyard, with elaborate eaves and brackets. Behind it was a short passageway, then a rectangular front room, 1.8 by 2.3 m, and 3.8 m tall at the highest point. The walls were covered with pictures, including one of a man and wife seated at a table on which were placed two large cups and saucers and a ewer. Another scene was of eleven female musicians. Another small passageway led to the rear chamber, hexagonal in shape, where the bodies were laid. It was covered with scenes of domestic life, such as a door partially open with a woman visible on the other side. Su, *Pai-sha Sung-mu*.

[94] In Szechwan graves were sometimes constructed of stone, pictures carved on the walls in relief. E.g., Ssu-ch'uan sheng po-wu-kuan et al., "Ssu-ch'uan Kuang-yüan shih-k'o Sung-mu ch'ing-li chien-pao."

[95] SMSSI 7:78–79.

[96] SMSSI 7:80–81.

[97] SMSSI 7:79.

[98] *Ching-wen chi* 48:619.

how pulleys and ramps could be used to raise and lower the dirt and objects.[99]

Among the objects placed in tombs, the most important to literati families were probably the epitaphs (*mu-chih ming*). It was common to ask someone known for his literary abilities to write the text on the basis of information the family supplied. Ch'eng I reported that his father told his family not to ask some worthy to write an epitaph, since the writer would be sure to exaggerate his modest accomplishments; instead they should inscribe the stone with the autobiography he had himself composed.[100]

Before tombs could be constructed, a site had to be chosen. Some Sung families maintained family graveyards, placing each body in a site that corresponded to its genealogical position.[101] Others had family graveyards, but sited each grave within it according to geomantic principles.[102] Some of Ssu-ma Kuang's thoughts concerning the siting of tombs were already given above in his memorial on the location for Jen-tsung's tomb. Both he and Ch'eng I were highly critical of contemporary geomancy.[103] The underlying presuppositions of geomancy go back to the ancient idea that the living benefit when their ancestors are comfortable. From Han times on, theories were elaborated about the forces of the earth and their effect on the living, drawn from several strains of cosmological thought, including yin-yang, five phases, *I-ching*, and other divinatory traditions. The two main schools of modern times (the school of forms and the school of the compass) claimed founders who predated the Sung, but their theories were not nearly as influential as the theories of several other masters, all of whom seemed to have worked within a framework variously called the "Five Surnames," "Five Notes," or "Five Sounds." This framework was already old in the Sung, Lü Ts'ai (d. 655) having criticized it at length in the early T'ang.[104] According to this way of thinking a particular location might be auspicious for someone in one category of surnames (based on its sound) but ill-omened for those in others.[105]

---

[99] SMSSI 7:79.

[100] ECC wen-chi 12:653. On epitaphs as literature, see Egan, *Literary Works of Ou-yang Hsiu*, pp. 49–63.

[101] E.g., *Kung-k'uei chi* 60:808–9; T'ai-yüan shih wen-wu kuan-li wei-yüan hui, "T'ai-yüan shih Nan-p'ing-t'ou Sung-mu ch'ing-li chien-pao."

[102] *Ti-li hsin-shu* ch. 13 reported that burying in genealogical order was prevalent in Ho-nan, Ho-pei, Kuang-chung, and Lung-wai—that is, in North China along the Yellow River. In other areas various geomantic theories were followed.

[103] Unlike Ssu-ma Kuang, Ch'eng I does not seem to have discounted all of the cosmological premises underlying geomancy. He allowed for a sort of amateur geomancy based on the idea that the comfort of the ancestors was linked to the comfort of the living descendants. "Father and grandfather, son and grandson, all share the same *ch'i*. According to this principle, when the one is at peace the other will be at peace; when the one is endangered the other will be endangered." Thus one should seek sites that would not be likely to be disturbed for centuries and where trees and plants flourished (ECC wen-chi 10:623). Anyone could select grave sites according to these criteria.

[104] *Chiu T'ang shu* 79:2720–21.

[105] These sounds were not rhymes or tones but based on the position of the tongue. One source

Ch'eng I ridiculed the theory of the five notes. He pointed out that this classification matched neither rhymes nor tones. It was without canonical basis, did not make sense in terms of the known history of surnames, and moreover could be disproved by history. As evidence, he gave cases of people who had lived very long in ancient times before there were any geomancers, proving that the geomancers' claim to be able to extend life spans did not hold up to scrutiny. Ch'eng I also objected to moving bodies, noting that "burial is hiding. Once the body is hidden, it cannot be moved. One must seek permanent rest." What those choosing grave sites should pay attention to, he argued, was genealogical order (*chao-mu*): "If they are not divided into *chao* and *mu* ranks, it is easy to confuse seniority. If the dead have consciousness, how could they be comfortable with this?"[106] Elsewhere he explained that the most senior burial should face south, with its head to the north, and the "accompanying" burials placed in front of it in two ranks, their heads also to the north.[107] Thus he wanted concentrated graves of the sort Shih Chieh, Han Ch'i, and his own family had constructed, rather than the scattered grave sites that frequently resulted from reliance on geomancers.[108]

Ch'eng I cited the example of his own family to prove geomancy's fallacies:

> In the world today there are a lot of works on divination and numerology, and of them, the books on geomancy are the most preposterous. When my grandfather was buried, we used a geomancer. My elders all had faith in him; only my late elder brother and I did not. Later we simply used the *chao-mu* method [of burying in genealogical order]. . . . After I used the *chao-mu* method for one site, one of my elders summoned a geomancer to the burial place. This man said, "This place will cut off those in the Shang class [which apparently applied to the Ch'eng surname]. Why did you make the grave here?" I answered, "It was exactly because I knew it was a place that cuts it off [in your theory]. I want to test what will happen." Note that the members of my family have increased several fold since then.[109]

This passage highlights the conflict reformers often faced in their own families. Ch'eng I's father, his father's younger brother, and probably his father's first cousin all played roles in this burial project.[110] How was a filial son and nephew to take a stand against the family's tradition of consulting geomancers when his seniors wanted it? Ssu-ma Kuang recounted a rather similar incident

---

explained that in pronouncing the *shang* note the tongue was extended, in the *cheng* it was against the teeth, in the *ch'üeh* it was contracted, and so on, so that some sounds were throat sounds, others teeth or lip sounds, and so on (*Ta Han yüan-ling mi-tsang ching* 3b–4a).

[106] ECC wen-chi 10:625.

[107] ECC i-shu 2B:56.

[108] On Han Ch'i's instructing his sons not to consult geomancers and thus disturb the pattern of the graveyard he had established, see *An-yang chi* 2:12b–13a.

[109] ECC i-shu 22A:290.

[110] ECC wen-chi 4:495–97, 500, 12:650.

with a different solution: his older brother Tan offered the local geomancer an especially high fee if he would report back to the Ssu-ma relatives that the place and time Tan had chosen were the most auspicious ones, "dressing it up according to the *Book of Burials*."[111]

A major complaint against geomancy was that it led to the delay of burials, sometimes for decades or even generations. Ssu-ma Kuang reported that

> When the descendants get old and decline they may forget the location of the coffin and abandon it without burying it. People want descendants in large part so someone will take care of their physical remains. When descendants act like this, wouldn't it be better to have no descendants and die by the road? Then some man of virtue might bury them. . . . If one really supposed that burial was able to affect human fortunes, how could those who are sons and grandsons bear to cause their parents to rot and suffer exposure in order to seek profit for themselves? There are no perverse rituals that hurt moral principles more than these.[112]

Delayed burial, delayed even for decades or generations, does indeed seem to have been pervasive in the Northern Sung in all social classes, as the experience of the Shih, Ch'eng, and Ssu-ma families suggests. In 1062 the government found over four hundred cases of imperial clansmen whose burials had been delayed twelve years or longer.[113] When burial was delayed more than a few weeks or months, people often did not want to keep the coffin in their homes. By Sung times it had become extremely common for families to bring the encoffined body to a temple to be left there until burial could be arranged.[114] Ssu-ma Kuang termed this a sin of great unfiliality because one could not count on the monks to look after the coffin and protect it from robbers.[115]

Although underground burial was the dominant practice in Sung China, it was not a universal one. A substantial minority were, instead, cremated, and their ashes either scattered over water, stored in urns aboveground, or buried in small graves.[116] In the early eleventh century Chia T'ung (ca. 1020) wrote that cremation had already become the custom among common people and

[111] SMWCKCCC 65:810.

[112] SMSSI 7:75.

[113] SS 124:2912.

[114] For instance, when his mother of eighty died in 1032, the high official Chang Te-hsiang (978–1048) had her coffin placed in a temple in the capital, hoping to get the chance to bring it back to be buried alongside his father's coffin in Fukien. After five years he decided instead to bury her near the capital (*Ching-wen chi* 60:815). The coffin of a widow of an official family who had outlived her sons, dying in 1027 at seventy-five, was left at a neglected Buddhist temple for eleven years until her grandsons were ready to arrange a joint burial (Li, "Nan-ching Chung-hua men-wai Sung-mu," pp. 343, 339).

[115] CL 27a; Ebrey, *Chu Hsi's Family Rituals*, pp. 84–85.

[116] On the history of cremation, see Ebrey, "Cremation in Sung China."

was gradually contaminating the practices of the educated.[117] Han Ch'i found that in central north China "customs are confused with those of the Ch'iang and Hu [barbarians]. When people die they are cremated and afterwards buried, though the poor deposit the bones in Buddhist shrines, where they accumulate for years in untold numbers."[118] Both Chia T'ung and Ssu-ma Kuang reported that educated families were especially prone to practice cremation when their members died away from home, Ssu-ma Kuang noting that sons and grandsons of officials thought it preferable to burn their parents' bodies so that their ashes could be returned home rather than to have them buried far away.[119] Buddhism clearly had much to do with the spread of cremation, as cremation had been the standard method of disposing of the dead in India, and Buddhist monks practiced it in China. Often the burnt remnants of eminent monks were preserved as relics through burial at the base of a stupa, a practice that had already gained popularity in India much earlier.[120] Moreover, crematoria were generally run by Buddhist temples, though it was also possible for people to cremate their own dead by constructing a pyre on open ground. Some Buddhist temples provided storage for the burnt remnants and others had pools of water where they could be scattered.

Both Ssu-ma Kuang and Ch'eng I saw cremation as a vile practice. Ch'eng I labeled cremation as a severe way of hurting a corpse. "Today if a fool or drunkard accidentally hits a person's ancestor's coffin, he will take great offense and want revenge. Yet he may personally drag his parent and toss him into the flames, finding nothing odd in it."[121] Ssu-ma Kuang noted that desecrating a stranger's corpse was a serious legal offense, and yet people were not offended by cremation.[122] Although cremation had been outlawed in 962, Ch'eng I complained that the law was not firm enough because it allowed soldiers who died on military campaigns to be cremated and also had rules prohibiting cremations within three *li* of a city, implying it could be done outside.[123]

Whether a body was buried or cremated, there would generally be a funeral procession. Most processions, of course, did not attract the crowds Ssu-ma Kuang's had, but they were still major undertakings. Carrying a heavy coffin required a large catafalque (a frame for suspending the coffin and distributing

[117] *Ku-chin shih-wen lei-chü* ch'ien 56:14a.

[118] *Han Wei-kung chi* 13:202.

[119] *Ku-chin shih-wen lei-chü* ch'ien 56:13a–14b; SMSSI 7:76. For an example of a Sung official cremated when he died away from home, see *Yu-hui t'an-ts'ung* 2:4a–b.

[120] See Schopen, "Burial 'Ad Sanctos' and the Physical Presence of the Buddha in Early Indian Buddhism."

[121] ECC i-shu 3:58.

[122] SMSSI 7:76.

[123] ECC i-shu 3:58.

its weight) and eight, sixteen, or more men to carry it.[124] In the procession, the coffin was preceded by a variety of people and objects. In 970 using Buddhists or Taoists or "people dressed up in strange colors" to lead processions had been banned, a rule that Wang Yung in the early thirteenth century said was violated everywhere.[125] After these various religious experts came carriages or sedan chairs carrying the epitaph, the soul seat, the portrait, the grave goods, and other miscellaneous objects. Then came the mourners, in order of degree of mourning.[126] Friends and relatives without mourning obligations, instead of joining the procession, might wait along the road for it to pass, setting out offerings to the soul. This custom went back to the Han and had reached quite elaborate proportions in the Sung. A memorial of 982 complained about the lavishness of these offerings.[127] It was this facet of funeral processions that most troubled Ssu-ma Kuang. He attributed its excesses to the regional commanders of the late T'ang who competed among themselves in ostentation. In his own day, he said, sacrificial tents set out along the route often reached thirty feet tall.

> People [use paper to] make birds, animals, flowers, trees, carriages, horses, and menservants and maids dressed in silk. When the catafalque passes, they burn the whole thing. They set out up to a hundred or more sacrificial foods, inedible because they have been dyed red or green. This custom has reached ordinary people who brag to each other about these displays. Sometimes the expenses reach several hundred strings of cash. Wouldn't it be better to give this money to the bereaved family as a contribution to their expenses?[128]

Vulgarity—the desire to display wealth—was thus again a major ground on which Ssu-ma Kuang condemned a practice. By contrast, Ssu-ma Kuang had no objections to making a sacrifice to the god of the soil when the procession reached the grave site, a practice not mentioned in the classics but which he accepted on the authority of the *K'ai-yüan li*.[129]

Funerary rituals did not end with burial. Once the dead were buried, they

---

[124] Government sumptuary rules allowed rank two, three, four, or five officials to have seventy-six bearers, officials rank six or seven thirty-two, down to sixteen for commoners (*Ch'ing-yüan t'iao-fa shih-lei* 77:31b–32b [p. 561]). The catafalque was covered with a tentlike awning keeping it shaded from direct sunlight. In K'ai-feng, catafalques and other paraphernalia needed for the procession could be hired for the occasion (*Tung-ching meng-hua lu* 4:25).

[125] SS 125:2917; *Yen-i i-mou lu* 3:24.

[126] Among the objects might be an empty carriage and wooden poles decorated with fanlike tops (SS 124:2910). This later was a classical flourish, but seems to have been in common use. See *Shih-wu chi-yüan* 9:341.

[127] SS 125:2917.

[128] SMSSI 7:85.

[129] SMSSI 8:91. Apparently geomancers often officiated at these ceremonies, as a geomancy manual commissioned by the government in 1051 gives full liturgies for the prayers and incantations to be recited (*Ti-li hsin-shu* ch. 14).

gradually came to be treated more as ancestors than as dead people, this transition marked by the switch from the soul cloth to a wooden tablet or plaque as a place for the soul to settle. In the classics the bereaved gradually altered their mourning garb, making several changes in synchronism with these sacrifices. In Sung times the custom of altering garments had died out as a regular practice. Neither Ssu-ma Kuang nor Ch'eng I advocated reviving it, though occasionally one of their contemporaries would do it as a pious imitation of the ancients.[130]

Ssu-ma Kuang provided liturgies for all six of the post-burial sacrifices. This liturgical schedule does seem to have been commonly followed by the educated, as they often composed prayers for these occasions. Ssu-ma Kuang reported that in many cases people followed the orthodox liturgical schedule but employed Buddhist monks to hold ceremonies, at least for three occasions—the "cessation of wailing," conventionally set at the one hundredth day; and the first and second sacrifices of good fortune, on the first and second anniversary of the death.[131] This practice, of course, he did not encourage.

According to the ritual classics, those in mourning were to restrict their activities for the entire mourning period. This entailed, for officials, retirement from office, and for others abstention from meat and wine and from participation in "auspicious" rituals such as weddings, cappings, and ancestral rites. These restrictions were gradually lessened over the course of the mourning period. In practice higher civil officials both in the capital and in the prefectures and circuits were usually summoned back after one hundred days, and in emergencies they could be summoned sooner. In such cases, the official could wear mourning garments at home, but in office wore official garb of light color without jewelry.[132] Lower officials normally were out of office for the full mourning period.

Abstention from meat and wine for the entire mourning period does not seem to have been widely practiced in Sung times. Ssu-ma Kuang complained that as recently as the Five Dynasties (907–960) it had been disreputable to be seen publicly eating meat or drinking wine while in mourning, but *shih-ta-fu* of his day did so without shame and without attracting attention, since the custom was so common.[133] Nevertheless, severe restrictions on activities and diet were admired as evidence of filial piety, as seen in the case of Ssu-ma Kuang's son K'ang. In epitaphs, it is quite common to find descriptions of both men and women abstaining in these ways.

The prohibition on participation in auspicious rites was more seriously observed. Even officials who had been summoned back to office after one hun-

---

[130] E.g., SS 294:9822.
[131] SMSSI 5:54.
[132] SS 125:2922–24.
[133] SMSSI 6:64–65.

dred days normally did not participate in major imperial rites.[134] The Sung code prohibited marrying while in mourning for a parent or grandparent and provided heavy penalties for violation—three years penal service in the case of a parent and a beating of a hundred strokes in the case of a grandparent.[135] As a consequence of this prohibition, it was not unheard of for marriage arrangements to be speeded up because a parent or grandparent was expected to die soon. If the wedding had not taken place before the death, many people seemed to think it was acceptable to carry it out a day or two after the death, before the mourning garments were donned, as the law only forbade those in mourning garments from marrying. Not surprisingly Ssu-ma Kuang strongly objected to this practice, claiming it was against the law.[136]

One of the few issues concerning the ritual sequence associated with funerals and mourning to be debated by scholars in the Sung was when to "associate" the tablet or plaque for the newly deceased ancestor with other ones in the ancestral hall. Ssu-ma Kuang had this performed the day after the sacrifice for the cessation of wailing, that is, about a week after the burial. He explained that the authorities gave divergent schedules, but the Chou practice was to do it at the cessation of wailing. In his liturgy after the plaque was "associated" it was returned to the soul seat for the rest of the mourning period.[137] Ch'eng I, however, argued for waiting to associate the tablet till the end of the mourning period, so that there would be a focus for the rites of "morning and evening wailing" that would last until the end of mourning.[138]

CONCLUSIONS

The major ways mortuary customs in Sung times differed from the rituals in the classics were recognized by Sung scholars and largely condemned. They labeled as vulgar or unfilial wakes, the burning of paper offerings, Buddhist services, cremation, geomancy, and celebrating weddings before mourning clothes were put on. To men like Ssu-ma Kuang the standard for judging mortuary practices was the expression of grief and concern for the dead. The music and feasting of wakes they interpreted as disrespectful; they could not accept the explanation of the participants that they were entertaining the dead, nor did they see the assemblage of friends and relatives amidst food and music as in any way aiding the bereaved in coping with their grief or adjusting to their new social status. Buddhist services they condemned primarily as heterodox but also as unfilial because assuming parents had been sinful was disrespectful. Ostentation they viewed as entirely inappropriate for funerals; it was

[134] SS 125:2924–26.
[135] *Sung hsing-t'ung* 13:16a–b.
[136] SMSSI 6:65.
[137] SMSSI 8:96–98.
[138] ECC i-shu 17:180.

bad enough at weddings. To Ssu-ma Kuang, dread, loathing, fear, and anger had no proper place in funerals. Unwillingness to touch a dead body or reluctance to put on mourning clothes were simply immoral.

In the last chapter Ssu-ma Kuang and Ch'eng I were seen to take opposed stands on many of the issues concerning ancestral rites. In this chapter, by contrast, they were shown to have very largely agreed on how weddings and funerals should be performed. They agreed on the practices to be condemned—cremation, Buddhist services, five-note geomancy, tying the hair. They even shared interests in technical details of how to construct tombs. In the last chapter I attributed the differences in their views to differences in their philosophical outlooks. I pointed to ways Ch'eng I's views on ancestral rites were largely congruent with his philosophical positions and Ssu-ma Kuang's views to his historical outlook. For weddings and funerals, however, they both took essentially historical approaches. Neither proposed creating new rites on the basis of moral principles or making any major modification in the ritual sequences established in the *I-li*.

The reason Ch'eng I was not more philosophical in his approach to weddings and funerals probably resides in the nature of the rites themselves and the ways they were tied to ideology and society. Ancestral rites could be approached in an academic way and could be revised relatively easily. If one's father had been a younger son, one would not even need the cooperation of cousins to reform how rites to him were performed. The rites, moreover, did not have to be expensive and could be planned well in advance. Any committed scholar had several opportunities a year to demonstrate proper ancestral rites, and a given performance of the rites would not have to take more than a few hours. Even if they were performed as solemnly as Confucian teachers said they should be, there was no reason they could not be pleasant occasions, ending in communal meals. Because ancestral rites were rites of confirmation and solidarity, they were a subject on which emotional detachment was possible, a subject that one could approach mainly on intellectual or philosophical grounds.

As was made evident repeatedly throughout this chapter, neither Ssu-ma Kuang nor Ch'eng I found it easy to be as detached about funerals or burials. Ssu-ma Kuang's objections to Buddhist services were not calmly reasoned refutations. Neither of them was dispassionate in assessing geomancy. Their reactions to geomancy seem to have been tied to the feelings each had about the importance of handling the physical remains of the dead in protective, comforting ways. Moreover, they had personal experience with how hard it was to get even close relatives to omit rites they believed were essential for the peace of the dead or the protection of the living.

Neither Ch'eng I nor Ssu-ma Kuang invented the emotional impact of funeral rites or inferred it from books: they found it around them. Yet their reactions to these practices were also shaped by books. Their ideas were not simply those current in their social milieu; not only did they disagree with each other on some points, but they both described how their closest relatives followed grave geomancy, a practice neither of them could abide. From books they seem to have acquired an uneasiness about the emotional force of rituals. Indeed, one might go so far as to say that their reaction, while based in their emotional response, was ambivalent about emotion. They were suspicious of frivolity and partying. They were uncomfortable when emotions were carried to extremes, with the possible exception of grief, whose excesses could be condoned. Like officials who wanted to tame local cults to powerful demons because religious fervor frightened them, Ssu-ma Kuang and Ch'eng I wanted to control the tendencies for people to let weddings and funerals become celebrations.

To assess the contributions of Ch'eng I and Ssu-ma Kuang to the Confucian discourse on family rituals, it is necessary to consider the content of the last chapter and this one together. As discussed in Chapter Two, the early Confucian discourse was characterized by several polarities concerning what made rituals authentic and effective. One of Ch'eng I's major contributions to the long-term Confucian discourse on family rituals was his defense of the internal pole of ritual thought. He emphasized that rites had to be regularly examined with regard to their correspondence with moral principles independent of the rituals. Indeed, he found the true source of authority in his own ability to recognize the moral principles upon which rituals could be created.

Ssu-ma Kuang's contribution to the Confucian discourse on family rituals was of a different sort. He stretched an existing genre (*shu-i*, etiquette books) to the point where one might easily say he created a new genre. The *Shu-i* that Ssu-ma Kuang wrote was unlike any earlier surviving ritual book. It was distinctly Confucian, yet it nearly ignored status distinctions, providing a single liturgy for officials of all ranks and the educated generally. Unlike T'ang *shu-i* it did not concentrate on what leading families did, but what Confucians should do, based on consideration of the classics and imperial manuals. In his book, Ssu-ma Kuang provided a thorough exploration of the relationship of ritual (*li*) to custom (*su*). He broke through the tradition of discussing Confucian rituals narrowly in terms of the classical texts and fully confronted the popularity at all social levels of customs that were not canonical in origin. In his *Shu-i* Ssu-ma Kuang examined all of the customary practices he saw as infiltrating the ritual behavior of the educated plus the worst of those largely confined to the uneducated. He offered no simplistic solutions, but attempted to analyze each individual case on the basis of how offensive the deviation was and how feasible doing away with it would be. He took an unbending stance against anything Buddhist, but in the case of other customs was willing to consider a wide range of factors before making recommendations on the admissibility of various compromises.

Taken together, the ideas of Ssu-ma Kuang and Ch'eng I on family rituals brought to the fore the poles of another tension in the Confucian discourse on family rituals. Ssu-ma Kuang emphasized combating heterodoxy and vulgarity: he worked to show that according to the established authorities much of what people commonly did was wrong. Ch'eng I, in the case of ancestral rites at least, was eager to find good impulses underlying behavior that was not canonical in any narrow sense. The contrast in their approaches presented scholars with alternatives. In assessing contemporary practice, should the scholar concentrate on what people did and identifying and rooting out what was wrong? Or should he devote his energies to evaluating the motivations behind ritual acts, so that ones basically good could be brought into the sphere labeled Confucian?

By titling this chapter "combating heterodoxy and vulgarity," I have tried to draw attention to a fundamental source of tension and ambiguity in the response of men like Ssu-ma Kuang and Ch'eng I to the ritual practices they found around them. They shared the Neo-Confucian sectarian view that Buddhism was to be rooted out, that it was an undesirable contaminate of Chinese civilization. It did not matter who practiced Buddhist rites; neither an educated official nor an illiterate peasant should cremate his parents or have sutras chanted for their salvation. They offered no alternatives or compromises on these points, nor did they ever imply that the offense was a lesser one the lower one descended on the social scale.

Nevertheless, Ssu-ma Kuang's *Shu-i* was not written in a style to reach readers without a classical education. It is filled with analyses of canonical injunctions and their contradictions. Ch'eng I's views are known from the oral instruction he gave to his disciples and the essays he wrote for much the same audience. Both asserted the importance of ritual to all social classes, and the need for everyone to perform authentic rituals. But neither seems to have gone much beyond the assertion of an ideal. Rather than shape common people's behaviors, they were trying to influence the interpretations of the well-educated: they were trying to get them to label certain types of actions vulgar and un-Confucian. It was not until Chu Hsi in the next century that a major scholar took the imperative to combat heterodoxy and vulgarity to mean that one should try to write for a broader audience.

Chapter Five

CHU HSI'S AUTHORSHIP OF THE *FAMILY RITUALS*

"The times are of major significance in ritual."[1] Were a
sage to appear, he would surely begin with current rituals
and make adjustments, selecting those features that were
simple, easy to understand, and possible to practice. He
would certainly not reinstitute today the most complicated
of the ancients' rituals.
—Chu Hsi (1130–1200)[2]

CHU HSI (1130–1200) was an extraordinary man. He was immensely learned
in the classics, commentaries, and histories; he wrote, compiled, or edited
almost a hundred books.[3] He considered himself to be a follower of the Ch'eng
brothers, but much had happened to change the mood of scholars since Ch'eng
I died in 1107. At the beginning of the twelfth century, during Hui-tsung's
reign (1100–1125), those who had opposed Wang An-shih's reforms plus their
descendants and disciples were banned from office; some were even forbidden
to enter the capital. Writings by the leaders of this movement were banned;
officials and candidates for office were no longer to cite such leading intellectuals of the prior generation as Ssu-ma Kuang, Ch'eng I, and Su Shih. Despite
this factional strife, the government took an activist stance on achieving Confucian goals, expanding its school system, for instance. In 1113 it issued a
new set of ritual rules, the *Cheng-ho wu-li hsin-i* [New forms for the five
categories of rites of the Cheng-ho period]. This book was the first government
manual to include liturgies for commoners for cappings, weddings, and funerals. It did not, however, include liturgies for their ancestral rites because when
the compilers asked the emperor to approve allowing commoners to sacrifice
to three generations of ancestors, he strongly objected.[4]

With the devastating military defeat by the Jurchen and the loss of north
China at the end of Hui-tsung's reign, the bans on the opponents of Wang An-
shih were rescinded. Yet the long reign of Kao-tsung in Hangchow (1127–

---

[1] Allusion to *Li-chi*, "Li-ch'i," 23:4a; Legge, *Rites* 1:396.

[2] YL 84:2178.

[3] On Chu Hsi as a philosopher, see Munro, *Images of Human Nature*, and the various chapters
in *Chu Hsi and Neo-Confucianism*, ed. Chan. On his activities as an educator, see the chapters in
Neo-Confucian Education, ed. de Bary and Chaffee.

[4] See Ebrey "Education through Ritual," pp. 293–96.

1162) also proved discouraging to scholars. They perceived the emperor as overly willing to compromise for peace and insufficiently willing to support the most visionary of scholar-officials. Unhappy with the reforms that had been imposed from the top, serious scholars were drawn to thinking about how they could effect change in the realms under their own control through personal self-discipline and education of their kinsmen and neighbors. Whereas in the early eleventh century the need to identify and oppose "heterodox" Buddhist practices had motivated many scholars' desires to reform family rituals, by the mid-twelfth century, when Chu Hsi lived, such reforms had the added appeal that they could be begun at the bottom.[5]

Chu Hsi's views on family rituals are revealed in a couple of dozen letters, even more conversations recorded by disciples, in scattered essays, prefaces, memorials, and notices, and in two surviving books, the *Family Rituals* and the *I-li ching-chuan t'ung-chieh* [The classic and commentaries of the *I-li*, organized and explained].[6] In terms of his larger orientations toward rituals, Chu Hsi differed from both Ch'eng I and Ssu-ma Kuang in significant ways. Chu Hsi cannot be characterized as giving priority to either the meaning behind a rite or the external authority of the form; he insisted on both. He once criticized the followers of Lu Tien (1042–1102) for "first seeking the moral principle in their discussions of ritual." In Chu Hsi's view, "The reason the ancients discussed the moral principles was that the forms were all present; everything they heard or saw conformed to ritual." Unfortunately in his day only one or two parts out of a hundred of the ancient rituals survived, so there was no basis on which to discuss their moral significance. "We must collect and analyze the scattered rituals, clarifying each detail and gradation, and when that is done infer the moral meaning."[7] He frequently criticized people for fabricating (*tu-chuan*) rituals, for making them up on their own authority.[8] On the other hand, Chu Hsi had a strong commitment to finding ways to foster

[5] On the intellectual mood of the first generation of the Southern Sung and its relationship to political events, see Liu, *China Turning Inward*. For Chu Hsi's relationship to his predecessors, see also Bol, "Chu Hsi's Redefinition of Literati Learning."

[6] In Ch'ing times, some doubts about Chu Hsi's authorship of the *Family Rituals* were raised. These are discussed in some detail in Chapter Eight. Like Ch'ien Mu, Ueyama Shumpei, Kao Ming, and Ch'en Lai, I think the weight of the evidence is very strong that the *Family Rituals* is Chu Hsi's book, although, like many of his other books, he probably had students draft some parts for him. See Ch'ien, *Chu Tzu hsin hsüeh-an* 4:165–73; Ueyama, "Shushi no 'Karei' to 'Girei kyōdon sūkai' "; Kao, "Chu Hsi's Discipline of Propriety"; and Ch'en, "Chu Tzu 'Chia-li' chen-wei k'ao-i."

Ch'ien Mu emphasizes, among other points, that there would have been no advantage to anyone to attribute a book to Chu Hsi shortly after his death as he was in official disfavor and his teachings labeled false teachings. Ch'en Lai gives particular weight to the conclusive evidence that Chu Hsi had written a liturgy for sacrifices that he discussed with friends in the early 1170s, arguing that if this part of the *Family Rituals* is genuine it is likely that the rest is as well.

[7] YL 84:2178.

[8] E.g., YL 84:2183, 90:2308; WC 46:9b.

practice of rituals, stronger it seems than either Ch'eng I or Ssu-ma Kuang. He recognized that ancient rituals could not simply be performed in his day. If a great sage were to arise, he would develop rituals for the current age. In the meantime, he and his students should start with the rites people actually performed in their day and introduce modifications.[9]

Because of its great influence in later periods, in this chapter I concentrate on Chu Hsi's *Family Rituals* and examine as fully as sources allow the social and cultural processes that led to Chu Hsi's writing it the way that he did. Let us begin with the book itself.

CHU HSI'S *FAMILY RITUALS*

Chu Hsi's *Family Rituals* is a work in five chapters—one on general principles and one each on cappings, weddings, funerals, and sacrifices. Most of it is straightforward liturgy with almost no attention to the canonical origins of rites or the disputes among scholars on what the classics meant or where one could deviate from them. The only part that discusses ritual in theoretical terms is the preface, which draws a distinction between the fundamental features of *li*, such as seniority, love, and respect, that must always be preserved, and the embellishments that are less important and can be adjusted to accord with circumstances, such as inadequate funds.

Chu Hsi's disciple Yang Fu described the sources Chu Hsi used to write the *Family Rituals*. The *I-li* was his basic source but he also consulted more recent books.

> For the capping ritual he largely drew from Mr. Ssu-ma. For the wedding ritual he consulted both Mr. Ssu-ma and Mr. Ch'eng. For funerals, he based himself on Mr. Ssu-ma but later thought Mr. Kao was best [i.e., Kao K'ang, 1097–1153]. On the association of tablets he drew from Heng-ch'ü's [Chang Tsai's] final testament. On burials he thought the *Shu-i* was too sketchy so used the *I-li*. For sacrifices he used both Mr. Ssu-ma and Mr. Ch'eng, which led to inconsistencies. For offerings at festivals, he modeled himself on the practices of Han Wei-kung [Ch'i]. As for making clear the greater and lesser descent-line systems, this was to teach the idea that those who love ritual will keep the sheep.[10] Further, the main ideas of the *Family Rituals* are all linked to this, and his other books did not have room for it, so the master was especially insistent on it.[11]

Although Yang Fu is correct in pointing to the variety of sources Chu Hsi used, Ssu-ma Kuang's *Shu-i* was clearly the most important. To write the *Family*

---

[9] YL 84:2177–78. Ch'ien Mu cites many passages in which Chu Hsi made this point in *Chu Tzu hsin hsüeh-an* 4:115–28.

[10] An allusion to a passage in the *Analects* (cited here in Chapter Two) indicating a desire to keep a practice simply because it is traditional even if it no longer seems to carry meaning.

[11] HLTC 19:2a.

Rituals, Chu Hsi took Ssu-ma Kuang's liturgies, simplified and reorganized them, omitted all of their explanations of how choices were arrived at, and supplemented them with some ideas from Ch'eng I and some he arrived at himself.

One of the most important of Chu Hsi's own ideas was to create a new first chapter to highlight the centrality of the offering hall and the more routine ceremonies held there, including daily "looking in," twice-monthly "visits," and more formal offerings on popular festivals like New Year and Middle Origin (*chung-yuän*). The term "offering hall" was new in this context. Since Chang Tsai and Ch'eng I had objected to the use of ancestral portraits, Chu Hsi apparently concluded that it was inapropriate to call the ancestral hall an image hall. Following Ch'eng I, he had tablets for four generations of ancestors, proposing that the most senior pair (the great-great-grandparents) be the furthest to the west, as the traditional *chao-mu* order (with the most senior pair in the center) required an odd number of generations. In this first chapter Chu Hsi also proposed a way to pay for the rites at the offering hall and at graves by regularly setting aside a portion of land to endow these rites.

In other chapters, Chu Hsi's debts to his predecessors were greater. For cappings, he followed Ssu-ma Kuang's *Shu-i* closely, though he omitted the divinations Ssu-ma Kuang described and substituted more modern clothing. For weddings, Chu Hsi differed from both Ssu-ma Kuang and Ch'eng I in combining some of the classical "six rites" of marriage, perhaps imitating the government's *Cheng-ho wu-li hsin-i* in this regard.[12] Although he quoted Ssu-ma Kuang's objections to negotiating the value of dowries, he left that passage under the discussion of "displaying the bedclothes" and did not use it as a reason to resist the customary use of marriage letters. Chu Hsi did not have the bride introduced to her husband's ancestral altar on the day of the wedding, as Ssu-ma Kuang did, nor did he retain the three-month delay, as Ch'eng I had, but compromised by making token use of the "three" and having the bride introduced on the third day. The most major change from the *Shu-i* for both weddings and cappings was the overlay of the lesser descent-line system. In the *Family Rituals* the presiding men at cappings and weddings were not to be the principals' fathers or grandfathers, as they were in the *Shu-i*, but whenever possible the great-great-grandfather's descent-line heir, a relative possibly as distant as a third cousin. Next choice was the great-grandfather's descent-line heir, possibly a second cousin, and so on. Chang Tsai and Ch'eng I had, of course, been strong advocates of reviving the *tsung* system, but neither

---

[12] He did not copy the *Cheng-ho wu-li hsin-i* exactly, however, as he combined rite one with rites two and three and rite four with rite five, while the government manual had combined rite two with rite three and rite four with rite five. Chu Hsi's familiarity with the *Cheng-ho wu-li hsin-i* is discussed below.

had ever explicitly said it should be incorporated into weddings and cappings.[13]

Chu Hsi's prescriptions for funeral rituals deviate remarkably little from Ssu-ma Kuang's except that he was more tolerant of divination for burial sites and described a recently developed method of preparing cement burial vaults. On the issue of when to associate the tablet for a recently deceased ancestor with the others in the ancestral hall, he sided with Ssu-ma Kuang rather than Ch'eng I.

In his chapter on ancestral rites, Chu Hsi retained Ssu-ma Kuang's description of the steps in the seasonal sacrifices, but expanded the scope of the rites in line with Ch'eng I's recommendations. He had rites to four generations of ancestors, and on all of the occasions mentioned by Ch'eng I. Chu Hsi can be interpreted as both cutting back on ancestral rites and as expanding them. Following Ch'eng I, he broadened ancestral rites by discarding status limitations, explicitly stating that the rites described in his book could be performed by gentlemen without office and by commoners,[14] thus violating the canonically derived rules enunciated in the *Cheng-ho wu-li hsin-i*. Yet he cut back on ancestral rites in two ways. He carefully specified that rites to early and first ancestors were not rites anyone could perform; they were only to be performed by the descent-line heir of a great line. Moreover, he did not envision each household setting up an offering hall with tablets for four generations of ancestors. Whereas Ssu-ma Kuang had each family head conduct rites, Chu Hsi had each descent-line heir do it in his home. Ch'eng I had argued that as everyone wore mourning for a great-great-grandfather, everyone should be able to make sacrifices to him, but he also advocated the descent-line heir system. Chu Hsi, reconciling these two imperatives, specified that only descent-line heirs could preside at ancestral rites, others to attend as observers whenever possible.

All considered, Chu Hsi introduced as many significant changes and new ideas as Ch'eng I had. In terms of content his most significant innovations were (1) to add offerings on popular festivals, (2) to call for setting aside land to endow sacrifices in offering halls and at graves, (3) to arrange the ancestral tablets from the west, (4) to extend the principles of the descent-line system to cappings and weddings, (5) to restrict rites to early and first ancestors to the heirs of great descent lines, (6) to reduce the number of steps in wedding rituals, (7) to have a bride introduced to her husband's ancestors on the third day, rather than the first day or the third month, (8) to omit some of Ssu-ma Kuang's divinations and add others, (9) to add a description of how to prepare

---

[13] On this difference between the *Shu-i* and the *Family Rituals*, see also Makino, *Kinsei Chūgoku sōzoku kenkyū*, pp. 2–27.

[14] CL 2b; Ebrey, *Chu Hsi's Family Rituals*, p. 6.

cement burial vaults, and (10) to take a noncommittal stand on grave geomancy.

The eventual popularity of the *Family Rituals* probably owed more to Chu Hsi's editorial hand than to these innovations in ritual procedures. Chu Hsi wrote the *Family Rituals* not as a study of the classics, but as a straightforward liturgy. He addressed it to a broader audience than earlier liturgical books, including the *I-li*, *K'ai-yüan li*, Ssu-ma Kuang's *Shu-i*, and the Sung government's *Cheng-ho wu-li hsin-i*. Perhaps because of the great growth in printing during the Northern Sung, Chu Hsi had a good appreciation of the importance of getting books into circulation and making them easy enough to consult so that people would actually use them. The *Family Rituals* presents its material in almost outline form, with the key steps of each rite readily apparent because they are in large type. Much more of the detail, including words to be spoken, descriptions of objects to be used, and so on, is in indented sections of small characters where it can easily be skipped. There are lapses in editing; for instance some objects and actions mentioned in the first chapter are not described or defined until the fifth chapter. Yet all considered this book was remarkably well put together if one assumes Chu Hsi's goal was to make it easy to consult. A person would not have needed a full classical education to have understood the *Family Rituals*.[15] The text is remarkably free of allusions. The only authorities cited at all frequently are Ssu-ma Kuang and Ch'eng I. Ssu-ma Kuang is cited over twenty times (the longer quotations being from his impassioned discussions of the flaws in popular customs). Citations from the classics are largely confined to an appendix to the chapter on funerals (taken verbatim from Ssu-ma Kuang's *Shu-i*).

To give a better sense of the *Family Rituals* as a liturgical text, let me summarize how Chu Hsi described the visits to the ancestral altar to be held on the first and fifteenth of each month. No earlier liturgy (at least no surviving one) provided instructions for the performance of these rites.[16] He may well have designed them himself by simplifying the seasonal sacrifices.[17] Chu Hsi specified the following steps, paraphrased and numbered here.

[15] The text does contain a few rare characters, carried over from the *I-li*, whose pronunciation and occasionally meaning are glossed. Even when the meaning is not given, one generally gets a general sense of it from context. That is, one knows the character refers to a kind of container or an item of clothing.

[16] Yang Fu, as cited above, said Chu Hsi based his description of rites at popular festivals on Han Ch'i's book, and since these twice-monthly visits are described together with rites at New Year and the winter solstice, it is possible that Chu Hsi drew on Han Ch'i's book for them.

[17] Chu Hsi's liturgy for these visits is clearly a simplification of the liturgies for the seasonal rites: the more elaborate seasonal rites are scheduled by divination not by the calender; purification for them lasts three days, not one; a much wider range of food and drink is offered; wine is poured three times, not once; and a liturgist reads a prayer before each pair of ancestors.

1. The day before the rite, the offering hall and sacrificial equipment are cleaned and the presiding man begins to observe purification by avoiding certain foods, sexual relations, and contact with those in mourning.

2. At dawn on the day of the rite, the door to the hall is opened. A dish of fruit is set out, and cups and saucers are set at each ancestor's place. Reeds are placed in front of the box of spirit tablets to absorb the libation of wine. Sand is placed in front of the incense table. Tables, wash basins, towels, and towel racks are all put in their correct places.

3. The participants put on formal clothes and line up, the men on one side and the women on the other. Each side is arranged in rows by generation and within rows by age.

4. The presiding man washes his hands, then opens the tablet case to take out the tablets for the ancestors. The presiding woman then does the same for ancestresses. If there are any associated tablets for uncles or other relatives without heirs, more junior participants arrange them.

5. The presiding man goes to the front of the incense table where he calls on the ancestral spirits to come down, then burns incense and bows twice.

6. Attendants, who could be sons, wash, then come up to hold the wine jar and decanter. With their assistance, the presiding man pours a libation onto the reeds, then prostrates himself. He bows twice before returning to join those in line.

7. All those in line bow twice.

8. The presiding man returns to pour wine for each of the ancestors, with his eldest son doing the same for any lower-ranking associated tablets.

9. The presiding woman, with the help of an attendant and the senior daughter-in-law, serves tea in much the same way.

10. The presiding man and woman both stand in front of the incense table and bow twice.

11. After they have returned to the ranks, the whole group takes leave of the spirits with two bows and leaves the room.[18]

It is easy to imagine that Chu Hsi and other Confucian scholars found moral significance in ceremonies of this sort. Participation in this rite twice a month, as Chu Hsi specified, would make principles of differentiation by gender, generation, and age seem a part of the order of things. It would reinforce the idea that even the highest-ranking person in the family had to serve the family's ancestors. Chu Hsi seems to have found moral value in almost any standardized, deferential behavior. His *Elementary Learning* [*Hsiao-hsüeh*] cites extensively from the *Li-chi*'s rules for greeting superiors, eating in their presence, and so on.[19] Therefore it is noteworthy that in the *Family Rituals* Chu Hsi did not belabor the moral meanings of this rite, or even the sentiments that

---

[18] CL 4b–5b; Ebrey, *Chu Hsi's Family Rituals*, pp. 12–15.
[19] For an analysis of this text, see Kelleher, "Back to Basics."

ought to animate the actions of the participants. Rather he gave a matter-of-fact description of how the rite is performed.

How did Chu Hsi come to write this particular book? Why did he rely so heavily on Ssu-ma Kuang and Ch'eng I? Why did he write in a simpler fashion? Why did he simplify some rites? Chu Hsi fortunately discussed ritual issues so often that it is possible to reconstruct answers to these questions.

Let me preview my argument. Evidence suggests that the draft of the *Family Rituals* that eventually was published was put together during the 1170s and early 1180s. Chu Hsi's earlier experiences thus are more relevant than those of the last fifteen years of his life. Chu Hsi's early life was lived at considerable distance from any cousins, and his connections to them seem to have been mediated by their common ties to graves. Chu Hsi's early service as a local official made him realize the need for straightforward guides to family rituals. Three times when he held such posts he urged the government to promulgate liturgies that the poor could follow.

During the period when Chu Hsi worked on the *Family Rituals*, he discussed his efforts to decide on key issues of family rituals with scholars he respected, most notably Chang Shih and Lü Tsu-ch'ien, who were also working on comparable texts. These men exchanged drafts of their works in progress and considered each other's arguments. Chu Hsi asked disciples to assemble materials and prepare drafts for his book. In all likelihood some of the inconsistencies and infelicities of the surviving draft are the result of asking students to make revisions without Chu Hsi having the chance to prepare a final version.

Chu Hsi lost his draft of the *Family Rituals* sometime before 1190. In the mid-1190s he returned to active research on rites, from 1197 devoting much of his efforts to his massive *I-li ching-chuan t'ung-chieh*. During this period he frequently discussed with his disciples the meaning of various passages in the classics concerning family rituals and how these were relevant to their own circumstances, showing that he still accepted most of what was in the *Family Rituals*. These discussions do not contribute to an understanding of the context in which the *Family Rituals* was written, but were commonly used in later periods to supplement or emend the text.

DATE WHEN THE *FAMILY RITUALS* WAS DRAFTED

Near the end of his life, Chu Hsi told his students that he had begun looking into how to perform family rituals at an early age:

> From the time I lost my father at fourteen *sui* till sixteen *sui* when I finished mourning, the sacrifices were all done according to my family's old ritual. Although the ritual was not fully elaborated, it was quite well arranged, and my late

mother managed the sacrifices very devoutly. When I was seventeen or eighteen I examined various authors' rituals to fill out the elaborations of our rituals.[20]

Two of the authors whose rituals he examined must have been Ssu-ma Kuang and Ch'eng I. During this period Chu Hsi was studying with Hu Hsien (1086–1162), a local Confucian teacher whom his father had recommended before he died. Chu Hsi once wrote to Hu asking for guidance on reconciling differences between the *I-li*, Ssu-ma Kuang's *Shu-i*, and Ch'eng I's writings:

> There are still two items I have doubts about concerning the parts of the *I-li* we discussed the other day, and would like to ask for your instruction. The *Shu-i* says that the groom salutes the bride, then comes down the west steps to the bride's sedan chair, and raises the curtain to wait. The other day when I saw you, you said that as the ancients used carriages, they could not climb the stairs, so they got into the carriage from the bottom of the stairs. Therefore there is the rite of "descending from the left staircase." Since today we use sedan chairs, I do not know if one simply goes directly to the hall or not. If this is done, the bride would first enter the sedan chair, then later leave via the western stairs. Also there is no mention of the rite of lifting the veil when the bride enters the groom's house and he leads her in. What should be done today? Please instruct me.

In reply, Hu Hsien agreed that Ssu-ma Kuang had not mentioned lifting the veil, but noted that Ch'eng I had mentioned it in his collected works.[21]

Whether these early studies had any effect on the *Family Rituals* that Chu Hsi eventually prepared is uncertain. The only definite statement about when Chu Hsi wrote the *Family Rituals* places it later, after 1169. Chu Hsi's disciple Li Fang-tzu (c.s. 1214), in his chronological biography of him, recorded that while in mourning for his mother Chu Hsi "exhaustively consulted the ancient and modern rituals, using them to make rituals for mourning, burial, and sacrifices. Later he extended it to capping and marriage to make a book titled *Family Rituals*."[22] Chu Hsi's mother died in 1169 and his mourning lasted through 1171. In the early 1170s, Chu Hsi sent Lü Tsu-ch'ien and Chang Shih drafts of a liturgy for sacrifices.[23] How long passed before Chu Hsi extended his work to cappings and weddings is not known.

Chu Hsi's disciple Ch'en Ch'un (1159–1223) wrote that in 1190, while Chu Hsi was serving as prefect in Chang-chou (Fukien), Ch'en asked him about the rituals of cappings, weddings, funerals, and sacrifices, and Chu Hsi answered:

---

[20] YL 90:2316. The sacrifices in question would have been the post-burial sacrifices. Note that as the only son, Chu Hsi should have presided at these sacrifices. Here he acknowledges that it was actually his mother who organized them, undoubtedly much more experienced in these matters than a youth of fifteen or sixteen.

[21] WC pieh 3:1a–b.

[22] CL (SKCS ed.) fu-lu 1a.

[23] TLC pieh 7:28a–b; NHC 20:2b–4a.

Wen-kung [Ssu-ma Kuang] wrote a guide, but it is rarely used today because it is verbose, complex, and long, making it hard to read. Often people become intimidated and give up before they even start to practice it. Disturbed by this, I once wanted to cut and edit the book, separating the main points from the details, to make a new book that people would find easy to understand and easy to follow. I almost had a finished volume, but while at a monastery it was stolen by a servant boy. I did not get to work on it again.[24]

Considering the number of scholarly projects Chu Hsi worked on, and the number he brought to completion, it is not surprising that he abandoned one after he lost his draft. Chu Hsi still had, however, a manual he used in his own family for ancestral rites, as Ch'en Ch'un was later able to compare some details in this text and the version of the *Family Rituals* later discovered.[25]

In a postface he wrote in 1194 to a book by Chang Shih, Chu Hsi confirmed part of what Ch'en Ch'un described. Chu Hsi discussed the need for *shih* to examine rituals carefully and make the effort to carry them out to improve interpersonal ethics and renovate vulgar customs. Neither Ch'eng I nor Chang Tsai had discussed the rites fully enough, and although Ssu-ma Kuang had written a complete book, "When the reader sees the detail of the steps and procedures, he will think that what cannot be easily comprehended often cannot be easily practiced, and be afraid even to try." Although the book circulated, "those who have copies merely store them in their trunks. No one has been able to put its instructions into practice." People did not understand that expressing respect was more important than the objects used, and that it was certainly better to perform the rites with minor adjustments than not at all. He went on:

I once had a desire to study other authorities' theories in order to edit Mr. Ssu-ma's book, making an appendix with corrections, additions, and subtractions, and arranging the material into categories. This reorganization would allow the reader to find the main points and from there go to the details, without fear that the steps would be hard to carry out. Even poor and humble people would be able to fulfill the major items of the rituals, abbreviating the elaborations without missing the original ideas. But because of illness I have not been able to accomplish this.[26]

In a conversation recorded in 1191 or later, Chu Hsi reported that he had never finished his work on sacrifices, having done no more than edit Ssu-ma

[24] PHTCC 14:1b.

[25] PHTCC 14:1b–2a. Ch'en Ch'un elsewhere recorded an undated conversation in which Chu Hsi made similar comments about the difficulties people had in using Ssu-ma Kuang's *Shu-i*, and how he had once compiled a "sacrificial ceremonies" that was easier to understand, but it had been stolen and he no longer had it (YL 90:2313). Presumably the same text is referred to here, the reference to "sacrificial ceremonies" either to a chapter in the whole book or a mistake.

[26] WC 83:15b–16a.

Kuang's work.[27] Huang Kan (1152–1221), one of Chu Hsi's closest disciples, also reported that Chu Hsi never finished the *Family Rituals*. In his biographical account of Chu Hsi he wrote: "Although the *Family Rituals* he compiled was widely used by contemporaries, he later had many thoughts for additions and subtractions that he never had time to make."[28]

In 1211 Ch'en Ch'un saw a copy of the *Family Rituals* at the home of Chu Hsi's youngest son Tsai, who asserted that it was the copy Chu Hsi had lost at a Buddhist temple. Chu Tsai said the book was recovered by a scholar who returned it on the day of Chu Hsi's funeral. Ch'en reported that this book had five parts (*pien*)—one on general principles and one each on cappings, weddings, funerals, and sacrifices—and that each part was divided into sections and each section into main points and details.[29] This description matches surviving editions of the *Family Rituals* very closely and is perhaps the best evidence that current editions of the *Family Rituals* are based on Chu Hsi's lost manuscript.

Yang Fu, another close disciple of Chu Hsi, summarized the history of the *Family Rituals* by saying that Chu Hsi worked on the *Family Rituals* during mourning for his mother, that after it was complete a servant boy stole it, and that the book only reappeared after Chu Hsi died.[30] There seems to be enough confirming evidence to accept Yang Fu's summary, with the understanding that Chu Hsi did not finish the work while in mourning.

CHU HSI'S FAMILY EXPERIENCES

Since the end of the T'ang dynasty, Chu Hsi's ancestors had been settled in Kuan village of Wu-yüan county, then the southernmost county in She prefecture, Chiang-nan East circuit (currently the northeast corner of Kiangsi province). Although the first ancestor to have moved there was an official, there is no sign of further official service until the early twelfth century when Chu Hsi's father Chu Sung and a kinsman a generation senior to him (Chu Pien) gained office.[31] Chu Sung, in the biography he wrote for his own father, reported that the family had a tradition of Confucian scholarship going back several generations, and it is entirely plausible that a literati life-style preceded official service by a generation or two if not longer.[32]

---

[27] YL 90:2313.

[28] *Mien-chai chi* 36:47a. For Chu Hsi to have continued to alter a manuscript for years after its first preparation does not seem to have been uncommon. Although he gave copies of his commentary to the *Ta-hsüeh* to friends and disciples in 1174, he continually altered it, not publishing it until fifteen years later in 1189. See Gardner, *Chu Hsi and the Ta-hsueh*, pp. 30–32.

[29] PHTCC 14:2b.

[30] HLTC 19:2a; cf. CL (SKCS ed.) fu-lu 1a–b.

[31] WC 98:12a–17a. A genealogy of Chu Hsi's ancestors is given in *Hsin-an ming-tsu chih* 2:42a. If any of the members of the Chu family of Wu-yüan had been officials, this source would have recorded it.

[32] *Wei-chai chi* 12:1b. Cf. *Wen-chung chi* 69:7b–8a. Chu Hsi made no claims of scholarly

In 1118 Chu Hsi's father Chu Sung qualified for office through the school promotion system briefly in force in that period. In about 1124–1125 Chu Sung was serving as sheriff of Cheng-ho county in Chien-chou (northern Fukien), and while there his own father Chu Sen died. The family was not well-to-do, having pawned one hundred *mu* of fields in their native Wu-yüan to cover the expenses of travel to Cheng-ho,[33] and rather than return Sen's body to be buried beside his ancestors, Chu Sung had him buried beside a Buddhist temple in Cheng-ho.[34] Later Chu Sung went on to hold posts elsewhere, and Chu Hsi was born in Yu-ch'i county, further south in Fukien. In 1137, out of office, Chu Sung moved the family to Chien-an county in Chien-chou (northern Fukien). When Chu Sung died in 1143, his body was moved neither to Cheng-ho, where Sen's body lay, nor to Wu-yüan, where earlier ancestors were buried, but to Wu-fu village in Ch'ung-an county in northwest Fukien, to a place Sung had picked out himself next to a Buddhist cloister, near where he had friends he could ask to care for his widow and orphans.[35]

Chu Hsi, thus, grew up in the south, not the north like Ch'eng I and Ssuma Kuang. This certainly affected some of his feelings about family rituals. Burial practices and kinship organization clearly varied considerably by region, and other customs probably did as well. Buddhist monasteries occupied a more dominant place in Chu Hsi's social and physical landscape; they owned a particularly large share of the land in Fukien where he lived, and provided the physical surroundings for much of literati social life in that area.[36]

When his father died, Chu Hsi, then fourteen *sui*, was the only surviving son. His father, on his deathbed, had not advised his wife to return to live with her brothers- and cousins-in-law in Wu-yüan. Rather he directed her to turn to a wealthy friend of his, Liu Tzu-yü (1097–1146).[37] The Liu family of Wu-fu had at least two branches. Liu Tzu-yü provided Chu Hsi and his mother and sisters with a house; his brother Liu Tzu-hui taught Chu Hsi; and one of his cousins married Chu Hsi's younger sister. The other branch provided another teacher, Liu Mien-chih (1091–1149), and a wife for Chu Hsi. Over the years Chu Hsi seems to have retained closer ties to these Lius than to any patrilineal relatives.[38]

---

accomplishments for his ancestors in WC 94:24b–25b. On education and wealth generally preceding official status, see Hymes, *Statesmen and Gentlemen*, esp. pp. 29–81.

[33] NP 1A:7.

[34] *Wei-chai chi* 12:2a.

[35] WC 94:25a.

[36] On Buddhist monasteries in Fukien, see Huang, *Sung-tai fo-chiao* pp. 119–64, and Chikusa, *Chūgoku bukkyō shakai shi kenkyū*, pp. 145–98. On Chu Hsi's visits to Buddhist monasteries for various social and intellectual purposes, see Chan, *Chu Tzu hsin t'an-so*, pp. 633–39.

[37] WC 88:2b, 8a–b.

[38] On Chu Hsi's ties to Liu Tzu-yü's side of this family, see WC 84:22b–23a, 87:6b–9a, 16a–b, 19b–20b, 88:2b–9a, 17b–28a, 90:1a–6a, 92:23b–25b, 94:26b–29a, 97:1a–16a, 26b–27b. On his ties to his wife's side of the family, see WC 90:21a–23a, 91:1a–2b. On this Liu family, see also Ch'en and Ho, *Chu Hsi p'ing-chuan*, pp. 5–8.

Chu Hsi's first contact with his kinsmen in Wu-yüan seems to have occurred in 1150, two years after he attained the *chin-shih* but before he was assigned to a post. In the spring he visited his ancestors' graves and had one hundred *mu* of land that had belonged to his father assigned to covering the expenses of caring for the graves and making sacrifices at them.[39] Having satisfied his sense of obligation by making this large donation, Chu Hsi did not return for another twenty-six or twenty-seven years. By that time he was a prominent scholar and stayed three months, lecturing at the local school and meeting with scholars. He recognized his kinship ties to the Chus who lived there, writing a preface to their genealogy, making an offering at the grave of the first ancestor to settle in the area, and marking the place with a stone.[40]

When Chu Hsi's mother died in 1169, he did not have her buried either with his father or with his grandfather, but "at the northeast corner of T'ien Lake by Rear Mountain in Ning-fu prefecture's Chien-yang county, one hundred *li* from [his] late father's grave at White Water."[41] Later that year, in the seventh month, Chu Hsi moved his father's body from where it had been originally buried, but not to place it next to his mother's. Instead it was to place the body in a spot more suitable according to geomantic divination. He explained his action this way:

When he was about to die [my father] wanted to be buried in Wu-fu [village] in Ch'ung-an [county]. The year after he died he was buried by the side of Ling-fan temple in that village. At the time I was young and ignorant; I was unfamiliar with divination of places. Later I worried that his body and spirit were not comfortable there, so on the fifth day of the sixth year of Ch'ien-tao I moved him to below Good Ledge at White Water in that village.[42]

Chu Hsi's family experiences help explain the way the *Family Rituals* treats geomancy, the descent line system, and the endowment of land for sacrifices. The burial customs he was used to were quite different from those of the Northern Sung literati from North China described in the last chapter. Lengthy delays in burial were not common in his family, perhaps because the climate precluded it, but people might specify in advance where they wanted to be buried, and some were willing to be buried apart from their ancestors.[43] Even

---

[39] NP 1A:7.

[40] NP 2A:61 dates this visit to 1176, twenty-six years after the first in 1150, but in WC 86:13b Chu Hsi said he had been gone twenty-seven years. During one or the other of these trips, Chu Hsi's kinsmen tried to get him to visit the most powerful of the local shrines, dedicated to the god Wu-t'ung, but he stubbornly refused (YL 3:53).

[41] WC 94:26a.

[42] WC 94:25a. The burial would not have taken place in the settled area of the village, but in the surrounding area under its administrative jurisdiction.

[43] Not all southerners scattered graves. Hung Mai (1123–1202) reported that his family's grave-yard had twenty thousand pine trees growing on it (*I-chien chih* i 10:270). See also Lu Yu's

husbands and wives might be buried apart. Chu Hsi was accustomed to these practices; even though they did not match the classics, he found very little in them that was objectionable.

Scattered grave sites, however, are more difficult to care for than concentrated family graveyards. Chu Hsi, at an early age, found a partial solution for his own case by assigning one hundred *mu* of land for the graves of his ancestors. It was common during the eleventh and twelfth centuries for families to set aside land to provide for the care of their graves, though they usually thought of the land as attached to a small private temple, supporting in perpetuity a monk to look after the graves and offer regular sacrifices.[44] It is conceivable that Chu Hsi's original donation was attached to a temple but his later biographer preferred not to record the act in a way that might be construed as support for Buddhist intrusion on ancestral rites. Or it is possible that Chu Hsi entrusted the property directly to the group of kinsmen descended from the first Chu to settle in the village three centuries earlier. Ever since Fan Chung-yen (989–1052) had endowed his kinsmen in this way, such endowments had carried great prestige as acts that made possible the promotion of ideal kinship solidarity.[45] One can easily imagine that Chu Hsi's relatives in Wu-yüan encouraged him to donate the land, not wanting him to sell it to outsiders. In his absence, they would naturally have had to manage the land, choosing the tenants or farming it themselves. The land was large enough that it could have served as the nucleus of significant descent-group formation, as many groups endowed rites with considerably smaller amounts of land.[46] Nevertheless, whatever choice Chu Hsi had in the initial endowment, it seems to have worked; when he returned a quarter century later, Chu Hsi was on good terms with his kinsmen.

The academic flavor of the discussion of the descent-line system in the *Family Rituals* reflects, I suspect, the fact that Chu Hsi never tried to put this system into practice. Chu Hsi was the descent-line heir of his father and grandfather.[47] He had little contact with his great-great-grandfather's and great-grandfather's descent-line heirs, apparently visiting them only twice, and surely he did not turn to them to manage the marriages of his younger sisters or children, as the *Family Rituals* instructs. Had he actually tried to follow the *Family Rituals* in these regards, he would undoubtedly have run into the sorts

---

(1125–1210) description of both scattered and concentrated graves of his ancestors, *Lu Fang-weng ch'üan-chi* wen 39:243; *Fang-weng chia-hsün*, p. 4.

[44] See the account Lou Yüeh (1137–1213) wrote of his mother's family's endowed grave-side temple, the third such at the site (*Kung-k'uei chi* 60:808–89), or Huang Kan's account of the temple that had been at his family's graves for centuries (*Mien-chai chi* 28:30b–34b).

[45] See Twitchett, "The Fan Clan's Charitable Estate."

[46] See, Ebrey, "Early Stages of Descent Group Organization," pp. 40–44.

[47] See WC 86:16a, where his announcement of his retirement to the family altar extends only to his grandparents.

of problems that led most authors of revised versions in later centuries to omit these provisions altogether.

CHU HSI'S LOCAL SERVICE

At eighteen Chu Hsi attained the *chin-shih* degree and at twenty-four *sui*, in 1153, took up his first post as registrar of T'ung-an county, further south in Fukien.[48] Like many Confucian scholars before him, Chu Hsi decided he should do something about the way common people performed family rituals. He submitted a memorial asking the court to issue regulations for wedding ceremonies:

> In the ritual and legal texts, weddings are important as they draw distinctions between men and women and prevent disorder at its source. Through inquiries I have learned that in this county there have not been proper wedding ceremonies for a long time. The common people of the villages and lanes who are too poor to provide betrothal gifts sometimes entice a [young woman], calling it "taking a companion to be a wife." Through practice it has become the custom and has spread even to the educated and rich families who also sometimes do it without fear or shame. Such behavior not only violates the ritual codes and throws the national laws into disarray, but it leads to jealousy, which can accumulate till violence erupts, so that people commit murder without remorse. How deeply pitiable is the ignorance of customary practice![49]

Chu Hsi then requested that the prefecture issue rules for wedding rituals from the *Cheng-ho wu-li* section for gentlemen and commoners and that observance of them be strictly enforced.

In a policy discussion written while in T'ung-an, Chu Hsi explained more fully his ideas on government-issued ritual rules. He began by stating, "Ritual is not difficult to carry out at the top, but those who wish to carry it out at the bottom face difficulties." At court the regulations are clear; there are, moreover, dozens of officials who can assist in interpreting them. However, at the prefectural and county level, both *shih-ta-fu* and commoners faced numerous obstacles in performing family rituals because the *Cheng-ho wu-li hsin-i* was inadequately known. Chu Hsi proposed selecting those parts of the *Wu-li* that applied to officials and commoners in the counties and prefectures, emending them to take into account more recent regulations, and issuing them under the title "Shao-hsing period edited digest of the rituals for officials and commoners of the Cheng-ho period." He wanted this digest printed and three copies sent to each prefecture and county: one for the government office, one for the

---

[48] On Chu Hsi's official service, see also Schirokauer, "Chu Hsi's Political Career" and "Chu Hsi as an Administrator."

[49] WC 20:1b–2a.

school, and one for a Buddhist or Taoist temple. It would then be up to local authorities to make sure that the provisions were widely explained "in the markets and villages." They should do this by making further copies of the digest and by selecting scholars who love ritual to lecture on the rites.[50]

In calling for vigorous efforts by local officials to let ordinary people know exactly what they should do in each of the family rituals, Chu Hsi was going beyond most of his predecessors. Men like Ou-yang Hsiu and Ssu-ma Kuang who labeled much of ordinary ritual behavior heterodox or vulgar did not try to write specifically for the local level or see to it that books were widely distributed. And those like Ts'ai Hsiang who did try to reform local practice generally did it through posting placards that explained the evils of undesirable customs and warned of punishments. Attacking the problem by printing and circulating liturgies had been briefly attempted under Emperor Hui-tsung.[51] Chu Hsi clearly saw this as the method most likely to succeed. He recognized that the way to standardize practice was to get standardized books into the hands of local leaders.

After Chu Hsi left T'ung-an in 1157, he did not have to face the problem of dealing with common people's ritual practices for many years, as he was not given another post in local administration until 1179 when he was appointed prefect of Nan-k'ang, in Kiangsi. While in that post he again submitted a memorial asking the government to promulgate ritual manuals for use at the local level. He noted that the prefecture's original copies of the *Cheng-ho wu-li hsin-i* had often been destroyed in the wars or broken up. Without copies, prefects and magistrates found it difficult to perform the rites that were their responsibility and they had no authoritative text for the people's cappings, weddings, funerals, and sacrifices.[52]

In 1190 Chu Hsi took up the post of prefect of Chang-chou in southern Fukien. Despite his earlier experiences, he seems to have been genuinely shocked at some of the customs he found in this area. His biographer reported:

In recent years, the customs of [Chang-chou] had deteriorated. The master found the common people so ignorant of ritual that they might not wear sackcloth or [head and waist] bands while in mourning for their parents. As soon as he arrived he gave instruction on ancient and modern ritual rules and laws to enlighten them. He also collected together the old procedures for mourning, burial, and marriage, and promulgated them, ordering the elders to explain them. Local custom also greatly honored Buddhist teachings, and men and women would gather in Buddhist temples for religious classes. Women who did not marry would live by themselves in cloisters. He prohibited all of these practices.[53]

[50] WC 69:17a–19a. See also Chu, "Chu Hsi and Public Instruction," pp. 256–57.
[51] SS 98:2423; *Sung ta-chao-ling chi* 148:548.
[52] WC 20:30b–31b.
[53] NP 4A:171.

Several of the notices Chu Hsi posted while in Chang-chou survive. In the sixth month of 1190 he put up a notice concerning proper mourning garments for parents. He reiterated the standard Confucian explanations of why one goes into mourning. Although in recent times people did not wear exactly the sorts of garments prescribed in antiquity, "According to the regulations on mourning in the legal code, if before mourning is over, one wears auspicious clothes or, forgetting one's grief, plays music, the penalty is three years penal service, or for performances [tsa-hsi], one year. Even for listening to music or participating in a feast, the penalty is sixty strokes." He noted that in recent times Emperor Hsiao-tsung (r. 1163–1189, d. 1194) had worn mourning for Kao-tsung (r. 1127–1162), but this remote area had not yet been influenced by the imperial example. Since it was his responsibility as prefect to promote proper behavior, he was announcing both to the educated *shih* and to the commoners that they must wear some sort of mourning garment, including hemp bands, and must not drink wine, eat meat, or, to use his euphemism, enter their bedrooms.[54]

Two months later he posted a placard prohibiting women from living in dharma cloisters. By way of explanation, Chu Hsi stated the standard Confucian explanation that the differentiation of men and women is basic to society. Men properly belong outside and women at home. The Buddhist teaching of celibacy is a perverse teaching, for "if everyone in the world fully followed this teaching, in less than a hundred years there would be no people in the world, only birds and beasts."[55] Returning these women to civil society would also help alleviate the problem of unmarried men kidnapping women in order to get wives. In response to the counterarguments he had been hearing, Chu Hsi said that at least the younger women whose appearance had not yet deteriorated should be returned to their homes and married according to the wishes of their seniors and the aid of go-betweens. To those who claimed that dowry expenses were prohibitive, he reminded them that there were costs to setting up daughters in cloisters, and some wedding costs could be shifted to the other side when the family budget required it. How could someone condemn men and women to a lonely life with no one to depend on out of worries over expenses?[56]

Chu Hsi, in part to communicate these sorts of prohibitions, tried to strengthen the mutual responsibility (*pao*) system. Each local unit would teach Confucian moral principles to its members. Chu Hsi specified, for instance, that they should teach people that proper marriages had to involve a matchmaker and a betrothal and that properly married wives had to be distinguished from common-law ones, who simply shared the same room publicly with a man, and from "elopers," who had run away to get married without using a go-between. Mutual responsibility groups should also teach the importance of burial within a month of death, that Buddhist services and Buddhist processions were not proper, and that it was wrong for those who came to condole to demand food or drink. (Apparently the customs Ts'ai Hsiang found in southern Fukien over a century earlier still persisted.) The mutual responsibility groups were also to teach people that they could not privately set up cloisters under the pretext of cultivating the dharma, nor should men and women gather in mixed-sex groups at temples to hear discussions of sutras.[57]

Chu Hsi's encounters with social reality, his discovery that common people did not perform rites the way his peers did, seems to have led to a persisting concern with developing forms of the rites that could more easily be put into practice. Chu Hsi saw a need for texts that would be easy to consult and that would be widely available in every county in the country. His experiences in trying to teach wedding rituals may also explain why Chu Hsi in the *Family Rituals* radically reduced the traditional "six rites" of weddings. There is no sign that he was copying *shih-ta-fu* practice in this regard, as all of the classical names for steps of the wedding process were commonly used by educated men in Sung times, and truncating this ritual proved difficult for them to accept. The *Cheng-ho wu-li hsin-i* had reduced the steps in the weddings for commoners, and Chu Hsi was not only familiar with this text, but thought it should be made more widely known precisely to help commoners know what constituted a legally and ritually acceptable marriage.

DISCUSSIONS OF FUNERALS AND ANCESTRAL RITUALS AMONG CHU HSI'S CIRCLE, 1169–1176

Chu Hsi was above all else a scholar and teacher, dealing with books and people who cared about books. A major component of the social context in which Chu Hsi developed his ideas about family rituals was his network of friends and students, men already committed to the Neo-Confucian tradition but often unsure which authority to follow. When these men had to bury their parents or marry their children they often wrote to each other to ask for advice.

During the years he was working on the *Family Rituals*, Chu Hsi discussed ritual issues in a great many of the letters he wrote to friends and students, the most important of whom were Chang Shih, Lü Tsu-ch'ien, Wang Ying-ch'en, Wu I, P'an Ching-hsien, and Ch'en Tan. In 1169 they were all middle-aged men; Wang Ying-ch'en was fifty-two; Ch'en Tan, forty-seven; Wu I, forty-

---

[57] WC 100:5b–8a. I tend to read these proclamations as revealing Chu Hsi's desires to use the authority at his disposal to regulate the daily life of commoners in ways he believed would be for their own good. For a different reading, emphasizing the development of voluntaristic local organizations that could serve to limit the intervention of the state in local affairs, see de Bary, *The Liberal Tradition in China*, pp. 32–34.

one; Chu Hsi, forty; Chang Shih, thirty-seven; and P'an Ching-hsien and Lü Tsu-ch'ien, thirty-four. In the eyes of later generations, Chu Hsi, Lü Tsu-ch'ien, and Chang Shih were three of the greatest Confucian thinkers of their age, but at the time Wang Ying-ch'en was treated as an intellectual peer, perhaps because he was older and a high official.

During the period discussed here, 1169–1176, Chu Hsi was largely out of office, busily engaged in several scholarly projects, completing two history books, *Tzu-chih t'ung-chien kang-mu* (1172) and *Pa-ch'ao ming-ch'en yen-hsing lu* (1172), a collection of the Ch'eng brothers' writings, *Ch'eng-shih wai-shu* (1173), a history of the Neo-Confucian movement, *I-lo yüan-yüan lu* (1173), and the *Reflections on Things at Hand* (*Chin-ssu lu*, 1175).[58] Several of these books were produced through collaboration with students and colleagues. Chu Hsi was at the heights of his intellectual powers during this period and not yet subject to partisan political attacks.[59]

Prior to 1169 Chu Hsi, Lü Tsu-ch'ien, Chang Shih, and Wang Ying-ch'en were all acquainted with each other. Chu Hsi had met Chang Shih in the capital in 1163, joined him in mourning his father in 1164, corresponded with him in 1167, and visited him in his hometown of Heng-yang (Hunan) in 1168.[60] Chang's father Chün (1097–1164) had been an eminent official, and Chang Shih entered office through *yin* privilege in about 1163.[61] A scholar of considerable standing, Chang Shih's collected works, edited by Chu Hsi, contain letters to Chu Hsi, Lü Tsu-ch'ien, P'an Ching-hsien, and Wu I.

In 1169 Chang Shih took up his first post after finishing mourning for his father. It was as prefect of Yen-ling in Chekiang. Shortly later, Lü Tsu-ch'ien also arrived there to serve as professor of the prefectural school. Lü Tsu-ch'ien was from perhaps the most eminent family of the Sung dynasty. From the very beginnings of the dynasty his ancestors had included many leading officials; during the late Northern Sung they also acquired strong credentials within the Neo-Confucian movement.[62] Lü Tsu-ch'ien seems to have met Chu Hsi in 1156 when Chu Hsi was holding his first post in T'ung-an and he was accompanying his father to Fu-chou.[63] In 1160, while in the capital awaiting reassignment, he got to know Hu Hsien and Wang Ying-ch'en. He qualified for

[58] NP 1B:47–57.

[59] On later attacks on Chu Hsi and his teachers, see Haeger, "The Intellectual Context of Neo-Confucian Syncretism," and Schirokauer, "Neo-Confucians under Attack."

[60] YL 103:2608; WC hsü-chi 5:12b; NP 1A:23, 1B:29. On Chu Hsi's relationship with Chang Shih, see also Chan, *Chu Tzu hsin t'an-so*, pp. 521–48.

[61] For Chang Shih's biography, see WC 89:1a–10b, SS 429:12770–75. On his philosophy, see Chiang, "Ch'un-ju Chang Nan-hsüan ti Hsiang-hsüeh."

[62] Leading officials and scholars included Lü Meng-cheng (946–1011), Lü I-chien (978–1043), Lü Kung-chu (1018–1089), Lü Hsi-che (1036–1114), and Lü Hao-wen (1064–1131). On Lü Tsu-ch'ien and his family, see P'an and Hsü, *Lü Tsu-ch'ien ssu-hsiang ch'u-t'an*, and Kinugawa, "Sōdai no meizoku."

[63] Chan, *Chu-Tzu hsin t'an-so*, p. 555.

office through *yin* in 1162 and later also attained the *chin-shih*. In 1169 Lü Tsu-ch'ien had just come out of mourning for his mother, which freed him to return to office and to remarry as his first wife had died in 1162. He married his first wife's younger sister, the marriage probably planned for several years, as Miss Han was then twenty-five *sui*.[64] Although only thirty-four *sui*, Lü already had considerable scholarly stature, having written studies of the *Ch'un-ch'iu* and *Tso-chuan*.

On the way to take up his post, Lü Tsu-ch'ien stopped in San-ch'ü to visit Wang Ying-ch'en.[65] Wang Ying-ch'en's ancestors, like Chu Hsi's, had come from Hui-chou, but more recent generations had settled further south in Yü-shan county in Hsin-chou. Wang Ying-ch'en had a kinship connection with Chu Hsi,[66] and was on friendly terms with many of the members of the Lü family a generation senior to Lü Tsu-ch'ien. Although he came from a family with no recent official service, at eighteen *sui* he passed the *chin-shih* examination in the first place, guaranteeing that he would be noticed. During his official career he became acquainted with Chang Shih's father Chün. Wang Ying-ch'en had an active career both in the provinces and at court and was known as a patron of scholars. When Hsiao-tsung succeeded to the throne in 1162, Wang Ying-ch'en played the major role in formulating the accession ceremonies. In 1164 while serving in Fukien he invited Li T'ung, one of Chu Hsi's teachers, to visit. Later he recommended Chu Hsi as his own replacement. In the beginning of 1169 he was minister of rites, but when Lü Tsu-ch'ien visited him he had been appointed prefect of P'ing-chiang (in Kiangsu) and must have been getting ready to move. Less than half of Wang Ying-ch'en's collected works survive, but the surviving part includes a letter each to Chang Shih and Lü Tsu-ch'ien and fourteen to Chu Hsi.[67]

Early in 1170 Chu Hsi buried his mother and later that year reburied his father.[68] This year P'an Ching-hsien's father died. P'an, like Lü Tsu-ch'ien, was from Chin-hua in Chekiang and from a large and well-established official family. While in the Imperial University he had made the acquaintance of Wang Ying-ch'en. A few years after he attained the *chin-shih* in 1163, he resigned to care for his elderly parents and never served in office again. Chu Hsi reported that he originally met P'an through Lü Tsu-ch'ien.[69] P'an Ching-hsien's writings do not survive, but there are letters to him from Chu Hsi, Lü

[64] TLC fu-lu 1:6b.

[65] TLC fu-lu 1:7a.

[66] Chu Hsi referred to himself as a distant maternal nephew, WC 87:5a. Chu Hsi's grandfather's and great-grandfather's wives were both surnamed Wang, so he may have been related to Wang Ying-ch'en through one of them.

[67] For Wang's biography, see SS 387:11876–82 and *Sung-Yüan hsüeh-an* 46:97–100. His collected works are the *Wen-ting chi*.

[68] WC 94:25a–26a.

[69] See WC 93:11b–13b for Chu Hsi's biography of P'an.

Tsu-ch'ien, and Chang Shih. After his father died in 1170 P'an wrote to Lü Tsu-ch'ien asking for advice on mourning procedures and requesting that Lü write the epitaph. Apparently P'an Ching-hsien had been with Lü Tsu-ch'ien and Chang Shih in Yen-ling, as Lü Tsu-ch'ien in his reply wrote "Prefect Chang is very sorry that you had to leave. Since [Chu Hsi] Yüan-hui is in mourning he cannot come, and now you also leave for mourning. It has become difficult to find opportunities for sincere discussions of learning."[70]

In his letter Lü Tsu-ch'ien praised P'an Ching-hsien and his brothers for helping restore the ancient rituals. With regard to P'an's questions, Lü Tsu-ch'ien urged P'an and his brothers to moderate their austerities, since people in their day did not have the same constitutions as the ancients; to avoid getting ill they should judge their stamina before limiting themselves to vegetables and water. For the details of the rites, he recommended Ssu-ma Kuang's *Shu-i*, noting that "on the whole it is very good. It would be excellent to become familiar with it."[71] He urged P'an Ching-hsien and his brothers to be meticulous in the funerary rites, but to pay most attention to the idea of the rite, eliminating any superfluous elaborations.[72] Lü Tsu-ch'ien went on to ask whether a burial plot had been found yet; he noted that the classical ritual was to put off "the cessation of wailing" until after the burial. "To call the one-hundredth day the cessation of wailing is a mistake that in recent ages has been passed down by custom. It is not the ritual."[73] For the burial procession, he thought that gongs and decorated pavilions were not too harmful, so long as the emphasis remained on the expression of grief. Lü Tsu-ch'ien went on to discuss other matters, and mentioned letters from Wang Ying-ch'en.[74]

To help P'an Ching-hsien further, Lü Tsu-ch'ien prepared a detailed liturgy for burial rites based on the *I-li* and Ssu-ma Kuang's *Shu-i*, noting where he had made additions. For instance, he thought that in the south graves should not have side niches for grave goods because this would weaken them. He noted that Ssu-ma Kuang had used prayer boards to represent the ancestors and said that if one wanted to follow the ancient system of tablets to consult Ch'eng I's collected works. He did not refer to any texts by Chu Hsi, probably because he had not yet seen any.[75]

In 1171 P'an Ching-hsien and Chu Hsi were still in mourning. Lü Tsu-ch'ien's second wife, whom he had married two years earlier, died and he buried her the next month. Chu Hsi wrote to condole.[76] Chu Hsi should have come out of mourning at the end of the year. The next year, 1172, Lü Tsu-

---

[70] TLC pieh 10:29a.
[71] TLC pieh 10:28b–29a.
[72] TLC pieh 10:30a.
[73] TLC pieh 10:30b.
[74] TLC pieh 10:30b–32a.
[75] TLC pieh 3:23a, 24b.
[76] TLC 10:10b–11a; WC 33:8b–9a.

ch'ien had to resign from office to go into mourning, as his father had died. While in mourning he revised the funeral and burial liturgy he had compiled two years earlier for P'an Ching-hsien. He also wrote a similar guide to sacrificial rites. It quotes numerous sources, including the *Cheng-ho wu-li hsin-i*, Tu Yen, Han Ch'i, Chang Tsai, Ch'eng I, and various T'ang guides. It also twice quotes a liturgy by Chu Hsi. Lü Tsu-ch'ien noted that all the major authorities except Ch'eng I extended sacrifices to only three generations, and that both Ssu-ma Kuang and the *Cheng-ho wu-li hsin-i* specified joint sacrifices when brothers live together and separate ones when they live apart. Lü thus rejected Ch'eng I on two of his key points, the *tsung* system and the number of ancestors. Lü had the seasonal rites performed on the solstices and equinoxes and arranged the tablets with the great-grandfather in the center, the grandfather on the east, and the father on the west. In all these regards his provisions differ from Chu Hsi's *Family Rituals*. In itself this is not surprising as Lü Tsu-ch'ien and Chu Hsi, in their extensive correspondence, often differed in their approach toward the classics and their selective appropriation of earlier scholars' ideas.[77] Lü Tsu-ch'ien apparently did not finish his sacrificial liturgy at this time, however, as Chu Hsi in a colophon notes that he was revising it up until his death.[78]

After his father's death, Lü Tsu-ch'ien continued to correspond with P'an Ching-hsien on funeral and burial ritual.[79] He also corresponded with Chu Hsi. In a letter to Chu Hsi he described receiving word of his father's illness and arriving home to find him already dead. He reported that his father had ordered them to conduct the funeral and burial entirely according to canonical regulations, which he and his brothers had obeyed. For the last several years he had been doing research on sacrificial rituals, but had not finished his work; he hoped after the heat let up to get a chance to discuss his ideas with Chu Hsi. The items and details (*t'iao-mu*) that Chu Hsi had prepared he had set aside sometime earlier, but hoped to find time to study them and perhaps put them into practice.[80] This may well have been the guide to the procedures for ancestral rites that Lü Tsu-ch'ien cited in his own liturgy. When Chu Hsi wrote to condole Lü Tsu-ch'ien, he lamented that he was too poor to send a contribution toward the funeral expenses and lived too far away to wail before the coffin.[81]

In 1173 Chu Hsi wrote to Wang Ying-ch'en on the issue of family shrines.

I received your request for discussion of the shrine system. I recently asked Ch'en Ming-chung [Tan] to borrow copies of the various ancient and modern works on

---

[77] See Chan, *Chu Tzu hsin t'an-so*, pp. 559–63.
[78] TLC pieh 4:1a–10b.
[79] TLC pieh 10:31a–37a.
[80] TLC pieh 7:28a–b.
[81] WC 33:11a.

sacrifices. Right now I am living alone with no one around with whom to discuss these issues. . . . The Chih-ho [1054–1055] system, while not matching the ancient one, got the idea, just not thoroughly enough. The Cheng-ho [1111–1117] system stuck closer to antiquity, but often got the gradation at the expense of the meaning.

In antiquity, of the five shrines of the feudal lords, the two *chao* and two *mu* were for the four generations from great-great-grandfather on down, that is, the mourning relatives. The "great ancestor" was the first to receive a fief, and his shrine was preserved indefinitely. Nowadays nobles have families, not states, and so should not have shrines for their first ancestors. Therefore the Chih-ho system of four shrines for the two *chao* and two *mu*, the four generations with mourning, with no shrine for the great ancestor, while different from the ancient system, does not violate its idea. . . . But this is just a discussion of the pluses and minuses of each version. If you wish to [construct a shrine], then the Cheng-ho rituals are what is carried out now. Those who serve as officials today and have the rank to establish shrines all use it. But the system of shrines is vaguely described, so it has not flourished as it did in T'ang, not to mention antiquity. Scholars who love ritual inevitably lament this. If we examine it according to Master Ch'eng's sayings, then "as one has mourning obligations to his great-great-grandfather, he must offer sacrifices to him. Even when there are seven or five shrines, the sacrifices stop at the great-great-grandfather, and even when there are three or one shrine or when sacrifices are made in the chamber, they must reach to the great-great-grandfather. It is just that the gradations vary." I suspect that this best captures the basic meaning of the sacrificial rites. . . .

As for rites at graves, Mr. Ch'eng also thought it had not existed in antiquity, but grew from custom. As it did not harm principle, he approved it at a simpler level than the seasonal rites.

This is a rough discussion, based on my limited experience and what I have read. Please give me your opinions. . . . I have written a draft of the rites for sacrifices in the chamber based on Mr. Ch'eng's theories, planning to carry them out in my family. But as I have been in mourning for several years in a row, I have not had a chance to give them a full test.[82]

In this letter Chu Hsi analyzes some of the issues concerning ancestral rites that most engaged eleventh-century scholars. He reveals his respect for earlier writings: his first impulse is to collect copies of earlier rules. He distinguished between understanding the ancient system and knowing what to do in his day. He recognized the authority of the government to establish how such rites should be performed by its officials. He also cited approvingly Ch'eng I's ideas on the number of ancestors to receive sacrifices and on sacrifices at graves, but saw room for further discussion and analysis.

Chu Hsi's next two letters to Wang Ying-ch'en continue the discussion of

[82] WC 30:15a–17a.

shrines and were probably written soon afterwards. The first discussed the opinion of a Mr. Sung that one should conduct seasonal rites to a maternal grandfather without heirs, probably referring to what we would call uxorilocal marriages (where the husband moves into the wife's family). Chu Hsi did not think one could be comfortable sacrificing to people of a different patrilineal group. He urged instead searching for a patrilineal kinsman of the grandfather's who could be set up as heir, providing financial help to him if necessary, but not performing the rites.[83] The next letter discussed what to do about offerings to the second and third wives of an ancestor or to his concubines in light of Ch'eng I's view that only the first wife's tablet should be on the altar, any others put elsewhere. Chu Hsi largely supported Ch'eng I, but was somewhat tentative, asking Wang Ying-ch'en to give his opinion. On burning prayers at graves, Chu Hsi cited a discussion by Chang Shih and was again quite noncommittal himself. He cited Wang Ming-ch'ing's (1127–1214) recently published *Hui-shih* as a source for Northern Sung scholars changing their clothes to more subdued ones on death-day anniversaries and Chang Tsai's somewhat different plan. He admitted that his own draft was confused on this point and that he was not sure which authority to follow.[84]

Wang Ying-ch'en does not seem to have been entirely convinced by these replies from Chu Hsi as he passed on the correspondence to Lü Tsu-ch'ien for his opinions. Lü Tsu-ch'ien responded in 1174, apparently siding with Chu Hsi on the issue of the sacrificial rites to successor wives but not so clearly on death-day anniversary clothes. Lü Tsu-ch'ien also noted that Chang Shih still had doubts on this issue.[85]

In the first of these letters to Wang Ying-ch'en, Chu Hsi mentioned asking Ch'en Tan to help him collect sources for research on sacrifices. Ch'en Tan was from Chu Hsi's home county of Chien-yang and received his *chin-shih* the same year he did (1148). Although older than Chu Hsi, he seems to have looked on himself as a disciple of Chu's. Unfortunately very little else is known about him and none of his writings survive.[86] Chu Hsi's collected works include four letters to Ch'en Tan on family rituals, one of which was written shortly after the first letter to Wang Ying-ch'en given above. Chu Hsi repeated the discussion of where to offer sacrifices for successor wives and concubine mothers and the clothes to be worn on death-day anniversaries. He also referred to the problem of sacrifices for uncles and brothers without heirs. He added a discussion of the offerings to first ancestors at the winter solstice, clarifying that it should be on the same day as the regular winter sacrifice. He

[83] WC 30:17a–b.
[84] WC 30:17b–18a.
[85] TLC pieh 7:6a–b.
[86] For brief biographies, see Chan, *Chu Tzu men-jen*, p. 210; *Min-chung li-hsüeh yüan-yüan k'ao* 20:6b.

noted that Wang Ying-ch'en had not yet replied to his letter, so he did not yet know Wang's thoughts on these issues.[87]

The letters to Ch'en Tan included in Chu Hsi's collected works just before and after this one concern funeral ritual, suggesting either that Ch'en Tan was also helping Chu Hsi prepare a text that covered funerals, or that he was himself in mourning. Chu Hsi discussed the "soul cloth," admitting that it was not ancient but was acceptable as one could not follow ancient ways completely. In this he was following Ssu-ma Kuang. On where to put the tablet between burial and the end of the mourning period, he advised Ch'en Tan to reexamine Ssu-ma Kuang's *Shu-i* and Kao K'ang's "Ritual for seeing off at the end" (*Sung-chung li*).[88] In the next letter, Chu Hsi referred to having discussed mourning garments in detail in a prior letter. He added that since the ancient system was not clearly understood, it was acceptable to use the hats and robes of their day.[89]

Besides enlisting Ch'en Tan to help him work on ritual texts, Chu Hsi apparently also enlisted Wu I, for Wu I and his friends prepared a draft on sacrificial rituals that Chu Hsi thought needed further deliberation.[90] Wu I was, like Chu Hsi and Ch'en Tan, from Chien-yang. None of his recent direct ancestors had been officials and he was orphaned early, but he studied under Hu Hsien as Chu Hsi had done. After Hu Hsien died, Wu I studied with the latter's kinsman Hu Hung (1106–1162) along with Chang Shih.[91] After Hu Hung died in 1162, Wu I remained loyal to much of his teachings.[92] No writings of Wu I's survive, but there are letters to him from Chu Hsi and Chang Shih. Wu I seems to have been as close to Chang Shih as to Chu Hsi, and perhaps looked on himself as an independent scholar, of comparable standing to these two, since they had been fellow students. In his letter to Wu I and his colleagues, Chu Hsi pointed to two principal problems. The first was the direction of the shrine. They had it facing east, following Ch'eng I. Chu Hsi cited classical evidence that the shrine faced south and argued that the person who recorded Ch'eng I's comment on this point must have made a mistake. Chu Hsi also discussed an item in their draft that had the sacrifice to the first ancestor at the winter solstice extending to all the tablets in the shrine. Chu Hsi commented that this sacrifice had been invented by Ch'eng I on the basis of moral principles and the succession of the seasons. If inconvenient today, it did not have to be carried out; omitting it would certainly be better than missing its meaning. Chu Hsi ended by requesting further comments from Wu I and his co-

---

[87] WC 43:5b–6a.

[88] WC 43:5a–b.

[89] WC 43:6a.

[90] Calling on students to help him prepare books was not uncommon for Chu Hsi. On his collaborative work on the *Elementary Learning*, see Kelleher, "Back to Basics," pp. 220–23.

[91] On Hu Hung, see Schirokauer, "Chu Hsi and Hu Hung."

[92] For Wu I's biography, see WC 97:45b–47a.

workers.[93] Chu Hsi's deference to Ch'eng I, thus, was far from absolute. He compared his remarks to evidence from the classics and was willing to dismiss some as interpolations and others as inventions, without much authority.

It must also have been in approximately this period that Chu Hsi and Chang Shih wrote to each other about their work on sacrificial rites. The earliest letter seems to be one Chang Shih wrote to Chu Hsi.

As for the sacrificial rituals that you have formulated, privately I have also long wanted to undertake such a task. But because the texts are incomplete and I have few people with whom to talk over the issues [I have not undertaken it]. Now to receive your careful and thorough work is very comforting. As the issues are not settled, I will give it a try, beginning at the winter solstice this year. But I still cannot avoid doubts on a few issues and would like to consult with you further on them.

The ancients did not sacrifice at graves. This was not an omission; they knew that the feelings and forms of ghosts and spirits could not receive sacrifices at graves. The spirit tablets are in shrines, and the grave contains the bodily soul [t'i-p'o]. How can sacrificing at the place that contains the bodily soul accord with moral principle? Who receives the sacrifice?[94] Those who insist on practicing this because of private feelings, even though they recognize that logically it does not work, are serving their ancestors hypocritically. Those who do not know its impossibility are ignorant. . . . I think that at the seasonal festival one can make a visit [to the grave], prostrate oneself, bow, stamp, shout, and wail, clean and sweep, and observe. One can also set out food offerings to the god of the soil to the left of the grave. This is my first doubt. . . .

Besides the seasonal rites, sacrifice to the first ancestor at the winter solstice, early ancestors at the beginning of spring, and deceased fathers in the last month of fall all express subtle moral principles. The sacrifice on New Year is also suitable. But is there room for discussion of what you call the "annual sacrifices and festival offerings"? Of them the Middle Origin one is extremely objectionable. This originated in Buddhist teachings. How can following customs go to the extreme [of accommodating this]? This is my second doubt.[95]

The following letter from Chu Hsi to Chang Shih was apparently written in response to the one above.

Your critique of [my work on] sacrifices is astute; on examining it I am gratefully awakened. At the beginning I also had doubts on the two issues you raise.

[93] WC 42:11a–12a. Ch'en, *Chu Tzu shu-hsin pien-nien k'ao-cheng*, tentatively dates this letter to 1170.

[94] Elsewhere, in distinguishing spirits (*shen*) from ghosts (*kuei*), Chang Shih wrote that "the *hun* energy becomes the spirit while the bodily soul becomes the ghost" (NHC 33:12b). He thus seems to have seen worship at graves as a kind of ghost worship, as opposed to spirit worship.

[95] NHC 20:2b–3b. On the Buddhist origins of sacrifices at Chung-yüan, see Teiser, *Ghost Festival*.

Then I noticed that the two [Ch'eng] masters had argued that following custom with regard to sacrifices at graves did not harm moral principle, so I did not want to leave it out lightly. As for "festival offerings," I can offer an explanation. Today's popular festivals did not exist in antiquity; thus even though the ancients did not sacrifice on those occasions, they were not bothered by it. Today people put emphasis on these occasions; they have feasts and music on these days, with special festival foods for each one, so the current feeling is that on these days one cannot help thinking of one's ancestors and also offering them the item. Although it is not an orthodox ritual, it is something that, given human feelings, cannot be omitted. But one should not exclusively use these occasions [to make sacrifices] and omit the orthodox rituals of the four seasons. Therefore my idea the other day was that once one has the orthodox sacrifices, there is no harm in also keeping these.

Now I have received your learned opinion that these are corrupting and not reverent. This really pinpoints their flaw. But if we wish therefore to do away with them, I fear we will stir up trouble. The longing heart [of the survivors] is not able to stop on its own. Thus I feel [reform] is not an easy problem. Moreover, when the ancients did not sacrifice, they did not presume to have feasts. So if today on the basis of the classics we do away with sacrifices at these popular festivals and yet the living eat, drink, and enjoy themselves according to custom, this conflicts with the ideas of serving the dead as one serves the living and serving the departed as one serves the survivors. [Omitting the offerings] could be done if one did away with [the festivals] altogether. I also worried that to make the point of doing away with something that at bottom does not harm moral principle not only would use-lessly disturb people but also, I feared, could not be carried out very widely. Thus people might stick to the rules and not perform this abolished sacrifice, but eat and drink the festival foods. This would gradually become the custom, so that in time [the discrepancy] would not be noticed. In terms of the principles of nature [t'ien-li], is this tolerable?

When the kings of the three [ancient dynasties] instituted rituals, as conditions had changed, they accorded with what suited the spirit of the times without vio-lating what was right according to moral principles. If the sages were to return and participate in this discussion, they would also have problems. In my opinion, besides the seasonal rites, one should offer at the shrine a large plate of the cus-tomary foods at the customary times, according to local tradition, following the same rituals used on the first of each month. This seems to accord with the need to do things in proportion and make compromises with feelings. It could be prac-ticed widely for a long time without arousing opposition.

As for sacrifices at New Year, they are also without canonical authorization; I simply employed the same reasoning.

When I was first deciding on the form for the seasonal sacrifices, I used the solstices and equinoxes. In that case the two winter solstice sacrifices would be annoyingly close.[96] Now I have changed to the system of divining to select days, using the idea of letting the gods decide rather than determining it oneself. There are a great many other places where I made revisions like these. Most of them are based on Messrs. Ch'eng, checked by reference to other authorities. Where I specially chose the theories of the two [Ch'eng] masters, I made a chapter on the theories of sacrifices. I also made another chapter on the prayers used in sacrifices.[97]

The copy I sent you previously has been refined a little further. I am recopying it to send to you. I would appreciate it if you could examine it and advise me of places that need corrections.[98]

In this letter Chu Hsi offers a full explanation of an innovative feature of the *Family Rituals*: the inclusion of a liturgy for ancestral rites as seasonal festivals. He also explained why he followed Ch'eng I on rites at graves and his general views on what sorts of deviations from the classics are justified. It is worth noting that while Chu Hsi seemed to defend his own views rather vigorously, Chang Shih's arguments apparently did have some effect on him, as he considerably toned down Ch'eng I's prescriptions for rites to early ancestors in the *Family Rituals* and downgraded the rites on popular festivals to offerings.[99]

Chang Shih was not fully convinced by Chu Hsi's arguments, for he wrote to Lü Tsu-ch'ien that he had made several changes in accordance with Chu Hsi's advice but was still uneasy about the issue of sacrifices at graves and the timing of the seasonal rites. "Normally when I go to the hills, I just bow to the ground, wail, and clean the area, and for the seasonal rites I use the solstices and equinoxes." He also thanked Lü Tsu-ch'ien for his researches, suggesting that Lü Tsu-ch'ien had sent him a copy of his own formulations of the rites. Chang also indicated that he planned to build a family shrine.[100]

It was also in 1174 that Lü Tsu-ch'ien arranged a marriage between Chu Hsi's eldest son Shu and P'an Ching-hsien's daughter. The year before, when Chu Shu was twenty-one *sui*, his father had sent him to study with Lü Tsu-ch'ien, who had him lodge with P'an Ching-hsien. In late 1174 Chu Hsi responded to a letter from Lü Tsu-ch'ien:

[96] The second winter solstice sacrifice was the one to first ancestors that Ch'eng I had proposed.

[97] The current edition of the *Family Rituals* schedules the seasonal sacrifices by divination, but it is not organized into three parts. Ch'eng I's ideas and the texts of prayers are inserted where appropriate.

[98] WC 30:29a–30a. Ch'en, *Chu Tzu shu-hsin pien-nien k'o-cheng*, p. 47, suggests an earlier date for this letter (1168), only possible if one assumes Chang Shih worked at least eight years on his guide to sacrificial rituals.

[99] CL 5b, 54b, 55b; Ebrey, *Chu Hsi's Family Rituals*, pp. 17, 167–72.

[100] NHC 25:3a.

As for the engagement ritual, we will do as you advise. In the spring we will go there and first complete this ritual. But [P'an Ching-hsien] Shu-tu's letter says that his daughter is just thirteen *sui*. This is not what I had been told. My son is full grown. My idea was to get him a wife soon. If we follow [Ssu-ma Kuang's] Wen-kung's etiquette, then next year we could have the wedding. I am now waiting for their response. Next I want to get a wife for my second son.[101]

Ssu-ma Kuang had argued that the legal minimum age for marriage for women of thirteen *sui* was too low, and set fourteen as a more reasonable minimum. Chu Hsi clearly wanted to adhere to his specifications, even at the expense of delaying the marriage of his full-grown son.[102]

In 1174 Chu Hsi completed a compilation of various authorities' writings on sacrificial rites. Only the postface has survived:

What precedes is *Sacrificial Rituals of the Ancient and Modern Authorities*, which I have compiled in sixteen sections. A person's life always comes from his ancestors. Therefore the desire to repay their origins is something no one with flesh and blood can lack. The ancient sage kings instituted the canonical rituals on the basis of this universal situation in order to fulfill this spirit and show love and gratitude. They gave them form and meaning, elaborating each step. When the Ch'in [dynasty] destroyed learning, ritual [texts] were the first to be destroyed. Since the Han, Confucian scholars one after the other have collected the fragments, preserving ten or twenty percent.

As the past and the present are different, and customs have changed, even rulers who promote Confucianism and value the Way and scholars who know the classics and love learning cannot entirely follow the ancient rituals to restore the greatness of the three [ancient] dynasties. Those who have formulated [rituals] in accord with their times for a single family or single state may not always have achieved the former kings' ideal of inventing [ritual] on the basis of moral principle, but there are not even many of these [books] that have survived until today.[103]

Chu Hsi thus admired earlier scholars who had formulated rituals for their time. He went on to explain that he was publishing all of their books that he had been able to collect as a convenience to the reader. He thought this would aid the court in its efforts to educate the people. From a letter to Cheng Po-hsiung (c.s. 1145), it is apparent that this book was arranged with one section for each authority, probably beginning with the classics. Meng Hsien was the seventh, Hsü Jun the eighth, the *Cheng-ho wu-li hsin-i* was the eleventh, Sun

---

[101] WC 33:28a. On Chu Shu, see Chan, *Chu Tzu hsin t'an-so*, pp. 54–57.

[102] Chu Hsi was still writing to Lü Tsu-ch'ien about arrangements for the marriage in late 1176, when he was already worried about his wife's illness (WC 34:1b–2b). As she died at the end of that year, the marriage must either have taken place just before she died or been delayed another two years until Shu was out of mourning.

[103] WC 81:6a–b.

Jih-yung the twelfth, Tu Yen the thirteenth, and Fan Tsu-yü, the nineteenth.[104] Another letter mentioned that the book gave the theories of Ssu-ma Kuang, Han Ch'i, Ch'eng I, and the *T'ang hui-yao*.[105] This book does not seem to have included Chu Hsi's own formulation of the sacrificial rites, the contents of which he had been discussing with his friends and students. In later years when he cited this compilation, it was as a source for other authors' ideas.[106]

This compilation of others' instructions did not satisfy all the needs Chu Hsi saw. In 1175 he wrote to Lü Tsu-ch'ien that he had been too busy to get much done on a set of instructions for family rituals that could be performed by rich and poor alike, to be made part of his revision of the *Lü Family Compact*.[107]

In 1176 Chang Shih finally finished his book on family rituals, based on judicious selection from the writings of Ssu-ma Kuang, Ch'eng I, and Chang Tsai. At the time he was serving as a local administrator in the remote region of Kuei-lin, Kwangsi. Chu Hsi noted in his epitaph for Chang Shih that while in Kwangsi Chang had worked hard at instructing the people in correct funeral, burial, and marriage procedures and in combating practices based in Buddhism, Taoism, or superstitious beliefs in ghosts.[108] After Chu Hsi saw a draft of this book, he wrote to Chang Shih urging him to make his ritual easier to put into practice but also objecting to the omission of the capping ceremony. In response Chang Shih defended his omission of capping but noted that some scholars in Ch'ang-sha were also uneasy about it. The step called "calling down the spirits" in the sacrificial liturgy Chang had omitted because he did not want to confuse ignorant people who believed in ghosts and shamans.[109] In his postface to the book, Chang Shih claimed that capping, defunct for so long, could not be restored, and so he had concentrated on the other three rites. Whereas the three authorities he used disagreed on particular points, they were identical in their desire to base themselves in the ancient teachings and combat heterodox doctrines. *Shih-ta-fu* were responsible for the state of ritual. If, after studying it, they carried it out among their own relatives, customs would gradually be improved.[110] In all of these regards, Chang Shih was echoing senti-

[104] WC 37:24b–25a. These various works were all still available in the early thirteenth century. See CCSLCT 6:179–81.

[105] WC 63:19a–20a. Cf. YL 90:2320.

[106] E.g., YL 90:2320.

[107] WC 33:29a. Ch'ien, *Chu Tzu hsin hsüeh-an* 4:172, and Ueyama, "Shushi no 'Karei,' " p. 222, assume that Chu Hsi was referring to his work on the *Family Rituals* in this letter. Ch'en Lai argues, probably rightly, that he was referring only to the section on rituals in the *Compact*. On the *Compact*, see Übelhör, "The Community Compact (*Hsiang-yüeh*) of the Sung and Its Educational Significance." On the date of this letter, see Ch'en, *Chu Tzu shu-hsin pien-nien k'ao-cheng*, pp. 131–32.

[108] WC 89:7b, 9b.

[109] NHC 24:3b–4a. For the religious views of these people, see Hansen, *Changing Gods in Medieval China*.

[110] NHC 33:9a–10a.

ments commonly expressed in the eleventh century. When this book was re-printed in 1194, Chu Hsi wrote a postface for it. In it he described Chang Shih's book as easier to follow than Ssu-ma Kuang's and noted that he also had once wanted to compile a book that would get rid of superfluous embel-lishments and provide a basic outline that even the poor and humble could follow.[111]

In 1176, however, Chu Hsi was still recommending to his students that they study Ssu-ma Kuang's *Shu-i*. During that year he visited Wu-yüan, where his ancestors prior to his grandfather were buried. During his three months there, he instructed students on several books, one of which was the *Shu-i*.[112]

This account of the interchange among Chu Hsi and his circle on how to conduct family rituals could be expanded to include more people,[113] or ex-tended a few years in time.[114] The circle did not last much longer, however, as its key members started to die—Wang Ying-ch'en at the end of 1175, Wu I in 1177, Chang Shih in 1180, and Lü Tsu-ch'ien in 1181. Enough has been presented, however, to show the bases on which these men discussed rites and some of the give-and-take that occurred. Given the relative fixity these issues acquired in later periods, when the *Family Rituals* was pronounced orthodox, it is refreshing to see how varied these men's opinions were in the 1170s. Chang Shih, Wang Ying-ch'en, Lü Tsu-ch'ien, and Chu Hsi all wanted to accommodate some popular practices, retain some canonical elements, and honor Ch'eng I. But they did not concur about when and where to do each of these. Chang Shih was happy with solar dates for seasonal rites and with omit-ting capping, but could not bring himself to accept sacrifices at graves or at the Middle Origin festival. Lü Tsu-ch'ien accepted solar dates but saw no reason to follow Ch'eng I on rites to four generations of ancestors or the *tsung* system. Wang Ying-ch'en was uncomfortable with following Ch'eng I on al-lowing the tablet of only one wife on the altar. Chu Hsi could not follow Ch'eng I on the direction of the ancestral shrine, but wanted to follow him on the occasions for rites unless convincing reasons could be found to do other-wise; and he was willing to go along with offerings at popular festivals and at graves, but not with giving up capping.

These letters reveal many of the bases on which Chu Hsi decided issues concerning rituals. They demonstrate that he saw decisions concerning rites

[111] WC 83:15a–16a. Parts of this postface were translated above.

[112] NP 2A:61.

[113] For instance, letters from Chu Hsi to Wang Yü (1142–1211) and Ts'ai Yüan-ting (1135–1198) on ritual matters may date to this period. See WC 44:8b–9a, 49:4a–6b, pieh chi 3:16a–b.

[114] Among the more relevant events of the next few years were the death of Chu Hsi's wife in 1176 (WC 34:22–32), Chang Shih's and Lü Tsu-ch'ien's advice to him the next year not to be misled by geomancers in managing her burial (NHC 23:4a; TLC pieh 8:11a), the death of Chang's wife in 1177, Chu Hsi's letters to Lu Chiu-ling on the association of tablets in 1177 or 1178 (WC 36:1a–3a), Lü's erection of a family shrine in 1180 (TLC fu-lu 1:15a, pieh 1:27a–33a), and Chu Hsi's service in Nan-k'ang from 1179 (WC 20:30b–31a).

not as simple ones that could be made according to self-evident moral principles, but as complex ones that required finding an optimal balance between desirable and undesirable features. When to perform the seasonal sacrifices provides a good example. In the Northern Sung Ssu-ma Kuang had retained the *I-li*'s provision of choosing a day that would be convenient and then divining with stalks for its acceptability. He argued that for officials divination was more convenient than the alternative practice of using the solstices and equinoxes because they might not be free on the solar date. He, however, did not object to the solar dates, saying that those who did not want to be bothered by divinations could use them. Many other guides, including three T'ang ones, used the solar dates, as did Chang Tsai and Ch'eng I.[115] Chang Tsai had provided a cosmological justification for use of these dates, saying that they were midpoints in the movements of yin and yang, and moreover made the time between sacrifices equal.[116] Among Chu Hsi's peers, both Chang Shih and Lü Tsu-ch'ien used the solar dates. Chu Hsi resisted, not it seems because he wanted to retain as many canonical elements as possible, nor because he wanted to retain as many divinations as possible (as he eliminated Ssu-ma Kuang's divinations for the date for capping and the date for the first and second sacrifice of good fortune one and two years after a death). According to his letter to Chang Shih, a major consideration was his desire to incorporate the three extra rites Ch'eng I had described without creating scheduling conflicts. Since Ch'eng I had called for rites to the first ancestor at the winter solstice, Chu Hsi wished to hold the winter sacrifice on a different day.

Elsewhere Chu Hsi showed considerable interest in divination, especially through the *I-ching*.[117] Yet in the *Family Rituals* he discarded divinations that were popular and added ones that were not. He made no mention, for instance, of the divinations commonly performed as part of the wedding process, even though these had canonical roots. Yet, rather than hold rites at graves on the date of the Clear and Bright festival, as was commonly done, he recommended divining to choose a date in the same month. Although there are no letters that discuss his choices on these issues, I suspect that a consideration may have been how far to follow popular customs. Just as Chang Shih was uneasy about rites at popular festivals, Chu Hsi may have considered moving grave rites to a different day as a way to separate them more clearly from popular customs and to associate them more with canonical practices. One could practice popular customs so long as they did not harm moral principles, but it was best to do them in a way distinct from common practice.

The concepts Chu Hsi used in discussing rites in these letters tended to be relatively traditional ones: according with the times or human feelings when

[115] TLC pieh 4:2b.

[116] CTC, p. 290.

[117] On Chu Hsi's interests in divination, see Chang, "An Analysis of Chu Hsi's System of Thought of *I*."

one wished to justify a deviation from the canon, "keeping the sheep" when one wished to retain a classical gesture rarely performed in his day. It was not his practice to discuss these rites in terms of *li*, *ch'i*, human nature, spiritual forces (*kuei shen*), or yin and yang, though one could link his cosmology to many of his views on rites.[118] His ideas about the way to decide on issues in rites is largely congruent with emphasis on book learning and "investigation of things" (*ko-wu*). These attitudes probably contributed to his distaste for invention of rituals without basis in the canons, inclining him more in the direction of Ssu-ma Kuang than Ch'eng I.[119]

Above all, Chu Hsi's persistent examination of earlier authors' ideas is linked to his interest in self-cultivation through submission to ritual. Chu Hsi's *Classified Conversations* includes 104 exchanges on the phrase in the *Analects*, "to overcome oneself and return to ritual."[120] For instance, Chu Hsi said, "In 'to overcome oneself and return to ritual,' ritual means that with rules one will have limits and be strict with oneself and so will not slip."[121] He also insisted that overcoming selfish impulses was not enough in itself; one also had to practice ritual. "The Buddhists can overcome the self and even have what can be termed selflessness, but they do not return to ritual. In the teachings of the sages, thus, returning to ritual is central."[122] When a student asked if one could attain the virtue of humanity through overcoming oneself and returning to ritual for one day (as one could interpret a statement in the *Analects*), Chu Hsi said that the effort would have to be expended anew each day.[123] For Chu Hsi ritual had more to offer the learner when it drew from and was treated as external authority.

In his correspondence through 1176, Chu Hsi did not discuss the descent-line system, even in his discussions of ancestral rites. It is thus not clear when Chu Hsi revised the *Family Rituals* to give such a prominent place to the descent-line system. I would tentatively suggest that his interest may have been greatest in the early 1180s when he discussed it with some students.[124] Part of

---

[118] My interpretation of Chu Hsi's views on family rituals seems largely compatible with Munro's analysis of Chu Hsi's views of human nature, which he convincingly links to Chu Hsi's cosmological conceptions. See his *Images of Human Nature*.

[119] On his intellectualist stance and appreciation of book learning, see Yü, "Morality and Knowledge in Chu Hsi's Philosophical System."

[120] YL 41.

[121] YL 41:1043.

[122] YL 41:1045.

[123] YL 41:1055.

[124] In the conversations recorded by Pao Yang from 1183 to 1185, Chu Hsi said that the lesser descent-line system should be established, and without it sacrifices could not be done properly, explaining, for instance, that when there were still relatives who owed mourning to an ancestor whose tablet was about to be retired, they should take charge of it (YL 90:2308). In a letter to Liu Ping, who died in 1185, Chu Hsi discussed ancestral rites in terms of the descent-line system (WC 40:3b–4b).

Chu Hsi's interest in the descent-line system may have come not merely from Chang Tsai's and Ch'eng I's writings but from the more recent experiments of Lü Tsu-ch'ien. Shortly before he died in 1181, Lü Tsu-ch'ien sent Chu Hsi a set of rules and procedures for a descent-line system for his own family. The accompanying letter said that there had in the past been practical difficulties in putting this system into practice, but he and his uncles were now planning to have joint rites, and after a few years of experimentation, would revise the rules.[125]

When Chu Hsi finished his draft of the *Family Rituals* is not clear, other than that it occurred before 1190. Nor is it clear which parts of the *Family Rituals* were written by him alone and which ones students drafted for him. The discussions of the early 1170s largely concern ancestral rites, an issue Chu Hsi had thought about at length himself and discussed with friends. It seems likely that the parts of the first and fifth chapters of the *Family Rituals* on ancestral rites were written by Chu Hsi. These are the more innovative parts of the text, the ones that give emphasis to the offering hall and integrate the ideas of Ssu-ma Kuang and Ch'eng I. The chapters on cappings, weddings, and funerals are much closer to Ssu-ma Kuang's *Shu-i* and may well have been drafted by one or more students according to principles that Chu Hsi outlined for them. Chu Hsi apparently did not find these rituals as problematic as ancestral rites. If he entrusted drafting them to students staying with him, that would account for the lack of letters concerning their content. It is also possible that Chu Hsi wrote these chapters shortly before they were lost. He certainly had the detailed knowledge of the rituals to have written them himself, as he was able to respond to almost any question a student asked about ritual procedures.

Late Work on Ritual

Chu Hsi lived at least ten years after losing the *Family Rituals*. The conversations recorded in the 1190s are not part of the context in which the *Family Rituals* was drafted. As they provided an important element in the way the text was used in later times, however, they deserve at least cursory treatment.

Many of the ideas Chu Hsi expressed in letters in the 1170s he continued to maintain through the 1190s. For instance, when a student Hu An-chih asked about the rituals of the four masters, Chu Hsi replied:

> The two Ch'engs and [Chang Tsai] Heng-chü largely used ancient rituals, whereas [Ssu-ma Kuang] Wen-kung based himself on the *I-li*, giving consideration to what can be carried out today. In sum, Wen-kung's work is relatively solid. Its content

[125] TLC pieh 1:27a. Interestingly, when Lü Tsu-ch'ien had formulated his earlier liturgy he had specifically justified younger sons performing sacrifices, so perhaps he had been convinced by Chu Hsi on the importance of the descent-line system.

is not that far from antiquity and it is seventy to eighty percent good. As for [Ch'eng I] I-ch'uan's rituals, the sacrifices can be used. For weddings, Wen-kung's are best.[126]

On another occasion when asked what book could be used for family rituals, he recommended Ssu-ma Kuang's *Shu-i*, and when asked to comment on Ch'eng I's work, said it was too incomplete.[127] Elsewhere he preferred Ssu-ma Kuang's work to Chang Tsai's as Chang Tsai was too prone to invent rituals rather than base himself on the *I-li*.[128] Yet Chu Hsi continued to view Ssu-ma Kuang's *Shu-i* as imperfect. In response to a question about the different authorities, he said the important thing was to simplify the rites so they would be easy to practice, and that people found Ssu-ma Kuang's *Shu-i* too difficult.[129] Once he gave an example of the difficulties this caused. Because the mourning garments described were so complex and unrelated to contemporary custom, those suddenly encountering a death had no possibility of following his descriptions and would simply follow general practice.[130]

Despite his close study of the ancient ritual texts, Chu Hsi remained willing to extend the ritual in the *I-li* to commoners. In a letter Chu Hsi confirmed his correspondent's inference that no separate rituals were needed for commoners because they could perform family rituals the same way *shih* did.[131] Chu Hsi saw ways ritual could be a tool of government, but unlike early Confucians like Hsün Tzu and the authors of the *Li-chi*, he was not so much concerned with how ritual taught political hierarchy, but with how it taught family hierarchy, which he saw as basic to morality.

Chu Hsi, of course, did not categorically reject "restoring antiquity"; rather he treated it as a direction toward which to work. When a student suggested that the ancient practice of giving five lengths of cloth for betrothal gifts would be awkward to follow in their day as it would seem too skimpy, he replied that to classify it as generous or skimpy was to discuss it in terms of profit and was therefore unacceptable. Moreover, if scholars gave up hope of restoring antiquity, there would be no one else who could change the course of customs.[132] Yet Chu Hsi also maintained that in many instances following "ancient" rituals would be simpler than following customs, especially for weddings.[133] Even for other rituals, if people would recognize that they should

[126] YL 84:2183.
[127] YL 89:2271.
[128] YL 84:2183.
[129] YL 89:2272.
[130] YL 84:2185.
[131] WC 63:17b–18a.
[132] YL 89:2273.
[133] YL 89:2274.

copy the main point of the rituals, not every detail, they would find that they were easy to carry out.[134]

Chu Hsi's sense of what would be easy to practice, of course, might not always match ours. In his *Shao-shih wen-chien lu*, Shao Po-wen had reported an incident in which his father Shao Yung retorted to Ssu-ma Kuang that he was a man of the present and so wore the clothes of the present.[135] Chu Hsi rejected this view and sided with Ssu-ma Kuang on the suitability of wearing the long garment in their day.[136] Moreover, Chu Hsi himself wore the long garment for visits to his ancestral altar.[137]

Not everything Chu Hsi did or said in the 1190s matches what he prescribed in the *Family Rituals*. In the *Family Rituals*, Chu Hsi described a burial method that did not use bricks, but when he buried his eldest son in 1192 bricks were used for the vault, though the cement made of lime, sand, and soil described in the *Family Rituals* was also used. For this burial Chu Hsi also did not use the figurines or containers of food that were described as standard in the *Family Rituals*.[138] When Chu Hsi wrote a brief liturgy for the marriage of his daughter or granddaughter, he added lifting the veil, an item not in the *Family Rituals*.[139]

Minor differences of this sort are outweighed by confirmation of both general attitudes and details. The *I-li ching-chuan t'ung-chieh* testifies to Chu Hsi's continued or renewed interest in the descent-line system, as a full chapter is devoted to it.[140] In the 1190s Chu Hsi several times repeated his objections to having a bride introduced immediately to her husband's ancestors, sometimes mentioning the idea given in the *Family Rituals* of using the third day instead.[141] He also confirmed his views on relatively small points in the wedding ritual, such as whether the bride or the groom should bow first and whether the groom should see his bride's parents when he went to fetch her.[142]

From Chu Hsi's conversations with his students, it is clear that sacrifices remained the ritual most open to debate among scholars. Chu Hsi confirmed that in his own family tablets were arranged from the west, as they are in the *Family Rituals*, and he defended this practice on several occasions.[143] Moreover, though Ch'eng I had once said commoners should use placards instead of spirit tablets, Chu Hsi said it would do no great harm for all to use tablets,

[134] YL 90:2313.
[135] See *Shao-shih wen-chien lu* 19:210.
[136] YL 87:2265.
[137] YL 89:2282.
[138] YL 89:2284, 2286.
[139] WC 69:31b–32b.
[140] *I-li ching-chuan t'ung-chieh*, ch. 5.
[141] E.g., YL 89:2273, 2274, WC 63:18a–b.
[142] YL 89:2274.
[143] YL 90:2304, 2314, WC 49:6a–b, 63:30b–31a.

as he specified in the *Family Rituals*.[144] Chu Hsi regularly repeated his approval of Ch'eng I's proposal that everyone sacrifice to four generations of ancestors.[145] He continued to disapprove of anyone other than a patrilineal relative continuing the ancestral sacrifices, and thus rejected adoption of strangers or affinal relatives.[146] He continued to approve of scaled-down sacrifices on popular festivals, once citing Han Ch'i as his authority on this.[147] He repeated to a student his response to Chang Shih two decades earlier, "On Tuan-wu are you able to avoid eating sticky-rice cakes? On double nine [festival] are you able to avoid drinking dogwood wine? Can you feel comfortable if you make no sacrifices on these days but enjoy [the foods] yourself?"[148] Chu Hsi also maintained his ambivalence on rites to early and first ancestors, once commenting that they seemed presumptuous, but also admitting that he had earlier accepted them.[149] Nevertheless, he continued to answer questions on sacrifice to first and early ancestors, such as how many places to set, showing that he did not rule out performing them in every case.[150]

Concerning funerals, Chu Hsi remained firmly opposed to Buddhist funeral services and cremation.[151] He reiterated the view that it was better to delay the end of mourning to the twenty-seventh month, even though Wang Su's preference for the twenty-fifth month was well-founded.[152] Chu Hsi also continued to support Ssu-ma Kuang's view of when to associate a recently dead ancestor's tablet in preference to Ch'eng I's.[153]

In the *Family Rituals*, Chu Hsi quoted large parts of Ssu-ma Kuang's condemnation of geomancy and the part of Ch'eng I's critique that allowed some cosmological basis for geomancy in that ancestors and descendants shared the same *ch'i*. He then left the issue largely up to his readers, saying current methods could be followed as ancient ones no longer were understood.[154] If anything, Chu Hsi's interest in geomancy seems to have grown in the 1190s.[155] After his son died in 1191, he wrote to Ch'en Liang (1143–1194) that he had selected a burial site, but as the "yin-yang expert" said not to excavate until

---

[144] YL 90:2311–12.
[145] E.g., YL 90:2317–18.
[146] WC 46:18a–b.
[147] YL 90:2320–21.
[148] YL 90:2321.
[149] YL 90:2313, 2318, WC 63:19b–20a.
[150] YL 90:2319.
[151] YL 89:2281.
[152] YL 89:2283.
[153] E.g., WC 63:2a–3a.
[154] CL 35a–b; Ebrey, *Chu Hsi's Family Rituals*, pp. 103–6.
[155] On Chu Hsi and geomancy, see also Ebrey, "Sung Neo-Confucian Attitudes toward Geomancy."

the next year, he was delaying burial.[156] Chu Hsi also defended geomancy to his students, as the following discussion reveals.

> In a discussion of geomancy [*ti-li*], [Chu Hsi] said, "Master Ch'eng also selected a place where the grass and trees were flourishing, so it is not the case that he did not select spots. Po-kung [Lü Tsu-ch'ien] by contrast merely picked a flat place at random, then performed the burial. If he did not know the principle [of selecting sites], his action was wrong, but if he knew and purposely did not use it, his action was especially wrong.[157]

Apparently Lü Tsu-ch'ien had concurred with Ssu-ma Kuang that one could bury virtually anywhere. In another conversation, Chu Hsi not only showed interest in the lore of graves, but assumed the possibility that underground wind would harm a coffin and this could in turn lead to the descendants of the one buried suffering financial losses.[158]

Where Chu Hsi laid out his views on geomancy most fully was in a memorial to the throne written in 1194. The issue was whether or not to bury the former emperor Hsiao-tsung (r. 1163–1189, d. 1194) at the site of the earlier Southern Sung imperial tombs in Shao-hsing. An official inspecting the imperial tombs had reported that the earth was shallow and water and rocks had appeared. Emperor Ning-tsung (r. 1195–1224) asked for debate on the issue, and Chu Hsi, then briefly holding a court post, submitted a memorial proposing that a new site be selected.[159]

> Your subject has heard that burial means hiding; it is the means by which to hide the physical remains of ancestors. . . . If the body is whole, the spirit [*shen-ling*] will attain peace, then the descendants will flourish and the sacrifices will not be cut off. This is a principle of how things spontaneously happen [*tzu-jan chih li*]. . . . All literati and commoners with even modest resources when burying their forebears consult widely among experts and visit famous mountains, comparing one site to the next to select the very best. Only afterward do they use a spot for burial. Should the selection be defective, making the spot inauspicious, then there will surely be water, ants, and ground wind that will damage the contents and cause the body and spirit to be uncomfortable. And descendants also have worries about death and extinction [of the descent line], which are very scary. Sometimes, although they obtain auspicious land, the burial is not solid enough or the coffin placed deep enough, so that during wars or disturbances, the body cannot escape being exposed. This is another major cause for concern. As

---

[156] WC hsü 7:8b.

[157] YL 89:2286.

[158] YL 89:2287.

[159] On this incident, see *Wen-hsien t'ung-k'ao* 126:1133B–1134A; *Sung hui-yao* li 37:24b–26a; Makio, "Shushi to fūsui shisō."

to places that have already been dug into many times, the *ch'i* of the earth will already be thin. Even if it is an auspicious spot, it will not have full power. Moreover, if one frequently carries out earthwork projects near the ancestral tombs, this will result in [the ancestors] being startled and shaken, which also leads to disasters. Although this is the theory of the experts, it is not without a rational basis.[160]

Chu Hsi went on to criticize some particular geomantic theories. He dismissed the theory of the five notes, noting that former Confucians had already refuted it (undoubtedly referring to Ch'eng I) and that it was no longer so popular anyway. It had been used for the burial of previous emperors, but the repeated misfortunes of the imperial family—including the failure of two emperors to have direct descendants and the interruption of the imperial succession with the loss of the north—was evidence enough that it was not efficacious. Thus Chu Hsi substantiated the validity of geomancy through negative evidence: faulty geomantic theories had been followed, and undesirable things had happened. Chu Hsi then argued that rather than improve the existing site in Shaohsing, where the *ch'i* of the earth had been weakened by repeated excavations, a new site should be found. Chu Hsi specifically recommended calling in experts: "If you wish to search [for a spot], then I venture to note that the most prominent scholars of geomancy in recent years have come from Chiang-hsi and Fu-chien. Even if they are not all fully proficient, surely there is one with a rough knowledge of the main points, who can make the tomb more or less flat and stable, who would be better than a couple of censors."[161]

There is no reason to think Chu Hsi was less than sincere in his defense of geomancy. If he had been arguing for using the existing tomb site, one might have supposed he was promoting frugality in burials, a long tradition among Confucian scholars, and only cloaking his argument in a geomantic vocabulary in order to sway his audience. But his proposal for starting a new imperial tomb area could only add expense (and certainly violated Ch'eng I's emphasis on burying in *chao-mu* order).

Chu Hsi's failure to follow his many predecessors in condemning geomancy is not entirely surprising given his overall cosmological beliefs. Chu Hsi was much more concerned with the metaphysical issues of the relationship of *li* and *ch'i* and the great ultimate than the Ch'eng brothers had been and saw divination as the way to reach beyond the current world.[162] As someone who took the *I-ching* seriously and who believed that all phenomena and their

[160] WC 15:34a–b.

[161] WC 15:37a. The tradition that Kiangsi and Fukien represent the two main schools of geomancy has continued into the present. See de Groot, *Religious System of China*, 3:1007–8.

[162] See Chan, "Chu Hsi's Completion of Neo-Confucianism," and Hsü, "A Comparative Study of Chu Hsi and the Ch'eng Brothers."

changes could be explained in terms of an organismic model of *li* and *ch'i*, Chu Hsi could accept the metaphysical assumptions of geomancy: that forces of the earth act on the remains of ancestors and these remains act at a distance on their descendants.

Chu Hsi's environment also contributed to his approach to geomancy. His father had already shown considerable interest in selecting grave sites and a willingness to scatter them. Chu Hsi's confidence in professional geomancers and their theories probably was reinforced by his respect for Ts'ai Yüan-ting (1135–1198), well known in his own time and in later ages for his geomantic knowledge.[163] Chen Te-hsiu (1178–1235) reported that whenever Chu Hsi ran into subtle points concerning "human nature or the Way of heaven" he would discuss them with Ts'ai Yüan-ting, and that he only made up his mind on abstruse points after these conversations.[164] Ts'ai himself followed the geomantic teachings of his father and honored his text, "A Treatise on the Production of Subtleties" (*Fa-wei lun*).[165] This treatise analyzed geomancy using the type of language that Chu Hsi used in discussing the *I-ching* or spirits and ghosts.[166] Ts'ai Yüan-ting is said to have helped Chu Hsi select a grave site for himself, and Chu Hsi's son-in-law and disciple Huang Kan also had Ts'ai find a site for him.[167]

CONCLUSIONS

In this chapter I have tried to show how complex a process authorship is. Chu Hsi had a remarkably retentive mind; when students asked questions on funeral ritual, he could cite the *I-li*, the *K'ai-yüan li*, Ssu-ma Kuang, and more recent authors like Kao K'ang. He wrote his *Family Rituals* with a knowledge of the content and organization of these books. Yet he wrote a book that differed in important ways from anything his predecessors had written. It was not merely his intellectual grasp of the implications of ideas that led him to do something different. His personal experiences as a family member, local official, and teacher had much to do with his shifts in content, purpose, and style.

If Chu Hsi's life and ideas had been no better documented than Ssu-ma Kuang's or Ch'eng I's, one could still have drawn many links between his *Family Rituals* and the environment in which he wrote it. The specific provi-

---

[163] See *Ssu-k'u ch'üan-shu tsung-mu* 109:921B; *Liu Chiang-tung chia-ts'ang shan-pen Tsang-shu* prefaces.

[164] *Hsi-shan wen-chi* 42:7b.

[165] This treatise is also sometimes attributed to Ts'ai Yüan-ting, an attribution the editors of the *Ssu-k'u ch'üan-shu* accepted. However, the prefaces included in *Ts'ai-shih chiu-ju shu* show that Ts'ai Fa wrote it. In 1166 Ts'ai Yüan-ting brought a copy of it to Chang Hsien, asking him to write a preface for it (*Ts'ai-shih chiu-ju shu* 1:45b–46a).

[166] Compare *Fa-wei lun* and Ch'ien, *Chu Tzu hsin hsüeh-an* 1:283–344.

[167] CLIC 5:46b; *Ts'ai-shih chiu-ju shu* 2:157a–158a; *Mien-chai chi* 4:12a.

sions in the book reflect Chu Hsi's respect for the classics, earlier scholars' writings, and special deference to Ch'eng I. The way it was written probably also reflects both the spread of printing and the emphasis Chu Hsi and other scholars of his day were placing on reforming society from the bottom up. To reform society from the bottom one had to get one's ideas across to the people at the bottom. With printing the most efficient way to do this was to get books into their hands.

Because Chu Hsi's life is so well documented, it is possible to link his book in more specific ways to his experiences as a local official and as a scholar who corresponded with other scholars. Graves can be used to illustrate some major ways Chu Hsi's experiences impinged on the development of his ideas. He grew up in a milieu in which graves were treated with religious reverence and where geomantic ideas were widely accepted. He twice traveled a couple hundred kilometers to visit his early ancestors' graves, including the grave of his "first" local ancestor. He made sacrifices at these graves and at the graves of his father and mother closer to home. His proposals concerning tomb construction clearly derived from the technically most advanced practices of his day, and his proposal to endow grave rites also reflected relatively recent developments in social organization. But of course he did not simply follow the times. He ended up denying the validity of the rites at graves of first ancestors except in the case of the descent-line heir of a great line. This stand may well have been influenced by the misgivings Chang Shih expressed, rooted at least in part in the classics. But Chu Hsi might well have continued to disagree with Chang Shih on this point if he had lived close enough to his ancestors' graves to make sacrifices there more regularly. From books Chu Hsi knew of Ssu-ma Kuang's and Ch'eng I's objections to geomancy, and even his friend Lü Tsu-ch'ien was a skeptic. Yet he was also familiar both with geomancy books and with scholars like Ts'ai Yüan-ting who professed them. One cannot say that his larger interest in cosmology led him to his interest in geomancy; it is just as possible that his emotional attachment to the significance of graves and their location, nurtured by his early experiences, made him receptive to geomantic theories, and from these theories to even more comprehensive cosmological schemes.

Chu Hsi's contributions to the Confucian discourse on ritual are of a high order. He had a rare ability to comprehend or encompass both ends of most of the traditional polarities. He followed Ssu-ma Kuang's lead in fully engaging the problems created by the distance between ritual and custom. The *Family Rituals* can be seen in part as an attempt to overcome the tendency for ritual and custom to diverge. He did not confine discussion of ritual to the ideal plane of perfect rituals, for he recognized that custom always intruded into practice.

On the issue of authority, Chu Hsi made efforts to encompass both the internal and the external poles. For the purposes of self-cultivation and education, he recognized the value of adhering to established external norms. Moreover, whenever possible he tried to identify an objective source—the classics, an imperial manual, or a more recent author—for every step. He insisted that people were not to go about designing their own rituals. Yet he repeatedly pondered the meaning of rites and was quite concerned to make sure adherence to form did not lead to distortion of the meaning or neglect of the feelings that should be expressed. He accepted most of Ch'eng I's inventions, but did not recommend that others imitate the process by which he had arrived at them. Nor did he reveal any contempt for adhering to forms for the simple sake of adherence, an attitude Ch'eng I sometimes revealed.

Equally important, Chu Hsi's writings brought to the fore a tension or polarity in the Confucian discourse on ritual that had largely been latent until his time: the tension between self-cultivation and the education of commoners. A scholar like Ch'eng I who stressed the inner feelings behind ritual had to look on ritual primarily in terms of the reflective individual. Chu Hsi, because he also saw the value of objective standards, could simultaneously look on ritual as something that ought to be taught to others, especially children and the less educated, without being entirely condescending; whether the learner was young or old, illiterate or well-versed in the classics, he would benefit from modeling his behavior on established standards.

The tension between personal self-cultivation and education of others becomes evident when one asks precisely what it was people should be told to do. The same liturgies might not meet the needs both of the classically educated and the illiterate. For self-cultivation, complexity in the prescribed rites was not a major impediment, as emphasis was placed on the process of working toward correct performance; one could honor the fixed, eternal validity of the norms specified in the classics, as Chu Hsi often encouraged his disciples to do. For education, however, it was essential that rites be practiced. Chu Hsi knew complexity discouraged practice, even among his peers, but more so among the common people without leisure or financial resources for complex rituals or the literacy to follow archaic texts. Moreover, to encourage practice, the fact that conditions vary and change over time had to be taken into account. In writing his *Family Rituals*, Chu Hsi stripped everything from Ssu-ma Kuang's *Shu-i* that was not essential in a guide to practice. But he did not write separate liturgies for the educated and uneducated.

Another way to put this is that Chu Hsi insisted that form, meaning, and practice were all essential to ritual. To deal adequately with all three, however, he ended up writing three books. Since he believed that meaning could best be grasped by careful and thorough study of the classical texts, he probably saw his study of the ritual classics, his *I-li ching-chuan t'ung-chieh*, as contributing most to the understanding of the meaning of the rites. His *Sacrificial Rituals of the Ancient and Modern Authorities* must have been concerned above all with form, with the exact details of how to arrange utensils and participants and the sequence of steps. His *Family Rituals* I see as primarily a work designed to foster practice. It could fill the need he unsuccessfully asked the government to fill: the need for a concise manual that would tell people precisely what they were supposed to do. It is not Chu Hsi's fault if his book found its greatest audience among literati who used it as a text to study as much as to put into practice.

Chapter Six

THE ORTHODOXY OF CHU HSI'S *FAMILY RITUALS*

Our dynasty reveres ritual as a means of transforming the
world. Mr. Chu's rituals, as a consequence, are
widely practiced.
—Liu Ch'iu (1392–1443)[1]

THE CONFUCIAN tradition had always been concerned with establishing correct or orthodox (*cheng*) principles, actions, and rituals. The classics were a
repository of correct knowledge, but scholars could differ widely in what they
inferred to be the messages of the classics, even on concrete issues such as
when or how to perform a ritual. From late Sung times on, the state and the
community of Confucian scholars worked in concert to build a less contestable
foundation for orthodoxy. They did this by attributing great authority to everything written by Chu Hsi. In no earlier period of Chinese history had a single
author's ideas carried such weight. The state declared Chu Hsi's commentaries to the Four Books the standard basis for the examinations, and scholars
revered him as the greatest interpreter of the wisdom of the sages.[2] Orthodoxy
was, thus, more narrowly delimited than in earlier centuries, yet, in comparative perspective, there remained remarkable room for maneuver. Chu Hsi's
writings were too voluminous for each book to be given equal stature or prominence. Moreover, even when a book was given attention and respect—as the
Family Rituals was—inconvenient items in it could be ignored or dismissed
when they posed problems for the state, the educated class, or specific groups
in it.

In this chapter I examine the roles played by the scholarly community and
the state in making Chu Hsi's *Family Rituals* the orthodox liturgy for family
rituals. I also try to discover what orthodoxy meant in practice. What did
scholars or officials mean when they labeled a liturgy orthodox? How did the
label affect the way people approached performing the rites described in it?

---

[1] *Liang-hsi wen-chi* 4:18b.

[2] On these developments, see Liu, "How Did a Neo-Confucian School Become the State Orthodoxy?"; de Bary, *Neo-Confucian Orthodoxy and the Learning of the Mind-and-Heart*, pp. 1–
66; and Chan, "Chu Hsi and Yüan Confucianism," and "The Ch'eng-Chu School of Early
Ming."

THE INITIAL CIRCULATION OF THE *FAMILY RITUALS*

Once the *Family Rituals* had been rediscovered soon after Chu Hsi's death, his disciples worked to promote, interpret, and circulate it. A copy that had found its way to Kuang-chou was published by Chu Hsi's disciple Liao Te-ming (c.s. 1169).[3] In 1216 another disciple, Chao Shih-shu, published the *Family Rituals* while serving as magistrate of Yü-hang (in Chekiang). In his postface for this edition, Chu Hsi's son-in-law and major disciple Huang Kan (1152–1221) said that the deterioration of custom had obscured Heavenly principles (*t'ien-li*), but that these could be regained through practice of the rituals in Chu Hsi's book.[4] Chu Hsi's disciple Ch'en Ch'un (1159–1223) wrote two colophons for an edition printed in Yen-ling (Chekiang) between 1216 and 1223, based on the Yü-hang edition but with corrections. In one he claimed: ''This book selectively brings the ancient into the present. Arranged with sections and titles, it is simple and clear. Because it is of the greatest significance for moral education, everyone ought to learn it, and every family ought to teach and practice it.''[5] In the other colophon Ch'en Ch'un discussed the limits of a literal approach even to this text. For instance, for burial Chu Hsi used lime for the cement vault around the coffin, but lime was not available in some localities. In such cases, Ch'en Ch'un urged, people should decide what to do by thinking about the main meaning of the whole text. If they do so, the book will be of use in reforming the ritual and custom of the age.[6]

In about 1230 Yang Fu, a disciple of Chu Hsi with particular expertise in ritual studies, wrote a commentary for the *Family Rituals*. Yang regularly amplified points by citing conversations or letters in which Chu Hsi had discussed the canonical authorities relevant to particular ritual practices.[7] When this evidence was at variance with the text of the *Family Rituals*, Yang favored the letters or conversations on the grounds that the *Family Rituals* was an early, unfinished work of Chu Hsi's. He even cited cases where Chu Hsi's own fam-

---

[3] PHTCC 14:2b, 5b. Liao's edition corrected misprints in the earlier Kuang-chou edition and incorporated material from Chu Hsi's draft manuscript on ancestral rites. His printing of Chu Hsi's *Family Rituals* while prefect of Kuang-chou is also mentioned in his biography in the Sung history (SS 437:12972). The date for the publication of this edition is based on Fang Ta-tsung's statement that it occurred ten years after the text was rediscovered in 1201 (CL [Ming ed.] preface).

[4] *Mien-chai chi* 22:7b–9a.

[5] PHTCC 14:6a–b.

[6] PHTCC 14:3a–4a.

[7] Yang Fu's knowledge of ritual is evident from his authorship of a fourteen-*chüan* work on sacrificial rituals and a seventeen-*chüan* compilation of illustrations of the *I-li* (*Sung-Yüan hsüeh-an* 69:51). He also helped finish Chu Hsi's *I-li ching-chuan t'ung-chieh*. The date for his commentary is based on Fang Ta-tsung's statement that it was done twenty years after Liao's edition had been published (CL [Ming ed.] preface). Yang Fu's commentary has been preserved in the *Hsing-li ta-ch'üan* (1415) and in a few rare Sung, Yüan, and Ming editions of the *Family Rituals*.

ily's practice differed from the *Family Rituals*. When Chu Hsi had not discussed an issue at length, Yang Fu cited other Sung authorities such as Ch'eng I, Chang Tsai, and Ssu-ma Kuang, or analyzed it himself, citing the relevant classics. Despite his respect for Chu Hsi's teachings, Yang Fu was ready to disagree with Chu Hsi and offer his own proposals, much the way Chu Hsi had disagreed with Ch'eng I or other earlier writers. For instance, Yang Fu believed that the wedding rite of "requesting a date" should not be omitted for the sake of simplification as Chu Hsi had done. Yang Fu showed virtually no concern with popular customs or the problems of local administrators, his interests instead being those of a punctilious ritualist who saw the classics as the final authority for ritual procedures.[8]

Chou Fu, in the postface to his own edition dated 1245, objected to the way Yang Fu had interspersed his notes through Chu Hsi's text. Chou Fu removed them to a separate appendix, arguing that Chu Hsi had wished the *Family Rituals* to be simple and easy to practice. Chu Hsi was perfectly capable of analyzing classical precedents, Chou argued, but had chosen not to in this book. Thus Yang Fu's "corrections" were tendentious and distorted Chu Hsi's original intentions.[9] Chou's edition with the appendix proved popular and was reprinted repeatedly through the late nineteenth century.

Ch'en Ch'un's letters provide good evidence of how the *Family Rituals* was used by Chu Hsi's followers in the early thirteenth century. In a long letter to a friend, Ch'en Ch'un discussed a series of issues concerning funeral ritual. For instance, he argued that it was impossible to reconstruct what was meant by the *I-li*'s description of mourning garments, but Ssu-ma Kuang's *Shu-i* and the *Family Rituals* both provided sensible adjustments to the times. On the issue of what clothes to wear when one must visit others while in mourning, an issue neither the *Shu-i* nor the *Family Rituals* addressed, Ch'en Ch'un cited the practice of one of Chu Hsi's sons-in-law. The siting of graves he discussed in the sorts of geomantic language Chu Hsi used in his memorial to the throne but without citing Chu Hsi. On the construction of tombs, however, he recommended following the *Family Rituals*, explaining how to make modification for a joint burial of a husband and wife and suggesting that bricks be substituted for the cement if lime was difficult to obtain.[10]

---

[8] Another scholar who shared Yang Fu's approach was Ch'e Kai (d. 1276). Bothered by the omissions in Chu Hsi's *Family Rituals*, he wrote a ten-*chüan Nei-wai fu-chih t'ung-shih* [Explanations of the mourning regulations for both patrilineal and nonpatrilineal relatives] to explain the mourning grades more comprehensively than Chu Hsi had done. His nephew, in his postface written in 1278, explicitly argued that even though Chu Hsi was the preeminent figure in *tao-hsüeh*, it was perfectly acceptable to write works that would supplement his (*Shuang-feng hsien-sheng nei-wai fu-chih t'ung-shih*, postface).

[9] CL (SKCS ed.) fu-lu 23b–24a. See *Ying-shu yü-lu* 1:28a for a Sung edition of Chou Fu's book.

[10] PHTCC 28:1a–6a. See also a letter he wrote discussing spirit tablets, citing the varying recommendations of Ssu-ma Kuang, Ch'eng I, and Chu Hsi (PHTCC 35:9b–10b).

By the end of the Sung a second, shorter, commentary had been written for the *Family Rituals* by Liu Kai-sun, identified as a later follower of Chu Hsi's (that is, one who had not studied with him personally). By this time some editions of Chu Hsi's *Family Rituals* had illustrations.[11] Who added the illustrations has never been determined, but it has long been recognized that Chu Hsi had nothing to do with them. Most likely they were adapted from another book to make descriptions of objects and room layouts in the *Family Rituals* somewhat more comprehensible.[12] Because diagrams and pictures are less ambiguous than text, these illustrations probably had considerable impact on how people interpreted the *Family Rituals*. The relative placement of people and objects were all made more concrete by the diagrams. The rules for mourning garments were much easier to grasp from diagrams, in part because the diagrams left out many of the exceptions and complications.

How many other Sung editions of the *Family Rituals* were published is unknown.[13] There was at least one in the early Yüan (while the Southern Sung still survived in Hang-chou), published by an ardent proponent of Chu Hsi's learning, Yao Shu (1203–1280), as part of his "urgent desire to transform people and perfect customs."[14] In 1305 the full text of the *Family Rituals* was copied into a Yüan collection of Chu Hsi's writings, the *Chu Tzu ch'eng-shu* as a single *chüan*, with occasional notes by the compiler, Huang Jui-chieh, and an appended chapter of twenty-nine illustrations. This is apparently the earliest version to survive.[15] Probably in the Yüan a third commentary was written, by a certain Liu Chang. Liu Chang, like Liu Kai-sun, rarely offered opinions; he did, however, cite Ssu-ma Kuang's *Shu-i* so often as to give the impression that he preferred that book's concern with canonical authority to Chu Hsi's practice-oriented approach.[16] Thus, by the end of the Yüan, the *Family Rituals* existed in several formats: in five chapters with no illustrations

---

[11] See *T'ieh-ch'in t'ung-chien lou ts'ang-shu mu-lu* 4:17b–18b; *Chi-ku ko chen-ts'ang mi-pen shu-mu*, p. 5; *Tung-hu ts'ung-chi* 4:25a–b; *Pei-ching t'u-shu kuan shan-pen shu-mu* 1:20a–b.

[12] On the illustrations, see CLIC preface 8a–9b.

[13] One edition with Yang Fu's commentary had a preface dated 1242 by Fang Ta-tsung (CL [Ming ed.]. See also *T'ieh-ch'in t'ung-chien lou ts'ang-shu mu-lu* 4:18a). Another was published in Ch'ao-chou (Kwangtung) before 1245 (HLTC 21:18b). References to Sung editions not clearly identifiable with any of those mentioned above are found in *Ch'ien Tsun-wang tu-shu min-ch'iu chi chiao-ch'eng* 1B:1a–b and *Wen-lu t'ang fang-shu chi* 1:18b. The thirteenth-century bibliography, CCSLCT 6:182, lists the *Family Rituals* as being one *chüan* in length, which may reflect yet another edition since all other references to Sung editions (if they give length) give it as five or ten *chüan*.

[14] *Mu-an chi* 15:175.

[15] It is reproduced as Appendix B of my translation, *Chu Hsi's Family Rituals*.

[16] Several Yüan and Ming illustrated versions with all three commentaries have survived. *Lü-t'ing chih-chien ch'uan-pen shu-mu* 2:14a mentions a ten-*chüan* Yüan edition. *Pei-ching t'u-shu kuan shan-pen shu-mu* 1:20a–b has a Ming edition in five *chüan*, with an additional chapter of illustrations; *Shang-hai t'u-shu kuan shan-pen shu-mu* 1:4a and *T'ieh-ch'in t'ung-chien lou ts'ang-shu mu-lu* 4:17b list a Ming edition in ten *chüan*.

and an appendix; in ten chapters with two commentaries and illustrations throughout; in five chapters with two commentaries and an extra chapter of illustrations; in ten chapters with three commentaries and illustrations in the first chapter; and probably others. For scholars who wished to treat the book as something to study, there were editions copiously annotated with references to the classics and the writings of the Neo-Confucian masters. For those concerned primarily with how to carry out the rituals, there were unannotated texts with illustrations.

To use the *Family Rituals* it was not necessary to buy or borrow a copy of one of these books. During the late Sung and Yüan, the *Family Rituals* was copied into many reference books, usually divided by subject (that is, rituals for weddings in one place, for funerals another). These reference books, apparently designed for wide audiences, provided such assorted information as the language to use in letters and contracts, lucky phrases to paste on doorposts, lists of auspicious and inauspicious days, and summaries of historical events. They were printed in less expensive format than scholarly books and reprinted many times. Sometimes the large and small type of the *Family Rituals* were both copied, in others only the large type.[17] The large type by itself provides a checklist of the sequence of steps for each rite, useful for those who expected to perform them in approximately the way they had seen others do, but who needed to check such details as whether after a death the soul seat is set up before or after rice is put in the mouth of the deceased.[18] The inclusion of the *Family Rituals* in these books undoubtedly contributed to spreading knowledge of its provisions.

Early in the Yüan period, revisions of the *Family Rituals* began to appear. Wu Hsia-chü (1257–1306), a great-grandson of one of Chu Hsi's disciples, compiled *Wen-kung chia-li k'ao-i* [An examination of discrepancies in Wen-kung's *Family Rituals*], a book which compared every detail in the *Family Rituals* to the provisions in the *I-li* and *Li-chi*.[19] Also in the Yüan period the famous Cheng communal family of Chin-hua used the *Family Rituals* to write their own briefer *Cheng Family Ceremonies* [*Cheng-shih chia-i*]. They explicitly noted where they had made changes. They dropped the distinction between eldest and younger sons in capping, held the "cessation of wailing" ceremony three months after the death rather than a few days after the burial,

---

[17] Reference books giving both large and small type text include *Hsin-pien shih-wen lei-chü han-mo ta-ch'üan* (1307) i chi 1:2b–3a, 6:4b–7a; ting chi 8:1a–12a; hsü chi 9:1a–9a; *Hsin-pien t'ung-yung ch'i-ch'a chieh-chiang kang* (Sung) jen-chi 2:1a–14a, 3:2a–8b. Ones giving only large type include *Hsin-pien shih-wen lei-yao ch'i-cha ch'ing-ch'ien* (1324) pieh-chi 471–72, 481–82, 557–60, 587–88; and *Shih-lin kuang-chi* (Sung) ch'ien-chi 10. *Chü-chia pi-yung shih-lei ch'üan-chi* i chi 3:88–103 provides large type and an abbreviated version of the small type.

[18] In *Chu Hsi's Family Rituals*, I give a running translation of the large type as an abstract for each chapter.

[19] *Hsin-an wen-hsien chih* 19:5b–7b.

omitted divinations for scheduling the seasonal sacrifices, added sacrifices to the stove god, omitted fall sacrifices to deceased fathers, and added sacrifices to recent ancestors on their birth dates. The two biggest departures from Chu Hsi's *Family Rituals* were having the family head preside rather than the descent-line heir and setting aside the four-generation rule on ancestral rites. Cheng Yung, in an essay he wrote in 1358 on their family's offering hall, justified these deviations. As he recounted, in antiquity ancestral sacrifices had been tied to land and rank, but Chu Hsi, in his *Family Rituals*, had designed the four-generation offering hall for use by everyone, without regard to rank or station. Yet because the Cheng family had remained undivided for ten generations, it could not follow the restriction of the *Family Rituals* to four generations, nor the ordering of the tablets from the left. Since one should "serve the dead as one serves the living," and since "ritual is created on the basis of moral principle and instituted on the basis of the conditions of the times," their actions were justified.[20] Both the scholarly community and the state granted tremendous honor to the Cheng family in the late Yüan and early Ming, thereby legitimating this flexible approach to putting the *Family Rituals* into practice.[21]

From this survey of Chu Hsi's *Family Rituals* in Sung and Yüan times, it is apparent that the scholarly community, especially Chu Hsi's personal disciples, did much to promote knowledge of the text. They published it, wrote commentaries for it, and espoused its use. These scholars often found it difficult to adjust to Chu Hsi's relatively uncluttered instructions for family rituals. The commentators were not worried that people would find the prescriptions too complicated, but that the authority and intellectual rationale for Chu Hsi's choices might not be apparent. Their efforts undoubtedly helped the book gain a following among scholars. Yet the success of the book was certainly not due solely to their efforts. Its reference value was quickly recognized, leading to its incorporation in encyclopedias within a few decades of its first publication. No previously available book met as well the need for straightforward instructions on what to do in each step of a rite. Still, when families like the Chengs of Chin-hua attempted to use the *Family Rituals* as guides to performance, they often had to make adjustments.

POLITICAL PROMOTION OF THE *FAMILY RITUALS*

During the Yüan period, the government recognized Chu Hsi's *Family Rituals* as legally relevant in two ways. The validity of a marriage was declared to depend on the performance of wedding rituals that conformed to its prescriptions.[22] Moreover, when the government issued prescriptions for wedding rit-

---

[20] *Cheng-shih chia-i*, 5b, 15a, 19b, 23b–24b, 27b–28b.

[21] On the honor given this family, see Dardess, "The Cheng Communal Family."

[22] *Ta-Yüan sheng-cheng kuo-ch'ao tien-chang* 30:1a (p. 1257).

uals (on the order of earlier government ritual manuals, such as the *K'ai-yüan li* and *Cheng-ho wu-li hsin-i*), the *Family Rituals* was consulted in issuing rules for wedding ceremonies for the Han (i.e., ethnic Chinese) population.[23]

The Ming government went considerably further. The year it was founded the first emperor declared that marriages among the people should conform to Chu Hsi's *Family Rituals*, and this rule was incorporated into the "Great Ming Commandment" of the same year.[24] The court relied heavily on the *Family Rituals* in establishing ritual regulations; the rules for officials and commoners in the *Ming chi-li* (1370) often conform closely to it and sometimes directly cite it. It is worth noting, however, that two major changes were made when the *Family Rituals*'s provisions were incorporated into these Ming official texts—the descent-line system was given less play in that the presiding man at weddings was not the descent-line heir; and distinctions according to rank were reincorporated as all officials could set up offering halls, whatever their ritual seniority within their own families. The descent-line system could be viewed as offensive to the prerogatives of the rulers: it challenged the priority of the ranks and honors conferred by the government as an official could be ritually junior to a cousin of commoner status. The descent-line system was moreover at odds with ordinary family practice as it undermined the authority of the family head.[25]

The distinctions according to rank in the Ming ritual codes were largely the same as those in the Sung dynasty's *Cheng-ho wu-li hsin-i*; that is, separate forms were given for cappings, weddings, and funerals for officials and commoners. For ancestral rites, full descriptions of the rites was given only for officials, but the *Ming chi-li* concluded its introduction to the description of ancestral rites for officials by stating that commoners could conduct approximately the same rites to their parents and grandparents in their homes. Thus commoners were restricted to two generations and not given permission to erect offering halls, but they could still use the basic liturgy of offerings and prayers.[26]

In subsequent years official approval was given to more extensive ancestral rites for both officials and commoners, coming closer to giving full approval to the model in the *Family Rituals*. In 1384 the government promoted the

[23] *T'ung-chih t'iao-ko* 3:12a–14b.

[24] *Ta-Ming hui-tien* 71:7a; *Ta-Ming ling* 1:33a.

[25] That is, in a complex family, if the family head died leaving both a younger brother and a son, in normal family practice his younger brother, the eldest surviving male and senior by generation, would become the family head, yet it was his eldest son who would succeed as descent-line heir.

[26] *Ming chi-li* 6:14a, 28:1a–24b; cf. *Ta-Ming hui-tien* 95:1a. Numerous minor differences between the *Family Rituals* and these Ming ritual manuals can also be noted. For instance, the *Ming chi-li* 28:15a, 26b, 32b, and *Ta-Ming hui-tien* 71:4b, 11b, for both officials and commoners, has the bride introduced to the ancestors on the second day of the wedding, not the third as in the *Family Rituals*.

circulation of a book titled *Kung-yeh lu* [A record on working hard at one's profession], written by a county magistrate as a means of improving customs. As this text described ancestral rites for commoners for three generations at the four seasons, popular festivals, and death-day anniversaries, the government was tacitly accepting these additions.[27] A century and a half later, in 1536, the government approved Hsia Yen's (1482–1548) proposal to recognize the right of commoners to sacrifice to four generations, not two or three, and to recognize the legitimacy of officials' and commoners' sacrificing to first and early ancestors. Approved practice was thus brought very close to the *Family Rituals*.[28]

Bringing Ming rules into line with the *Family Rituals* made sense considering the approval given to the text itself. In 1391 a recent recipient of the *chin-shih*, Hsieh Chin (1369–1415), wrote a memorial urging imperial publication of the *Family Rituals* along with other guides to family propriety, such as the *Family Instructions* of Yen Chih-t'ui, Chu Hsi's *Elementary Learning*, the *Lü Family Compact*, and the Cheng family's "Family Rules."[29] According to the *Ming-shih*, "During the Yung-le period [1403–1424], the *Wen-kung chia-li* was distributed throughout the realm."[30] Perhaps copies were sent to prefects or magistrates, or perhaps this is a reference to the fact that the *Family Rituals* (with the commentaries by Yang Fu, Liu Kai-sun, and Liu Chang) was included in the officially sponsored compendium of Neo-Confucian writings, the *Hsing-li ta-ch'üan* [Great compendium on nature and principle] first issued in 1415.[31] This work was distributed to schools and academies throughout the country and became a basic source for orthodox Neo-Confucianism, widely read by those studying for the examinations.

Imperial support for the *Family Rituals* in the early Ming was not without ambiguities. Ming T'ai-tsu (r. 1368–1398) looked on ritual as a means of social control, a way of reinstituting hierarchical order to society. Confucian scholars encouraged him in this vein, certainly preferring rule through ritual

[27] CLHT 5:2a–6a.

[28] *Wu-li t'ung-k'ao* 115:44a–47b. Hsia Yen said that Chu Hsi had removed rites to early and first ancestors from his *Family Rituals* on the grounds that they were presumptuous. Actually Chu Hsi's original *Family Rituals* includes them; it was Ch'iu Chün who excised them. Hsia Yen apparently used Ch'iu Chün's text (discussed in the next chapter).

[29] *Wen-i chi* 1:13a. The Cheng "family rules" (*chia kuei*) are distinct from the *Family Ceremonies* discussed above and more concerned with management of family property and related issues of discipline. On Hsieh Chin, see Chan in DMB, pp. 554–58.

[30] *Ming-shih* 47:1224.

[31] Apparently the HLTC editors copied everything in the ten-chapter edition with the three commentaries by Yang, Liu, and Liu. I was able to look at a Ming edition of this text in the Shanghai Library. My comparison of the first chapter found the commentaries identical to those in HLTC, with minor editorial changes (*fu-chu* = Yang Fu *yüeh*; *tseng-chu* = Liu Kai-sun *yüeh*; *pu-chu* = Liu Chang *yüeh*; Hsien-sheng *yüeh* = Chu Tzu *yüeh*; etc.). There are, however, not as many illustrations in the HLTC edition as there were in this Ming edition.

to his very harsh penal methods.[32] The emperor strongly asserted the classical principle (iterated in the *Chung-yung*) that rituals are established by the Son of Heaven.[33] In 1374 when his thirty-two-year-old consort née Sun died without children, he asked the officials in charge of ritual to report on the classical precedent for mourning in such cases. When they reported three days later that the *Chou-li* and *I-li* had a son wear one year mourning for his mother when his father was still alive, and none for a concubine-mother, the emperor insisted they had to be wrong. "Mourning one year for mothers is at odds with human feelings. Today's impractical scholars can only see one side of the issue. Clearly they praise the past to denigrate the present. Moreover, ritual issues from the Son of Heaven. The superior puts it into practice and the inferiors imitate."[34] As a consequence he issued new rules for mourning that had every son mourn his mother (including mothers who were concubines) three years, whether or not his father were alive, and had a son mourn for one year his father's concubines who had borne half-siblings.[35] Thus imperial patronage for Confucian ritual was also imperial control over ritual and the Confucians who saw themselves as experts in its provisions.

Scholars nevertheless continued to encourage imperial promotion of the *Family Rituals*. In 1488 Ho Ch'in (1437–1511), a Confucian teacher just recalled to office after a long period of retirement, submitted a lengthy memorial on how to promote Confucian forms of government. His fourth point was the need to promote ritual and music to transform the populace. "When customs are good, it is easy for people to do good and difficult for them to do evil." He acknowledged that the first Ming emperor had instituted rituals, but as that period had been chaotic, further refinements were necessary. The current emperor rejected Buddhist techniques and "carried out the correct principles of Mr. Chu's funerals and burials," but the people had not yet been transformed and were still deluded by heterodox teachings. One reason for this was that officials themselves did not follow the correct rituals, leading the rich and extravagant to greatly exceed the regulations. Some would drink wine and eat meat at sacrifices or perform Buddhist services. Some would perform weddings while in mourning or openly allow music. The rites of sacrifices were neglected even by gentry families who all followed contemporary custom: "Few make wooden tablets, but many attach paper pictures with labels on

---

[32] Cf. Dardess, *Confucianism and Autocracy*, pp. 196–204; Farmer, "Social Regulations of the First Ming Emperor."

[33] *Li-chi*, "Chung-yung," 53:9b; Legge, *Rites* 2:324.

[34] *Hsiao-tz'u lu* 1a–2a.

[35] This text also draws heavily on the *Family Rituals*, quoting it for the description of mourning garments. The *Family Rituals* itself had children mourn their mothers three years, following the government regulations in effect since the T'ang (see *T'ung-tien* 89:487A–488A), but still classed their mourning obligation as "even sackcloth" rather than the deepest "untrimmed sackcloth." Moreover Chu Hsi in discussions made it clear that he thought this rule applied to concubine-mothers, not only legal mothers.

them. Few sacrifice according to ritual, but many invite in a shaman to confuse them.'' Moreover, those who sacrifice to heterodox spirits at home will pray to "excessive cults" outside. Correcting this situation, he argued, required further efforts to proclaim and carry out the principles already set out in such books as the *Hsing-li ta-ch'üan*.[36]

Local officials often shared Ho Ch'in's views of the educational value of proper rituals and took it upon themselves to promote the use of the *Family Rituals*. When Ting Chi (1446–1486) was magistrate of Hsin-hui (Kwangtung), he issued rules for rituals based on the Ming regulations and the *Family Rituals* and selected elders to teach these rituals to the common people. P'an Fu (1454–1526), as magistrate of Ch'ang-le (Kwangtung), similarly taught the common people to practice the *Family Rituals* of Master Chu. When the scholar Lü Nan (1479–1542) was banished to assistant prefect of Chieh-chou (Shansi), he promulgated the *Lü Family Compact* and Chu Hsi's *Family Rituals*.[37] Hai Jui (1513–1587), while magistrate of Ch'un-an county (Chekiang), issued thirty-one rules for commoners to observe, one of which was

> Throughout the county all cappings, weddings, funerals, and ancestral rites must be based on [Ch'iu Chün's revised] *Family Rituals with Specifications of Procedures*. At funerals it is not permitted to invite Buddhists or Taoists to set up Buddhas. For weddings it is not permitted to use many plates or boxes of pork, lamb, candies, or cakes, and it is not permitted to give generous thank-you gifts to the matchmakers. Matchmakers who demand such gifts should be sent to the officials to be dealt with.[38]

During the Ch'ing period, the *Family Rituals* continued to receive imperial support. In 1662 the great scholar Huang Tsung-hsi (1610–1695) advised using the *Family Rituals* to compile a standard manual of ritual for all subjects.[39] In 1684 Wei Hsiang-shu (1617–1687) recommended that it be used in compiling a Ch'ing dynasty ritual code.[40] By this point the Ch'ing government had decided to become a serious patron of traditional Confucian learning and Chinese culture, and did issue guides to the private performance of family rituals.[41] As in the case of the Ming, these were based extensively on the *Family Rituals*. In addition, the *Family Rituals* was included in abridged form in the digest of the *Hsing-li ching-i*, issued in 1715.[42] It was also extensively copied

[36] *I-lü chi* 8:19a–26b. Quotes pp. 19a–b, 20b–21a. On Ho Ch'in see also P'ei and Ch'in in DMB, pp. 509–10.

[37] *Ming-shih* 281:7210; 282:7254, 7243.

[38] *Hai Jui chi*, pp. 188–89. On Hai Jui see also Handlin, *Action in Late Ming Thought*, pp. 54–64.

[39] *Ming-i tai-fang lu*, p. 14.

[40] *Huang-ch'ao ching-shih wen-pien* 54:10a–b.

[41] The first edition of the *Ta-Ch'ing hui-tien* was commissioned in 1684; the first edition of the *Ta-Ch'ing t'ung-li* was commissioned in 1736.

[42] On this book, see Chan, "The *Hsing-li ching-i* and the Ch'eng-Chu School of the Seventeenth Century."

into the *Ku-chin t'u-shu chi-ch'eng* [Collectanea of ancient and modern documents], an imperially compiled collection of excerpts from important authorities on a wide range of subjects, finished in 1725. Its standing as the orthodox manual can be seen from its place in this compendium, which generally only cited three manuals of rites: the *K'ai-yüan li*, the *Family Rituals*, and the *Ming hui-tien*.[43] No new manual written in Ming or early Ch'ing times was considered worthy of inclusion.

Successive dynasties issued liturgies for family rituals in part because of tradition: governments determined ritual forms as part of establishing their claims to legitimacy, much as they issued calendars and law codes. Yet throughout this period many scholars and officials retained the belief, already common in the Sung, that promulgating models for ritual performance was not simply a symbolic gesture but was one of the most effective means of promoting good behavior among the common people. Chu Hsi had emphasized the need for simple liturgies so that common people could be instructed in ritual, and many latter-day Confucians reiterated his argument. On this issue there was no disagreement in principle among scholars out of office, officials at court or in the provinces, and the rulers.

Imperial patronage of Chu Hsi's *Family Rituals* provided an example of proclaiming the orthodoxy of the *Family Rituals* while modifying or ignoring many of its specific details. No government action conveyed the message that people needed to adhere to each detail. After all, calling for adherence to both the *Family Rituals* and to official regulations that differed in many particulars made it impossible to expect literal adherence to either. Simultaneous support for divergent books provided tacit approval of the view that adherence to the *Family Rituals* meant adherence to its broad outlines or "basic meaning," or even adherence to Confucian or "ancient" forms of these rites as opposed to Buddhist forms.[44] Of course, it also made it relatively easy for people to decide to adhere to the book. They would be judged by their intentions more than their actions.

CHU HSI'S *FAMILY RITUALS* AND THE EDUCATED ELITE

In the early Ming, Confucian scholars did not simply advocate that the state promote use of the *Family Rituals*; many also tried to use it themselves as a guide to their families' ceremonies. A few examples, given here in chronolog-

---

[43] Privately compiled works of the period also gave considerable prominence to the *Family Rituals*, but did not so totally neglect other works. The *Wu-li t'ung-k'ao* and *Tu-li t'ung-k'ao* both cite SMSSI and *Cheng-ho wu-li hsin-i* in addition to the CL.

[44] Indeed, the necessity of following Confucian forms was itself undermined by Ming emperors' frequent affirmation that "the Three Teachings are One," a view quite at odds with the militantly Confucian thrust of Chu Hsi's *Family Rituals*. On imperial endorsement of Three Teachings (Buddhist, Taoist, and Confucian) syncretism, see Langlois and Sun, "Three Teachings Syncretism and the Thought of Ming T'ai-tsu."

ical order, should suffice to show the sorts of efforts they made. Hua Tsung-hsüeh (1341–1397) wrote a set of family instructions that included liturgies for sacrifices based closely on the *Family Rituals*. He advised his sons that for mourning and funeral matters the *Family Rituals* was the best source but admitted that it did not have to be adhered to exactly. For instance, contemporary methods of sealing the coffin were superior and could be followed, but the current practice of putting a pearl rather than food in the mouth of the corpse was vulgar and should not be adopted.[45] The Confucian teacher Ts'ao Tuan (1376–1434), influenced by the *Family Rituals*, took a strong stance against Buddhist funerals.[46] Hsü Chien (1390–1450), among others, built an offering hall along the lines advocated by the *Family Rituals*.[47] Yang Shih-ch'i (1365–1444), one of the leading officials of the early fifteenth century, not only built an offering hall for his four generations of ancestors, "honoring Master Ch'u's rituals in all regards" for the rites held there, but also left instructions to his sons to carry out his funeral according to Chu Hsi's prescriptions: "I have never employed Buddhists or Taoists. After I die they should not be used either. Simply rely on the *Family Rituals*. . . . For the text of the sacrificial reports, also use the *Family Rituals*; do not write new ones."[48]

For the most committed Confucian scholars, adherence to the *Family Rituals* was treated as a form of self-discipline and self-cultivation. Scholars might be praised for following the *Family Rituals* for cappings, weddings, funerals, and sacrifices, or for following forms based on careful consideration of both ancient rituals and Chu Hsi's *Family Rituals*.[49] Some teachers put particular emphasis on this sort of discipline. Ho Ch'in (1437–1511), whose memorial was cited above, taught his students to practice ancestral rites. Before each of the seasonal rites, he would have them memorize and recite the text of Chu Hsi's chapter on the seasonal sacrifices and explain its meanings. Once when a merchant wished to study with him, Ho taught him first the *Elementary Learning* and the *Family Rituals*, then the Four Books, then Chu Hsi's *Digest of the Comprehensive Mirror*. Later this man acted as funeral manager for local commoners, making sure they excluded all heterodox practices.[50]

More common than Ho Ch'in's emphasis on ancestral rites was an emphasis on funeral rituals. Wang T'ing-hsiang's (1474–1544) writings are particularly revealing in this regard. A poet, philosopher, and active official, Wang had

---

[45] *Lü-te chi*; *Tu-li t'ung-k'ao* 81:41a.

[46] *Ts'ao Yüeh-ch'uan chi* 1a–3a, 18b–20a. On Ts'ao, see also Ch'ing in DMB, pp. 1302–3.

[47] *Hsi-yüan wen-chien lu* 4:36a–37a.

[48] *Tung-li wen-chi* 2:24a–25b; *Tung-li hsü-chi* 53:25b–27b, quote 25b–26a.

[49] E.g., *Ming-shih* 282:7248, 7250.

[50] Ho Ch'in himself made an offering hall on the model of the *Family Rituals*, going back only to his father, since his father was a younger son and the first to move north to Liao-yang. Later, when Ho discovered that the descent-line heir of his great-great-grandfather was poor and unable to perform proper rites, he felt justified in taking on these rites himself (*I-lü chi* 1:17a, 2a–b, 9a, 7:13a–b).

served in local administration for many years, then rose to hold high posts in the capital.[51] Among Wang's letters and essays are many discussions of details of rituals, especially funeral rituals. He answered questions such as: "When burial has been delayed beyond the normal period for a reason, what rituals should be followed?" "May one sacrifice during the three years of mourning?" "What should one do if his father and mother both die?" "What should one do if too poor to manage a burial?"[52] In providing answers, Wang regularly cited the *Family Rituals*, but also felt free to disagree with it—for instance, opposing its arrangements of ancestral tablets.[53] When Wang retired to mourn his mother from 1524 to 1527, he wrote a manual for funeral ritual based on the *I-li* and the *Family Rituals*, referring to the differences in emphasis and detail in the then-extant revised versions by Wang Yüan, Feng Shan, T'ang To, and Ch'iu Chün. For instance, after describing the preparation of the body before encoffining, he added a note explaining that he had returned to the *I-li*'s provision for marking the places for wailing before washing the body because later on there would not be enough time: "During the washing and dressing, the sons and daughters leave the room to wail, standing on the east and west; so it is clear that the room should not still be confused without places marked."[54]

The effort required to adhere to the *Family Rituals* also sharpened people's recognition that others were not following it as closely. Yang Shih-ch'i, for instance, noted that many contemporary *shih-ta-fu* tended to abbreviate Chu Hsi's sacrificial rituals.[55] Liu Ch'iu (1392–1443) described how Chu Hsi had made the offering hall the centerpiece of his *Family Rituals*, thereby unifying the practice of ancestral rites for both superiors and inferiors, and how the Ming had promoted his book, so that families of officials and literati had taken to using this method for serving their ancestors. Yet rich families not of literati status, he found, seldom adopted it.[56]

By the sixteenth century, it was widely expected that *shih-ta-fu* would adhere in some basic way to the *Family Rituals*; as a consequence this adherence came to be taken as an indicator of literati status. Local gazetteers in describing the customs of the county or prefecture often stated that the *shih-ta-fu* conformed to Chu Hsi's *Family Rituals* while the commoners still followed Buddhist or other vulgar forms. For instance, the gazetteer for Huang-chou (Hupeh), dated 1500, reported that because of the influence of the reigning

[51] On Wang T'ing-hsiang, see Fang's entry in DMB, pp. 1,431–34.

[52] *Wang-shih chia-ts'ang chi* ch. 36.

[53] Ibid. 35:12b–14b.

[54] Ibid Sang-li pei-tsuan 1:11b. Wang also wrote letters on points of ritual, such as a letter to Liu Yüan-fu on whether the son or the husband should be chief mourner for a woman, bringing in the *I-li*, *Li-chi*, the *Family Rituals*, and his own earlier writing (*Tu-li t'ung-k'ao* 53:13a–14a).

[55] E.g., *Tung-li hsü-chi* 1:18b–20a, 3a–4b, 4:21b–23b.

[56] *Liang-hsi wen-chi* 4:18b–19a, 6:16b.

dynasty, the area's gentlemen (*shih-jen*) largely followed the *Family Rituals* for capping and weddings, though there were still a few who used Buddhist ceremonies for funerals and sacrifices.[57] The 1527 gazetteer for Chiu-chiang (Kiangsi) reported that in Te-hua county capping was only carried out in *shih-ta-fu* families, and that these families had recently taken to following Chu Hsi's *Family Rituals* for funerals, thereby influencing the commoners, who customarily had "entertained the corpse" for several days.[58] The 1541 gazetteer for Chien-ning (Fukien) reported that *shih-ta-fu* carried out the capping ritual, the seasonal rites, and most of the wedding ritual. In the Hung-chih period (1488–1505) several local scholars had attempted to reform funeral practices with the result that the *Family Rituals* was followed in funeral ceremonies as well. Unfortunately, we are told, in the Chia-ch'ing period (1522–1566), a couple of *shih-ta-fu* families allowed Buddhist services, with the consequence that the commoners took to using them again. Nevertheless, for laying out and oblations, the *Family Rituals* was uniformly followed.[59] Similar references linking adherence to the *Family Rituals* to *shih* or *shih-fa-fu* status appeared in gazetteers through the rest of the Ming and Ch'ing period.[60] In references of this sort, the point is that the educated abstained from Buddhist services or practiced capping; they may well have ignored the descent-line system, truncated the double laying out, or arranged spirit tablets in a different order than Chu Hsi had described.

THE *FAMILY RITUALS* AND DESCENT-GROUP ANCESTRAL RITES

While promoting adherence to the *Family Rituals* both for themselves and for the population at large, scholars also had to come to terms with the ways instructions in this text ran counter to other goals. Like Ssu-ma Kuang, Ch'eng I, and Chu Hsi in the Sung, scholars in later periods had to balance the value of adhering to established authorities against the demands of their elders, the needs of their families, and the limits of their resources. Many conflicts could be overcome by interpreting the text in terms of its "basic meaning," an approach with a long pedigree. The practice that proved most troubling in this regard was sacrifices to early ancestors in halls, a common practice of Ming descent groups. Because this conflict illustrates both how ideas were interpreted in terms of existing social formations and how social groups were modeled after ideas, it is worth extended analysis.

A descent group, as the term is used here, is a group of households defined in terms of descent from a common patrilineal ancestor. Descent groups normally performed some ancestral rites in common. Through the Ming and

---

[57] *Huang-chou fu-chih* 1:17b.
[58] *Chiu-chiang fu-chih* 1:19b.
[59] *Chien-ning fu-chih* 4:2a–b.
[60] See Brook, "Funerary Ritual and the Building of Lineages in Late Imperial China."

Ch'ing period descent groups varied enormously in size, wealth, and form of organization. Almost all groups visited the graves of common ancestors in the spring, or spring and fall, and held group ancestral rites there. Some compiled genealogies. Some built shrines or offering halls either at their ancestors' graves or near their residences.[61]

Chu Hsi's *Family Rituals* makes no mention of these sorts of large descent groups, a social phenomenon only beginning to gain importance in his time. Nor does it say anything either to discourage or promote the compilation of genealogies, an activity that was pursued with great vigor in the Yüan and early Ming.[62] Other practices associated with descent groups received at least ambiguous support from Chu Hsi's *Family Rituals*. The *Family Rituals* encouraged annual grave rites by including liturgies for them in the chapter on sacrifices. Moreover, in the first chapter it advised endowing ancestral rites by regularly setting aside some land at times of family division. The *Family Rituals* specified that such land should be used for the regular hall-based ancestral rites for four generations, then later for the rites at graves. The fields set aside to support ancestral rites were to be legally registered as inalienable, permanent property.[63]

Descent groups whose primary ritual focus was sacrifices at graves could, thus, easily turn to Chu Hsi's *Family Rituals* for ideological support and convenient liturgies, even if slightly misconstruing Chu Hsi's intentions.[64] Even Chu Hsi's closest disciples interpreted the text that way. Ch'en Ch'un wrote a letter that discussed the issue of sacrifices to first ancestors; in it he cited the *Family Rituals* as authorizing such rites at graves by great descent lines each year. Yang Fu, in his early thirteenth-century commentary to the *Family Rituals*, argued that Chu Hsi's reference to "storing" the first ancestor's tablet at his grave implied that there was a second offering hall there for the early ancestors.[65] Chao Chü-hsin, a Yüan period scholar, drew on the *Family Rituals*'s authorization of grave rites to encourage burying relatives together. As Chao noted, an offering hall modeled on Chu Hsi's *Family Rituals* could only go back four generations, but at graves sacrifices could go back to the first ancestor, making them especially important. To make graves a more appropriate site for such rites, he advocated burial in generational (*chao-mu*) or-

---

[61] On descent groups see the various chapters in *Kinship Organization in Late Imperial China*, ed. Ebrey and Watson.

[62] For Yüan genealogy writing, see Morita, "Sōgen jidai ni okeru shūfu"; for Ming see Taga, *Chūgoku sōfu no kenkyū*, 1:165–298.

[63] CL 4b; Ebrey, *Chu Hsi's Family Rituals*, pp. 10–11.

[64] Chu Hsi had rites to first ancestors presided over by the heir of a great descent line. He probably saw these great lines as ones going back to antiquity, such as the line descended from Confucius. He certainly never implied that every descent group could consider itself a great line for he saw rites to early ancestors as presumptuous on the part of all those not heir to a great line.

[65] PHTCC 25:9a–10a; HLTC 19:9a.

der.[66] Chao's essay and diagram came to be regularly included in most Ming and Ch'ing revised versions of the *Family Rituals*.

Descent groups orientated toward graves were common in Yüan, Ming, and Ch'ing times, and Neo-Confucian rhetoric was often employed to give legitimacy to the efforts of educated men to foster such groups. Hu Han (1307–1381) described the orderly burial ground of a descent group whose first ancestor had moved south with the Southern Sung, eight generations earlier. He also praised a man who wanted to unite his scattered kin and so bought land to enable them to rebury their ancestors in one place. Ts'ao Tuan (1376–1434) in the early Ming instructed his family to adopt Chao's burial plan permanently. Ch'en Ch'üeh (1604–1677) in the seventeenth century belonged to a large descent group, with some two hundred adult male members, that had its ritual activities focused on two grave sites. Ch'en wrote at length on how these grave rites should be conducted, and he strongly advocated to others the benefits of burying kinsmen together, much as Chao Chü-hsin had in the Yüan.[67]

By the Yüan period there were also many descent groups whose ritual activities were focused on free-standing ancestral halls.[68] Yüan and Ming scholars knew that these halls violated principles Chu Hsi had articulated because Chu Hsi placed the offering hall within the home and limited offerings there to four generations of ancestors. Some scholars, therefore, tried to get people to abandon these practices. Wu Hai (fourteenth century) urged a group that had an offering hall for twenty-one generations of ancestors to reform it to accord more closely to canonical principles. He suggested that they record information about their ancestors in a genealogy and use the hall for descent-group meetings rather than sacrifices.[69] The leading Neo-Confucian scholar Wu Ch'eng (1247–1331) urged restricting ancestral rites to Chu Hsi's plan on the grounds that four generations was really very generous in light of the much more stringent restrictions in the classics.[70] Other scholars simply ignored this discrepancy between what Chu Hsi had called for and what they found around them; when they wrote to glorify the efforts of their friends or kinsmen to found or perpetuate large-scale lineages, they would cite Ch'eng I's advocacy

[66] CLHT 6:18a–24b.

[67] *Hu Chung-tzu chi* 9:128–29, 4:53–54; *Ts'ao Yüeh-ch'uan chi* 12b; *Ch'en Ch'üeh chi* wen 7:190–94; pieh 7:490–92.

[68] It is difficult to date with any precision the spread of offering halls to first ancestors of sizable descent groups (ones with depths of more than five generations). Certainly there was considerable regional variation, and such construction could come in waves, descent groups imitating or competing with each other. Without adequate leadership, or new endowments, descent groups could decline and their halls fall into disuse or be taken over for other purposes. On descent-group shrines, see especially Makino, "Sōshi to sono hattatsu," and Tso, "Tz'u-t'ang tsu-chang tsu-ch'üan ti hsing-ch'eng chi ch'i tso-yung shih-shuo."

[69] *Wen-kuo chai chi* 2:41–42.

[70] *Wu Wen-cheng chi* 46:7b–8b.

of rites to first ancestors, his call to "collect agnates," or Ou-yang Hsiu or Su Hsün on genealogies.

The prominent scholar Sung Lien (1310–1381) provided explicit justification for going beyond Chu Hsi on offering halls. He approved of offering halls to first ancestors of large descent groups on the hallowed grounds of creating rituals on the basis of moral principles and on the basis of its effects: "It not only makes descendants remember their roots, but it also regulates feelings and fulfills the idea of 'bringing together agnates.' "[71] Sung Lien reported with approval one case of a man from a very large descent group with eleven generations' depth and over a hundred current male members. In 1365 this man established a shrine in his own house for their first ancestor. Acknowledging that according to Chu Hsi rites for early ancestors should be held in the spring, he chose New Year instead as it was the only time convenient to get kinsmen to bow before the shrine, have a feast, and record any newborns in the genealogy.[72] In another case Sung Lien reported that the descendants of a disciple of Chu Hsi had originally set up an offering hall according to Chu Hsi's *Family Rituals*, with tablets for those without descendants on the side, offerings made in the middle month of each season, and "visits" twice a month. However, in the Yüan–Ming transition the property had been transferred to a school and then to the Ming government, so the shrine no longer existed. In 1372 they built a shrine outside the city, endowing it with a hundred *mu* of land, so that the spring and autumn rites would continue. Again Sung Lien evoked the idea of creating rituals on the basis of moral principles, and added that it was filial sons and benevolent men who established shrines to sacrifice to their ancestors.[73]

Scholars' efforts to provide rationales, based on the classics, moral principles, and human feelings, for rites to first ancestors in halls continued through the Ming and into the Ch'ing period. Lü Nan (1479–1542), for instance, argued that Ch'eng I's theory was superior in nearly all regards to Chu Hsi's: it was close to the classics, unified superiors and inferiors, allowed expression of filial piety, and was suited to present times.[74] Hsia Yen, as seen above, urged the emperor to recognize the right to sacrifice to first ancestors. Li Kuang-ti (1642–1718), a strong supporter of Ch'eng–Chu Confucianism, nevertheless justified going against Chu Hsi on rites to first ancestors on the grounds that Chu Hsi's view simply reflected his personal situation:

Master Chu, to avoid disorder, lived as a migrant in Min [Fukien]. His agnates lived far away in Wu[-yüan, Hui-chou]. Therefore, to feel comfortable with his

[71] *Sung Hsüeh-shih wen-chi* 10:183–84. On Sung Lien see Mote's entry in DMB, pp. 1,225–31.

[72] *Sung Hsüeh-shih wen-chi* 10:183–85; cf. 24:455–56, 71:1119–21.

[73] Ibid. 49:857–58.

[74] *Ching-yeh hsien-sheng li-wen* 1:5. On Lü Nan, see Ching's entry in DMB, pp. 1,100–13.

rituals, Master Chu did not dare to sacrifice to his first ancestor alone. If at that time he had lived amidst lots of agnates and they had already built an ancestral hall like people today have, would Master Chu have been able to get rid of it and not make sacrifices at it? I am certain that he then would have followed I-ch'uan's [Ch'eng I's] theory.[75]

Through the fifteenth century the growing acceptance of rites to first ancestors does not seem to have led to any significant changes in the text of the *Family Rituals*. After all, most people did not belong to well-organized descent groups with halls to first ancestors; they could follow the *Family Rituals* without much difficulty, especially if they took a flexible approach to its interpretation. None of the three main revised versions of the fifteenth century (discussed in the next chapter) refers to adaptations suitable for large descent groups other than stating that the rites to first ancestors in the chapter on sacrifices could be taken to mean the first ancestor to move to the present location, the common practice of descent groups. The earliest emendations more specifically for descent groups are found in the anonymous commentary included in the expanded version of the *Hsing-li ta-ch'üan*, published repeatedly from 1534 on. This author seems to have understood great descent lines as the large descent groups of his day. For instance, in his notes to the section on rites to first and early ancestors (which Chu Hsi had described as rites performed in an ordinary household-based offering hall), this commentator distinguished between forms appropriate to lesser descent lines (i.e., with four generations of ancestors) and great descent lines (going back to first ancestors). In sacrifices to first and early ancestors held by a greater descent line, women should not participate. "At the sacrifices at an altar for four generations of parents, the descendants will all be closely related, so for men and women to assemble in the same hall will not cause embarrassment. At sacrifices to first and early ancestors, the descendants will be distantly related and moreover numerous. Therefore women do not join the ranks. This is nothing other than natural principles."[76]

One consequence of stretching the *Family Rituals* to sanction hall-based rites to first ancestors is that descent groups could then use its liturgies for rites and benefit from the social prestige of adherence to an orthodox standard. By the Ch'ing period descent groups often claimed with pride that they adhered to Chu Hsi's *Family Rituals*. For instance, the "family models" dated 1705 included in the genealogy of the Ku lineage of Kuei-chi (Chekiang) extolled the importance of ritual in general and the value of the *Family Rituals* in particular. "Master Chu Wen-kung selected the key points of cappings, weddings, funerals, and sacrifices to write the *Family Rituals*. It is truly the correct way to establish oneself and the great method for regulating one's family. For

[75] *Jung-ts'un chi* 21:8a–b.
[76] HLTC (expanded ed.) 21:17b.

our descendants to master and practice it not only will reflect well on their predecessors, but will provide a model for future generations."[77]

In most cases, descent groups undoubtedly modified the liturgies for ancestral rites in the *Family Rituals* to suit their own needs, much as the Cheng communal family had in the Yüan period. Lu Shih-i (1611–1672) approved of Chu Hsi's emphasis on the descent-line heir, but objected to the complexity of the ancestral rites, which he saw as beyond the means of poor scholars. He therefore wrote a modified version for his own descent group. Group rites four times a year were impractical, in his opinion, so he developed a plan for the whole group to assemble at New Year, the descendants of the great-great-grandfather in the spring, of the great-grandfather in the summer, of the grandfather in the fall, and of the father in the winter.[78] Mao Ch'i-ling (1623–1716) wrote a liturgy for ancestral rites drawn from both the *Family Rituals* and from the ritual rules then used by descent groups.[79] Others downplayed the differences between Chu Hsi's plan and descent-group practice. Li Wen-chao (1672–1735), who wrote a detailed commentary to the *Family Rituals*, said he could see nothing excessive or wrong in an ancestral hall for an entire descent group.[80]

Compiling revised versions of the *Family Rituals* could even be seen as a way to promote the strength and solidarity of a descent group. Ko Yin-sheng donated ten *ch'ing* of land to establish a descent group of his kinsmen. In 1561 he wrote a revision of the *Family Rituals* for their use. Unlike others who ignored the descent-line heir that Chu Hsi had so stressed, in his revision Ko Yin-sheng stressed the heir's role as leader of the descent group, responsible for managing the land and holding cappings and weddings.[81] Similarly in 1842 when Jen Jo-hai wrote a revision of the *Family Rituals*, he explicitly related his efforts to the reform and development of his descent group. He had their ancestral hall rebuilt and wrote up a group compact on proper funeral and mortuary practices. For instance, anyone who did not attend the funeral of a relative within the mourning grades would be punished by having to kneel in the ancestral hall the next day.[82]

It is ironic that the *Family Rituals*, which largely limited sacrifices to four generations, came to play a large role in the rhetoric and liturgies of descent groups of much greater depth. Sacrificial equipment used by descent groups, including spirit tablets, were often based on descriptions in the *Family Rituals*. The steps of ancestral rites and the script given by Ch'iu Chün, were often

---

[77] Taga, *Sōfu no kenkyū*, p. 619. For other examples, see pp. 627, 638, 727, 793. See also Liu, "An Analysis of Chinese Clan Rules," pp. 69–70.

[78] *Ssu-pien lu chi-yao* 10:8a–9b.

[79] *Chia-li pien-shuo* ch. 11–12.

[80] *Chia-li shih-i* 1:8b.

[81] *Chia-li chai-yao*.

[82] Jen, *Ssu-li ts'ung-i*.

followed, in part perhaps as a matter of convenience, in part perhaps in a desire to be orthodox or "ancient." Since scholars regularly repeated the principle that ritual should accord with human feelings, or could be modified in light of moral principle, or should be changed to match conditions, those performing Chu Hsi's rites out of context probably felt no sense of irony in their actions.

Some sense of the influence of the various editions of the *Family Rituals* on descent-group rites can be seen in Justus Doolittle's description of a large ancestral hall in Fu-chou and the rites held there in the mid-nineteenth century. The hall had been built near the end of the eighteenth century and was well endowed. For the sacrifice held at the autumn equinox, offerings were made of a pig, a goat, five kinds of green vegetables, five kinds of fruit, five kinds of grain, some pig hair and blood, all of these foods uncooked, an additional ten dishes of cooked food, and ten cups each of tea and wine. A master of ceremonies directed the men participating, telling them when to kneel, bow, and rise up. The presiding "man" was a boy of six or eight who was the eldest son of the eldest son, back to their first migrant ancestor (that is, the descent-line heir). He made three libations of wine, pouring it onto straw as described in the *Family Rituals*. The master of ceremonies knelt to chant the text of a prayer, with all of those participating also kneeling. "During the progress of the worship they all knelt down five times, and while on their knees bowed down their heads simultaneously three times. There was no weeping, no smiling, and no talking, except by the professor of ceremonies. All was orderly, still, solemn, and reverent." When the ceremony was over, the cooked foods formed the basis of a feast for those participating.[83]

In the case of descent-group rites, social practice and orthodox ideas continually modified each other. Chu Hsi, by incorporating Ch'eng I's ideas on rites to early ancestors and rites at graves into the *Family Rituals*, and supplementing them with advice on setting aside inalienable land to pay for rites, gave qualified approval to ritual activities associated with the elementary sorts of descent groups already appearing in the Sung. His sanction in turn made it easier for educated men to take leadership roles in their descent groups as they did not have to look on the key ritual activities of these groups as uncanonical or as usurping the privileges of rulers. When a local group of agnates produced

[83] Doolittle, *Social Life*, 1:230–35, quotation, p. 235. See also Kulp's more generalized description of descent-group rites in Kwangtung in the early twentieth century (*Country Life in South China*, pp. 302–5). His description also included a master of ceremonies, hair and blood, and the reading of prayers. It also mentions some features of the *Family Rituals* not in Doolittle's description (such as bowing according to rank, and someone responding as a representative of the ancestors). But it also includes popular practices such as firecrackers and music not in the *Family Rituals*. Hsu, *Under the Ancestors' Shadow*, pp. 190–91, describes a solemn lineage ancestral rite in which all the males lined up in rows in order of seniority, with a master of ceremonies giving orders for kneeling and bowing.

literate men, these men would try to give the group the prestige associated with classical terms and ideas, and reinterpreted it in terms of the classical descent-group ideology. Old words were given new meanings as writers searched for ways to find in orthodox sources justifications for the practices they wanted to preserve. Yet educated men also made efforts to introduce approved practices and perhaps especially approved rituals. Thus the accommodation of rites to early ancestors at graves or halls allowed the educated to shape social and cultural phenomena occurring among commoners and often to control it. This process was a dynamic one, changes in local social organization leading to intellectual changes, which led to changes in elite behavior and transformation of the local organization, which also led in time to further accommodations at the intellectual level, such as the willingness by late Ming to look on any descent group as the equivalent of a "great line."

CONCLUSIONS

The popularity of the *Family Rituals* as a reference book, as a handy guide to the sequence of steps in weddings and funerals, did not rest simply on its orthodoxy. Yet the honor granted Chu Hsi and his teachings did shape how people approached this text and its contents. Some topics that Chu Hsi and his friends debated, such as whether to make sacrifices on popular festivals, no longer were much discussed, the *Family Rituals* accepted as orthodox. The honor granted this book also shaped how people approached performing family rituals, especially, perhaps, the more public and consciously constructed ones like descent-group ancestral rites. It would not have been socially as useful to claim adherence to the *Family Rituals* if the text itself had not been promoted as authoritative. The Yüan, Ming, and Ch'ing governments, in promoting the use of the *Family Rituals*, were not only following the suggestions of scholars, they were also serving the interests of the educated elite. The *Family Rituals*, which ignored political rank, was a valuable counterbalance to the imperial ritual manuals, which never fully abandoned distinctions between officials and those without political rank.

The orthodoxy of the *Family Rituals* was a remarkably elastic one. As a source of knowledge about what to do, the *Family Rituals* was much less ambiguous than the classics. Yet people did not try to put it into practice in a mechanical way. It was the basic meaning or underlying intention of the text that was held up for emulation, not each specific step. The Ming government, by certifying both its own rules and the *Family Rituals* itself, despite the many discrepancies between them, was tacitly admitting that in ritual more than one way could be acceptable. Even Confucian scholars did not feel obliged to adhere narrowly to the *Family Rituals*, as the orthodoxy of the *Family Rituals* in no way undermined the orthodoxy of the classics themselves. Consequently they always had the option of finding justifications for practices at variance with the *Family Rituals* in the classics.

The text of the *Family Rituals* became so well known that it had a pervasive effect on the Confucian discourse on ancestor-oriented rituals. Even when people were acting in ways that contradicted the *Family Rituals*—as they were in building halls for group rites to distant ancestors—the *Family Rituals* was taken into account. Scholars thus were motivated to assert that Chu Hsi had somehow implied the existence of such halls (as Yang Fu did), or would not have objected to them if he had lived near relatives who built them (as Li Kuang-ti did).

The orthodox status of the *Family Rituals* is central to the subjects discussed in the next three chapters. As will be seen in the next chapter, it shaped the way those who wished to revise it approached their work. Most preferred subversion from within to attack from without; they revised Chu Hsi in Chu Hsi's name rather than draw attention to the ways they were changing his provisions. Ming T'ai-tsu's concern to preserve for himself the right to decide on matters of ritual also led many prudent authors to incorporate the major government regulations into their revisions of the *Family Rituals*.

Chapter Seven

REVISED VERSIONS OF THE *FAMILY RITUALS* WRITTEN DURING THE MING DYNASTY

> There are some who criticize [the *Family Rituals*] on the
> grounds that it does not fit the present in such details as
> having commoners perform the triple [capping], the steps
> of the visit to the ancestral temple in weddings, the
> procedures for dressing the body, laying out, libations, and
> burials, and the utensils used for presenting food during the
> seasonal sacrifices.
> —Wang Tso, 1450[1]

CHU HSI wrote the *Family Rituals* as a liturgy, as a step-by-step guide to practice. He thought he had written it in a clear and direct style that would facilitate both the performance of Confucian rites among his peers and the instruction of the common people. He knew he had made compromises at many points and explicitly argued that compromises were necessary to foster practice. Through the Ming his original text was repeatedly reprinted, and there were even new commentaries written for it.[2] Nevertheless, revised versions proved even more popular. During the Ming dynasty, when the *Family Rituals* gained the standing of a classic, writers took to reshaping it to suit their audiences. Authors responded to the demands of book buyers. If Ming law required a different mourning garment for a certain relative than Sung law had, Ming rules should be in the book rather than outdated Sung ones. Because people wanted to be able to turn quickly to whatever information they needed at the moment, authors added numerous subheadings and illustrations. The authors of these books, whatever their claims, were not merely repackaging Chu Hsi's ideas. Writing revised versions of the *Family Rituals* was a way to shape how people talked about rituals and thus also how they experienced them and how

---

[1] CLHT preface, 13b. Wang Tso was explaining why several scholars had written revised versions of the text.

[2] The two new commentaries are in the sixteenth-century annotated edition of the HLTC (1534 or earlier). One, called *Chi-lan* (collected observations), consists entirely of explanations of people and events referred to either in the text or in earlier commentaries. The other, called *Pu-chu* (supplemental notes), is very extensive, as long or longer than Yang Fu's original commentary. Its author had clearly thought about how to perform the actions described in the *Family Rituals*, and often explained in great detail how he imagined the physical arrangement of people or objects.

they acted. In their revised versions, authors incorporated many ideas and practices from outside the Confucian tradition, narrowly defined. Ordinary people, by resisting certain sorts of reforms and welcoming others, were influencing the content and direction of the Confucian discourse on family rituals.

With a few notable exceptions, the authors of these revised versions were not nationally famous scholars or statesmen. Of the forty-eight Ming authors listed in the appendix, only Teng Yüan-hsi (1529–1593) is among the two hundred thinkers recounted in the *Ming-ju hsüeh-an* [Records of Ming scholars]. Only seven have brief biographies in the *Ming shih* [Ming history]. Here I scrutinize their books not because of the originality of their ideas, but because their books played a key role in mediating between society and ritual performance. When people turned to "the *Family Rituals*" for guidance on how to perform a rite, more often than not they turned to one of these "edited" versions. These books thus interpreted the *Family Rituals* for people, selecting some features to retain, others to omit, and many to modify. By specifying how they modified the performance of the rites, authors were encouraging others to make the same adjustments and to label them Confucian.

The most common reason authors gave in their prefaces for writing these books was that the original *Family Rituals*, even with its commentaries, was not easy enough to use. The Ming emperors, concerned to protect their prerogatives in matters of "deliberating on" or "instituting" rituals, might object to a subject who wrote his own guide; they would be less likely to take offense at those who professed to be making imperially patronized works like the *Family Rituals* more accessible or more consistent with Ming regulations. Moreover, given the social utility of adhering to "Master Chu's *Family Rituals*," a book that subtly altered what this book was taken to mean would have a greater impact than a new liturgy by an obscure author. It might also have a larger book-buying audience and thus prove more profitable to the publisher. Yet revised versions were by no means all alike. Over time they veered in two directions, reflecting a tension apparent from the time of Yang Fu and Chou Fu in the thirteenth century—one direction was toward ever shorter and more accommodating versions, the other toward ever more precise and canonically based versions.

FIFTEENTH-CENTURY REVISED VERSIONS

A list of forty-nine Ming revised versions of the *Family Rituals* whose titles have been preserved is found in the Appendix. Many of these books probably had only a single printing, but it is impressive that people kept writing and printing new ones. Nineteen of the forty-nine Ming revised versions are still extant. Little is known of most of the others other than their titles and sometimes the dates and place of origin of the author. Their titles frequently contain the character *yao* ("essential," twelve cases), *i* ("easy," six cases), and *chien* ("simplified," five cases), suggesting that many of them were designed to be easier to use or more to the point than the original *Family Rituals*. Another phrase used in several cases is *ts'ung-i*, "following what is appropriate," implying that one need not carry canonical principles to the point of unreasonableness.

At least seven revised versions of the *Family Rituals* were written during the fifteenth century, including three of the most durable and influential ones. The authors of these books often saw themselves as spreading Neo-Confucianism to ordinary people and fighting heterodoxy. For instance, during the Yung-le period (1403–1424), Li Lun of Wen-chou (Chekiang) set up a "community compact" (*hsiang-yüeh*), a descent-group shrine, a charitable school, and charitable fields so that "his agnates and fellow villagers all took him as their teacher. He wrote *Chia-li cho-chung* [*Family Rituals* considered] based on solid research."[3] In other words, writing this book was associated with organizing his kinsmen along the Neo-Confucian model and also with local paternalistic leadership of commoners in general. Another example is Fu K'uang, of T'ai-chou (Chekiang) in the mid-fifteenth century. When he took up his post as a teacher in I-yang (Hunan), he found that the people there believed in ghosts, so he "taught them the orthodox learning and wrote *Chia-li chi-yao* [Edited essentials of the *Family Rituals*] to show to them; local customs were greatly transformed."[4] Fu K'uang, thus, was following Chu Hsi's lead in emphasizing reform of local ritual practice as part of local government service. The prominent scholar Lo Lun (1431–1478), in his preface to Hsieh Hsing's (1420–1493) *Chia-li yao-lu* [Record of the essential of the *Family Rituals*, similarly saw this book as part of Hsieh's efforts to promote correct rituals among the population of the county he was governing.[5]

The earliest of the surviving fifteenth-century revised versions of the *Family Rituals* is the *Chia-li chi-shuo* [*Family Rituals* with collected discussions]. Its author, Feng Shan, came from Wu-hsi, passed the *ming-ching* examinations during the Yung-le period, and served a fairly short career in office. In his preface dated 1434, Feng Shan reported that two years earlier when his father died, he had tried to conduct the funeral in a way free of vulgarities. He had used the *Hsing-li ta-ch'üan* version of the *Family Rituals*, much better printed than the editions previously available to him. Shortly afterward two men in his home community, one a scholar and the other a doctor, left final instructions that their funerals should be patterned on the *Family Rituals*, and their sons came to Feng Shan for advice. It was to meet this demand that he began

---

[3] *Le-ch'ing hsien-chih* 6:43b–44a.

[4] *T'ai-chou fu-chih* 109:3a–4a.

[5] *I-feng wen-chi* 3:25b–26b.

writing his book. Feng Shan explained that he had shortened the text where possible, substituted current government regulations for outdated ones, and used Yang Fu's emendations in place of Chu Hsi's original text where Yang Fu said Chu Hsi had changed his mind later in life. Where Feng Shan believed that ancient and modern needs differed (in other words, where he disagreed with Chu Hsi's provisions), Feng added hypothetical questions and answers to discuss the issue.[6]

As a result of his revisions, Feng Shan's book is much easier to read and understand than Chu Hsi's original *Family Rituals*. Material is better organized, especially in the "general principles" section where Chu Hsi assumed knowledge of matters not introduced until the chapter on sacrifices. Every chapter has dozens of subheadings, such as (from the first chapter) "great descent lines," "lesser descent lines," "early deaths," "sacrificial fields," "birth of sons," and "form for prayer boards." Chu Hsi's language in the large type is usually retained, but the small type is freely paraphrased, abridged, or even omitted. Tedious material is summarized in diagrams and brief definitions of rare characters or technical terms are given in small type.

The most interesting parts of Feng Shan's book are the hypothetical questions he posed about the *Family Rituals*, showing the problems people faced in using it. For instance, after instructions on reporting the birth of the first main-line son to the ancestors, Feng Shan posed this question:

> In the *Family Rituals*, only wine and fruit are used in making reports [to the ancestors]. In recent times everyone has parties with music for events like cappings and weddings. If on the authority [of the *Family Rituals*], one eliminated the sacrifice [to the ancestors] and yet the living eat and drink and have a good time in the customary way, can one feel comfortable?

He gave this answer:

> Under the subheading of popular festivals [in the chapter on general principles], there is Chu Hsi's answer to Chang Nan-hsüan [Shih]: "People today consider the customary festivals important and on these days there is always feasting and music. One cannot but think of one's ancestors [on such occasions], so although making offerings to them is not the canonical ritual, it is necessitated by human feelings."[7] If we extend this line of argument, since today one cannot eliminate feasting and music on occasions like cappings and weddings, one could hardly be so unconcerned with one's ancestors as to make a report with only wine and fruit without the full sacrifice ceremony. Following the procedure used at the seasonal sacrifices would be appropriate.[8]

[6] The 1589 edition does not have this preface, but it is in the 1479 edition.
[7] This is not in the original text, but in Yang Fu's commentary in HLTC 19:7b.
[8] CLCS 11b–12a.

It should be noted that this passage is not inserted in the chapters for cappings or weddings, where it would directly challenge Chu Hsi's instructions, but after reports for the birth of sons.[9]

Feng Shan's book proved both popular and influential. It was reprinted several times through the sixteenth century and circulated in enough copies so that several editions survive today. Through the Ch'ing it was frequently cited by other authors. Yet it was not without its critics. In 1450 T'ang To complained that Feng Shan had divided up Master Chu's original text, "confusing it with the customs practiced in the countryside."[10] T'ang To nevertheless freely copied (without attribution) most of the hypothetical questions and answers into his own *Chia-li hui-t'ung* [*Family Rituals* systematized]. T'ang To also mentioned another current book, the *Chia-li i-lan* [*Family Rituals* made easy to consult] by Wang Yüan (c.s. 1404), which for some unexplained reason had been burned by the Ministry of Justice during the Cheng-t'ung period (1436–1449) and was no longer available.[11] T'ang quoted at length from Wang's book many times, showing that Wang Yüan had found precise adherence to the *Family Rituals* too difficult for his contemporaries to practice. For instance, Wang Yüan argued against opening and closing the door during sacrificial rites and going to each place to set out offerings and give prayers. People commonly omitted this and it was, in fact, not needed as it was based on the defunct custom of letting the impersonator eat. Omitting it, he claimed, was comparable to the way Chu Hsi omitted the ancient wedding rites of "asking the name" and "presenting the lucky divination" on the grounds that they were too complicated. His main goal was to cut unnecessary details from the rites to attract more people to its practice. He observed that among his own relatives "the young truncate the parts of their service to their ancestors that they find too complicated." He had written his simplified version for the sake of his own family: "I do not dare to institute a change or to set up a model for other people. Men of virtue who love antiquity should still pass down in their families practices based on Wen-kung's *Family Rituals*."[12] Wang Yüan, in other words, classed Chu Hsi's manual as "ancient," much like the *I-li*, to be used in a literal fashion only by the most committed. Since Chu Hsi himself

[9] Similarly, under weddings, after the groom arrives home with the bride, Feng Shan inserted a question concerning whether it was acceptable to follow the common custom of having the bride immediately introduced to the ancestors in the offering hall and quoted Chu Hsi out of context to suggest that he saw no great harm in it. Yet on the third day Feng Shan also included the original instruction that had the introduction delayed until then (CLCS 48a–b, 51a–b).

[10] CLHT fan-li.

[11] Wang Yüan's biography in *Ming-shih* 281:7196 does not mention this book but describes Wang as active in reforming customs while serving as a local official. The book does not seem to have been burned because Wang had fallen into trouble, and so probably was burned because of something in the text itself that violated some government rule or regulation.

[12] CLHT 9:1a–2a.

had applied the principle of simplification at places in his manual, extending it further toward the same goal should be acceptable.

T'ang To, the author of the next surviving version, was a Confucian teacher from a family of military officers, both his father and a nephew serving as commanders.[13] The rationale for his *Chia-li hui-t'ung* is given in its six prefaces and postfaces. Chu Hsi's later opinions needed to be considered, and adjustments made for elements in his book that were obsolete or inappropriate for commoners. One author of a preface praised T'ang for writing a text appropriate for the present, not one mired in antiquity.[14] In his own preface, T'ang To brought up the need to gain uniformity in customs, which was difficult because of the prevalence of Buddhism and Taoism, the variability of local customs, and people's tendencies toward ostentation or negligence in performing rites. T'ang acknowledged that the *Hsing-li ta-ch'üan* had been issued to schools, but his book was also needed because the *Family Rituals* was still not accessible to common people.[15] By citing the need for uniformity, T'ang was evoking a principle that the state authorities very much approved.

T'ang To quoted Chu Hsi, Yang Fu, the two Lius, and a dozen other Neo-Confucian scholars to amplify points in the liturgy. He began each chapter with Chu Hsi's "large type" text presented without interruptions, but afterwards gave specifications that sometimes quoted Chu Hsi's "small type," sometimes paraphrased him, and often were simply quotations from other authors. Sometimes when he departed from Chu Hsi's prescriptions, he cited the strength of custom, but more often he did not bring attention to his departures. For instance, he had the father or mother preside at a child's wedding without mentioning that Chu Hsi had had the descent-line heir perform that role, perhaps patterning himself on the *Ming chi-li* in this regard. T'ang To clearly disapproved of grave geomancy, but rather than accuse Chu Hsi of error, he overwhelmed Chu Hsi's noncommittal stance with long, explicit condemnations by well-respected scholars.[16]

One feature of T'ang To's text stands out as a useful innovation. At sacrifices he had an assistant keep everyone on schedule by calling out the steps to be performed, such as "Invoke the spirits," "Urge the spirits to eat," or "Bow prostrate." Considering the complexity of these rites, having someone direct them would make them easier to perform. In making this addition,

---

[13] CLHT preface 14a–b.

[14] CLHT preface 14b.

[15] CLHT preface 16b–17b.

[16] These included Chen Te-hsiu (1178–1235) on geomancy leading to friction between branches of a family as each tried to maximize its own benefits, the parts of Ch'eng I's and Ssu-ma Kuang's essays omitted in CL, comments by Lü Ts'ai (early T'ang), Hsieh Ying-fang (1296–1392), an anecdote about Chu Hsi, and a long quote from Lo Ta-ching (thirteenth century). Finally as an alternative to geomancy T'ang included the long illustrated proposal for burying agnatic kinsmen in a common graveyard, arranged according to generation, composed by Chao Chü-hsin in the Yüan (CLHT 6:10a–24b).

T'ang To was probably copying the practice of state sacrifices conducted by local officials, or even the ceremonies performed by Taoist priests as their liturgical texts often included scripts of this sort.

The next surviving revised version of the *Family Rituals* was the one that would become standard, used more widely than Chu Hsi's original text. It is the *Chia-li i-chieh* [*Family Rituals* with specifications of the procedures] by Ch'iu Chün (1421–1495), a leading official and political thinker from Kwang-tung.[17] Ch'iu apparently wrote his version of the *Family Rituals* while in retirement from office to mourn a parent, publishing it in 1474.

In a note placed after Chu Hsi's preface to the *Family Rituals*, Ch'iu Chün refuted the argument made by Ying Pen (1272–1349) a century and a half earlier that the *Family Rituals* was a forgery, not written by Chu Hsi himself. Ying Pen's argument was based on the apparent discrepancy in dates. In 1194 when Chu Hsi wrote the colophon to Chang Shih's compilation of the three authorities' rituals, he said he had wanted to revise Ssu-ma Kuang's book but had not been able to because of illness. Huang Kan, in his postface to the *Family Rituals*, said that Chu Hsi had used the books of former Confucians, but still was undecided on some points, and also that in his late years he had discussed family, community, noble, and royal rituals, but had died before making a final draft. Therefore the statement in the chronological biography that Chu Hsi had written the *Family Rituals* in 1170 did not make sense. A reference to Chu Hsi's finishing a *Family Rituals* in four *chüan* and the inclusion of the preface to the *Family Rituals* in his collected works would be due, Ying suggested, to disciples adding these items, taking them to belong to Chang Shih's book. Ch'iu Chün's response is worth quoting:

> One may infer from Mr. Ying's remarks that the *Family Rituals* was an unfinished book, or one that, though finished, is not entirely usable. But can one infer that this book did not exist? If this book did not exist, it would mean someone fabricated the preface. But no one other than Master Chu could have written the words of the preface. The idea that a disciple added it, thinking it belonged to the Chang book, is nonsense. Even worse is the citation of Mien-chai's [Huang Kan's] remark in his postface about an unfinished draft. This refers to the [*I-li*] *Ching-chuan t'ung-chieh*, not the *Family Rituals*. [Chu Hsi's] remark in the preface to [Chang Shih's] *Three Authorities' Ritual Models* means nothing more than that he had not had time to compare each of the authorities to make emendations, so he would have no final worries. It does not mean that the book did not exist. Huang [Kan], Ch'en [Ch'un], Li [Fang-tzu], and Yang [Fu] all were direct disciples who had received instruction from Chu [Hsi] in person. Not one of them was suspicious of the book. And yet Mr. Ying, who lived in the Yüan *Chih-cheng* period [1341–1368], one morning wildly argued that the book was not compiled by Master Chu! Surely to say it was produced by a disciple is a forced interpreta-

<hr>

[17] See Chu, "Ch'iu Chün (1421–1495) and the *Ta-hsüeh yen-i pu*."

tion. . . . Because I worry that scholars might be misled by these arguments, I have recorded his points and roughly refuted them.[18]

Like Feng Shan and T'ang To, Ch'iu Chün saw combating heresy as his ultimate goal, but unlike them he stressed the special responsibility of the *shih-ta-fu* in this battle.

> The reason Confucian learning is not influential is that it is brought into disarray by heterodox teachings. These have gained sway because Confucian scholars have lost their control over ritual. . . . [Heterodox teachings] took advantage of our losing control over our rituals to steal the secondary parts of our funerals and ancestral rites and make them into their services for transferring merit and prayer. Even our *shih-ta-fu* known for their ability as writers and their familiarity with the classics willingly follow [heterodox] procedures and restrictions without considering it wrong. No wonder the whole world's population mindlessly follows them, satisfied that [such practices] are normal.[19]

Part of the problem, Ch'iu claimed, was with the punctilious traditionalists who could never approve of anyone's performance. "When they hear of someone who performed a ritual, they say, 'his performance of X was not in accord with the ritual,' or 'his performance of X ritual distorts antiquity.' Some even say, 'The incompleteness of his performance is worse than my nonperformance.' " Ch'iu saw himself as combating this sort of attitude by making the *Family Rituals* easier to understand and practice.[20]

Ch'iu did not make the text easier by shortening it. To the contrary, he expanded it greatly, his text reaching eight *chüan* and over four hundred double pages. But he did make it easier to use through his rearrangements and additions and his adoption of several of Feng Shan's and T'ang To's best features.[21] To facilitate performance, for each rite Ch'iu provided a list of the people and equipment to secure in advance and a "specifications of procedures." The latter is the script to be used by one or two "masters of ceremonies" (*li-sheng*) in directing the rite, with notes inserted to explain what each person does in response to the oral order. This script is considerably more

[18] CLIC preface 4b–6a. Yang Shih-ch'i identified the author as Ying Pen, reported that his comments were found as an addendum to Chang Shih's *San-chia li-fan*, and saw more sense in them (*Tung-li hsü-chi* 18:1a–b).

[19] CLIC second preface 2a–b.

[20] CLIC second preface 2b–4a.

[21] Like Feng and T'ang he often abridged or changed the small type, and included the full texts of letters and prayers. He also added many not even referred to in the *Family Rituals*. Like T'ang To and the *Ming hui-tien*, Ch'iu Chün curtailed the overlay of the descent-line system, using the descent-line heir for presiding man at neither cappings nor weddings. He added a full description of procedures for reburials and for domestic rites to the stove god, drawing on the *Ming chi-li* and perhaps also the *Cheng Family Ceremonies* (CLIC 6:31a–39a, 7:38a–39a). He also made up for omissions in the *Family Rituals*, adding Ssu-ma Kuang's "Miscellaneous Proprieties for Capping," and writing himself a "Miscellaneous Proprieties" for weddings and for sacrifices to parallel the "Miscellaneous Proprieties for Funerals" that Chu Hsi had taken from the *Shu-i*.

detailed than T'ang To's; for instance for the twice-monthly visits to the offering hall, the master of ceremonies says: "Stand in order," "Wash hands," "Open the cases," "Take out the tablets," "Resume positions," "Invoke the spirits," "Presiding man, go to the front of the incense table," "Kneel," "Burn incense," and so on. The notes explain such things as "the men stand on the left, the women on the right, each generation making one line," "the presiding man takes out the ancestors' tablets, the presiding women the ancestresses' tablets; for the others, a son and his wife take out associated tablets and put them to the left of the regular seat."[22] Ch'iu Chün justified revising Chu Hsi's text by adding masters of ceremonies on the grounds of its effectiveness. As many young men were not well versed in complicated rituals, "without someone to lead, call out, and assist, it is impossible to do everything precisely."[23] Ch'iu Chün's introduction of masters of ceremony seems to have accorded well with the practical realities of ritual performance. By Ch'ing times, at least, it often seems to have been common for people to be able to find men such as local school teachers able to take on these roles. Justus Doolittle, in the mid-nineteenth century, described educated men who would serve as "professors of ceremony." "The common people are not obliged by law to use these directors of worship. Custom makes their employment reputable and fashionable in wealthy and literary families. For instance, when making a sacrifice of food to the dead, if a teacher of the rites is at hand to instruct one when to kneel and when to rise up, when to begin doing a particular act or to cease from doing it, everything is performed with less confusion than though he were to act according to his own memory or judgment of what was proper and becoming under the circumstances."[24]

Ch'iu's *Chia-li i-chieh* was first published in Canton in 1474; it was reprinted several times within his lifetime in Peking, Fukien, and Canton.[25] Although when Ch'iu wrote the *Chia-li i-chieh* he seems to have had in mind primarily *shih-ta-fu* families like his own, by 1487, when he wrote his major treatise on statecraft, the *Ta-hsüeh yen-i pu* [Supplements to the *Extended Meanings of the Great Learning*], he recognized the educational potential of the book for commoners. After discussing the importance of correct family rituals among ordinary people to governance, he remarked that Chu Hsi's aims in these regards were not achieved in his time but were faring better under the current dynasty.[26] In discussing the problems of Buddhist funerals, he described his book as already having some impact in his home region.[27]

[22] CLIC 1:3b–4a.

[23] CLIC 2:1b.

[24] Doolittle, *Social Life*, pp. 250–52 (quote p. 251). On masters of ceremony, see also Hayes, "Specialists and Written Materials in the Village World," p. 103; Naquin, "Funerals in North China," pp. 64–66.

[25] Chu, "Ch'iu Chün," p. 446.

[26] *Ta-hsüeh yen-i pu* 49:4b.

[27] *Ta-hsüeh yen-i pu* 51:8b.

Ch'iu's book proved highly popular, in part no doubt because of Ch'iu's reputation as a scholar, but probably also because it met the needs of scholars, teachers, and local officials. Highly educated men were naturally the most avid book-buyers and also the most eager to perform elaborate Confucian rituals. These book-buyers shared the concerns of the Sung and Yüan commentators in the philosophical and historical basis for provisions of the rites, but also needed clear, straightforward, easy-to-follow instructions on performance. They liked the highly explicit step-by-step approach of Ch'iu Chün's *Specifications for Procedures*, coupled as it was with respect for Chu Hsi's original intentions and classical precedent.

SIXTEENTH-CENTURY SCHOLARLY REVISIONS

As discussed in the last chapter, during the early Ming adherence to the *Family Rituals* became a part of self-discipline and self-cultivation for many scholars. During the sixteenth century, several authors of revised and expanded versions of the *Family Rituals* went even further than Ch'iu Chün had in trying to meet the concerns of highly educated scholars. Two books attempted to combine the key features of Ch'iu Chün's book with the commented version of the *Family Rituals* in the *Hsing-li ta-ch'üan*, with due consideration also to the *Ming hui-tien*. The author of one such book, Wei T'ang, a local official in Hsiao-shan (Chekiang), reported having worked on the book off and on for twenty years, having discovered in his youth that while Ch'iu Chün's text was in circulation, people did not pay careful attention to the notes; for instance, the wording of the texts they used in funeral ceremonies was often at variance with it.[28] Another late Ming version to take this tack was issued by the Hui-chou (Anhwei) prefectural government, and authored by Weng Cheng-ch'un (1553–1627). Probably to discourage people from calling in priests or shamans, it provided the texts for prayers to ancestors and the stove god to use when severely ill.[29] An unusual feature of this book is the very frequent indication of the pronunciation of characters, especially ones used in prayers, perhaps to help people read prayers in a standard, official pronunciation, rather than in local dialects. Many of the words whose pronunciation is provided are common ones (such as *ch'ien*, "to move"; *chien*, "to offer"; *huan*, "official"; *chiu*, "mother's brother"; *pi*, "brush/pen"; and so on). The publication of this book seems to have been aided by ardent followers of Chu Hsi, as the preface is followed with ten pictures of major events in his life, the last

[28] *Wen-kung chia-li hui-ch'eng* (1557). Wei's book is even longer than Ch'iu Chün's, but instead of Ch'iu Chün's citations of the classics, Wei T'ang included the sorts of citations from Chu Hsi, Ch'eng I, and other Sung scholars that were in the HLTC commentaries. Ming authors, some quite obscure, were also cited in abundance.

[29] *Weng T'ai-shih pu-hsüan Wen-kung chia-li* 8:30b–33a.

being one of him in mourning clothes in front of his mother's tomb, with a caption indicating that this was when he wrote the *Family Rituals*.

Teng Yüan-hsi (1529–1593), a well-known scholar of the classics and history from Kiangsi, attempted in his *Chia-li ch'üan-pu* [*Family Rituals* selected and supplemented], to combine the basic features of Chu Hsi's *Family Rituals* with Chu Hsi's *Elementary Learning*.[30] He began with two chapters on family ethics that included many quotations and stories Chu Hsi put into his *Elementary Learning*. In the sections on each of the family rituals, Teng put quotations from the classics first, then Chu Hsi's text, which he labeled "contemporary etiquette" (*chin-i*), treating it as a commentary on the classics.[31]

The demand for substantial revised versions of the *Family Rituals* was great enough for authors (or booksellers) to appropriate each other's books and reissue them with at best modest revisions. Lo Wan-hua (1536–1594), a man who placed first in the *chin-shih* examinations of 1568 and rose to the post of minister of rites, published his *Chia-li t'ung-hsing* [*Family Rituals* for common circulation] in 1573. It was extensively indebted to Ch'iu Chün's book but included lists of pronunciation of characters, new sample letters for cappings and weddings, new illustrations, and more extensive citation of Ming government regulations. Twenty-six years later, P'eng Pin, in Fukien, published a nearly identical text under his own name, retitled *Chia-li cheng-heng* [*Family Rituals* with correct balance]. The major difference between the two texts is that the second one begins with ten illustrations from another source.[32]

SIXTEENTH- AND SEVENTEENTH-CENTURY SHORT VERSIONS

A strong countercurrent against Ch'eng-Chu Neo-Confucianism appeared in mid to late Ming, identified with Wang Yang-ming (1472–1529) and his followers. Wang Yang-ming turned away from the scholarly or intellectualist side of the Ch'eng-Chu tradition, especially from lengthy study of the classics, arguing that people could find moral truth within themselves. He never argued against filial piety or the rituals that had come traditionally to be associated with the embodiment of filial piety such as mourning and ancestral rites. Yet he was not at all in the tradition of the punctilious ritualists and did not give importance to adherence to fine points of ritual.[33] Family rituals receive more attention from Wang Yang-ming as a component of moral education for the common people. As an official, he worked to revive the "community com-

[30] On Teng, see Goodrich's entry in DMB, pp. 1,280–82.

[31] He made an exception for funerals, explaining that they had to be performed in trying circumstances that did not allow leisurely consultation of the classics.

[32] These are similar to those in *Weng T'ai-shih pu-hsüan Wen-kung chia-li*, but as the date of that book is uncertain, it is not clear whether one copied from the other or both from a third source.

[33] Tu, *Neo-Confucian Thought in Action*, pp. 5, 167–72; Ch'ing, *To Acquire Wisdom*, pp. 96–97.

pact," one element of which was the promotion of correct wedding and funeral rituals.[34]

Wang Yang-ming's attitude toward the *Family Rituals* is made clear in a
letter he wrote to Tsou Shou-i (1491–1562), who was then working on a book
on family rituals, probably his *Yü su-li yao* [Essentials for instruction in customs and rituals].[35]

> I have received your letter stating that customary rituals should on the whole be
> based on Wen-kung's *Family Rituals*, but simplified and brought closer to human
> feelings. This is excellent! No one but you, sincere in your intention to transform
> the people and perfect their customs, would be willing to work so indefatigably
> on this task. With regard to the survival of ancient rituals, nowadays even old
> teachers and scholars cannot penetrate the theories. Ordinary people, finding them
> complex and difficult, set them aside and do not practice them. Therefore, those
> in positions of authority today who wish to lead the people to ritual are not ham-
> pered by the need to make [the liturgies] more detailed; rather all they need to do
> is make them simple and clear so that they will be easy for people to carry out.

Wang Yang-ming, like Chang Tsai and Ch'eng I, emphasized that the details
of rites could be modified by those who understood them properly. He put
particular emphasis on understanding their relationship to human feelings.

> With regard to such issues as the order of the places for the four generations of
> ancestral tablets, and the ways tablets are grouped, certainly one may make minor
> adjustments to correspond to current desires and practice. Give each matter care-
> ful consideration and bring it into accord with human feelings. For all the people
> in the world, past and present, have the same feelings. When the ancient kings
> instituted rituals, they based them on human feelings, giving them order and em-
> bellishment. This is the reason that they can remain the standard for untold gen-
> erations. When we find something contrary to our hearts, something that makes
> us uneasy, either it is a case where the transmission [of the ancient ritual] is faulty,
> or where the difference in manners and customs from ancient to modern times
> makes different practices appropriate. In these cases one can use moral principles
> to create rituals that the ancient kings did not have or pass down. If one simply
> sticks to ancient forms, one will be blindly following practices not based in one's
> heart. This is ritual that is antiritual. It is practicing the obscure and repeating the
> unexamined.
>
> In recent ages the learning of the mind-and-heart was not taught, so human
> feelings were lost and discussing ritual became difficult. But when moral knowl-

---

[34] See Chan, trans., *Instructions for Practical Living and Other Neo-Confucian Writings*, pp.
302–3. See also de Bary, "Individualism and Humanitarianism in Late Ming Thought," pp. 150–
57.

[35] On Tsou Shou-i, see the entry by Ching in DMB, pp. 1,310–12. His *Yü su-li yao* is listed in
Ch'ien-ch'ing t'ang shu-mu 2:25a.

edge [*liang-chih*] resides in people's hearts, the passage of time is insignificant. If you follow the moral knowledge in our hearts to arrive at [the form to be followed], then I am sure it will not be far from the mark [literally, "it will not be like making sandals without knowing the size of the foot and ending up with baskets"].

Wang Yang-ming went on to oppose the influence of the early Ming emperors' insistence on their prerogatives in matters of ritual and scholars' acquiescence to imperial claims.

> The idea that only the Son of Heaven can deliberate on ritual to institute forms is a current theory not based on an analysis of ritual. This idea arose because in later ages ritual decayed to such an extent. Therefore I have purposely advocated simplification on the sole grounds that I wish to make [ritual] easy to understand and practice. In addition to cappings, weddings, funerals, and ancestral rites, you should add the community compact, which is also an extremely good supplement to popular mores.[36]

Later in the letter, Wang Yang-ming discussed the arrangement of the tablets in the offering hall in the *Family Rituals* and mentioned that he himself followed the alternative pattern given in the *Cheng Family Ceremonies*, though even this might be too elaborate for ordinary people with small rooms. He also discussed the problem of ancestral rites for childless uncles, pointing out that it was difficult for a man to take on those responsibilities without arousing the suspicion of relatives who would think he was making a claim on the property.

Wang Yang-ming's concern to simplify rituals seems to have stimulated many new revisions of the *Family Rituals*. As discussed in Chapter Five, Chu Hsi had wanted a manual that prefects and magistrates could use to guide commoners. After Wang Yang-ming several authors came closer to achieving this goal by producing exceptionally short and simple versions of the *Family Rituals* and by giving close consideration to what people actually did and how it could be transformed. These briefer versions probably also reflect changes in society since Sung times. The audience for them undoubtedly drew from that large segment of the population with enough education to read books of a general nature but who had not received the full classical education in preparation for the examinations. This audience expanded rapidly during the Ming along with the expansion of the economy and the increase in the circulation of books.[37] Comments on local customs in these revised versions often show a close knowledge of the routine practices of ordinary, uneducated families, a knowledge much deeper than Chu Hsi or his disciples revealed. This knowledge probably reflects increases in interaction across class lines and more po-

---

[36] *Wang Yang-ming ch'üan-shu* shu-lu 3:43–44.
[37] See Rawski, "Economic and Social Foundations of Late Imperial Culture."

rous social boundaries around elite families by mid-Ming times.[38] The growth of descent groups—both in size and numbers—probably contributed to this trend as descent groups brought educated men into increased contact with illiterate cousins in contexts in which family rituals were being performed.

There are too many of these brief revised versions to describe them all in detail. Chu T'ing-li (1492–1566) had studied with Wang Yang-ming before gaining the *chin-shih* in 1523. In 1536 while serving as a local official in Honan, he made an abridgement of Ch'iu Chün's text, writing a *Chia-li chieh-yao* [Essentials of family rituals] that covered all of the family rites in less than ninety double pages. Chu blamed the deficiencies of popular customs first on the *shih*, who should lead the people, then on teachers, who should be examples for the *shih*, and then on local officials.[39] Wang Shu-kao's (1517–1600) *Chia-li yao-chieh* [Essential details of the *Family Rituals*], published in 1571, had been originally written as a simplified version of the *Family Rituals* for the use of his own descent group, with emphasis on "ease of practice," but when he received an appointment as a prefect of Ta-ming (Hopei), he had the book published for distribution in that locale, getting the agreement of the local elders to put its provisions into practice. The book contains little that was new, but did reduce the text to a very manageable forty-two double pages. Sung Hsün's (c.s. 1559, d. 1591) *Ssu-li ch'u-kao* [First draft of the four rituals], written in 1573, did not use the words "Family Rituals" in the title, but like other books described here was a simplified version of the *Family Rituals*, written, as Sung reports in his preface, by comparing different versions. Its relaxed view of popular practices can be seen in its advice to consult an almanac to choose a suitable day for a capping.[40] Chu T'ien-ch'iu, who had seen Ch'iu Chün's *Chia-li i-chieh*, did not copy much from it, concentrating instead on making his text succinct. His *Chia-li i-chien pien* [*Family Rituals* compiled to be easy and simple], published in 1593, omitted the first chapter, incorporating its contents under sacrifices, and managed to cover all four rituals in thirty-seven double pages. Cheng Pi-cho's *Chia-li huo-wen hsü-chih* [Queries and essential knowledge concerning the *Family Rituals*] is unusual in mentioning regional differences in customs.[41] Cheng mentioned, for instance, that in his area of Fukien people did not have different mourning clothes for hot and cold weather, as they did in Kiangsi. He also described as superior the local

---

[38] This shift had probably begun in Chu Hsi's time (see Hymes, *Statesmen and Gentlemen*, pp. 114–99), but does not seem to have reached him to any large degree. By the Yüan and early Ming, however, many more scholars seem to have been in intimate contact with illiterate commoners.

[39] *Chia-li chieh-yao*, preface.

[40] *Ssu-li ch'u-kao* 1:1a.

[41] The author mentioned that his book was based on an earlier work issued by the Fukien government, the *Ssu-min pien-yung chia-li i-chieh* [*Family Rituals* simplified for the convenience of the four classes of people].

custom of using ash instead of charcoal as a moisture-absorbing substance inside coffins. He discussed many popular customs, accepting some (such as placing flowers and candles on incense tables) but objecting to others. Not to pay a condolence visit to a close relative who died of a contagious disease out of fear of catching it was totally unacceptable, he asserted, but one could keep the visit short or send a son or other member of one's family as one's representative.[42]

These sixteenth-century short versions are notable not simply because they were short—the "large type only" versions in some reference books were equally short—but because they show considerable empathy for common people and common practices. Something of the mindset behind this approach can be seen in Lü K'un's (1536–1618) *Ssu-li i* [Doubts about the four rituals]. Lü K'un was a scholar deeply impressed by the need to bring the basic Confucian message to ordinary people, even women.[43] In this book, Lü argued against many of the instructions in the *Family Rituals* as well as others in the *I-li* and *Li-chi*. For instance, he objected to addressing the young men being capped in language they could not understand, to telling people when and how to wail, to the excessive numbers of bows and prostrations at sacrifices, to giving up work while in mourning, to curtailing mourning for concubines, to making too many distinctions among brothers based on their seniority, to not giving women personal names, and to seventy-year-old men remarrying. Having a neighbor act as a chief mourner in preference to a married daughter he saw as unnatural. Not eating for three days after the death of a parent he considered senseless, since "mourning is for the parent; it is not for other people or for ritual or for oneself" and surely the parent would not wish to see one get sick.[44]

Much of the specifics of what Lü wrote was close to the earlier comments by Feng Shan, T'ang To, and Ch'iu Chün, all of whom were willing to incorporate elements of contemporary practice into the sphere labeled Confucian ritual. Nor was Lü K'un simply justifying all contemporary practice, for he still objected to such practices as "dotting" an ancestral tablet to mark the transfer of the soul to it, holding Buddhist services, playing music or giving elaborate meals at funerals, negotiating dowry and betrothal gifts, and so on.[45] But Lü K'un differed from his predecessors in that he drew attention to his disagreements with Chu Hsi. Moreover, he offered a consistent rationale for his choices between custom and ritual in terms of emotions and naturalness. Reflecting the spirit of the late Ming, he contended that ritual should not re-

[42] *Chia-li huo-wen hsü-chih* 2b, 8a, 11a.

[43] See Handlin, *Action in Late Ming Thought*, pp. 103–212.

[44] *Ssu-li i* 3:2b, 4:10a–10b.

[45] *Ssu-li i* 3:3a–b, yü-yen 5b.

strict or suppress emotions, but provide a means for their full expression.[46] In this he is reminiscent of the Six Dynasties writers who also wished to reconcile expressing emotion and fulfilling ritual norms.

One follower of Lü K'un, Lü Wei-ch'i (1587–1641), manifested a particularly deep knowledge of local customs.[47] His *Ssu-li yüeh-yen* [Brief sayings on the four rituals] consists of statements concerning proper procedures to which are appended discussions of the way "little people" (*hsi-min* or occasionally *hsiao-min*) or "rural custom" (*hsiang-su*) diverged from these norms and how those with ambitions to revive old rites or reform customs could effect change. For instance, he discussed the practice among peasants (*t'ien-chien hsi-min*) of men marrying their brother's widows, unaware that it was illegal. He posed a hypothetical question about what poor people should do when they needed such "borrowed" marriages to care for their old parents. He responded that in extreme circumstances the widow might remarry after one hundred days, so long as burial had taken place, but never for any reason could she be married to her late husband's brother.[48] The popularity of Buddhist services on the seven sevens and one hundredth day could be countered, Lü proposed, by holding ancestral sacrifices on these days, even though, strictly speaking, one was not to make sacrifices while in heavy mourning.[49] Lü discussed at length the prevalence of entertainment at funerals, including musicians, singers, dancers, and various sorts of drama and opera. Since others often paid for these performances as diversions for the bereaved, it was difficult for the bereaved to stop them. Like-minded men would have to get together to agree on a halt to this practice.[50] Lü was also aware that ordinary people's family altars were not strictly devoted to the ancestral cult, commonly also including pictures or images of Buddhist or Taoist gods as well.[51] Lü Wei-ch'i's short book turned out to be one of the more influential later works on family rituals. It is cited by several later authors, and was reprinted not only as an independent work, but also as an appendix to Ch'iu Chün's *Chia-li i-chieh*.[52]

[46] On the intellectual atmosphere of this time, see de Bary, "Individualism and Humanitarianism."

[47] On Lü Wei-ch'i, see Handlin, *Action in Late Ming Thought*, pp. 196–209.

[48] *Ssu-li yüeh-yen* 2:2b. Although Lü is not explicit in this regard, he may be suggesting that the widow could marry, the money received as brideprice being used to get a wife for her ex-husband's brother, so there would be a wife to care for the old parents. The other possibility is that he was envisioning a uxorilocal marriage, a new husband being brought in for the widow to do the work of her previous one.

[49] *Ssu-li yüeh-yen* 3:1b.

[50] *Ssu-li yüeh-yen* 3:4a–5a.

[51] *Ssu-li yüeh-yen* 4:3b.

[52] Early Ch'ing followers of the Wang Yang-ming school continued to produce short versions of the *Family Rituals* suited to ease of practice. Sun Ch'i-feng (1585–1675) in 1671, at the age of eighty-eight wrote a *Chia-li cho* [*Family Rituals* considered]. In his preface and postface he

In general, these short versions of the *Family Rituals*, though tolerant of popular customs like burning mock money, maintained a firm line against Buddhist practices. Given the great popularity of syncretism in the late Ming, this consistency is noteworthy.[53] Rituals could be abbreviated and practices of unknown origin could be incorporated, but all authors accepted the principle that family rituals were to be Confucian, not Buddho-Confucian. The promotion of family rituals was still linked to combating heterodoxy.

ANCESTRAL RITES AS DESCRIBED IN REVISED VERSIONS

To give some sense of what it would have meant to have consulted a revised version of the *Family Rituals* rather than the original, let me summarize the changes commonly made in revised versions concerning how to perform the most important of the ancestral rites, the seasonal sacrifices. All revised versions altered in some way how ancestral rites would be organized, bringing the description of the ceremony closer into line with what was commonly done or what the authors thought could in fact be done. Many, for instance, specified holding the seasonal sacrifices on the solstices and equinoxes or popular festivals rather than divining for a day.[54] Almost no author, it seems, was satisfied with Chu Hsi's arrangement of ancestral tablets. Authors would either recommend the plan of the Cheng communal family (which added a tablet for the first ancestor in the center, then had ancestors on the west, the most senior toward the middle, and the ancestresses on the east, in similar order), or the plan given by Ch'iu Chün and adopted in the *Ming hui-tien* (in which the two more senior generations are in the center, flanked by the two more junior generations).[55] Some authors mentioned substituting paper tablets for

---

claimed that he was returning to Chu Hsi's idea that what was fundamental in rites was expressing love and respect. He therefore tried to avoid overly complicated procedures that detracted from this goal. He quoted Lü K'un and Lü Wei-ch'i several times, like them regularly considering how feelings entered into the rituals and the need to keep expenses down. His basic manual was a concise thirty-three double pages.

[53] On this syncretism, see Ch'ien, *Chiao Hung and the Restructuring of Neo-Confucianism in the Late Ming*, pp. 2–25.

[54] Commented versions of the *Family Rituals* noted that Ssu-ma Kuang had said it was all right to follow the practice of using the solstices and equinoxes, already established by the T'ang, and that Chu Hsi, in a conversation with disciples, had concurred with Ssu-ma Kuang on this point (HLTC 21:13b). Some Ming versions of the *Family Rituals* simply called for holding the rites on these days, with no discussion of divination. Ch'iu Chün gave both alternatives and recommended reporting to the ancestral altar the date of the rites, even when solar dates were used (CLIC 7:2b). T'ang To went so far as to suggest that the sacrifices could be held on popular festivals so long as there was one in each season. He proposed five sacrifices a year: on New Year, then the Ch'ing-ming festival for the spring, the double five festival for the summer, the mid-autumn festival for the fall, and the winter solstice for the winter (CLHT 9:7a).

[55] Ch'iu Chün reversed the order of each couple, putting the wives to the west of their husbands, so that a daughter-in-law would never be next to her father-in-law—she would either be next to

wooden ones for economy or to allow younger sons to conduct rites without making duplicate tablets.[56] Almost all revised versions eliminated repeating the prayers before each pair of ancestral tablets on the grounds that it was tedious and time-consuming. Instead they provided a single prayer to all ancestors to shorten and simplify the ceremony.[57] As discussed above, Ch'iu Chün urged recruiting masters of ceremonies to call out the steps of the rites, a revision most authors of detailed liturgies after him adopted. Changes less commonly made included such accommodations as burning mock money, omitting opening and closing the door when the ancestors eat, displaying portraits of the ancestors during the sacrifice, and omitting the slaughter of sacrificial animals as an unnecessary canonical flourish.[58]

At the same time, authors of revised versions did not change the most fundamental features of Chu Hsi's *Family Rituals*. None of them omitted purification, invoking the spirits, or pouring libations of wine to them, the triple offering with a woman making the second offering, use of written prayers, or the offering of a varied meal including cooked meat, grain, and vegetables. Nor did they allow the intrusion of Buddhist ideas or practices. No revised version altered the emphasis on differentiation among family members. It is common in anthropology to treat ancestral rites as rites of solidarity concerned especially with reproducing the bonds among the kinsmen defined by links to a common ancestor. Yet in all liturgies the distinctions among family members are much stressed and the focus of the ritual is on the interaction of the presiding man and the tablets, not on the other members of the family, who are treated more like an audience. To the extent that solidarity is sought it is an organic solidarity based on differentiation, not one based on stripping people of their ordinary social roles.[59]

Seasonal sacrifices performed according to Ch'iu Chün's revised versions or any of the other relatively scholarly revisions indebted to it clearly would have looked different than one based strictly on the original *Family Rituals*. A ceremony punctuated by the shouted orders of two alternating masters of ceremony would not be experienced in the same way as one in which the main participants either acted silently or kept telling each other what to do. Seasonal sacrifices performed according to one of the briefer, more accommodating revised versions would have been somewhat further from Chu Hsi's plan. The

---

her son, grandson, or her husband's grandfather, making quite explicit the need for the ordering of the dead to correspond to the ordering of the living (CLIC 1 t'u 40b–43b).

[56] HLTC (expanded version) 21:12b; CLHT 9:7b.

[57] CLCS 154b–155a; CLHT 9:16b–17b; CLIC 7:12b–13b.

[58] CLIC 156a–b; CLHT 9:7b, 19a; 9:1a–2a; 1:10a; 9:13b; HLTC 21:15a–b.

[59] It is true, of course, that a man who might in ordinary life be the family head, deferring to no one in the household, had to prostrate himself before his ancestors, but this was no more than what he would do before officials or other superiors. And the descent-line heir was not necessarily the family head. He could be a young boy.

biggest difference is that such a ceremony would have fewer allusions to canonical sources and the practices of the emperor and more to the everyday ways people approached gods. Burning mock money, calling out the steps of the rites, representing the ancestors by likenesses and not simply written names all brought ancestral sacrifices closer in form to temple-based worship. Ancestors, thus, would share a little more in the nature of gods. The relationship of descendants to their ancestors would seem a little more like the relationship of parishioners to local gods, or of the faithful to Kuan-yin and other common deities. Yet even in these cases ancestral sacrifices still involved written prayers, offerings of assorted cooked food, distinctions by generation, age, and gender, and a special place for the ritually senior descendant and his wife. The seasonal sacrifices still fit in much the same place within the larger scheme of service to the dead—distinct from service to the recent dead or distant ancestors, and more elaborate than the more casual, more frequent visits, reports, and offerings also presented to the four generations of recent ancestors.

CONCLUSIONS

All of the books discussed in this chapter had authors, even if these authors tended to downgrade their role to editor or reviser. Had more information been available concerning the background, experiences, and opinions of each author, it would have been possible to treat authors the ways I treated Ssu-ma Kuang, Ch'eng I, and Chu Hsi in earlier chapters. But lack of information on individual authors and the social and cultural processes of authorship was compensated by the abundance of information about the books they published. Here I have looked at their books not as independent works, but works that have meaning largely in terms of each other and Chu Hsi's original *Family Rituals*. These authors shaped what people took to be the messages of Chu Hsi's *Family Rituals*. Certain ways of recasting his text were done so often that one cannot explain them simply as an author's whims. Rather they must reflect the demands of various audiences: educated gentlemen, local teachers, men willing to act as masters of ceremonies, and even families with modest literacy and modest goals for orthodoxy. These revised versions of the *Family Rituals* thus reveal the ways Confucianism as an evolving intellectual tradition could absorb and put new constructions on ideas and practices of nonelite origins.

Through the fifteenth century authors of revised versions were largely working within Chu Hsi's intellectual framework. They accorded Chu Hsi's text special honor—more than he had granted Ssu-ma Kuang's—but they continued to search for better compromises that would get more people to perform Confucian rites. These authors also continually experimented with format, trying to present complex materials in ways that would make their books easy to consult when needed.

During the sixteenth century these fifteenth-century books—at least Feng Shan's, T'ang To's, and Ch'iu Chün's—still circulated, showing that this approach retained a large audience. Indeed, several late Ming books were essentially revisions of Ch'iu Chün's text.[60] The new books written in the late Ming, however, were for more specialized audiences. Perhaps the tension between designing rituals for popular education and for literati self-cultivation had become too great. Or perhaps the expectations of the book-buying public had been raised and they now demanded books designed for more specific needs. Whatever the explanation, while some scholars expanded the *Family Rituals* to give priority to quotations from the classics, others turned to preparing much simpler texts, suitable for those who did not need much detail. Purchasers of these short versions may have found them adequate because they could call on masters of ceremony to handle the more complex parts of the rites. Or they may have been satisfied with a basic reference book because all they wanted was a checklist of the proper sequence of steps, expecting to perform the steps more or less the way everyone else they knew did.

Historically both the ever-more-expanded and the ever-more-simple versions are significant but in different ways. The expanded ones, with their emphasis on canonical sources, were going in the direction of the ritualism of the seventeenth century, discussed in the next chapter. The simple versions carried to the furthest extreme the well-established tendency to simplify procedures and interpret canonical injunctions flexibly in terms of their "basic meanings," thus accommodating popular customs that "did not harm moral principles" toward the larger goal of fighting heterodoxy. On issues of family rituals, through the Ming the Confucian tradition maintained a distance from Buddhism, but otherwise tended to be encompassing rather than exclusionary. Confucianism did not splinter into sects and subsects, all differing in their

---

[60] A *Chia-li i-chieh* published in 1530 with a preface by Yang Shen (1488–1559) simply appropriated all of Ch'iu Chün's text. Ch'en Jen-hsi's (c.s. 1622) *Chia-li i-chieh* also offers little that does not appear in Ch'iu Chün's book. A seven-*chüan Family Rituals* edited by Chiang Kuo-tso and four others in 1602 rearranged Ch'iu's text significantly, adding new commentaries and removing to a final chapter all of the diagrams, which were newly drawn and given full explanations (*Wen-kung chia-li*, 1602 ed.).

A late Ming book that purported to be Ch'iu Chün's book is actually a considerably altered version. In general, the features that made Ch'iu Chün's text scholarly were omitted while those that made it convenient were kept. This book accepted more popular customs than Ch'iu Chün had, allowing, for instance, the bride to be introduced to the ancestral altar immediately after her arrival rather than on the third day. It also quoted from T'ang T'o's and Feng Shan's books, which Ch'iu Chün had not, and like them cited Ming regulations much more often than Ch'iu had. Although the surviving edition was published in 1770, all the government regulations quoted are from the Ming, and no Ch'ing authors are cited, suggesting that it was first written in the late Ming.

ideas of how to mourn properly. Scholars and commoners alike were content with flexible understandings of Confucian ritual behavior.

The tendency of the Confucian discourse on rites to accommodate, encompass, and absorb contributed to the integration of Chinese society in late imperial times. It countered pressures toward social cleavages between the educated and uneducated in Chinese society by labeling much of what people commonly did "Confucian ritual." The most highly educated could consult the detailed guides, but there were also versions of the *Family Rituals* that suited the needs of those unconcerned with such issues as contradictions between the Tso-chuan and the *I-li* for the sequence of wedding rites. Simplified guides would reassure such people that they only needed to make modest adjustments to their practices to participate more fully in traditions dating back to the sages.

Chapter Eight

INTELLECTUALS' REEVALUATION OF THE *FAMILY RITUALS* IN THE CH'ING DYNASTY

In the present age, all honor Master Chu's *Family Rituals*,
but much of it was fabricated without any basis.
—Li Kung, 1703[1]

IN THE MING dynasty, Chu Hsi's *Family Rituals* came to be looked on as orthodox by the state, by the Confucian scholarly community, and by the educated elite more generally. Acquiring the status of a near-classic certainly made the *Family Rituals* a more influential book. In the seventeenth and eighteenth centuries many intellectuals turned against the *Family Rituals*, even when they were convinced of the importance of ritual. By the end of the seventeenth century more and more scholars were aware that Chu Hsi had adapted elements of ancient ritual to meet the circumstances of his time, and decided that his solutions were not necessarily the best for their day, some five hundred years later. Even though the government still honored the *Family Rituals*, these scholars concluded that they should set it aside and seek in the classics justifications for forms of rites better suited to their families and descent groups. At the highest intellectual levels, the need to overcome the divide between ritual and custom was largely superseded by the need to identify correctly what constituted ritual. This chapter will look at how the *Family Rituals* lost favor among intellectuals and some of the consequences of this development for the ways texts mediated between ritual and society in the Ch'ing period.

The seventeenth century saw a strong return to punctilious traditionalism, or to use more positive terms, to the search for external or objective sources of authority that could establish for people how to act. This trend was part of a more general rejection of both the individualism and iconoclasm of late Ming Neo-Confucianism and of eclecticism and syncretism of all sorts. The followers of Wang Yang-ming may have been active in teaching common people basic Confucian ethics and simplified versions of family rituals, but by the early seventeenth century their teachings were also seen as tending to weaken observance of norms. Scholars identified with the Tung-lin movement saw these trends as dangerously undermining the hierarchical foundations of Chi-

---

[1] *Li Shu-ku hsien-sheng nien-p'u* 3:37b.

nese society. They urged instead that educated men be willing to work hard at moral cultivation. Rituals did not have to be easy to practice. These trends, already evident in the last decades of the Ming, were if anything intensified by the collapse of the dynasty and the conquest by the alien Manchus.[2]

With the resurgence of punctilious ritualism, a few seventeenth-century scholars attempted to follow the details of Chu Hsi's *Family Rituals* rather than its general spirit. Ch'en Ch'üeh (1604–1677), for instance, gave up the right to sacrifice to his father, since he was a younger son.[3] Chang Chia-ling in 1666 wanted to organize his family's ancestral rites along the lesser descent-line system, even though he was not the descent-line heir and would have to get the cooperation of cousins.[4] In 1668 Yen Yüan (1635–1704) followed the *Family Rituals* literally when mourning his grandmother.[5] This literalist approach to Chu Hsi's *Family Rituals* did not last long. After Yen Yüan found himself mentally and physically exhausted by the mourning rites described in the *Family Rituals*, he investigated the sources for Chu Hsi's provisions, only then learning that they were not simply rewordings of the classics, but Chu Hsi's adaptations. He concluded that he might be able to create rituals better suited to his day by going back to the classics themselves.[6]

Those who wanted to take a literalist approach to the *Family Rituals* were burdened not merely with severe mourning restrictions, but also the lesser descent-line system. As noted earlier, most revised versions of the *Family Rituals*, including those in the *Ming chi-li* and *Ming hui-tien*, downplayed the overlay of this system, returning to Ssu-ma Kuang's use of the family head as presiding man for cappings, weddings, and sometimes even ancestral rites. A few authors were even willing to see the offering hall as a descent-group hall to a first ancestor of a greater descent line, rather than a lesser one. The seventeenth-century desire to adhere to the forms of ancient rituals—rather than their spirit or underlying ideas—meant that many of these compromises were no longer acceptable to the well-educated. Turning back to the classics, scholars wrote erudite inquiries into the propriety of various adaptations of the lesser descent-line system. Some scholars thought the lesser descent-line system could not be revived because it was an integral part of the Chou feudal system and tied to hereditary status. Others debated whether the heir was most correctly the eldest son of the primary line or the one with office. Arguments based strictly on the classics were mixed with ones that drew from the social realities of the time.[7] Wang Wan (c.s. 1655), for instance, objected to having

[2] See Chow, "Ritual and Ethics," pp. 140–45, 158, 234–36.
[3] *Ch'en Ch'üeh chi* wen 7:195.
[4] Chow, "Ritual and Ethics," pp. 237, 246–47.
[5] Tu, "Yen Yüan," pp. 518–19.
[6] Chow, "Ritual and Ethics," pp. 455–62.
[7] Ibid., pp. 288–321.

descent-line heirs manage ancestral rites because many were commoners unable to assume leadership in the rituals when other kinsmen were officials.[8]

In its early stages, at least, this seventeenth-century return to the classics had many historical precedents. Ssu-ma Kuang wrote his *Shu-i* in large part to try to get educated families to abandon Buddhist ceremonies and other practices not based in the classics. Some of Chu Hsi's followers were uncomfortable with the compromises in the *Family Rituals*, especially Yang Fu, who in his commentary elaborated on canonical specifications. In the Ming, scholars like Wang T'ing-hsiang and Teng Yüan-hsi gave more weight to the classics than the *Family Rituals*, even as guides to practice. Until Lü K'un in the late Ming, however, scholars had used positive rhetorical styles, claiming they were achieving the true purposes of the *Family Rituals*.

In the Ch'ing, negative styles, explicitly rejecting Chu Hsi and his writings, became common. Scholars began to criticize the *Family Rituals* on the grounds that Chu Hsi's scholarship was inadequate, that he had not relied on the most authentic of the classics or interpreted them accurately, or that he was misled on issues such as geomancy. Mao Ch'i-ling (1623–1716), for instance, objected to Chu Hsi's use of the *I-li* as his prime authority. In discussing ritual, Mao argued, one must start with the *Changes*, *Poetry*, and *Documents* (the earliest of the classics), then check the *Spring and Autumn Annals*. If these books were silent on the subject, one should consult the *Analects* and *Mencius*. Only as a last resort should one use the ritual classics, which were clearly later in date.[9] A follower of Mao's, Cheng Yüan-ch'ing (b. 1660), in 1712 wrote a massive *Chia-li ching-tien ts'an-t'ung* [Classical sources for family rituals compared and unified], which methodically presented all of the authoritative sources for each step of each rite, beginning with the earliest classics and continuing with later authoritative guides such as the *K'ai-yüan li*, *Cheng-ho wu-li hsin-i*, *Chia-li*, *Ming chi-li*, and *Ming hui-tien*. All of the Ming authors of revised versions, even Ch'iu Chün, were ignored, but a few Ch'ing classical scholars, most notably Mao Ch'i-ling and Hsü Ch'ien-hsüeh (1631–1694), were quoted at length.[10] Cheng reported that he began his project after discovering first that Ch'iu Chün's *Chia-li i-chieh* was not always faithful to Chu Hsi's *Family Rituals*, then on further research that the *Family Rituals* was not always faithful to the *I-li* and *Li-chi*.[11]

---

[8] *Huang-ch'ao ching-shih wen-pien* 58:8a–b.

[9] *Chia-li pien-shuo* 16:15a. On Mao, see Tu Lien-che's entry in Hummel, ed., *Eminent Chinese of the Ch'ing Period*, pp. 563–65. On his ritual scholarship see also Kitamura, "Mau Kirei no reigaku."

[10] A handwritten copy of this book, heavily edited by Mao Ch'i-ling, apparently to give to a printer, survives in the Shanghai Library. Whether it was ever actually published is unclear. Hsü Ch'ien-hsüeh, a nephew of Ku Yen-wu, was the author of a massive study of funerary ritual, the *Tu-li t'ung-k'ao*.

[11] *Chia-li ching-tien ts'an-t'ung* preface. A similar book was the *Ssu-li ho-ts'an*, compiled in 1726 by 188 men in Hui-chou. Its substantial fifteen chapters are quite respectful of Chu Hsi's

Wang Fu-li, in his *Chia-li pien-ting* [*Family Rituals* with discussions and stipulations], completed in 1707, also began each section with quotations from the classics, followed by discussions of significant issues either from the classics or more modern authorities, such as Wang Yang-ming, Mao Ch'i-ling, Lü Wei-ch'i, and many others less famous. He cited four scholars' condemnations of Chu Hsi's views on geomancy, particularly taking him to task for burying his father and mother far apart. Wang Fu-li's book also included examples from history, relevant laws, appropriate days, and forms for letters and prayers.[12] Wang Fu-li pointed out that he had so significantly altered Chu Hsi's text that Chu Hsi's words did not add up to more than five out of his three-hundred-odd pages.[13]

Li Kung (1659–1733) provides an example of a scholar whose approach to family rituals was shaped by these seventeenth-century intellectual trends.[14] From an educated but not an official family in north China (Li county in Hopei), Li Kung studied with the most prominent scholar of the area, Yen Yüan, well-known for having rejected the authority of Chu Hsi's *Family Rituals*. In 1680 Li Kung studied the ritual classics and Teng Yüan-hsi's highly scholarly *Chia-li ch'üan-pu* with Yen Yüan. He made a study of the rites for capping, weddings, funerals, and sacrifices, and set up schedules for his own performance of rites.[15] When his legal mother died in 1692 he conducted the funeral according to Chu Hsi's *Family Rituals* and Yen Yüan's emendations.[16] In the 1690s Li Kung had opportunities to discuss ritual with several other leading authorities on the subject, including Hsü San-li, Mao Ch'i-ling, Wang Fu-li, and Wan Ssu-t'ung. Li Kung later recounted a conversation he had with Wang Fu-li, perhaps when they met in 1695. Wang had insisted on the impor-

---

specifications but give first place to the ritual classics themselves. It gives particular attention to combating Buddhist and Taoist customs, quoting in full two long memorials from Ming times on these subjects.

[12] *Chia-li pien-ting* 7:44b–50b. When the *Ssu-k'u ch'üan-shu* was compiled in 1773–1782, this book was rejected because it drew on yin-yang ideas for the specification of lucky days (*Ssu-k'u ch'üan-shu tsung-mu* 25:208–9).

[13] By the eighteenth century even those who still liked the *Family Rituals* were more likely to pay attention to canonical precedents. Li Wen-chao (1672–1735) wrote a new commentary to the *Family Rituals* in which he provided extensive discussions of Chu Hsi's deviations from the classics, sometimes accepting them and sometimes arguing for a return to the classical rules. For instance, at the beginning of the funeral rituals he posed the question of why Chu Hsi omitted prayers to the five deities that were in the *I-li*. He defended Chu Hsi on the grounds that since the time of the classics Buddhism and Taoism had changed people's conceptions of prayer, and if prayers were called for, people would probably bring in shamans (*wu-chu*) (*Chia-li sang-chi shih-i* 1a). In general, where Yang Fu or other earlier commentators turned to Chu Hsi's or Ch'eng I's writings and conversations to explain Chu Hsi's choices in the *Family Rituals*, Li Wen-chao analyzed them instead through close reading and analysis of relevant passages in the classics.

[14] For a biography of Li Kung, see J. C. Yang in Hummel, ed., *Eminent Chinese*, pp. 475–79.

[15] *Li Shu-ku hsien-sheng nien-p'u* 1:8b–11a.

[16] Ibid. 2:23a.

tance of ritual being practiced. Words like benevolence and filial piety were empty unless they were put into practice through ritual. Ritual was not what the ancients did but what should be done in their time. Those who insisted on complicated procedures were only discouraging the practice of ritual.[17] Mao Ch'i-ling's attitude seems to have had even greater effect on Li Kung, however. Li Kung wrote that until he met Mao Ch'i-ling in 1698 his ritual performances, even the funerals for his father and legal mother, had still contained elements of the rituals of the Sung, by which he seems to have meant Chu Hsi's *Family Rituals*.[18] When Li Kung wrote a study of funeral rituals, he quoted Mao Ch'i-ling extensively. In 1700 Li Kung met Wan Ssu-t'ung, and was impressed by his study of the ancient system of ancestral halls.

Over the years Li Kung continually revised his own family's ritual performances in line with the theories he was studying. In 1690 he worked out a plan for organizing his agnatic kinsmen and instituted common sacrifices to their first ancestor each year at the Clear and Bright festival. He revised this ceremony four years later, first having a sacrifice at the family offering hall, then a joint ceremony with all the kinsmen at the grave of the first ancestor.[19] In 1693 he modified his family's traditional offerings to household gods (stove, well, gate, and so on) in light of Yen Yüan's argument that the classics provided no support for the ordinary practice of these rites.[20] In 1700 he put into practice a new plan for twice-monthly visits and sacrificial rites, plans which he revised several times in later years.[21]

In 1703 Li Kung wrote to his younger brother on the subject of family rituals. He explained that his attitude toward reading books differed slightly from that of his teacher Yen Yüan. His goal was to examine the past to make an adjustment for the present. "For the rituals of cappings, weddings, funerals, and sacrifices, one cannot become familiar with the procedures without practice, and cannot select what is appropriate without scholarly investigations." He had instituted rituals to be practiced. "In the present age all honor Master Chu's *Family Rituals*, but much of it was fabricated without any basis. Carrying it out will lead to errors. Investigations of what would be appropriate are urgently needed. But within the seas only Mao Ho-yu [Ch'i-ling] understands ritual and music and Wang Chi-yeh [Ssu-t'ung] comprehends texts on ritual."[22]

In 1705 Li Kung wrote a treatise on sacrificial rituals that discusses all major points concerning when, where, and how to sacrifice.[23] Although he had done

---

[17] *Lun-hsüeh* 2:9b–10a.
[18] *Hsüeh-li* 3:1a.
[19] *Li Shu-ku hsien-sheng nien-p'u* 2:20b–21b, 27a.
[20] Ibid. 2:26a–b.
[21] Ibid. 3:17a–b, 4:6a, 5:17a, 55b.
[22] Ibid. 3:37a–b.
[23] Ibid. 4:4b.

careful research into ancient rituals, he often ended up proposing compromises much like those Chu Hsi had proposed. For instance, he agreed that the ancestral shrines (*miao*) could not be revived and offering halls (*tz'u*) were more suited to an age in which rank was not inherited. He approved of scholars (*shih*) sacrificing to four generations.[24] He also accepted sacrifices at graves, considering them especially important for families without offering halls. And whereas Yen Yüan had returned to the classical practice of a ten-day purification before sacrifices, Li Kung said this was beyond his ability and followed a three-day regime, which was what Chu Hsi's *Family Rituals* had given.[25] In fact, Li Kung in some ways approved of more popular customs than Chu Hsi had; for instance, he aproved of mock money offerings and the descent-group shrines common in the south.[26] Moreover, his disagreements with Chu Hsi seem on the whole trivial. For instance, he disapproved of the *Family Rituals*'s calling the places where ancestral tablets were put "niches" as this term was used by Buddhists.[27] The only disagreement of much significance was his rejection of Chu Hsi's simplification of the wedding rituals; he argued for retaining all of the six rites and repeated many of Mao Ch'i-ling's arguments on the timing of the introduction of the bride to her husband's ancestors.[28]

Li Kung's example shows that renewed attention to the classical authorities for ritual practice did affect the ritual practices of some well-educated and committed scholars and their kinsmen. But it also shows that there were limits to how far even the most committed scholars could go in putting their investigations of ancient texts into use. Few, if any, were willing to make major changes in how ancestral rites had come to be performed in households and descent groups, even though the classical bases for these rites were weak. Commitment to studying the classics as a guide to their own ritual performances, however, did have some effects. It led scholars to concentrate their efforts on their own families. Early Ch'ing ritualists like Li Kung, concerned with textual research, did not emphasize strategies for educating common people or reforming their customs, central concerns of many Sung and Ming scholars.

WANG MAO-HUNG'S ATTACK ON THE *FAMILY RITUALS*

Wang Mao-hung (1668–1741) was a strong supporter of Chu Hsi's philosophy and author of a chronological biography of him. Like many of his contemporaries, he found the *Family Rituals* unsuited to kinship organization as he knew it. But unlike them, he was not satisfied to set Chu Hsi's *Family Rituals* aside

[24] *Hsüeh-li* 4:1a–2a.
[25] *Hsüeh-li* 4:14b–15a.
[26] *Hsüeh-li* 4:3b–4b, 17a.
[27] *Hsüeh-li* 4:2b.
[28] *Hsüeh-li* ch. 2.

as an unsatisfactory book, based on too many compromises between authentic rituals and temporally bound customs. He took a different tack: he decided the book could not be by a person as intelligent as Chu Hsi. Wang wrote a highly polemical attack on the authenticity of the *Family Rituals*, opening with the declaration, "The *Family Rituals* is not Master Chu's book." He admitted that the *Family Rituals* was mentioned in Huang Kan's biography of Chu Hsi, that its preface was in Chu Hsi's collected works, that its completion was recorded in the first chronological biography by Li Fang-tzu, and that the story of its loss and rediscovery was found in the appendix to the *Family Rituals* compiled by Yang Fu and Chou Fu before 1245. He also noted that the book had been honored and used without suspicion ever since the Sung. He then brought up the following doubts about its authenticity:

1. The chronological biography said the book was written while Chu Hsi was in mourning for his mother, but Chu Hsi's preface makes no reference to being in mourning. Moreover, the author of the chronological biography, Li Fang-tzu, had not yet met Chu Hsi when Chu Hsi's mother died and so could not have personally observed him working on the book.

2. Ch'en Ch'un did not give the name of the man who gave back the lost copy to Chu Hsi's son, or state exactly where he had acquired the book.

3. In his biography of Chu Hsi, Huang Kan mentioned only that Chu Hsi wished to revise his *Family Rituals*, saying nothing of his mother's funeral or the loss or recovery of the text. Moreover, Huang Kan wrote this biography some twenty years after Chu Hsi's death, and may not have wished publicly to cast doubt on the *Family Rituals*, even if privately he was suspicious.

4. In letters discussing family rituals, Chu Hsi never explicitly mentioned this text by name. Some of the references that seem to be about the *Family Rituals* could be about Chu Hsi's *I-li ching-chuan t'ung-chieh*.

5. In the postface written in 1194 to Chang Shih's book on family rituals, Chu Hsi said he had wanted to do a revision of Ssu-ma Kuang's book, but had grown old without getting the chance. How could even an old man forget the *Family Rituals* if he had finished it some twenty years earlier?

6. The *Family Rituals* emphasized the descent-line system, not mentioned by Ch'eng I, Chang Tsai, or Ssu-ma Kuang, or by Chu Hsi in his preface.[29]

Wang Mao-hung wrote a second, fuller attack on the *Family Rituals*, in it arguing that many of its items did not make sense and therefore could not have been written by a scholar as learned as Chu Hsi.[30] For instance, he contended that the plan given for sacrificial fields was unworkable because descendants do not all have equal wealth and would not be willing to give over part of their

---

[29] This essay appears several places, of which the most accessible are *Chu Tzu nien-p'u k'ao-i* 1:35a–43a; *Ssu-k'u ch'üan-shu tsung-mu* 22:180–81; and *Huang-ch'ao ching-shih wen-pien* 54:14b–15b. It is also in Wang's works, *Po-t'ien ts'ao-t'ang ts'un-kao* 2:1a–7a.

[30] *Po-t'ien ts'ao-t'ang ts'un-kao* 2:7b–19b.

land for each of their many ancestors. Wang also objected to departures from Ssu-ma Kuang's *Shu-i* on such issues as whether to choose days for sacrifice by divination. He criticized omissions in the *Family Rituals*, such as the lack of any instructions about what to do with a new bride when both her parents-in-law had already died. Above all, Wang objected to the whole overlay of the descent-line system. For instance, he argued that the descent-line heir should not preside at weddings.

> The "Wedding ritual" [section of the *I-li*] always has one's own father or elder brother preside over the marriage. The wording is very clear. If a younger son has no elder brother [living], he simply gives the orders himself. Even though this is not stated it can be inferred. In [Ssu-ma Kuang's] *Shu-i*, if there is no father or grandfather, then the male family head serves. When the family head is the eldest brother, this would match the ritual. When he is an uncle or cousin, then it would be slightly in disagreement with ritual, but if the father is dead, to have the family head replace him does not lose the idea of the ritual. Now the *Family Rituals* throughout has the heir of the great-great-grandfather's descent-line act as presiding man. This means that a living father cannot preside at his child's wedding. It has the father instruct his child, recognizing that this item could not be changed, but it insists that the descent-line heir report it at the offering hall. If he does not know of the instruction, he would not be able to make the report. How confusing! Therefore I say this is not Master Chu's book.[31]

Some of Wang's points are wrong (such as the assertion that Sung Confucians said little about the descent-line system), and others have little to do with authenticity, as Chu Hsi was as capable as anyone of impractical ideas and could hardly be expected to take into account forms of kinship organization rare in his time. Scholarly refutations of Wang's attack will be discussed in the next section. It needs to be noted, however, that his arguments found a receptive audience in the eighteenth century, when the authenticity of many authoritative works was challenged.[32] It was given added publicity by citation in the catalogue of the imperial library issued in 1782.[33] From that time on, many scholars referred to the *Family Rituals* as a reputed work of Chu Hsi, leaving some doubt as to its actual authorship.

THE *FAMILY RITUALS* IN THE EIGHTEENTH AND NINETEENTH CENTURIES

Even after Wang Mao-hung's attack on the authenticity of the *Family Rituals*, the book in its various versions continued to circulate widely and to engage the interest of the scholarly community. Ch'in Hui-t'ien's (1702–1764) huge

[31] Ibid. 2:12b–13a.

[32] On this development, see Elman, *From Philosophy to Philology*.

[33] *Ssu-k'u ch'üan-shu tsung-mu* 25:208–9.

Wu-li t'ung-k'ao [Comprehensive studies of the five classes of rituals] quoted the *Family Rituals* in full under each of the relevant rituals, regularly referring to it as Master Ch'u's book. This work even included the editorial comment that "the *Family Rituals* is a book that *shih-ta-fu* living at home cannot be without for a single day."[34] The compendium of statecraft writings put together by Ho Ch'ang-ling (1785–1848) in 1826 did quote Wang Mao-hung's attack on the *Family Rituals*, but also included the comments of seventeenth- and eighteenth-century scholars who advocated its use or treated it as an authoritative text.[35] Scholars still often used the *Family Rituals* as a model for their own behavior; Lu Yao (1723–1785), for instance, instructed his sons to set up a four-generation ancestor hall on the model of the *Family Rituals*, not a large one to a distant ancestor designed to show off their wealth.[36]

Through the nineteenth century, numerous versions of the *Family Rituals* were in circulation. Both Chu Hsi's original five-*chüan* text and Ch'iu Chün's expanded text were frequently reprinted. A new commentary was even written. In 1732 five scholars published an edition focused less on practice than on Chu Hsi's text as an important document. The commentary they prepared was designed to make Chu Hsi's text more intelligible to people living over five hundred years after his time by explaining terms, giving their pronunciation, and providing simple punctuation.[37]

Revised versions of the *Family Rituals* also continued to be written, and these books were in many regards like Ming ones, with some concentrating on simplifying procedures, others providing the reader with useful samples of prayers, letters, and other reference materials.[38] Ts'ai Shih-yüan (1681–

[34] *Wu-li t'ung-k'ao* 115:3b. The author of this comment then went on to note that some items were difficult to put into practice and could be modified.

[35] *Huang-ch'ao ching-shih wen-pien* 54:5a–6a, 61:1a–b, 7a, 62:11a, 15b, 64:18b for comments by Ch'en Tzu-chih (1687), Liu Chen (1635–1690), Wu Ting (1744–1809), Lu Yao (1723–1785), Ch'ai Shao-ping (1616–1686), and T'ien Lan-fang (1628–1701).

[36] *Huang-ch'ao ching-shih wen-pien* 66:12b–13a.

[37] *Chu Tzu chia-li* (1732 ed.).

[38] How many revised versions were written in the eighteenth and nineteenth centuries is difficult to estimate. Although in general one would expect more books from Ch'ing times to survive than from Ming times, discovering such books is actually harder because they are not classified in China as rare books and therefore are not listed in rare book catalogues. Ch'ing books with "family rituals" in their titles are largely reference books. The *Chia-li ta-ch'eng* [*Family Rituals* made comprehensive], issued in 1735, devotes much less space to the elements in the rituals than the documentary forms needed: the engagement letters, announcements of deaths, and so on. The *Chia-li hui-t'ung* [*Family Rituals* systematized], also published in 1735, is very similar in scope though not identical, probably reflecting common borrowing from earlier reference books. The 1750 *Chia-li t'ieh-shih chi-ch'eng* [A collection of family rituals and form letters] is much like the two 1735 books, though it includes quite ample discussions of funeral ritual. The 1895 *Chia-li ch'üan-chi* [Complete collection of family rituals] is devoted largely to documentary forms. The books more closely based on Chu Hsi's *Family Rituals* in Ch'ing times were usually called by titles containing the term "four rituals" (*ssu-li*).

1731), a scholar from Fukien who rose to high office in the capital, was a strong supporter of Chu Hsi's learning and once argued that Chu Hsi's *Family Rituals* was totally suited to daily use. He also wrote a revised version of it that, he said, eliminated useless elaborations and conformed to what was easy to practice in local custom.[39] At least three separate books written in the nineteenth century were given the same title, *Ssu-li ts'ung-i* [Following what is appropriate in the four rituals], an allusion to a line in the *Li-chi* chosen to indicate that the author was going to neither extreme of sticking too closely to the classics or blindly following custom.[40]

By the late eighteenth century educated men who wanted to perform family rituals properly confronted a bewildering range of opinion, much of it intolerant in tone. This is brought out well by Wu Hsien-shen, a literatus with no official title who was living in Peking in 1793 when he wrote his *Chia-li chi-i* [Collected discussions on the *Family Rituals*]. In his preface he pointed out that ancient rituals, current customs, and human feelings all had to be taken into consideration in deciding on rituals. Before giving his own opinions on any particular point, he cited Chu Hsi's text and then a wide assortment of later opinions from authors like Ch'iu Chün, Lü Nan, Sung Hsün, Lü K'un, Teng Yüan-hsi, Lü Wei-ch'i, T'ang Shu (1497–1574), Mao Ch'i-ling, Chu Tung-hsiang (late seventeenth century), and Ku Yen-wu (1613–1682). In his own comments he dealt also with actual practice and the ways it might or might not be modified. For instance, in his discussion of when a bride should be introduced to her husband's ancestors, Wu began by quoting the *Family Rituals*'s statement that this occurs on the third day. As a commentary to that he cited a passage from Chu Hsi's *Classified Conversations* saying that to wait three months was too long. Next Wu quoted Teng Yüan-hsi to the effect that

[39] *Ch'ing hsüeh-an hsiao-chih* 5:130; Kao and Ch'en, *Fu-chien Chu Tzu hsüeh*, p. 405.

[40] The earliest of these three was published by Jen Jo-hai in 1842 and reprinted in 1859. Jen paid particular attention to the problem of balancing antiquity (*ku*) and custom (*su*). In capping, weddings, funerals, and sacrifices, the author asserts in the preface, it is necessary to make compromises between what changes and what continues, "neither to pervert the ancient nor to get mired in it, to neither follow customs nor be afraid of them." One source of guidance for such compromises was the forms for rituals issued by the Ch'ing government (*Ta Ch'ing t'ung-li*), and Jen regularly brought these into his discussion.

Two years later, in 1844, in a different part of the country (T'ung-ch'eng), Su Tun-yüan (1801–1857) published his book with this title, a concise forty-two page manual. His preface states that the *Chia-li i-chieh* was considered too complicated by most people who therefore followed custom, which in the case of funerals and sacrifices often meant that they violated the meaning of the ritual or followed Buddhist or Taoist forms. Su noted that most people did not realize how far Ch'iu Chün's text was from Chu Hsi's original, and in his efforts to simplify he turned to the Pai-lu tung ed. of Chu Hsi's original *Family Rituals*. This book was apparently popular for it was republished by Su's son in 1851.

The third *Ssu-li ts'ung-i*, by Lin Ch'üan, printed in 1893, was not based on either of these two books. It was a much larger book, with many appended discussions and considerable emphasis on the regulations issued by the Ch'ing government.

it would be better to have the bride introduced immediately. Then he quoted at length from Mao Ch'i-ling. Mao had stated that there was no source predating the Warring States period that clearly established when the bride should be introduced. Mao had then analyzed several passages in the classics as interpreted by various commentators, finally favoring the validity of the traditional three-month wait and dismissing Chu Hsi as a sloppy scholar. Wu Hsien-shen, in giving his own opinion, admitted that Mao's interpretation was clever, but Wu ended up defending Chu Hsi:

> The book *Family Rituals* was compiled by Wen-kung [Chu Hsi] on the basis of the *I-li*. The honorable Ch'iu Wen-chuang [Chün] elaborated and explained it. Master Chu once said, "Ancient rituals are difficult to carry out. If they are to be acted on in later ages, one must consider what is appropriate from past and present. Where the ancients were very complicated, how could we teach people to perform [the step]?" He also said, "As for wanting to carry out ancient rituals today, I worry that conditions and the text do not match. It would be better to start from the rituals people perform today and reform them." We can see that when Master Chu edited the *Family Rituals*, he considered the classical evidence and the suitability of ancient and modern forms. The whole world honors his book, and it should not be discussed lightly. I have also recorded Mao's theory to let later people see how different ancient and modern rituals of husband and wife are.

Still Wu Hsien-shen was not arguing for literal adherence to the *Family Rituals*. Custom also had to be considered:

> In current custom, the day after the bride arrives, some have her first introduced to her parents-in-law, then to the ancestral altar; some have her first introduced to the ancestral altar, then to her parents-in-law. There are also some who have her give obeisance at the offering hall as soon as she arrives. Mr. Sung of Shang-ch'iu [Sung Hsün] said, "On the next day [the bride] is introduced to the ancestral altar, to her parents-in-law, and to various seniors. To have her first introduced to the ancestral altar honors the ancestors. To have the introduction to the ancestral altar and the parents-in-law on the same day saves trouble." Now I honor the idea in the *Family Rituals* but modify it with Sung's and Teng's theories combined. One ought, the day after the bride arrives, introduce her to her parents-in-law, then any elders present; next have the parents-in-law present her in the offering hall.[41]

Other educated men, concerned with practice, also came to the defense of the *Family Rituals*. In the early nineteenth century Lu T'ung-shen attempted to refute Lü K'un's criticisms. In 1823 he wrote *Ssu-li i i-lun* [Skeptical essays on (Lü K'un's) *Doubts on the Four Rituals*] in four *chüan*. He examined each of Lü K'un's points in considerable detail, frequently faulting him for his understanding of the classics, but even more for trying to substitute the local

[41] *Chia-li chi-i* 13b–16b.

custom of his particular place for the models Chu Hsi had derived from the classics. Over and over he pointed out that customs in his area (I-hsing, Kiangsu) or the whole south were quite different than what Lü K'un described as customary, and sometimes these differences made it easier to retain Chu Hsi's features. He expressed great admiration for descent-group organization in his area, which he thought made it possible to retain the descent-line heir system. He also said girls in his area had their hairdos changed when engaged and hairpins added the day before the wedding, making it possible to conduct pinning ceremonies.[42]

In the mid-nineteenth century Ku Kuang-yü (1800–1867) and Hsia Hsin (1789–1871) independently wrote essays refuting Wang Mao-hung's attack on the authenticity of the *Family Rituals*.[43] Hsia Hsin noted that Ch'iu Chün had already refuted an earlier attack on the *Family Rituals*'s authenticity. Both Hsia and Ku pointed out that the reference in Chu Hsi's chronological biography to his writing the *Family Rituals* while in mourning for his mother was misleading. Although Chu Hsi probably worked on the *Family Rituals* while in mourning for his mother, he did not produce a finished version then. The draft status of the *Family Rituals* would account for Chu Hsi's failure to mention it as a finished book. These scholars found it implausible that Chu Hsi's closest disciples and his son could have been fooled by a forgery. They point out how often in letters or conversations Chu Hsi discussed the practical issues of how to perform rites in his day, showing his strong interest in the subject matter of the *Family Rituals*. Chu Hsi also frequently referred to writing he was doing on particular rites in ways that correspond to the text of the *Family Rituals*, something I showed here in Chapter Five.

Ku Kuang-yü also cited the testimony of Ch'en Ch'un, which was apparently unknown to Wang Mao-hung.[44] Ch'en Ch'un was explicit about talking to Chu Hsi in 1190 while the latter was prefect of Chang-chou about the draft of the *Family Rituals* that Chu Hsi had lost. Ch'en also reported that in 1211 he saw a copy of the *Family Rituals* at the home of Chu Hsi's youngest son Tsai, who asserted that it was the copy Chu Hsi had earlier lost. Ch'en reported that this book had five parts, one on general principles and one each on cappings, weddings, funerals, and sacrifices, and that each part was divided into chapters, and each chapter into main points and details. Ch'en later discussed minor differences between this draft and an early printed version.[45]

Ku Kuang-yü pointed out Wang's error in saying neither Ch'eng I nor Chang Tsai had stressed the descent-line system, since the two of them were major advocates of it. The fact that the early references to the *Family Rituals* were not as complete as one would like did not mean they were false; only

---

[42] *Ssu-li i i-lun*, passim.

[43] *Shu Chu chih-i* 7:10b–13a; *Ssu-li ch'üeh-i* 1:1b–5b.

[44] *Ssu-li ch'üeh-i* 1b–2b.

[45] PHTCC 14:2b.

that, since the authenticity of the book was not in doubt, their reference to its provenance were brief. Twentieth-century scholars who have looked into the issue of the authorship of the *Family Rituals* have largely accepted the judgments of Hsia Hsin and Ku Kuang-yü.[46]

CONCLUSIONS

The seventeenth-, eighteenth-, and nineteenth-century debates about family rituals and their relations to textual sources and social situations are historically significant on several grounds. The high Ch'ing is often perceived as a period when the state worked hard to achieve social and intellectual conformity. This period witnessed a severe censorship of published texts, an expansion of efforts at inculcating basic Confucian social norms in the general population, and a tendency toward conservatism on such issues as widow chastity. And yet issues widely considered to be matters of morality, such as who could or could not preside at ancestral rites to particular ancestors, were openly debated. The Ch'ing government continued to support Chu Hsi's philosophy and indirectly to support the *Family Rituals*. But it did not try to silence those who disagreed. Scholars freely criticized each other's views; they did not even feel compelled to accept and defend all the views of their own teachers.

Did the intellectual debate on Chu Hsi's *Family Rituals* undermine its influence on the performance of rituals? I suspect not. History cannot be easily turned back. By the seventeenth century the influence of the *Family Rituals* had diffused through society. Numerous versions of it were in circulation. It had influenced the liturgies incorporated in other sources, such as the imperial codes, the instructions in reference books, and the ritual rules in descent-group genealogies. Even educated men, when getting ready to celebrate a son's wedding, would be unlikely to first spend a few months searching through the *Tso-chuan*; they needed some sort of handbook or liturgy. Many of them were uncomfortable with the contentions and rigid style of the intellectual leaders and continued to prefer to emphasize the "main idea."

The only possible way critics of Chu Hsi's *Family Rituals* could have undermined its influence would have been if they had introduced something to supplant it. This they could not easily do. The classics posed so many philological problems that it was difficult to gain consensus even on small points like how long mourning should properly last, much less more major ones like the descent-line heir system. Those who believed guidebooks should match their own circumstances, especially their own forms of kinship organization, would have to produce books tailored to their own needs and thus unsuited to people in other circumstances. Scholars who rejected liturgies as inevitably simplifications or compromises were also abandoning the goal of influencing

---

[46] See Chapter Five, note 6.

those who could only choose between consulting a liturgy, asking their neighbors, or getting a master of ceremonies to handle matters for them.

At another level, however, the debate in high intellectual circles unintentionally confirmed much of the Confucian discourse on family rituals. These
debates were conducted within conservative parameters. Confucian scholars
freely debated whether to adhere to the provisions of a text five hundred years
old, one two thousand years old, or the very oldest ones available, not whether
texts were relevant to establishing proper ritual practices; they debated
whether the bride should be introduced to her husband's ancestors on the first,
second, or third day, not whether brides should be brought to their husbands'
homes and introduced to their ancestors. These debates, therefore, by brack-
eting many of the most crucial cultural assumptions underlying Chinese family
rituals may have in fact served to strengthen the capacity of family rituals to
communicate basic social and cosmological principles.

Chapter Nine

CONFUCIAN TEXTS AND THE PERFORMANCE
OF RITUALS

> To have the bride first introduced to the ancestral altar
> honors the ancestors.
> —Sung Hsün (d. 1591)[1]

FAMILY RITUALS evolved in China in a context that included texts: the ritual classics, the commentaries to them, the imperial ritual codes, the decrees and edicts that set status limitations on the performance of rituals, the criminal codes that outlawed some practices, the essays and memorials that debated fine points of ritual, the etiquette books that specified the language to use in ritual documents, and the liturgies, such as Chu Hsi's *Family Rituals* and its many revisions, that specified exactly how to perform the rites. In this chapter I outline and assess the ways these texts, especially the liturgies, influenced the performance of family rituals at all social levels. For imperial rituals one might posit an identity between the texts prescribing rituals and the performance of rituals.[2] In the case of domestic rites, however, texts and rituals clearly existed in tension with each other, neither fully determining the form or content of the other.

Confucian texts were a force toward continuity both in the underlying structure of the rites and the terms by which steps were labeled. Yet these texts did not prevent or confine change. The Confucian discourse, seen as the set of texts available in any given period, kept growing and changing. There were relatively invariant texts, such as the *I-li* and *Li-chi*, but these texts could be given new commentaries and could be read in new ways. One could even take short sentences out of context and build new structures on them, as those in the Sung advocating the *tsung* system had done. The *Family Rituals* proved far from an invariant text. Not only did revisions introduce elements that had their origins in customary practice, but familiarity with these new books must have led people to read the old book in new ways. Chu Hsi among many others had validated distinguishing core elements from details, and thus gave approval to the process of interpretation that allowed the same texts to mean

---

[1] *Chia-li chi-i* 16a–b.

[2] See Zito, ''Re-presenting Sacrifice: Cosmology and the Editing of Texts.''

different things to different people and allowed change and variation to be read as continuity and sameness.

The growth and evolution of the Confucian discourse on rites was not entirely parallel to changes in what people commonly did, as the connection between rules and behavior is never a simple one. Not everyone would have responded the same way to being told that music is inappropriate at weddings or that a father should be mourned in the first degree. How each person responded would have depended on the context in which he learned the rule; his understanding of its relevance to his personal situation; his intuitive sense of what adhering to the rule would do to the ritual and through the ritual to his relations with friends, neighbors, and relatives; and probably many other factors. The Confucian discourse was, after all, only one component of Chinese culture. For many centuries Confucian scholars and the state issued texts that interpreted and evaluated ritual behavior, but they did not have a monopoly even on how to frame the issues, as other discourses such as Buddhism, property law, popular religion, and the lore of ghosts also existed. In this chapter I look at the ways the Confucian discourse worked in conjunction with these other discourses to create both continuities and diversities in the practice of family rituals. It is commonly recognized that rituals can create both awareness of difference and feelings of solidarity. Ancestral rites, for instance, because they are done in similar ways in all families, convey the message that all families are essentially similar. Yet at the same time the rites are performed in bounded units; each performance announces where one family or descent group ends. Weddings, in more complex ways, symbolize the differences between men and women and wife-givers and wife-takers, while simultaneously overcoming them through the union of the bride and groom. In a somewhat analogous fashion, I argue, Confucian liturgies served both to bring out the similarities in the ways people throughout China practiced family rituals and to facilitate certain types of variation and distinction.

CONTINUITIES AND UNIFORMITIES: THE CONFUCIAN CORE

Detailed evidence concerning the ways common people or even the educated routinely performed domestic rituals in the Ming and early Ch'ing period is frustratingly incomplete. Novelists and short-story writers might describe a ceremony if it figured in a plot. Other writers would mention when people deviated from standards, but did not see any need to write about practices that largely conformed to authorized models. If on visiting a distant county a writer found that people placed food before the coffin or inscribed ancestral tablets approximately as Chu Hsi's *Family Rituals* specified, he would not see any reason to write an essay about it, especially if people in his home county had the same customs. Gazetteer accounts of local customs often make general statements about the ritual procedures of the educated, the rich, or the common people of the region, but when they describe people's behavior in terms that resemble provisions in the *Family Rituals* one can never be sure how much of the account is normative rather than descriptive.

The observations of foreigners and trained ethnographers, mostly made during the last century and a half, provide more precise evidence.[3] From their accounts, we know that at the end of the imperial period common practice across the country bore many general resemblances to the steps described in Confucian texts. Ancestral rites included periodic offerings of food and drink at domestic altars, as they had since ancient times. They also included practices common since at least the Sung and specified in Chu Hsi's *Family Rituals*, such as offerings on death-day anniversaries and major festivals. Continuities in wedding ceremonies included negotiations by matchmakers, exchanges of gifts, the highly ceremonial transfer of the bride to her husband's home where the new couple consumed wine and food together and the bride was introduced to her husband's parents, relatives, and ancestors. For funerals and burials, major continuities included ritualized wailing, mourning garments that visibly indicated the proximity of kinship to the deceased, setting food and drink near the coffin until burial, postponing burial days, weeks, or months to prolong mourning, restrictions on social activities during deepest mourning, use of heavy coffins, ceremonial funeral processions to the graveyard, and post-burial sacrifices to the deceased.

A variety of partial explanations can be offered to account for these continuities. Family rituals are, after all, not the only feature of Chinese culture that persisted over time. There were continuities in the structure of the state, the core values of Confucianism, the patrilineal and patriarchal organization of the Chinese family, and the composition of the elite. The close ties of ritual forms to all of these other features of Chinese civilization would mean that forces leading to continuities in one would indirectly foster continuities in the others.

Nevertheless, I would contend that without the existence of texts, especially texts that labeled the steps of the rites and described them in fairly concrete language, the continuities and uniformities in Chinese ritual practices could not have been so great. Relatively simple rites, such as the rite to the stove god, may have spread over China in surprisingly similar forms without texts playing a large role in standardizing them.[4] In such cases the ideas behind the rites could have spread the way folktales spread. And some very common elements of family rituals—such as burning incense and mock money as offerings—seem to owe their spread to their association with temple-based worship of gods rather than to Confucian texts. Yet even quite complex features

---

[3] See the sources cited in Chapter One, notes 11–13.

[4] See Chard, "The New Year Stove Rituals and the Stove God Scriptures in Domestic Popular Religion."

of family rituals persisted for many centuries. Would there have been essentially universal agreement about the mourning grade for the wife of a grandfather's first cousin through his paternal grandfather if there were no texts to consult? Would the idea that one puts on mourning garments on the third day have been so widely recognized without texts? Would the practice of offering three cups of wine to the ancestors, rather than one, two, or four, have been as widely recognized as standard without books that specified it? Jack Goody has argued that in preliterate societies, such as those in Africa, rituals will vary greatly even across relatively short distances, but in literate societies similar structures can be found in places separated by great distances.[5] China was a society with a highly literate elite, a widespread respect for books, and an abundance of books on ritual. People bought revised versions of the *Family Rituals* in sufficient numbers that booksellers kept producing new ones and reprinting old ones. Texts are not as malleable as oral traditions. Each generation reads them somewhat differently, but they cannot simply give them any meaning they choose. The texts constrain them.

Over the course of the imperial period, more and more texts became available to contribute to continuities. From the Han through the T'ang dynasties, the most important texts were the classics, their commentaries, and government ritual codes, none of which would have circulated very widely. To assume that these texts contributed to the perpetuation of recognizably similar ritual forms in the society at large is to assume that there was a considerable trickle-down effect: officials and others with classical educations modeled their ritual performances on these books in varying degrees, and the great prestige these people had in Chinese society led others who never read the books to imitate them.

With the advent of printing, a greater variety of books—and more copies of each book—became available. Ssu-ma Kuang saw a need for a book that would be easier to consult than the classics or government manuals. Printing allowed his book to gain a wide circulation among the well-educated, fostering an awareness of discrepancies between canonical norms and common practices. Yet within a century it was supplanted by a new and much simpler liturgy, Chu Hsi's *Family Rituals*. This was the first ritual manual to receive wide circulation. New books like these not only tended to introduce elements that had their origins in the practices common in the author's milieu, but they changed how people read the old books.

With the wider circulation of various versions of the *Family Rituals*, one began to get, I suspect, a different relationship between ordinary people's ritual performances and texts. From the sixteenth century on there were books

[5] He wrote, for instance, "Writing is surely critical to the fact that Hinduism (even taking into account the variety of local cults and local manifestations) exists in recognizably similar forms throughout the subcontinent, whereas in Africa or New Guinea local variance in religious belief and ritual action is enormous" (*The Logic of Writing*, p. 7).

available that people with only a few years of schooling could easily read. Such people could, in turn, serve as experts to those totally illiterate. The influence of texts, in other words, would not have to be mediated through the visible example of the classically educated. People who never saw a liturgical book would still know that such books existed, and that rituals were most effective when performed according to the ways that books specified. The chance to consult the exact wording in books might lead to a more rigid or mechanical approach, but this would be counteracted by the greater variety of books available to consult.

As I see it, the wide circulation of various versions of the *Family Rituals* in Ming and Ch'ing times contributed to the standardization of ritual performance in three ways. They conveyed a sense of the unquestionable, utterly essential features of the rites. They publicized the correctness of a few practices that in time gained widespread acceptance. And they legitimated much of what people commonly did, labeling it Confucian. The process by which practices that did not have canonical origins were incorporated into Confucian liturgies has been given so much attention in chapters three to seven that nothing more needs to be added here. But the ways liturgies conveyed notions of the essential features of the rites and fostered adoption of new practices deserves attention.

The practices that persisted for centuries were almost invariably ones that even the most probing thinkers did not question. Ch'eng I objected to setting the number of ancestors to receive sacrifices by social or political rank; he did not question the assumption that making offerings of food and drink was the right way to treat ancestors. Chu Hsi and later Mao Ch'i-ling debated what day the bride should be introduced to her husband's ancestors, but neither questioned that she should be introduced to them. Lü K'un thought feelings should play more of a role in determining how long to wail in the early stages of a funeral; but he did not question that wailing was an appropriate response to the death of a close relative. The writers of Confucian texts, in other words, while intellectually aware that rituals were man-made, did not push this insight to the point of questioning the most fundamental premises of these rituals. Every text in circulation that presented some ritual procedures simply as what one does and others as items of contention strengthened the hold of the unexamined practices. Even Buddhism could not dislodge this unexamined layer.

One of the more effective ways the unchallengeable features of the rites were conveyed was through the labels for the steps in rites. Over the centuries these names proved resistant to change. People recognized the general meaning and place in the ritual sequence of such steps as "presenting the gift" or "welcoming in person" in weddings, "setting out the soul seat," "dressing the body," and "putting on the mourning garments" in funerals. Even the simplest liturgy reinforced knowledge of these labels; indeed, the simpler the liturgy the more it resembled a checklist of the names of the steps, briefly defined. To accept that these were the steps of the ritual was to accept much about its form and meaning.

Unexamined practices were tightly linked to unexamined beliefs and assumptions, each reinforcing the other. Despite a strain of agnosticism about the powers of ancestors to receive offerings and repay their descendants going back to the late Chou, no Confucian scholar ever proposed abandoning offerings of real food and drink and substituting purely verbal tokens of respect. Nor did scholars make an issue of adding tea and incense when they became part of the standard way of serving gods. The use of real food and drink made the relationship of the living to their ancestors analogous to other relations involving provision of food; it evoked notions of the dependence of those receiving the food, perhaps coupled with the deference of those (generally women) who present it. Homologies between the offerings made to gods and those made to ancestors similarly conveyed understandings of the spiritual nature of ancestors. Buddhist and Taoist sects propagated their ideas through the written word, publishing popular tracts of many sorts.[6] In this they were more like Western traditions such as Christianity. The religious ideas about the dead intrinsic to ancestor worship, however, were not spread by tracts of these sorts. Confucianism was widely recognized as the tradition that underlay the ancestor cult, yet Confucian tracts urged filial piety, loyalty, sincerity, and study; they did not analyze ancestors as spirits or the metaphysical basis of their power over and dependence on descendants. Indeed such topics had been avoided since the time of Confucius. More important to creating common understandings of the nature of ancestors were the rites themselves and thus indirectly the liturgies which described in matter-of-fact ways how they should be performed.

Confucian liturgies contributed to uniformity in more direct ways as well, as some of the steps or procedures introduced in them eventually gained popularity. Ancestral halls, ancestral tablets, and sacrificing to three or four generations of ancestors all appear to have gradually become commonplace after texts describing them as standard gained wide circulation. Jesuit missionaries in the late sixteenth and seventeenth centuries reported that even people who did not believe in a literal way in what they were doing still called down the souls of their ancestors to reside in their spirit tablets and gave them food and drink.[7] Later observers seem in almost total agreement that every household had some sort of ancestral altar, at least a table along the wall of the main room of the house or a shelf on a wall. Wooden tablets, moreover, seem to

---

[6] See Overmyer, "Values in Chinese Sectarian Literature."

[7] See Rowbotham, *Missionary and Mandarin*, pp. 119–75; Dunne, *Generation of Giants*, pp. 282–302. See also the views of nineteenth-century missionaries in Huc, *The Chinese Empire*, pp. 220–24; Martin, *The Lore of Cathay*, pp. 264–78; and Moule, *New China and Old*, pp. 193–222. See also Weller, *Unities and Diversities*, pp. 125–27, for the tendencies of those with high school educations in a Taiwan township to scoff at the idea that ancestors could grant favors.

have been extraordinarily common, even among the poor, all over China, though paper tablets and portraits were also in use. The construction of these tablets often corresponded closely to the description in the *Family Rituals*. Doolittle found tablets very close to those described in the *Family Rituals* in mid-nineteenth-century Fukien, as did Johnston in Shantung in the early twentieth century.[8] The basic inscriptions on tablets, moreover, largely conformed to the *Family Rituals*. Descriptions of ceremonies, where they exist, also largely match the *Family Rituals*.[9]

Why did people come to adopt practices advocated in books? Ancestral tablets may well have been adopted because of their intrinsic advantages over other objects in common use. Ever since the decline in the use of impersonators to represent the ancestors in the Chou period, people felt a need to use a physical object to stand for each ancestor and to serve as its receptacle when it was summoned. Portraits made good sense, and their use was reinforced by the common practice of Buddhist, Taoist, and popular temples of representing deities with painted or sculpted likenesses. Yet inscribed tablets also had advantages. Symbolically the emphasis on name rather than likeness fit well with the core idea that ancestral rites concern patrilineality. Moreover, tablets were less expensive than portraits and more durable than strips of paper.

I suspect that the relatively positive way ancestral rites were presented in the *Family Rituals* also contributed to the acceptance of various measures introduced. Certainly the underlying message of these sections is that ancestral rites should be performed as Confucian ceremonies by the appropriate kinsman and thus by implication should not be entrusted to outsiders, including Buddhist or Taoist clergy.[10] Yet ancestral rites were not presented as an occasion for making choices. People were told to add to their ritual repertoire; they were not chided about what they should cease doing. It is probably always easier to get people to add new practices than to give up ones that their parents had performed.

Familiarity with the *Family Rituals* could lead to adoption of bookish forms of ancestral rites at relatively modest social levels. Wang Ken (1483–1541) offers an example. He came from a family of salt farmers and traders and ended his formal schooling at age ten. At twenty-five, however, having visited the Confucian temple at Ch'ü-fu, he became inspired with Confucian goals of

[8] Doolittle, *Social Life*, 1:219–21; Johnston, *Lion and Dragon*, pp. 277–79.

[9] For a fictional description of a domestic ritual, see Hawkes, trans., *The Story of the Stone*, 2:567–71. See also the descriptions of descent-group ceremonies cited in Chapter Six, note 83.

[10] The practice of entrusting ancestral rites to Buddhist monks seems to have declined after the Sung, but it did not disappear entirely. See Brook, "Gentry Dominance in Chinese Society," esp. pp. 221–23, for small Buddhist shrines with a resident monk established at graves in Ming times; Gray, *China*, p. 307, for death-day rites at Buddhist monasteries; Fei, *Peasant Life in China*, p. 76, for monks who kept the genealogical records for peasants to help them with ancestral rites; and Burkhardt, *Chinese Creeds and Customs*, p. 152, for private Buddhist chapels in modern Hong Kong that would care for ancestral tablets.

self-cultivation and social renovation. His biographer reports that in 1517, at age thirty-five *sui*, he became aware that it was wrong to have figures of Buddhas or gods on an ancestral altar and also that according to Chu Hsi's *Family Rituals* the altar should have the spirit tablets of four generations. He then spread these ideas to many other people in his community.[11]

Variation Outside the Confucian Core

A survey of the way Chinese in the nineteenth and twentieth centuries performed weddings or funerals could easily emphasize variation instead of uniformity. People in some places reported a relative's death to the local temple of the city god, in other places to temples of other gods; in some places bodies were laid out with the head to the south, in other places with the head to the door.[12] In some places, after a bride had entered the groom's home, she had to step on a saddle; in other places she had to find paper flowers hidden in a drawer.[13] If we grant that Confucian texts had something to do with continuities and uniformities in ritual practices, what about differences?

Variations in the ways people performed family rituals can be divided into three types: cases where Confucian liturgies either did not say what people should do or specified it only in vague ways; cases where Confucian liturgies presented in a matter-of-fact way a certain protocol, but many people did not follow it; and cases where Confucian liturgies mentioned a common deviation and explicitly condemned it but many people did not give it up. The relationship of texts to performance was different in each of these cases.

Confucian texts left many features of rites sketchy. One could not decide at which temple to report a death by consulting a Confucian text, because these texts do not list this step at all. Nor could one turn to these texts to decide whom to invite to a wedding. In Chu Hsi's *Family Rituals* wedding feasts are described as follows: "The presiding man entertains the guests. [*Note*: The male guests are in the outer quarters, the female guests in the inner hall.]" Virtually any sort of sex-segregated entertainment could be construed to fit this liturgy. It would not matter what food was served, how many guests were invited, how many of them were relatives, or what sorts of relatives they were. Ancestral rites at graves offer another example. Confucian liturgies specified the sequence of the steps for these sacrifices, but said nothing about who should participate, allowing considerable differences in the size and nature of the groups performing the rite. Ambiguities and silences of these sorts in the

[11] *Wang Hsin-chai hsien-sheng ch'üan-chi*, nien-p'u 2:5b. At this point Wang Ken had not yet met Wang Yang-ming. On Wang Ken, see Ching's entry in DMB, pp. 1382–85.

[12] See Walshe, "Some Chinese Funeral Customs," pp. 33–36.

[13] Freedman, "Rites and Duties," p. 268; Ahern, "Affines and the Rituals of Kinship," pp. 286–87.

liturgies left considerable room for people to use rituals for ends that conflicted with Confucian conceptions of family relations.[14]

People also ignored a fair share of what *was* specified in various versions of the *Family Rituals*. Most revised versions of the *Family Rituals* called for performing ancestral rites once in each season and also at popular festivals, but the "seasonal rituals" do not seem to have been as common in general practice as the ones associated with popular festivals. My suspicion is that many people had no sense that they were deviating from a fixed norm in this regard. Even scholars often thought that Chu Hsi's *Family Rituals* should be interpreted in a relatively free way, in terms of its underlying moral meaning. Probably the ritual experts commoners would consult were just as liberal in their interpretations of liturgical handbooks, dismissing many elements as trivial detail or antique versions. Thus there were probably many people whose ritual practices were molded to some degree by Confucian texts but who did not know that these texts called for ancestral rites both at popular festivals and once each season.

Another example of an injunction in the *Family Rituals* that seems to have had little impact was the requirement that people keep on their altars "associated" tablets for childless great-uncles, uncles, and brothers. From Chu Hsi's letters and conversations, we know that he saw this way of continuing sacrifices as a substitute for uxorilocal marriage and adoption of strangers or matrilateral or affinal kin. By Ch'ing times, uxorilocal marriage and adoption of outsiders appear to have been less common among the educated class than they had been in Sung times, but not because people were content to see their nephews make offerings to them as associated tablets. Rather they seem to have worked harder to find acceptable agnatic heirs. Among the common people, however, neither uxorilocal marriage nor adoption of outsiders seems to have abated to any great extent.[15]

One reason the *Family Rituals* may not have had greater impact in this regard are the contradictions with the customary law of property transfer, which linked receiving property and making offerings. The law allowed posthumous adoption, the adoptee chosen by the widow in consultation with her husband's patrilineal relatives. He would take over the role of heir in ancestral rites, would support the widow, and would eventually assume full control of the property. Any nephew who made a tablet and put it on his family altar would be interpreted by cousins as making a claim on the ancestral property. If he could not serve as heir because he was his own father's only heir, he would

---

[14] On some of the ways grave rites could be manipulated, see Rubie S. Watson, "Remembering the Dead."

[15] On regional differences in common people's views toward adoption of sons of other surnames and uxorilocal marriages in the nineteenth and twentieth centuries, see Wolf and Huang, *Marriage and Adoption in China*, pp. 202–5, 216–18.

do better to put his efforts into pressuring the one who did take over the property also to take on the rites.

A second contradiction was with the *Family Rituals*'s own "basic meaning," to borrow Chu Hsi's way of thinking. All versions of the *Family Rituals* communicate that an heir is essential: he is the priest needed to perform funeral rites, death-day rites, and periodic sacrifices. How could anyone who had tried to adhere to the *Family Rituals* in his service to his own forebears feel comfortable with no heir specifically responsible for rites to him, hoping instead that a nephew primarily responsible for the rites to his own father would look after him as well? A distant patrilineal relative who could be made full heir (i.e., heir to the property as well as the rites) would certainly be preferable, and probably many people thought a daughter's son or other nonagnatic relative would also be better. The internal contradictions in the text, in other words, helped generate deviations from the authorized standard.

A similar internal contradiction probably explains the continuing prevalence of introducing a bride to her husband's ancestors on the first day of the wedding.[16] If the bride was to be incorporated into her husband's family, she had to be introduced to its members in a way that would help her understand her place in the hierarchy of the family. Living members could be introduced in order of generation and age. To leave the ancestors to some later time apparently seemed to most people to give them a lesser place, even if there were canonical grounds for doing so. In other words, it was difficult to introduce a practice simply because it had canonical resonances when the surface meaning of its symbolism seemed to be at odds with what weddings were all about, indeed at odds with the ancestor-orientation of other rites in the *Family Rituals*. As Sung Hsün wrote, introducing the bride immediately to the ancestors honors the ancestors.[17]

If the deviations discussed above are classed as minor, one cannot take the same view of all deviations. Many practices were condemned in various versions of the *Family Rituals* as heterodox, vulgar, superstitious, or silly. One hesitates to dismiss as irrelevant the efforts of so many scholars and officials, over so many centuries, to "reform customs." Still the effects of their efforts were not just what they wanted, or thought they wanted, since later writers kept echoing their complaints.

With regard to weddings, the practice most widely condemned as vulgar in successive versions of the *Family Rituals* was treating the marriage as a financial transaction to be negotiated. From Ssu-ma Kuang on, authors of liturgies

---

[16] Introducing her to the ancestors on the second day, however, seems to have gained (or retained) some popularity. See the passage from Wu Hsien-shen cited near the end of the last chapter and Doolittle, *Social Life*, 1:86; Fielde, *Corner of Cathay*, p. 42. Note also that the second day was specified in some authorized texts, such as the *Ming chi-li* 28:15a, 26b, 32b, and *Ta-Ming hui-tien* 71:4b, 11b.

[17] *Chia-li chi-i* 16a. See Chapter Eight for Wu Hsien-shen's lengthy discussion of this issue.

regularly added the step called "delivery of the dowry." They sensed that this custom could not be banned, but they thought that with moral effort people could expend considerable sums on weddings without letting the financial transactions intrude into such matters as which spouse to choose and how to treat the new relatives. But for recent times there is abundant evidence that the financial side of marriage arrangements was openly discussed among ordinary people and that it did impinge on which spouse was chosen and how daughters-in-law were treated.[18] The reason the exchange side of marriages did not decline significantly undoubtedly has much to do with the nature of the Chinese family and marriage system. Families were as much units that held property in common as units that worshipped ancestors together. Family property largely passed along a patriline to sons and grandsons, but not along a single-stranded line as all brothers were to share equally in the family estate when it was divided. The provision of dowries from this property, thus, conflicted with the goal of passing it down within the patrilineal group. The side receiving the daughter and her dowry also had concerns over property, and not just the property they laid out for betrothal gifts. A wife who came in as an outsider could be suspected of favoring her own children over her husband's brothers' children, leading to petty disputes that would some day precipitate division of the family property and the split-up of the household. Thus it is not surprising that the uncertainties and anxieties attendant to any wedding often found expression in quarrels over money.[19]

For funerals, the two practices most vigorously condemned in successive versions of the *Family Rituals* were Buddhist services and feasting. Buddhist funeral services have continued through the imperial period and up to the present in Taiwan and Hong Kong.[20] In the mid-nineteenth century Justus Doolittle, familiar particularly with the area around Fu-chou, Fukien, reported that because these services were expensive they were not common among the poor, but he estimated that half of the mercantile families, eighty percent of the rich, and thirty to forty percent of the literati had monks perform services to transfer merit to the dead on each seventh day until the forty-ninth day.[21] J. J. M. de

[18] See Mann, "Grooming a Daughter for Marriage"; Rubie S. Watson, "Wives, Concubines, and Maids"; Wolf, *Women and the Family in Rural Taiwan*, pp. 119–24; and Ocko, "Women, Property, and the Law in the PRC."

[19] See also Weller, *Unities and Diversities*, pp. 33–37, on ideology and pragmatics in weddings. Tensions between the ways of thinking about family and family property embedded in the notion of *chia* (family as a property-holding unit) and ideas more strictly tied to the descent line are major themes in Ebrey, "Conceptions of the Family."

[20] Taoists also often performed funeral rituals comparable to Buddhist ones, but these were less often the target of Confucian complaints either because they were viewed as derivative (Taoists had simply made over Buddhist services into something they could call their own) or because Taoism itself was not perceived to be as threatening as Buddhism, since it was indigenous and based on many of the same cosmological principles as Confucianism.

[21] Doolittle, *Social Life*, 1:184, 191.

Groot, writing a couple of decades later on the basis of his observations in nearby Amoy, said that no other class exceeded the literati or would-be literati in spending money for the sake of alleviating the suffering of their close relatives through Buddhist services.[22] (Some of those de Groot called "would-be literati" may have been Doolittle's "rich.") Many other foreign observers and ethnographers have described these rites simply as a standard part of what Chinese routinely did for funerals. Revised versions of the *Family Rituals* invariably lamented the popularity of these rites, so it seems unlikely that many literati were ignorant of objections to them in the Confucian discourse. Moreover, some educated men made purposeful efforts to exclude Buddhist rites as a way of demonstrating their Confucian education. Such efforts, discussed in Chapter Six, not infrequently evoked the *Family Rituals* by name. A typical gazetteer entry would report that the *shih-ta-fu* of a prefecture followed the *Family Rituals* and thus did not perform Buddhist funeral services; a biography would note that a man adhered to the *Family Rituals* and did not call in monks for a parent's funeral.

What made the hold of Buddhist services so stubborn? From T'ang times on elementary Buddhist ideas, particularly karma and transmigration, were widely accepted in Chinese society, as can be seen from casual references to them in fiction, drama, and folklore. The idea that the dead pass through a series of courts where they are judged before reincarnation seems if anything to have become more widely held after the Sung, and was communicated in popular religious tracts, in plays performed at funerals, in pictures on temple walls, and in the sermons of monks and priests.[23] For the bereaved, the belief that they could help their dead loved ones avoid suffering was a strong motivation to hold Buddhist services. Hybridized rites, ones that drew on both Buddhist and Confucian cosmologies, allowed people to express the principles that were compelling to them. For the large majority of the population who took these Buddhist conceptions for granted, purely Confucian rites could only serve to express allegiance to Confucianism as an ideology; they would have been detached from their conceptions of death and afterlife and thus emotionally unsatisfactory.

And emotions are not an insignificant element in funerals. Canonical rituals provided survivors with ways to work through feelings of guilt about not having done more for the dead in the context of the ideas about death and afterlife of the late Chou and Han. The bereaved were encouraged to make the dead as comfortable as possible, try to arrest the decay of the body, and supply the dead with food, drink, and models of useful goods. After the assimilation of folk Buddhist cosmology, these steps were not enough because the desire to

---

[22] De Groot, "Buddhist Masses for the Dead," p. 31.

[23] See Eberhard, *Guilt and Sin in Traditional China*, pp. 24–59.

help dead relatives had been given new cultural constructions: people wanted to help them expiate sins.

The hold of Buddhist services was probably also strengthened by the role monks played as funeral experts. Buddhist priests claimed a special knowledge of death and the afterworld and efficacious ways to help the dead.[24] In a society in which fears of ghosts and the forces of death were pervasive, Buddhist monks were probably often called on to manage funerals not simply because survivors worried about the rebirth of the dead, but because they wanted someone else to take over responsibility for conducting ceremonies correctly, a task Buddhists were willing to perform.[25] Confucian scholars saw caring for the dead as a filial duty and could neither offer their own services as experts nor encourage delegating major tasks to anyone other than the descendants. The only "priests" in the Confucian ancestral cult were the heirs.

Finally, one should not overlook the way participation of monks and nuns added to the magnificence of funerals. The eighteenth-century novel *Hung-lou meng* [Dream of red mansions] describes in detail the elaborate funeral for a young wife. Canonical flourishes were not omitted, but neither were Buddhist and Taoist services. The coffin was kept in the house compound for forty-nine days (corresponding to the Buddhist seven-sevens before rebirth), during which time 108 monks performed Buddhist ceremonies for the salvation of the soul and 99 Taoist priests performed ceremonies for absolution.[26] In the twentieth-century novel *Chia* [Family], the funeral for the family patriarch, presented as a staunch Confucian, involved hanging pictures of the courts of the underworld, a Taoist priest who "opened the road," and 108 Buddhist monks who wandered around holding sticks of lit incense.[27]

Many ways of displaying wealth through ritual are condoned or even encouraged in Confucian liturgies, such as the construction of offering halls, the provision of well-made coffins and well-supplied tombs, and the presentation of numerous varieties of carefully prepared foods for ancestral rites, culminating in family feasts. Nevertheless, the impulse to demonstrate wealth does not seem to have been effectively channeled into these practices, even among literati and officials. By late Chou times mourning for parents had become the greatest occasion for demonstrating filial piety, and no other rite ever came close to replacing it. As discussed above, those of high standing, obliged to show that they had spared no expense in performing their duties, were often the most likely to deviate from the *Family Rituals* on the issue of Buddhist

[24] Cf. Teiser, *Ghost Festival*, pp. 203–8.

[25] For discussion of the value of funeral experts in the context of modern Kwangtung, see James L. Watson, "Funeral Specialists in Cantonese Society." It is my general impression that the attitudes toward death pollution he describes are at the extreme end of the Chinese spectrum; elsewhere and in earlier periods these feelings do not seem to have been as intense.

[26] Hawkes, trans., *The Story of the Stone*, 1:258–94, esp. 260, 275.

[27] Shapiro, trans., *The Family*, p. 252.

services. The inability of the rich and high-ranking to give up Buddhist services would naturally have conveyed messages to the uneducated at least as powerful as the text of the *Family Rituals*: these services were efficacious and brought honor.

The *Family Rituals* included Ssu-ma Kuang's condemnation of "entertaining the dead," an activity that generally involved boisterous feasting, with music or other entertainment, either shortly after the death or the night before the burial, and revised versions of the *Family Rituals* regularly lamented the continuing popularity of such funerary entertainment. From the observations of Westerners, however, it appears that funeral entertainment did not persist in the forms described in the Sung. Rather, by the nineteenth century, these activities seem to have been amalgamated into Buddhist or Taoist funeral services, which in their grander forms could include elaborate plays, such as Mu-lien's descent into the underworld.[28]

Funeral feasts were at great odds with the Confucian image of how a mourner should behave, so voluminously described in the *Li-chi*. Mourners should be so dazed by grief that they notice very little around them; they should be so indifferent to food or drink that they eat only small amounts of the coarsest foods. There was thus no grounds on which feasting could be relabeled a Confucian ritual. Moreover, the legal codes from the Sung through the Ch'ing all specified heavy punishments for these sorts of activities. I suspect that the reason funeral feasts and entertainment persisted probably relates to their role in funerals as rites of passage. In the *Family Rituals* and other distinctly Confucian texts, there is a group dimension to some steps in the funeral rites, but the group is defined strictly in terms of kinship. The only ones who gather for wailing are patrilineal relatives and their wives within the five grades of mourning and a more restricted circle of mourning relatives with other surnames, such as aunts, sisters, and daughters who had married out, plus their children. Friends, neighbors, and other relatives are expected to come to condole, but one at a time. The only time they would assemble together would be during the funeral procession. Yet gathering together a full complement of friends, relatives, and neighbors plays an important part in the rite of passage for the survivors and the community; each side begins the process of reestablishing social ties in the now-altered situation. The music that seems to have been a major feature of these feasts not only helped channel emotions, it helped create feelings of solidarity with others present. Loud sounds, especially drumming, are common at funerals cross-culturally and are often associated with ideas about ghosts.[29]

Another way to put this is that Confucian liturgies, bound as they were to

---

[28] See the various chapters in Johnson, ed., *Ritual Opera, Operatic Ritual*.

[29] On the anthropology of funeral rites, especially on notions of rites of passage, emotion, and music, see Huntington and Metcalf, *Celebrations of Death*.

Confucian moral philosophy, were better able to give form to some emotions than others. Fasting, wailing, and other austerities could give form to approved feelings of grief and guilt. So could attentive preparation of the body and its final resting place. Feelings given no legitimacy in Confucian doctrine—loathing for the decay of the corpse, fear of ghosts, relief that the burden of caring for a sick or unpleasant relative was over, ambivalent anticipation of taking on new authority, and the desire to reassert life, growth, and fertility in the face of death and decay—could find some expression through canonical forms, but noncanonical forms often seem to have served these purposes better.

POPULAR CUSTOMS AND CLASS DISTINCTIONS

The failure of Confucian scholars to achieve all of the reforms that they asserted were morally necessary could be attributed to their inability to understand their society adequately: they talked past the bulk of the population, telling them to give up meaningful ritual practices without offering satisfying substitutes.[30] Many authors of more accommodating versions of the *Family Rituals* did indeed charge the authors of more punctilious ones with this sort of short-sightedness. Confucian scholars were remarkably astute in recognizing that people created rituals, and that rituals served social, political, and psychological functions. But this insight encouraged tinkering. Scholars did not see how closely ritual forms were tied to the groups that performed them, nor that rituals work by a logic different than ordinary discourse. Thus they assumed that steps in rituals could be set aside without altering the social arrangements that they expressed, validated, or masked.

Confucians' limited understanding of ritual might not have mattered much if they had had a way to enforce adherence to specified standards. But as mentioned in the introduction, China had no ecclesiastical authorities to rule on the permissibility of various ritual practices or to discipline parishioners who performed weddings or funerals in deviant ways. The Chinese state publicized correct forms but set up no procedures for monitoring adherence to them. The state was able to suppress certain types of religious activities it labeled heterodox, but generally it did so by suppressing the groups that practiced them, an approach unsuited to family rituals. The scholarly community as an independent entity had even less capacity than the state. It did not even have the organizational basis to establish definitive understandings of what ritual rules meant in practice.

[30] Weller, for instance, argues that elite, ideologized interpretations of ghosts had relatively limited impact on the ways ordinary people thought or acted; ordinary people's context-specific modes of thinking were simply too far from the more abstract and moralized interpretations supplied by the intellectual elite for them to be influenced by them (*Unities and Diversities*, esp. pp. 125–43).

Confucian scholars may have viewed their inability to reform rituals practices as failure; from our perspective, however, it can be seen as adding an important element to the larger social and cultural system. As Sherry Ortner put it, "To say that society and history are products of human action is true, but only in a certain ironic sense. They are rarely the products the actors themselves set out to make."[31] In this case, scholars set out to reform customs but ended up by refashioning the dynamics of class distinctions. By identifying some very popular practices as heterodox or vulgar, scholars were creating an advantageous way to assert status. From the time of Confucius through the Ming and Ch'ing dynasties the identity of the educated class (*shih* or *shih-ta-fu*) was very much tied up with issues of ritual. As the bearers of culture, they should regulate their lives by the rules of the inherited culture, a principle element of which was ritual in all its meanings. It would be difficult to claim to be an educated man without full mastery of polite forms of address, ways to greet, condole, or congratulate others, or bodily ways to show deference and respect. They had little choice but to be attentive to the rituals associated with filial piety and reverence for ancestors.

From Sung times on, the absence of significant legal barriers to social mobility made ritual behavior one of the best ways to assert, fight over, and acknowledge social status in Chinese society. For families already well-established, with successful degree candidates or officials, adherence to a distinctly Confucian schedule of rituals validated their standing and helped make it a part of their family life, reducing the danger that the next generation would fail to carry on literati traditions. For those aspiring to acceptance into literati circles, imitation of literati ways was essential, and the more public sides of family rituals, perhaps especially weddings and funerals, provided excellent opportunities to do this. Yet the prestige of following Confucian ritualized behavior did not bring about uniform behavior, even among those with adequate means. Those with wealth wanted to display it through ritual performance, as discussed here with regard to Buddhist services. To demonstrate or claim superiority the educated could perform steps or procedures known to be rooted in the classics but not commonly done, such as wearing garments modeled on classical texts or practicing divination at moments no longer common or by methods no longer in general use. When canonical flourishes of these sorts gained widespread popularity (as spirit tablets did), they naturally lost their utility as special marks of cultivation and it became necessary to revive other canonical forms. Thus there was always a tension built into the efforts to accommodate popular customs and bring them into the domain of Confucian rituals. If the process went too far, it could become difficult for the educated to assert their merit through any means other than wealth, a situation hardly to their advantage. The Chinese class system and Confucian liturgies

---

[31] Ortner, "Theory in Anthropology since the Sixties," p. 157.

thus worked together to assure that there would always be considerable diversity in ritual practices.

Confucian doctrine was ambivalent on the propriety of creating status distinctions through the performance of family rituals. Within Confucian social ethics it was perfectly legitimate to assert that the *shih* should take the lead in matters of ritual. It was up to them to "civilize" the rest of the population by showing how rituals should be properly done, a point made in many a preface to a liturgy. The ultimate goal, they asserted or implied, was to achieve perfect harmony throughout the realm by getting everyone to regulate their lives according to ritual. Even though it was axiomatic in Confucianism that rituals express distinctions, for family rituals, at least since Sung times, these distinctions were confined to the kinship and political spheres. Family rituals should express distinctions of gender, descent priority, generation, and age. All Confucian thinkers agreed that the emperor's rituals should be distinct from those of all lower-ranking people, and most probably acknowledged the government's right to decree special forms for officials. But wealth and ancestry were not relevant. Everyone in the population, no matter how humble, had parents and ancestors; no Confucian scholar asserted that the poor or illiterate should follow different procedures for weddings, funerals, or ancestral rites than the rich or educated. By asserting that everyone should perform rites the same way, scholars freed themselves to perform them in rather distinct ways. In their own minds they were not expressing differences of class: they were demonstrating moral cultivation and commitment to the Confucian tradition.

CONCLUSIONS

In the Confucian tradition, uniformities in ritual practice were viewed as unquestionably desirable. The fundamental features of the rites were tied to enduring moral truths unaffected by social change. For people of all social stations to participate in the same overall structure was a way to integrate them into a common moral system, leading to social and political harmony. Change was inevitable, but slowing it down was better than speeding it up. People who altered their mourning garments several times during the mourning period according to the schedule in the classics were doing something of value, no matter how bookish their actions seemed. Efforts to adapt rites so that they could match current social arrangements or sentiments were justified by a desire to preserve the true core of the rites by whatever expedient would work, not by any notion that rites ought to change. To tell Confucian scholars that by writing and circulating liturgies they had preserved the core features of the rites would be to tell them that they had done their job well: They had fostered a Confucian society.

By contrast, from a modern Western point of view, it is easy to fall into looking on continuities as signs of ossification or stagnation. We criticize many of the rituals in our own society on the grounds that they are antiquated, based on social distinctions no longer relevant to us. Rituals are assumed to work best when there is a tight relationship between their symbolic content and the social groups that perform them. Yet continuities and uniformities themselves carry meanings. If rituals are judged according to what they do, then continuities and uniformities in ritual procedures can be seen as masking variability in actual social arrangements. Chinese family rituals, considered as a set of symbols, worked to deny change and variation. They were performed in similar ways in families otherwise quite different. Over time, the relationships of ancestors to property changed considerably. Aristocratic descent lines in the Chou had their identity tied to estates they could not alienate and that would pass to the eldest son. Peasant families in the early T'ang had very limited ability to transfer property to their descendants because of the government's policies of reallocating land every generation under the equal-field system. Peasant households in the most commercialized areas of Ming and Ch'ing times could freely divide, sell, or pawn their land, and at family division land had to be divided equally among all sons. The ancestral rituals people performed obscured these differences. They posited that all sons are obligated to their ancestors no matter what, in fact, they received from them. Changes in marriage practices also occurred over Chinese history, such as changes in the relative amounts of money spent on betrothal gifts and dowry and in the frequency and acceptability of uxorilocal marriage, divorce, and the remarriage of widows. Sung and later Confucian liturgies accommodated those changes not perceived as threatening to patrilineal or patriarchal principles. Thus, delivery of the dowry and post-wedding visits to the bride's family were added to Confucian liturgies. But Confucian liturgies never gave alternative forms for different types of marriages. There were no separate liturgies for uxorilocal marriages, men's remarriages, or marriages of widows or divorcées. Rather than provide ritual elaboration to these sorts of differences, Chinese family rituals masked them. All sorts of parent-child relations were presented in terms of an invariant model of filial obligation. All sorts of marriages were presented as minor variations on the ritually true form. Rituals need not reflect actual social circumstances: they can function most powerfully when they create images of a "true" order at considerable odds from the actual social order. Thus the continuities and uniformities in Chinese family rituals were a part of the ritual system, conveying as much meaning as any specific step.

Chapter Ten

CONCLUSIONS

CONFUCIANISM and Chinese society each evolved over time, influencing and being influenced by the other, in a context that also included a wide assortment of non-Confucian ideas and practices. Neither Confucianism nor Chinese society was the mirror image of the other. Nor was one the active agent, generating the other. The history of Confucianism cannot be adequately told until its connections with Chinese society are better understood. Similarly, a full history of Chinese society requires assessing the role played by ideas communicated through books. Here I have placed in social context one strand of Confucian writing as a step toward a fuller understanding of both Confucianism and Chinese society.

To uncover connections between Confucianism and Chinese society I have examined lower-order ideas. Ritual, filial piety, the authority of the sages and the classics, and the problems of governing were all central concerns of Confucianism. These concerns were implicit in the Confucian discourse on family rituals; their presence is evident in even the simplest liturgical manual. The history of the Confucian discourse on family rituals could, thus, be narrated strictly in terms of the working out of key Confucian concepts. The views of major writers like Ssu-ma Kuang, Ch'eng I, Chu Hsi, Lü K'un, and Mao Ch'i-ling on specific items concerning family rituals were generally congruent with their writings on other topics. Moreover, the opinions and approaches of more minor writers, like the authors of brief versions of the *Family Rituals*, often correspond to broad intellectual trends. In this book, however, I have tried to avoid assuming that an author's ideas about how to perform rituals flowed from his more general views on morality, filial piety, or metaphysics. His lower-order ideas on what food to offer to ancestors, what materials to use in constructing a coffin or tomb, or when and how to make offerings at graves would have been powerfully influenced by personal experience. Through books that detailed these lower-order ideas, writers were both representing ritual activity as they knew it and fostering its reproduction by those who read their books. Moreover, lower-order ideas could shape higher-order ones. Thinking about the details of ritual provided a way to think about behavior and morality in general. Perhaps it was thinking about the status limitations in the classics that led Ch'eng I to question the truth value of books; perhaps it was thinking about bodies and graves that led Chu Hsi to some of his more general ideas on cosmology; perhaps it was thinking about wailing at funerals that led

Lü K'un to speculate on human nature and emotions. Thus, rather than present the Confucian discourse on family rituals simply as a set of ideas, in this book I have offered a social history of it, a history that emphasizes the social and cultural dimensions of the acts of writing, circulating, and consulting texts. Let me briefly review what has been learned of each of these processes before considering some of the larger implications of this story for an understanding of Chinese society.

Authorship

To analyze why authors wrote the books they did, I have looked at the interplay between what they drew from other books and what they drew from the society around them. No author examined every principle underlying the rituals he prescribed. Some principles, such as patrilineality and patriarchy, were so diffused through their society and expressed in so many forms, including the rituals the authors had participated in since childhood, that they never became problematical. When knowledge acquired from books and knowledge acquired from personal experience clashed, reflective men analyzed the discrepancies. Where the two largely agreed, there was nothing much to ponder. Thus the most basic principles of social organization current in an author's society generally came to find expression in his writings nearly automatically.

From the books they read and Confucian scholarly culture, writers came to take for granted several basic Confucian premises concerning ritual. Because weddings, funerals, and ancestral rites were *li*, there was no room for doubt that they should be performed in formalized, traditionally specified ways. Adherence to canonically derived form was good for the participants' moral development and at the same time improved the harmony and order of society. But *li* were man-made and therefore alterable. From the time of Hsün Tzu at least, scholars were aware that rituals were not god-given but had been created by human beings; they also realized that rituals carried meanings and wanted them to carry ethically desirable meanings. This intellectual framework provided possibilities for invention but at a cost. Scholars often proposed changes that did not make sense in ritual terms. They did not see that rituals have their own autonomy, that if they are to compel feelings and understandings on the part of participants, only actions that make sense within the logic of the ritual can be incorporated into the ritual structure. Blind to this, scholars objected to relatively harmless practices like introducing brides on the first day of the wedding. Moreover, they often failed to notice the close connection between noncanonical customs, like marriage letters specifying the size of dowries, and such features of the family and kinship system as the tensions generated by property transfers.

The books that scholars read stimulated them to write new books. Chu Hsi and his friends and disciples discussed discrepancies between the classics, government ritual codes, and the writings of Ch'eng I, Chang Tsai, and Ssu-ma Kuang. Conflicting evidence worried them, even on small points such as exactly when to install an ancestral tablet in the altar after burial, for they were trying to use these men's writings to decide what to do themselves. Struggling with these issues was a major reason Lü Tsu-ch'ien, Chu Hsi, and Chang Shih all compiled their own ritual guides. In a similar way, it was after he tried to use Chu Hsi's *Family Rituals* as a liturgical guide for funeral rituals for himself and his neighbors that Feng Shan wrote a revised version of the text.

Logical contradictions in earlier books were not, of course, the primary reason authors decided to write new ones. Authors' social environments and personal experiences shaped what they found unsatisfactory in earlier books. In Chapter Three I argued, for instance, that Northern Sung scholars took an interest in rethinking the rules for ancestral rites because the old government rules did not work to their benefit and they did not want to perform ancestral rites the ways commoners did, for ancestral rites were powerful ways to celebrate ancestry and assert family standing. I also suggested that personal experiences, like the scattering of Ch'eng I's family and the joint organization of Ssu-ma Kuang's family, shaped individual authors' opinions concerning which customs were harmless and which revivals were feasible.

Encounters with social reality could lead to innovative ideas; they could also lead to absorption and reinterpretation of ideas of nonelite or at least noncanonical origins. In the Northern Sung, ways were found to discover filial piety motivating much of what occurred in ancestral rites. Thus rites at New Year, at graves, and on death-day anniversaries came to be included in Confucian liturgies. In the Ming scholars found equally sound motives underlying burning mock money, introducing brides on the first day of the wedding, and eliminating distinctions between the wives of elder and younger sons. Philosophical bases for such accommodations also came to be articulated. Chang Tsai and Ch'eng I took strong stands against the absolute authority of the wording of the classics. Chu Hsi and Wang Yang-ming argued that it was entirely appropriate to simplify rites to encourage wider practice.

CERTIFICATION AND CIRCULATION

After texts were written, they needed to circulate to have much influence on how people performed rituals or how later authors wrote new texts. Throughout Chinese history the government and the community of Confucian scholars both played major roles in promoting the circulation of key texts. The Han and later the T'ang governments were actively involved in establishing the *I-li* and *Li-chi* as canonical texts and authorizing certain readings of them as correct, working in conjunction with Confucian scholars whom they patronized. Certification of the classics probably was one reason it became so common for scholars to look to texts to decide the proper or authentic way to perform rituals. Debates over how rituals should be performed were generally couched in terms of how one should interpret ambiguous or apparently contradictory passages in the classics. Despite occasional challenges to the importance of books, these assumptions remained strong. The reason some late Ming and early Ch'ing writers felt deceived when they discovered that Chu Hsi's *Family Rituals* was not simply a digest of the classics is that they had such high expectations for the truth value of authorized texts.

Also with the help of scholars, successive dynasties issued ritual codes; in government circles these codes were granted even more authority than the classics because they were more finely honed and because the distinctions encoded in them represented the ones the government wanted expressed. As seen in Chapters Three and Four, the T'ang government's *K'ai-yüan li* still carried considerable influence among scholar-statesmen of the Northern Sung, such as Ssu-ma Kuang. Chu Hsi recognized the authority of the early twelfth-century *Cheng-ho wu-li hsin-i*. He explained to Wang Ying-ch'en that he had a variety of ideas about how the family shrine system should best be actualized, but if one were actually going to build a family shrine, then the *Cheng-ho wu-li hsin-i* was the authoritative text. He also wanted the government to issue a guide designed for common people on the basis of this imperial manual.

During the late Sung and Yüan, as discussed in Chapter Six, followers of Chu Hsi played key roles in getting the *Family Rituals* published and circulated. They also began the process of interpreting the text; they wrote commentaries to it that gave it particular readings and they discussed with each other how literally to adhere to its specifications and how to recognize its core ideas. From early Ming times on the imperial government joined the Confucian community in promoting this book, not only by helping circulate it but also by incorporating much of its language and specifications into its own ritual codes. Scholars went along with these government efforts; most Ming authors of revised versions of the *Family Rituals* incorporated into their texts the government's rules, such as the Ming government's schedule of mourning grades. The Ming government contributed to the elastic interpretation of the *Family Rituals* by pronouncing as orthodox both Chu Hsi's *Family Rituals* and its own code, even though the two differed in such particulars as the day to introduce a bride to her husband's ancestors. It thus added its backing to the notion that adherence to details need not be fussy.

Within the Confucian community, there was always some ambivalence about letting the government validate texts. Chang Tsai and Ch'eng I largely ignored the *K'ai-yüan li* and even the politically sponsored commentaries to the classics. They tried to rethink key issues concerning family rituals on the basis of their own understandings of the main ideas of the classics, one might even say their own understandings of man's place in the cosmos. And even though their views would tend to undercut the importance of books, their disciples and later followers, such as Chu Hsi, saw to the circulation and promotion of their writings, acting on their own without government assistance. Through the Ming and Ch'ing periods, scholars working independently of the government also subtly undercut the authority of both government manuals and the various versions of the *Family Rituals* by focusing on the details in the ritual classics. If it was necessary to go back to the classics to decide the authenticity of each step, other sorts of guides were no more than convenient summaries of particular men's interpretations: they had no ultimate truth value.

The third party to the process of certifying and circulating liturgies for family rituals was made up of book buyers and the booksellers willing to give them what they wanted. Judging by the sorts of books that came to circulate, buyers wanted books that were easy to consult, with diagrams, illustrations, and subheadings. Liturgies that purported to be updated versions of Chu Hsi's *Family Rituals* dominated the market, undoubtedly because this text was so famous. Even though family rituals were done at home, in distinctly local contexts, people did not want local handbooks, explicitly presented as guides to the performance of rituals as done in Fukien or Shantung; rather they wanted ones that presented the rituals in them as correct for everyone. At the same time, people wanted liturgies that would guide them through the steps of the rituals they wanted to perform; they did not want liturgies that would constrain them to perform rituals in unfamiliar ways. To put this another way, they wanted to be told that rituals close to what was commonly done by those around them were orthodox, universally valid ones.

Authorship in China worked much like authorship elsewhere: author's ideas were shaped by all of their experiences. The processes through which books came to be recognized as authoritative, however, seem rather distinctive. It combined elements of tight control with elements of free competition. In the Ming authors were hesitant to defy imperial authority or challenge the orthodoxy of the *Family Rituals*. Yet they could rewrite it, and these rewritten versions competed rather freely for audiences. Until the seventeenth century this competition worked overwhelmingly through positive rhetorical means. New books did not dwell on the failings of the other books available. Authors rewrote what they did not like and asserted that they had preserved the essential features of earlier books and presented them more effectively. Asserting identity was preferred to asserting difference.

INFLUENCE ON RITUAL PERFORMANCE

In the period before printing, covered in only cursory fashion in this book, copies of the key texts on family rites must have been relatively scarce. Not all educated men, not even all officials, would have had personal copies of the *I-li* and *Li-chi*; fewer still would have had copies of the various government ritual codes. Men with classical educations were familiar with the content of the ritual classics, but they might not be in a position to consult the wording of the text when it was time to perform a rite. The influence of authorized texts, then, must have been in the main indirect. Men educated in the Confucian tradition accepted that there were authoritative texts and tried to conform to the specifications in them. Others imitated them so that the influence of texts on common people's rituals was mediated by example, through a trickle-down effect.

From Han times on, the influence of the *I-li* and *Li-chi* on ritual behavior was limited by the inevitable tendency for old forms to lose meaning as ideas changed. Newer ideas about heirship, privilege, death, and emotions all weakened the fit between the rituals prescribed in old texts and the forms of ritual behavior that could serve to handle personal or family crises. Over time a great many practices of noncanonical origin came to seem more compelling than canonical ones. Some of these noncanonical forms were gradually absorbed into the Confucian discourses (ancestral rites on popular festivals, for instance), some coexisted with the Confucian discourse in varying degrees of tension (geomancy, for instance), and some were resolutely rejected by it (Buddhist services, for example). In no period of Chinese history did the Confucian discourse on family rituals have complete cultural hegemony.

As printing brought about a revolution in the supply of books, more and more people had access to texts as physical objects that could be consulted when needed. It became more common for scholars to have copies of the classics in their libraries as well as copies of other relevant books, such as Ssu-ma Kuang's *Shu-i*, Ch'eng I's writings, and Chu Hsi's *Family Rituals*. As simplified versions of the *Family Rituals* came to be written in large numbers, access to Confucian liturgies naturally increased. Even those with only a few years' schooling could read these books, since they never used highly allusive language. By Ch'ing times illiterate people who wished to know how to perform a ritual properly could usually find someone with a copy of one of these books to consult.

Whether people's contact with Confucian liturgies was direct, mediated by others' reports of them, or mediated even more indirectly by the example of other people's performances, they would learn a variety of different things from these liturgies. In Chapter Nine I stressed the significance of the unexamined layer of these books: the features of the rites that were never brought into contention, that were treated simply as what one does. Confucian liturgies did not influence the performance of family rituals solely at this deeper level, for quite a few of the innovations or adjustments to ancestral rites proposed in the Sung came to be widely followed. Ancestral halls, ancestral tablets, and sacrificing to four generations of ancestors all came to be widely practiced after they were advocated in books.

Confucian liturgies also contributed to the reproduction of certain kinds of variation in family rituals. Their omissions left room for manipulation and the expression of conflicts. Contradictions in the texts themselves fostered deviation from what they said on the surface. And labeling some otherwise very attractive practices as heterodox or vulgar fostered class differences, for only those whose status depended on a reputation for refinement would be motivated to give up otherwise familiar and satisfying practices.

TEXTS IN THE FORMATION OF CHINESE CULTURE

Texts on family rituals shared many characteristics with other sorts of texts. Like scriptures, legal codes, and histories, liturgies represented complex social realities by eliminating most of what goes on. Of all the activity that occurs simultaneously in a ritual, of all of the sights, sounds, and smells, a few elements were identified as meaningful and described in a sequential fashion. Like other sorts of texts, liturgies decontextualized and generalized. Authors found themselves wanting to specify not what is to be done by rich families, large families, happy families, or their own family, but by all or very broad categories of families.

Like the popular scriptures of Buddhism, Taoism, and popular religion, Confucian liturgies circulated widely. The people who owned these various texts did not, however, treat them alike. There is no sign that anyone considered Confucian liturgies sacred objects, to be reverently chanted or placed on an altar. There was nothing in them that had to be repeated word for word in order to be efficacious. The only other Confucian texts that circulated in comparable numbers were moral tracts concerned with developing awareness that certain behaviors are right or wrong. Such tracts invited disagreement by continually pointing out that the vast majority of people did not do as they should, as they were selfish, cruel, thoughtless, and indulgent. Liturgical texts, by contrast, are how-to handbooks. Most versions of the *Family Rituals* concentrated on specifying exactly what one should do at each step in a rite, not the moral sentiments that should motivate the acts. Their language is concrete and rarely polemical. In no sense did specifying that both wine and tea be offered to ancestors imply that there were people who used only one. The rhetorical structure of liturgical texts probably served to convey basic moral premises more effectively than tracts could.

Ritual texts, like other sorts of texts in China and elsewhere, fostered continuities over time and space. Texts can survive for centuries, much of their meaning retained. They can be read by people thousands of miles apart. Thus texts are a naturally conservative force; consulting them before performing a ritual leads people to retain wordings or procedures that might well have been forgotten without texts. What was specified in texts, thus, was always in danger of falling out of sync with what people felt; texts were not rewritten as quickly as new ideas and institutional arrangements were introduced. This potential was mitigated, in the Chinese case, by failure of authorities to rule on what sorts of behavior violated the ban on music at weddings and feasting at funerals. The government did try to clear up ambiguities in the mourning grades, but did so because these rules affected punishments for criminal offenses, not because the government monitored mourning behavior. The Confucian scholarly community as a whole debated how literally to interpret inconvenient rules, but never achieved consensus on all issues in contention. Once printing made it possible for many liturgical books to circulate simultaneously, the marketplace came to play a major role in determining the reading of old rules. By writing a commentary to an established text or a revised version of it, one could give it a new reading. The conservative bias of respect for books was thus in China balanced by a willingness to rewrite old books and accept the new versions as equivalent.

CONFUCIAN TEXTS AND CHINESE SOCIETY

If we grant that Confucian texts had much to do with both the uniformities and the diversities in the ways Chinese have performed family rituals, what does that add to our understanding of Chinese society? If rituals shape how people interpret themselves and those around them, in what ways did the Confucian discourse on family rituals shape Chinese social life? The ways this discourse was used to express and create class distinctions were discussed in the last chapter. In even more explicit ways, Confucian liturgical texts fostered the reproduction of other social distinctions, most obviously ones of gender. All of the rites described in Confucian liturgies show ways male and female are parallel and yet male is superior to female. There were initiation ceremonies for both boys and girls, but the ceremony for girls was clearly a lesser version of the ones for boys. A girl was pinned by her mother and another female relative, whereas a boy was capped by the descent-line heir and a respected friend of the family. In weddings, the bride and groom are compared to the two halves of a broken wine cup, yet it is the bride who is brought to the groom's house and introduced to his ancestors. During funerals, gender distinctions were repeatedly acted out. When a man died he had two main mourners, his wife and his eldest son. Thus the subordination of a wife is equated with the subordination of a child. The wife and son performed many of the same acts, but the son took the lead and only he could meet friends of his father who came to condole. When a woman died, her son and his wife would play these roles; her husband would be something of an anomalous bystander, like a parent who survived a child. Funerals also visibly manifested the patrilineal bias in kinship reckoning. Brothers' children and sons' children played more major roles in the funeral than sisters' children and daughters' children. Brothers were thus more crucial than sisters and sons than daughters.

Of all the rites, ancestral rites were the most balanced with regard to participation. Just as many women and girls would participate as men and boys; each would occupy half of the room. Toward the front would be both a presiding man and a presiding woman. On the altar tables would be tablets for both male and female ancestors. But this balance was still hierarchical. The men and the ancestors were on the more honored side. The presiding man took the leading role, doing many more of the ritual acts than the presiding woman. And ancestors were always addressed before ancestresses.

Male-female differentiation in family rituals simultaneously reflected ordinary life, validated it, and made it seem part of the nature of things. Most Confucian scholars recognized that these rituals represented male and female hierarchy and complementarity and they were generally careful when modifying a rite to make sure not to disturb this symbolism. Yet the relatively obvious nature of the gender symbolism in these rituals need not have undermined its power.

Confucian texts and the rituals based on them did not simply convey social distinctions. At another level, they overcame them by fostering commonalities in the ways people performed rituals. In early modern Europe, according to Peter Burke, the efforts of clerical elites to reform and reinterpret popular culture had the unintended consequence of widening the split between the cultures of the educated and uneducated. "The reforms affected the educated minority more quickly and more thoroughly than they affected other people and so cut the minority off more and more sharply from popular traditions."[1] In my reading of the evidence, this did not happen in China. From the eleventh century on, Neo-Confucian scholars called for the reform of popular customs, and their message reached the educated in more potent form than the uneducated. At times such men added canonical flourishes to their ritual performances to assert their cultural superiority. Yet over time class differences in the performance of family rituals seem to have narrowed rather than widened.

I see three main reasons class differences did not widen in China. One was that ordinary people came to adopt or imitate many facets of the orthodox models. Another was that the educated elite as a whole was never able to rid their behavior of all non-Confucian customs, for non-Confucian customs were too attractive. The third reason, and perhaps the most important in comparative terms, was the willingness of Confucian scholars to legitimate the practices common among ordinary people, as long as the practices were not Buddhist or non-Chinese in origin. The Confucian approach to popular ritual practices since the eleventh century encompassed two opposed tendencies— to reject heterodoxy on the one hand and to discover essentially good impulses underlying as many practices as possible on the other. Efforts of men like Chu Hsi to maintain a balance between these two tendencies prevented outright

---

[1] Peter Burke, *Popular Culture in Early Modern Europe*, p. 243. His comments are not specifically directed to popular rituals, but to popular culture in general, including drama and festivals.

rejection of everything vulgar. Ch'ien Mu recently wrote that Chinese civilization, comparatively speaking, valued "similarity and convergence rather than difference and divergence."[2] Identifying common ground was for most scholars more intellectually satisfying than identifying contradictions. The tendency to bring more and more of what people did into the realm labeled Confucian countered pressures toward social cleavages between the educated and uneducated by emphasizing commonalities across class lines rather than differences.

Accommodation can, of course, be viewed as capitulation. Silently omitting the canonical ban on music at weddings was letting custom take priority over the text of the classics. Eliminating prayers for each pair of ancestors was currying favor with the busy or lazy. Yet tactically accommodation seems to have worked. Until the seventeenth century, Confucian discourse and ritual practice evolved in parallel: Confucian writers, while always drawing the line at some practices, accepted enough of what was going on for their books to retain plausibility. Confucian rituals were prevented from becoming so ossified that their performance only served to display social distinctions.

A narrowing of class distinctions in ritual performance was a significant factor in creating cultural cohesion within the enormous expanse of China. It allowed people who spoke mutually unintelligible dialects and knew very little of each other's daily work lives to see each other as Han Chinese. Throughout Chinese history the performance of family rituals was taken as a marker of ethnic identity. Han Chinese wore mourning garments of undyed cloth; they made offerings to patrilineal ancestors; they sealed betrothals by the parents' exchanging gifts; they did not marry their brothers' widows. Non-Han people inside and outside of China's political borders were known to follow divergent customs. If ordinary peasants were to inhabit a cultural sphere as distant as that of barbarians, Confucian scholars' authority would be threatened. How much more comforting to see the poor using what resources they had to perform a simplified version of rituals that could be labeled Confucian. Every time a family hired a sedan chair for a wedding or paraded to the grave in mourning garments, it was acting out allegiance to both Han Chinese identity and the Confucian moral order.

[2] Ch'ien Mu, "A Historical Perspective on Chu Hsi's Learning," p. 32.

A LIST OF REVISED VERSIONS OF THE
FAMILY RITUALS

THE FOLLOWING list is limited to books whose titles contain the words *chia-li* [family rituals]. Many books with other sorts of titles were also revisions of Chu Hsi's *Family Rituals*, but cannot be identified as such merely from their titles. Books that begin *Ssu-li* [Four rituals] were often guides to family rituals based closely or loosely on the *Family Rituals*. For instance, the *Ssu-k'u ch'üan-shu tsung-mu* (25:208–9) decribes four such books, two of Ming and two of Ch'ing dates. The eight-*chüan Ming ssu-li chi-shuo*, written in 1612, "was largely modeled on Master Chu's *Family Rituals*, with cross-references to the *Ming hui-tien*." A few such books are discussed in Chapters Six, Seven, and Eight.

Under the date column, the date the book was first published is given if known, otherwise the author's dates are given.

The two symbols * and ** stand for "extant and seen" and "reportedly extant but not seen," respectively.

Title	chüan	Author	Date	Source
A. Yüan (1279–1368)				
1. *Wen-kung chia-li k'ao-i* 文公家禮考異	2	Wu Hsia-chü 吳霞舉	1257–1306	19
B. Early Ming (1368–1450)				
2. *Chia-li chü-yao* 家禮舉要	4	Li Chen 黎貞	fl. 1368–98	7, 24
3. *Chia-li i-lan* 家禮易覽		Wang Yüan 王源	c.s. 1404	3, 7
4. *Chia-li cho-chung* 家禮酌中		Li Lun 李倫	fl. 1403–24	43
*5. *Chia-li chi-shuo* 家禮集說	12 or more	Feng Shan 馮善	fl. 1403–24	1, 7, 9, 14, 25, 29, 32, 37, 42
*6. *Chia-li hui-t'ung* 家禮會通	10	T'ang To 湯鐸	1450	7, 9, 14, 27
7. *Chia-li ts'ung-i* 家禮從宜		Feng Ch'ing 豐慶	c.s. 1439	7

Title	chüan	Author	Date	Source
C. Mid-Ming (1451–1550)				
8. *Chia-li p'ang-fu* 家禮旁附		Fang Hsieh 方瀣	c.s. 1453	7
*9. *Chia-li i-chieh* 家禮儀節	8	Ch'iu Chün 丘濬	1474	many
10. *Chia-li yao-lu* 家禮要錄		Hsieh Hsing 謝省	1420–93	22
11. *Chia-li ts'ung-i* 家禮從宜	4	Yang Tzu-ch'i 楊子器	1458–1513	7
12. *Chia-li k'ao-i* 家禮攷異		Yü Pen 余本	1482–1529	7
13. *Chia-li pien-su* 家禮砭俗		Wang T'i 汪禔	1490–1530	7
*14. *Wen-kung chia-li i-chieh* 文公家禮儀節	8	Yang Shen 楊慎	1530	6, 20, 28, 29, 32, 38
*15. *Chia-li chieh-yao* 家禮節要		Chu T'ing-li 朱廷立	1536	14, 17
16. *Chia-li chi-yao* 家禮輯要		Fu K'uang 符匡	fl. 1506–21	40
17. *Chia-li chu-pu* 家禮註補		Lo Chao-p'eng 羅兆鵬	*chü-jen* 1549	2, 24
*18. *Chia-li k'ao-ting* 家禮考訂	4	Fang Yüan-huan 方元煥	fl. 1522–66	7
D. Late Ming (1551–1644)				
*19. *Wen-kung chia-li hui-ch'eng* 文公家禮會成	8	Wei T'ang 魏堂	1557	14, 37
*20. *Chia-li chai-yao* 家禮摘要	5	Ko Yin-sheng 葛引生	1561	10, 15
21. *Chia-li t'u* 家禮圖		Tsou Meng-lung 鄒夢龍	16th cent.	41
*22. *Chia-li ch'üan-pu* 家禮銓補	10	Teng Yüan-hsi 鄧元錫	1529–93	7, 9, 14
23. *Chia-li chi* 家禮輯		Wang Jen-chung 王任重	c.s. 1568	13
*24. *Chia-li yao-chieh* 家禮要節	1	Wang Shu-kao 王叔杲	1571	14, 30
*25. *Chia-li t'ung-hsing* 家禮通行	8	Lo Wan-hua 羅萬化	1573	29
**26. *Chia-li chi-yao* 家禮集要		Ling-hu Tsung 令狐鏓	1516–82	14

Title	chüan	Author	Date	Source
*27. *Chia-li i-chien pien* 家禮易簡編	1	Chu T'ien-ch'iu 朱天球	1593	7, 14, 37
*28. *Chia-li cheng-heng* 家禮正衡	8	P'eng Pin 彭濱	1599	7, 14, 29, 36
29. *Chia-li chien-yao* 家禮簡要	1	Li T'ing-chi 李廷機	c.s. 1583	7, 13
30. *Chia-li chieh-yung* 家禮節用		Wang T'ing-hsiu 王廷繡	1573–1619	40
31. *Shih-min pien-yung chia-li chien-i* 士民便用家禮簡儀			1607	31
*32. *Tsun-chih chia-li* 遵制家禮	4	Feng Fu-ching 馮復京	1573–1622	14, 30
*33. *Weng T'ai-shih pu-hsüan Wen-kung chia-li* 翁太史補選文公家禮	8	Weng Cheng-ch'un 翁正春	1553–1627	14, 36, 37
34. *Chia-li i-chien* 家禮易簡		Hsiao Ssu-li 蕭嗣立	*chü-jen* 1618	24
*35. *Chia-li i-chieh* 家禮儀節	8	Ch'en Jen-hsi 陳仁錫	c.s. 1622	29
36. *Chia-li pu-chien* 家禮補牋		Liang Ch'ao-chung 梁朝鐘	c.s. 1643	24
**37. *Chia-li wei-feng* 家禮維風	8	Sang Kung-yang 桑拱陽	ca. 1628–44	14

E. Ming (dates unknown)

Title	chüan	Author	Date	Source
38. *Ssu-min pien-yung chia-li i-chien* 四民便用家禮易簡		Fukien government		4
*39. *Chia-li huo-wen hsü-chih* 家禮或問須知	1	Cheng Pi-cho 鄭必著		29
40. *Chia-li chieh-wen* 家禮節文		Chang Mao 張茂		13
41. *Chia-li i-chieh* 家禮儀節	1	Cheng Yü-ming 鄭宇明		13
42. *Wei-su chia-li* 維俗家禮		Liu Meng-hsi 劉夢錫		2
*43. *Chia-li cheng-heng* 家禮正衡		Chou Ying-ch'i 周應期		29, 43
44. *Chia-li k'ao* 家禮考		Liu Min 劉閔		5

Title	chüan	Author	Date	Source
45. *Chia-li tsuan-yen* 家禮纂言	2	Tu Ju-shu 杜汝恕		43
46. *Chia-li chü-yao* 家禮舉要		Chang Shih-chun 張世準		40
47. *Chia-li i-hsing* 家禮易行		Huang Ch'in 黃芹		7
48. *Chia-li tsuan-yao* 家禮纂要		Hsü Hung-kang 許宏綱		8
49. *Chia-li shih-chien* 家禮是簡		Lu Ch'iao 陸僑		7

F. Ch'ing

Title	chüan	Author	Date	Source
50. *Chiao-ting Wen-kung chia-li* 校定文公家禮	4	Ying Hui-ch'ien 應撝謙	1615–83	11
*51. *Chia-li cho* 家禮酌	1	Sun Ch'i-feng 孫奇逢	1671	16
*52. *Chia-li ching-tien ts'an-t'ung* 家禮經典參同		Cheng Yüan-ch'ing 鄭元慶	b. 1660	14, 37
*53. *Chia-li pien-ting* 家禮辨定	10	Wang Fu-li 王復禮	1707	26, 30, 38
54. *Chia-li i-chieh chi-yao* 家禮儀節輯要	8	Li Shih-ta 李士達	1721	5, 32, 39
*55. *Chia-li shih-i* 家禮拾遺	5	Li Wen-chao 李文炤	1672–1735	12, 13, 15
**56. *Chu Tzu chia-li chi-yao* 朱子家禮輯要	1	Ts'ai Shih-yüan 蔡世遠	1681–1731	23
*57. *Chia-li hui-t'ung* 家禮會通	4	Chang Ju-ch'eng 張汝誠	1734	34, 1985 rprt.
*58. *Chia-li ta-ch'eng* 家禮大成	8	Lü Tzu-chen 呂子振	1735	1975 rprt.
*59. *Chia-li t'ieh-shih chi-ch'eng* 家禮帖式集成	4	Ch'en Ming-sheng 陳鳴盛	1750	1
*60. *Chia-li t'ieh-shih chi-ch'eng* 家禮帖式集成		Ch'en Ch'in-sheng 陳琴生	1770	18
*61. *Chia-li chi-i* 家禮集議	1	Wu Hsien-shen 武先慎	1793	17
62. *Chia-li tsuan-yao* 家禮纂要		Ch'eng Tzu-yüan 程梓園		21
63. *Ts'ung-i chia-li* 從宜家禮		Huang I-chung 黃宜中		35

Title	chüan	Author	Date	Source
64. *Chia-li i-chih* 家禮易知		Lu T'ing 盧挺		24
65. *Tseng-pu chia-li pien-ting* 增補家禮辨定	10	Ch'en Lan-chih 陳蘭芝		24
*66. *Chia-li ch'üan-chi* 家禮全集	6	Liang Chieh 梁傑	1895	17

Sources:

1. Academia Sinica Library, Taipei.
2. *Chao-ch'ing fu-chih* 21:1b.
3. *Chia-li hui-t'ung* preface.
4. *Chia-li huo-wen hsü-chih* 39b.
5. *Chiang-ning fu-chih* 54:32.
6. *Chiang-su sheng-li kuo-hsüeh t'u-shu kuan t'u-shu tsung-mu* 4:52–53.
7. *Ch'ien-ch'ing t'ang shu-mu* 2:24a–b.
8. *Chin-hua ching-chi chih* 3:17a.
9. Chinese Academy of Social Sciences Library, Peking.
10. Ch'ing-hua University Library, Peking.
11. *Ch'ing-ju hsüeh-an.*
12. *Ch'ing shih i-wen chih (Ch'ung-hsiu)*, p. 29.
13. *Ch'üan-chou fu-chih* 74:16b–48b.
14. *Chung-kuo ku-chi shan-pen shu-mu.*
15. *Chung-kuo ts'ung-shu tsung-lu*, pp. 460–61.
16. Columbia University East Asian Library.
17. Harvard-Yenching Library.
18. Hayes, "Specialists and Written Materials in the Village World," p. 81.
19. *Hsin-an ming-tsu chih* 2:8b.
20. *Hsü wen-hsien t'ung-k'ao* 159:4135B.
21. *Huang-ch'ao ching-shih wen-pien* 54:14a–b.
22. *I-feng wen-chi* 3:25b–26b.
23. Kao and Ch'en, *Fu-chien Chu Tzu hsüeh*, p. 405.
24. *Kuang-chou fu-chih* 90:10a–b.
25. *Kuo-li chung-yang t'u-shu kuan shan-pen shu-mu* 1:24.
26. *Kyoto daigaku bungakubu Kanseki bunrui mokuroku*, p. 59.
27. *Kyoto daigaku jimbun kagaku kenkyūjo Kanseki mokuroku*, p. 259.
28. *Mei-kuo kuo-hui t'u-shu kuan ts'ang Chung-kuo shan-pen shu-mu*, pp. 33–34.
29. Naikaku bunko Library, Tokyo.
30. Nanking Library.
31. Niida Noboru, *Chūgoku hōseishi kenkyū: Dorei nōdō hō, kazoku sonraku hō*, p. 438.
32. *Pa-ch'ien chüan lou shu-mu* 2:19a.
33. *Pei-ching t'u-shu kuan shan-pen shu-mu* 1:20a–b.
34. Princeton University Gest Oriental Collection.
35. *Sang-fu tsa-shuo* 5a–6b.
36. *Seikado bunko Kanseki bunrui mokuroku*, p. 87.
37. Shanghai Library.
38. *Ssu-k'u ch'üan-shu tsung-mu*, 25:207–9.
39. *Sung-chiang fu hsü-chih* 37:2a.
40. *T'ai-chou ching-chi chih* 3:11b–12a.
41. *Te-an fu-chih* 19:3b.
42. University of California, Berkeley, East Asian Library.
43. *Wen-chou ching-chi chih* 4:20b–21a.

GLOSSARY

Chang Ao　張敖　(9th cent.)

Chang Chia-ling　張嘉玲　(17th cent.)

Chang Chün　張浚　(1097–1164)

Chang Fang-p'ing　張方平　(1007–1091)

Chang Shih　張栻　(1133–1180)

Chang Te-hsiang　章得象　(978–1048)

Chang Tsai　張載　(1020–1077)

Chang Tuan-i　張端義　(1179–1250)

Chao Chü-hsin (Chi-ming)　趙居信　(季明)　(14th cent.)

chao-mu　昭穆

Chao Shih-hsia　趙師夏　(c.s. 1190)

Chao Shih-shu　趙師恕　(ca. 1200)

Chao Tzu　趙咨　(fl. 1505)

che-chung　折中　or　折衷

Ch'e Kai　車垓　(d. 1276)

Ch'en Ch'üeh　陳確　(1604–1677)

Ch'en Ch'un　陳淳　(1159–1223)

Ch'en Liang　陳亮　(1143–1194)

Chen Te-hsiu　真德秀　(1178–1235)

cheng　正

Cheng Chung　鄭眾　(d. 114)

Cheng-ho wu-li hsin-i　政和五禮新儀

Cheng Hsüan　鄭玄　(127–200)

Cheng Pi-cho　鄭必著　(ca. 1600)

Cheng Po-hsiung　鄭伯熊　(c.s. 1145)

Cheng Yü-ch'ing　鄭餘慶　(748–820)

Cheng Yüan-ch'ing　鄭元慶　(b. 1660)

Cheng Yung　鄭泳　(14th cent.)

Ch'eng Fan　程璠　(1019–1075)

Ch'eng Hao　程顥　(1032–1085)

Ch'eng I　程頤　(1033–1107)

Ch'eng Tuan-i　程端懿　(Sung)

Ch'eng Yü　程羽　(913–984)

chi　祭

Chi K'ang　嵇康　(223–262)

chi-t'ang　祭堂

chia　家

Chia I　賈誼　(195–165 B.C.)

Chia Kung-yen　賈公彥　(fl. 650s)

Chia-li chi-shuo　家禮集說

Chia-li chi-yao　家禮輯要

Chia-li chieh-yao　家禮節要

Chia-li ching-tien ts'an-t'ung　家禮經典參同

Chia-li cho　家禮酌

Chia-li cho-chung　家禮酌中

Chia-li ch'üan-pu　家禮銓補

Chia-li hui-t'ung　家禮會通

Chia-li huo-wen hsü-chih　家禮或問須知

Chia-li i-chieh　家禮儀節

Chia-li i-chien pien　家禮易簡編

Chia-li pien-ting　家禮辨定

Chia-li yao-chieh　家禮要節

chia-miao　家廟

Chiang Ko　江革　(1st cent.)

Chiang Kuo-tso　蔣國祚

chien (to offer)　薦

chien (simplified)　簡

Ch'in Hui-t'ien　秦蕙田　(1702–1764)

ch'ing　卿

ch'ing-ta-fu　卿大夫

Ch'iu Chün　丘濬　(1421–1495)

Chou Fu　周復　(13th cent.)

Chou-li　周禮

chu　主

Chu Hsi　朱熹　(1130–1200)

Chu Kuang-t'ing　朱光庭　(1037–1094)

Chu Pien　朱弁　(d. 1144)

Chu Sen　朱森　(11th cent.)

Chu Shu　朱塾　(1153–1191)

Chu Sung　朱松　(1097–1143)

Chu T'ien-ch'iu　朱天球　(16th cent.)

Chu T'ing-li　朱廷立　(1492–1566)

Chu Tsai 朱在 (1169–1226+)

Chu Tung-hsiang 朱董祥 (late 17th cent.)

chung 重

Chung-yung 中庸

Fan Chung-yen 范仲淹 (989–1052)

Fan Tsu-yü 范祖禹 (1041–1098)

Fang Ta-tsung 方大琮 (1183–1247)

Feng Shan 馮善 (15th cent.)

fu-chün 府君

Fu K'uang 符匡 (16th cent.)

Fu Pi 富弼 (1004–1083)

hai 亥

Hai Jui 海瑞 (1513–1587)

Han Ch'i 韓琦 (1008–1075)

Han I 韓億 (972–1044)

Han Yü 韓愈 (768–824)

Ho Ch'ang-ling 賀長齡 (1785–1848)

Ho Ch'in 賀欽 (1437–1511)

Hsia Hsin 夏炘 (1789–1871)

Hsia Yen 夏言 (1482–1548)

hsiang-su 鄉俗

hsiang-yüeh 鄉約

hsiao-min 小民

Hsieh Chin 謝縉 (1369–1415)

Hsieh Hsing 謝省 (1420–1493)

Hsieh Ying-fang 謝應芳 (1296–1392)

hsin-sang 心喪

Hsing-li ta-ch'üan 性理大全

Hsü Chi 徐積 (1028–1103)

Hsü Ch'ien-hsüeh 徐乾學 (1631–1694)

Hsü Jun 徐潤 (T'ang)

Hsü San-li 許三禮 (1625–1691)

Hsün Tzu 荀子 (ca. 310–ca. 220 B.C.)

Hu An-chih 胡安之

Hu Han 胡翰 (1307–1381)

Hu Hsien 胡憲 (1086–1162)

Hu Hung 胡宏 (1106–1162)

Hu Yüan 胡瑗 (993–1059)

Hu Yung 胡泳 (1138–1175)

Hua Tsung-hsüeh 華悰韡 (1341–1397)

Huang Jui-chieh 黃瑞節 (Yüan)

Huang Kan 黃榦 (1152–1221)

Huang Tsung-hsi 黃宗羲 (1610–1695)

hun 魂

Hung Mai 洪邁 (1123–1202)

i (easy) 易

i (etiquette) 儀

i-i ch'i-li 以義起禮

I-li 儀禮

ju-jen 孺人

Juan Chi 阮籍 (210–263)

K'ai-pao t'ung-li 開寶通禮

K'ai-yüan li 開元禮

Kan Ju-lai 甘汝來 (1684–1739)

Kao K'ang 高閌 (1097–1153)

Kao T'ang 高堂 (2nd cent. B.C.)

Ku Kuang-yü 顧廣譽 (1800–1867)

Ku Yen-wu 顧炎武 (1613–1682)

Kung-yeh lu 功業錄

K'ung Ying-ta 孔穎達 (574–648)

Kuo Shu-yün 郭叔雲 (12th–13th cent.)

li (principle, pattern) 理

li (ritual) 禮

Li-chi 禮記

Li Fang 李昉 (925–996)

Li Fang-tzu 李方子 (13th cent.)

Li Kuang-ti 李光地 (1642–1718)

Li Kung 李塨 (1659–1733)

Li Lun 李倫 (15th cent.)

Li T'ung 李侗 (1093–1163)

Li Wen-chao 李文炤 (1672–1735)

liang-chih 良知

Liao Te-ming 廖德明 (c.s. 1169)

Liu Chang 劉璋

Liu Ch'iu 劉球 (1392–1443)

Liu Hsiang 劉向 (d. A.D. 9)

Liu Kai-sun 劉垓孫 (ca. 14th cent.)

Liu Mien-chih 劉勉之 (1091–1149)

Liu Te 劉德 (d. 131 B.C.)

Liu Tsung-yüan 柳宗元 (773–819)

Liu Tzu-hui 劉子翬 (1101–1147)

Liu Tzu-yü 劉子羽 (1097–1146)

Lo Lun 羅倫 (1431–1478)

Lo Ta-ching 羅大經 (13th cent.)

Lou Yüeh　樓鑰　(1137–1213)
Lu Ch'en　盧諶　(274–340)
Lu Shih-i　陸世儀　(1611–1672)
Lu Tien　陸佃　(1042–1102)
Lu Ts'an　陸粲　(1494–1551)
Lu T'ung-shen　路同申　(19th cent.)
Lu Yao　陸耀　(1723–1785)
Lu Yu　陸游　(1125–1210)
Lü I-chien　呂夷簡　(978–1043)
Lü K'un　呂坤　(1536–1618)
Lü Nan　呂柟　(1479–1542)
Lü Pen-chung　呂本中　(1084–1145)
Lü Ts'ai　呂才　(d. 655)
Lü Wei-ch'i　呂維祺　(1587–1641)
Ma Jung　馬融　(79–166)
Ma Tuan-lin　馬端臨　(1254–
　1324/25)
Mao Ch'i-ling　毛奇齡　(1623–1716)
Meng Hsien　孟銑　(T'ang)
Ming chi li　明集禮
miao (shrine)　廟
Ou-yang Hsiu　歐陽修　(1007–1072)
p'ai　牌
P'an Fu　潘府　(1454–1526)
Pao Yang　包揚　(12th–13th cent.)
pi-li　鄙俚
p'o　魄
Pu-chu　補注
pu-hai i-li　不害義理
San-chia li-fan　三家禮範
*Shao-hsing tsuan-tz'u Cheng-ho
　min-ch'en li-lüeh*　紹興纂次政和民
　臣禮略
Shao Ku　邵古　(986–1064)
Shao Yung　邵雍　(1011–1077)
shen-pan　神板
shih (gentleman, officer)　士
Shih Chieh　石介　(1005–1045)
Shih li　士禮
shih-shih　適士
shih-su　世俗
shih-ta-fu　士大夫
Shih Tzu-chih　時紫芝　(11th cent.)
shu-i　書儀
Shu-sun T'ung　叔孫通　(2nd cent.
　B.C.)

Ssu-li ch'u-kao　四禮初稿
Ssu-li i　四禮疑
Ssu-li i i-lun　四禮疑疑論
Ssu-li ts'ung-i　四禮從宜
Ssu-li yüeh-yen　四禮約言
Ssu-ma K'ang　司馬康　(1050–1090)
Ssu-ma Kao　司馬諕　(968–1030)
Ssu-ma Kuang　司馬光　(1019–
　1086)
Ssu-min pien-yung chia-li i-chien　四民
　便用家禮易簡
su　俗
Su Ch'e　蘇轍　(1039–1112)
Su Hsün　蘇洵　(1009–1066)
Su Shih　蘇軾　(1036–1101)
Sun Ch'i-feng　孫奇逢　(1585–1675)
Sun Fu　孫復　(992–1057)
Sun Jih-yung　孫日用　(Sung)
Sung Ch'i　宋祁　(998–1061)
Sung Hsiang　宋庠　(996–1066)
Sung Hsün　宋纁　(c.s. 1559,
　d. 1591)
Sung Lien　宋濂　(1310–1381)
Ta-hsüeh yen-i pu　大學衍義補
Ta-Ming ling　大明令
Ta-T'ang K'ai-yüan li　大唐開元禮
Tai Sheng　戴聖　(Former Han)
Tai Te　戴德　(Former Han)
T'ang hui-yao　唐會要
T'ang Shu　唐樞　(1497–1574)
T'ang To　湯鐸　(15th cent.)
Teng Yüan-hsi　鄧元錫　(1529–
　1593)
tien　奠
t'ien-li　天理
ting　丁
Ting Chi　丁積　(1446–1486)
tsa-hsi　雜戲
Ts'ai Hsiang　蔡襄　(1012–1067)
Ts'ai Yüan　蔡淵　(1156–1236)
Ts'ai Yüan-ting　蔡元定　(1135–
　1198)
Ts'ao Pao　曹褒　(2nd cent.)
Ts'ao Tuan　曹端　(1376–1434)
Tsou Shou-i　鄒守益　(1491–1562)
Ts'ui Mien　崔沔

Ts'ui Sun 崔損
Ts'ui Yu-fu 崔祐甫
tsung 宗
tsung-tzu 宗子
ts'ung-i 從宜
Tu Yen 杜衍 (978–1057)
Tu Yu 杜佑 (735–812)
Tu Yu-chin 杜有晉 (T'ang)
T'ung-tien 通典
Wang Chien 王儉 (452–489)
Wang Ch'ung 王充 (A.D. 27–ca. 100)
Wang Fu-li 王復禮 (18th cent.)
Wang Hung 王弘 (379–432)
Wang Jung 王戎 (234–305)
Wang Kung-ch'en 王拱辰 (1012–1085)
Wang Mao-hung 王懋竑 (1668–1741)
Wang Pi 王弼 (226–249)
Wang Shu-kao 王叔杲 (1517–1600)
Wang Su 王肅 (195–256)
Wang Tan 王旦 (957–1017)
Wang T'ing-hsiang 王廷相 (1474–1544)
Wang Wan 汪琬 (c.s. 1655)
Wang Yang-ming 王陽明 (1472–1529)
Wang Ying-ch'en 汪應辰 (1118–1176)
Wang Yüan 王源 (c.s. 1404)

Wei Hsiang-shu 魏象樞 (1617–1687)
Wei Piao 韋彪 (1st cent.)
Wei T'ang 魏堂 (16th cent.)
Wen-kung chia-li 文公家禮
Wen-kung chia-li hui-ch'eng 文公家禮會成
Wen Yen-po 文彥博 (1006–1097)
Weng Cheng-ch'un 翁正春 (1553–1627)
Wu Ch'eng 吳澄 (1247–1331)
wu-chu 巫祝
Wu Hai 吳海 (14th cent.)
Wu Hsia-chü 吳霞舉 (1257–1306)
Wu Hsien-shen 武先慎 (18th cent.)
Wu I 吳翌 (1129–1177)
Wu-li t'ung-k'ao 五禮通考
Wu Yü-pi 吳與弼 (1392–1469)
Yang Fu 楊復 (13th cent.)
Yang Shih-ch'i 楊士奇 (1365–1444)
yao (essential) 要
Yao Shu 姚樞 (1203–1280)
Yeh Meng-te 葉夢得 (1077–1148)
Yen Chih-t'ui 顏之推 (6th cent.)
Yen Yüan 顏元 (1635–1704)
yin (privilege) 蔭
Ying Pen 應本 (1272–1349)
Ying Shao 應劭 (fl. 180s)
ying-t'ang 影堂
Yü su-li yao 諭俗禮要

SOURCES CITED

Primary Sources

An-yang chi 安陽集. 50 ch. By Han Ch'i 韓琦 (1008–1075). SKCS ed.

Chang Tsai chi 張載集. By Chang Tsai 張載 (1020–1077). Peking: Chung-hua shu-chü, 1978.

Chao-ch'ing fu-chih 肇慶府志. 22 ch. (1833). Edited by T'u Ying 屠英 (c.s. 1801) et al. Chung-kuo fang-chih ts'ung-shu ed. Taipei: Ch'eng-wen ch'u-pan-she, 1967.

Ch'en Ch'üeh chi 陳確集. By Ch'en Ch'üeh 陳確 (1604–1677). Peking: Chung-hua shu-chü, 1979.

Cheng-ho wu-li hsin-i 政和五禮新儀. 220 ch. Edited by Cheng Chü-chung 鄭居中 (1059–1123) et al. SKCS ed.

Cheng-shih chia-i 鄭氏家儀. 6 ch. By Cheng Yung 鄭泳 (fourteenth century). In *Hsü Chin-hua ts'ung-shu* 續金華叢書, edited by Hu Tsung-mao 胡宗楙. Taipei: I-wen yin-shu-kuan reprint.

Chi-ku ko chen-ts'ang mi-pen shu-mu 汲古閣珍藏秘本書目. 1 ch. By Mao I 毛扆 (1640–1686). TSCC ed.

Chia-fan 家範. 10 ch. By Ssu-ma Kuang 司馬光 (1019–1086). Chung-kuo tzu-hsüeh ming-chu chi-ch'eng ed.

Chia-li 家禮. 1 ch. By Chu Hsi 朱熹 (1130–1200). In *Chu Tzu ch'eng-shu* 朱子成書, 1341 ed. (reproduced in Ebrey, trans., *Chu Hsi's Family Rituals*).

Chia-li 家禮. 5 ch. By Chu Hsi 朱熹 (1130–1200). Ming ed., with preface by Fang Ta-tsung 方大琮 (1183–1247) dated 1242, in the Peking Library.

Chia-li 家禮. 5 ch. By Chu Hsi 朱熹 (1130–1200). SKCS ed.

Chia-li: For other editions of the *Chia-li*, see Appendix A of Ebrey, trans., *Chu Hsi's Family Rituals*.

Chia-li chai-yao 家禮摘要. 5 ch. By Ko Yin-sheng 葛引生. In *Tung-shan Ko-shih i-shu* 東山葛氏遺書, 1561.

Chia-li cheng-heng 家禮正衡. 8 ch. By P'eng Pin 彭濱. 1599 ed.

Chia-li chi-i 家禮集議. 1 ch. By Wu Hsien-shen 武先慎 (eighteenth century). 1793 ed.

Chia-li chi-shuo 家禮集說. By Feng Shan 馮善 (ca. 1400–1434). Ts'ui-ch'ing t'ang, 1589 ed.

Chia-li chi-shuo 家禮集說. By Feng Shan 馮善 (ca. 1400–1434). 1479 ed., in the National Central Library, Taipei.

Chia-li chieh-yao 家禮節要. 1 ch. By Chu T'ing-li 朱廷立 (1492–1566). Preface 1536.

Chia-li ching-tien ts'an-t'ung 家禮經典參同. By Cheng Yüan-ch'ing 鄭元慶 (eighteenth century). Handwritten copy in the Shanghai Library. Preface 1712.

Chia-li cho 家禮酌. 1 ch. By Sun Ch'i-feng 孫奇逢 (1585–1675). In *Sun Hsia-feng ta-ch'üan-chi* 孫夏峰大全集. 1884 ed. of Chien-shan t'ang.

Chia-li ch'üan-chi 家禮全集. 6 ch. By Liang Chieh 梁傑. 1895 ed.

Chia-li ch'üan-pu 家禮銓補. 10 ch. By Teng Yüan-hsi 鄧元錫 (1529–1593). 1610 ed.

Chia-li hui-t'ung 家禮會通. 4 ch. By Chang Ju-ch'eng 張汝誠 (eighteenth century). Fu-chou Chi-hsin t'ang ed.

Chia-li hui-t'ung (Wen-kung) 家禮會通(文公). 10 ch. By T'ang To 湯鐸. Nanking: Ch'ih-chung t'ang, 1450 ed.

Chia-li huo-wen hsü-chih 家禮或問須知. 1 ch. By Cheng Pi-cho 鄭必著. Ming manuscript copy held by the Naikaku bunko, Tokyo.

Chia-li i-chieh 家禮儀節. 8 ch. Anon., attrib. to Ch'iu Chün 丘濬. Reprint of Pao-ch'ih lou 1770 ed. In *Ch'iu Wen-chuang kung ts'ung-shu* 丘文莊公叢書.

Chia-li i-chieh 家禮儀節. 8 ch. By Ch'iu Chün 丘濬 (1421–1495). 1618 ed.

Chia-li i-chieh 家禮儀節. 8 ch. Attrib. to Yang Shen 楊慎 (1488–1559). Preface 1530. Late Ming reprint.

Chia-li i-chieh 家禮儀節. 8 ch. By Ch'en Jen-hsi 陳仁錫 (c.s. 1622). Late Ming ed.

Chia-li i-chien pien 家禮易簡編. 1 ch. By Chu T'ien-ch'iu 朱天球. Preface 1593.

Chia-li pien-shuo 家禮辨說. 16 ch. By Mao Ch'i-ling 毛奇齡 (1623–1716). In *Ming-pien chai ts'ung-shu* 明辨齋叢書. 1846 ed.

Chia-li pien-ting 家禮辨定. 10 ch. By Wang Fu-li 王復禮. Preface 1707.

Chia-li sang-chi shih-i 家禮喪祭拾遺. 1 ch. By Li Wen-chao 李文炤 (1672–1735). In *Tu-li ts'ung-ch'ao* 讀禮叢鈔, edited by Yen Jo-ch'ü 閻若璩 (1636–1704) et al. Taipei: Wen-hai ch'u-pan-she's Kuo-hsüeh chi yao, reprint ed. 1967 (fascimile reproduction of 1891 ed.).

Chia-li shih-i 家禮拾遺. 5 ch. By Li Wen-chao 李文炤 (1672–1735). In *Li-shih ch'eng-shu* 李氏成書. Ssu-wei t'ang ed.

Chia-li ta-ch'eng 家禮大成. 8 ch. By Lü Tzu-chen 呂子振 (eighteenth century). Taipei: Hsi-pei ch'u-pan-she, 1975 reprint of 1735 ed.

Chia-li t'ieh-shih chi-ch'eng 家禮帖式集成. 4 ch. By Ch'en Ming-sheng 陳鳴盛. 1750 ed. of Yu-wen t'ang.

Chia-li t'ung-hsing 家禮通行. 8 ch. By Lo Wan-hua 羅萬化 (1536–1594). 1573 ed.

Chia-li yao-chieh 家禮要節. 1 ch. By Wang Shu-kao 王叔杲 (1517–1600). 1571 ed.

Chia-yu chi 嘉祐集. 15 ch. By Su Hsün 蘇洵 (1009–1066). Wan-yu wen-k'u ed.

Chiang-ning fu-chih 江寧府志. 56 ch. Edited by Yao Nai 姚鼐 (1732–1815). Taipei: Ch'eng-wen ch'u-pan-she reprint of 1811 ed.

Chiang-su sheng-li kuo-hsüeh t'u-shu kuan t'u-shu tsung-mu 江蘇省立國學圖書館圖書總目. 44 ch. Shu-mu ssu-pien ed. Taipei: Kuang-wen shu-chü, 1970.

Chien-ning fu-chih 建寧府志. Shanghai: Ku-chi shu-tien reprint of 1541 ed.

Ch'ien-ch'ing t'ang shu-mu 千頃堂書目. 32 ch. By Huang Yü-chi 黃虞稷 (1629–1691). Shu-mu ts'ung-pien ed. Taipei: Kuang-wen shu-chü, 1967.

Ch'ien Tsun-wang tu-shu min-ch'iu chi chiao-cheng 錢遵王讀書敏求記校證. By Ch'ien Tseng 錢曾 (1629–1701). Edited by Kuan T'ing-fen 管庭芬 (1797–1880) and Chang Yü 章鈺 (1865–1937). Shu-mu ts'ung-pien ed. Taipei: Kuang-wen shu-chü, 1967.

Chih-chai shu-lu chieh-t'i 直齋書錄解題. 22 ch. By Ch'en Chen-sun 陳振孫 (ca. 1190–1249＋). TSCC ed.

Chin-hua ching-chi chih 金華經籍志. 27 ch. By Hu Tsung-mao 胡宗楙. Taipei: Chin-hsüeh shu-chü, 1970 reprint of 1925 ed.

Chin shu 晉書. 130 ch. By Fang Hsüan-ling 房玄齡 (578–648) et al. Peking: Chung-hua shu-chü, 1974.

Chin-ssu lu chi-chieh 近思錄集解. By Chu Hsi 朱熹 (1130–1200) and Lü Tsu-ch'ien 呂祖謙 (1137–1181). *Chi-chieh* by Chang Po-hsing 張伯行 (1651–1725). TSCC ed.

Ching-wen chi 景文集. 62 ch. By Sung Ch'i 宋祁 (998–1061). TSCC ed.

Ching-yeh hsien-sheng li-wen 涇野先生禮問. 2 ch. By Lü Nan 呂柟 (1479–1542). TSCC ed.

Ch'ing hsüeh-an hsiao-shih 清學案小識. 15 ch. By T'ang Chien 唐鑑 (1778–1861). Taipei: Kuo-hsüeh chi-pen ts'ung-shu, 1935.

Ch'ing-ju hsüeh-an 清儒學案. 208 ch. By Hsü Shih-ch'ang 徐世昌 (1858–1939). Taipei: Shih-chieh shu-chü, 1966.

Ch'ing-shih i-wen chih (ch'ung-hsiu) 清史藝文志(重修). 4 ch. By P'eng Kuo-tung 彭國棟. Taipei: Commercial Press, 1968.

Ch'ing-yüan t'iao-fa shih-lei 慶元條法事類. 80 ch. By Hsieh Shen-fu 謝深甫 (twelfth century). Taipei: Hsin-wen-feng, 1976 reprint of Seikadō manuscript copy.

Chiu-chiang fu-chih 九江府志. 6 ch. Shanghai: Ku-chi shu-tien, 1982 reprint of 1527 ed.

Chiu T'ang shu 舊唐書. 200 ch. (945). By Liu Hsü 劉昫 (887–946) et al. Peking: Chung-hua shu-chü, 1975.

Chu Tzu ch'eng-shu 朱子成書. By Chu Hsi 朱熹 (1130–1200). Edited by Huang Jui-chieh 黃瑞節 (twelfth century). 1341 ed. in the National Palace Museum, Taipei.

Chu Tzu chia-li 朱子家禮. 5 ch. By Chu Hsi 朱熹 (1130–1200). SKCS ed.

Chu Tzu chia-li 朱子家禮. 5 ch. By Chu Hsi 朱熹 (1130–1200). Edited by Shih Hsüeh-ch'eng 史學成 et al. 1732 ed. of Shou-ch'ang chiang-t'ang.

Chu Tzu nien-p'u 朱子年譜. 4 ch. By Wang Mao-hung 王懋竑 (1668–1741). TSCC ed.

Chu Tzu nien-p'u k'ao-i 朱子年譜考異. 4 ch. By Wang Mao-hung 王懋竑 (1668–1741). Taipei: Han-ching reprint of *Yüeh-ya t'ang ts'ung-shu* ed.

Chu Tzu yü-lei 朱子語類. 140 ch. (1270). By Chu Hsi 朱熹 (1130–1200). Peking: Chung-hua shu-chü, 1986.

Chu Wen-kung wen-chi 朱文公文集. 100 ch. By Chu Hsi 朱熹 (1130–1200). Ssu-pu ts'ung-k'an ed.

Chü-chia pi-yung shih-lei ch'üan-chi 居家必用事類全集. 20 ch. Anon. Kyoto: Chumon, 1979 reprint of Japanese 1673 ed.

Ch'üan-chou fu-chih 泉州府誌. 76 ch. By Huang Jen 黃任 (1683–1759) et al. Tainan: Teng-wen, 1964 reprint of 1870 ed.

Ch'üan T'ang wen 全唐文. 1,000 ch. By Tung Kao 董誥 (1740–1818) et al. Tainan: Ching-wei shu-chü 1965 reprint of 1814 ed.

Ch'üeh-sao pien 却掃編. 3 ch. By Hsü Tu 徐度 (d. 1156). TSCC ed.

Chung-kuo ku-chi shan-pen shu-mu 中國古集善本書目. Shanghai: Shanghai ku-chi ch'u-pan-she, 1985.

Chung-kuo ts'ung-shu tsung-lu 中國叢書綜錄. Edited by Shanghai t'u-shu kuan 上海圖書館. Peking: Chung-hua shu-chü, 1959–1962.

Ch'ung-wen tsung-mu 崇文總目. 5 ch. By Wang Yao-ch'en 王堯臣 (1001–1056) et al. TSCC ed.

Erh Ch'eng chi 二程集. 25 ch. By Ch'eng Hao 程顥 (1032–1085) and Ch'eng I 程頤 (1033–1107). Peking: Chung-hua shu-chü, 1981.

Fa-wei lun 發微論. 1 ch. By Ts'ai Fa 蔡發 (1089–1152). SKCS ed.

Fan T'ai-shih chi 范太史集. 55 ch. By Fan Tsu-yü 范祖禹 (1041–1098). SKCS ed.

Fang-weng chia-hsün 放翁家訓. 1 ch. by Lu Yu 陸游 (1125–1210). TSCC ed.

Feng-su t'ung-i 風俗通義. 10 ch. By Ying Shao 應劭 (second century). In *Feng-su t'ung-i chiao-shih* 校釋. *Chiao-shih* by Wu Shu-p'ing 吳樹平. Tientsin: Tien-chin jen-min ch'u-pan-she, 1980.

Hai Jui chi 海瑞集. By Hai Jui 海瑞 (1513–1587). Edited by Ch'en I-chung 陳義鍾. Peking: Chung-hua shu-chü, 1962.

Han shu 漢書, 120 ch. By Pan Ku 班固 (32–92). Peking: Chung-hua shu-chü, 1962.

Han Wei-kung chi 韓魏公集. 20 ch. By Han Ch'i 韓琦 (1008–1075). TSCC ed.

Ho-shan chi 鶴山集. 109 ch. By Wei Liao-weng 魏了翁 (1178–1237). SKCS ed.

Hou-Han shu 後漢書. 120 ch. By Fan Yeh 范曄 (398–445). Peking: Chung-hua shu-chü, 1963.

Hsi-shan wen-chi 西山文集. 55 ch. By Chen Te-hsiu 真德秀 (1178–1235). SKCS ed.

Hsi-yüan wen-chien lu 西園聞見錄. 107 ch. By Chang Hsüan 張萱 (1558–1641). Taipei: Hua-wen shu-chü reprint of 1940 ed.

Hsiao ching 孝經. 9 ch. Shih-san ching chu-shu ed.

Hsiao-tz'u lu 孝慈錄. 1 ch. By Chu Yüan-chang 朱元璋 (1328–1398). In *Huang-Ming chih-shu* 皇明制書. Tokyo: Koten kenkyūkai, 1966 reprint (facsimile of Ming ed.).

Hsin-an ming-tsu chih 新安名族志. 2 ch. By Ch'eng Shang-k'uan 程尚寬 et al. Microfilm of Ming Chia-ching ed.

Hsin-an wen-hsien chih 新安文獻志. 100 ch. Edited by Ch'eng Min-cheng 程敏政 (1445–1502+). SKCS ed.

Hsin-pien shih-wen lei-chü han-mo ta-ch'üan 新編事文類聚翰墨大全. By Liu Ying-li 劉應李 (d. 1311). 1307 ed.

Hsin-pien shih-wen lei-yao ch'i-cha ch'ing-ch'ien 新編事文類要啓劄青錢. 51 ch. (Yüan). Tokyo: Koten kenkyūkai, 1963 reprint (facsimile of 1324 ed.).

Hsin-pien t'ung-yung ch'i-cha chieh-chiang kang 新編通用啓劄截江綱. 68 ch. Edited by Hsiung Hui-chung 熊晦仲 (Sung). Sung ed. in Seikadō Library.

Hsin T'ang shu 新唐書. 225 ch. By Ou-yang Hsiu 歐陽修 (1007–1072) and Sung Ch'i 宋祁 (998–1061). Peking: Chung-hua shu-chü, 1975.

Hsing-li ta-ch'üan 性理大全. 70 ch. Microfilm of the National Central Library's 1415 ed.

Hsing-li ta-ch'üan 性理大全. 70 ch. Sixteenth-century expanded edition in the University of Chicago Library.

Hsü tzu-chih t'ung-chien ch'ang-pien 續資治通鑑長編. 600 ch. By Li T'ao 李燾 (1115–1184). Taipei: Shih-chieh shu-chü, 1961.

Hsü tzu-chih t'ung-chien ch'ang-pien 續資治通鑑長編. 520 ch. By Li T'ao 李燾 (1115–1184). Peking: Chung-hua shu-chü, 1985.

Hsü wen-hsien t'ung-k'ao 續文獻通考. 250 ch. Shih-t'ung ed. Taipei: Hsin-hsing shu-chü reprint.

Hsüeh-li 學禮, 5 ch. By Li Kung 李塨 (1659–1733). Pai-pu ts'ung-shu chi-ch'eng ed.

Hsün tzu chi-chieh 荀子集解. 20 ch. By Hsün Tzu 荀子 (ca. 310–220 B.C.). *Chi-chieh* by Wang Hsien-ch'ien 王先謙 (1842–1918). Taipei: Shih-chieh shu-chü, 1978.

Hu Chung-tzu chi 胡仲子集. 10 ch. By Hu Han 胡翰 (1307–1381). TSCC ed.

Huang-ch'ao ching-shih wen-pien 皇朝經世文編. 120 ch. Edited by Ho Ch'ang-ling 賀長齡 (1785–1848) and Wei Yüan 魏源 (1794–1856). Shanghai: Huan-wen shu-chü, 1902 ed.

Huang-chou fu-chih 黃州府志. 10 ch. Shanghai: Ku-chi shu-tien reprint of 1500 ed.

I-chien chih 夷堅志. 207 ch. By Hung Mai 洪邁 (1123–1202). Peking: Chung-hua shu-chü, 1981.

I-feng wen-chi 一峯文集. 14 ch. By Lo Lun 羅倫 (1431–1478). SKCS ed.

I-li 儀禮. 50 ch. Shih-san ching chu-shu ed.

I-li ching-chuan t'ung-chieh 儀禮經傳通解. 66 ch. By Chu Hsi 朱熹 (1130–1200), Huang Kan 黃榦 (1152–1221), and Yang Fu 楊復 (twelfth–thirteenth centuries). SKCS ed.

I-lü chi 醫閭集. 9 ch. By Ho Ch'in 賀欽 (1437–1511). SKCS ed.

Jung-ts'un chi 榕村集. 40 ch. By Li Kuang-ti 李光地 (1642–1718). SKCS ed.

Ku-chin shih-wen lei-chü 古今事文類聚. 236 ch. By Chu Mu 祝穆 (thirteenth century). SKCS ed.

Ku-chin t'u-shu chi-ch'eng (Ch'in-ting) 古今圖書集成, 欽定. 10,000 ch. (1725). Edited by Ch'en Meng-lei 陳夢雷 (1651–ca. 1723) et al. Peking: Chung-hua shu-chü, 1934 reprint of Palace ed.

Ku-liang chuan 穀梁傳. 20 ch. Shih-san ching chu-shu ed.

Kuang-chou fu-chih 廣州府志. 163 ch. Edited by Shih Ch'eng 史澄 et al. Taipei: Ch'eng-wen ch'u-pan-she, 1966 reprint of 1879 ed.

Kuei-erh chi 貴耳集. 3 ch. By Chang Tuan-i 張端義 (1179–1250). TSCC ed.

Kuei-t'ien lu 歸田錄. 2 ch. By Ou-yang Hsiu 歐陽修 (1007–1072). Peking: Chung-hua shu-chü T'ang Sung shih-liao pi-chi ts'ung-k'an ed., 1981.

Kung-k'uei chi 攻媿集. 112 ch. By Lou Yüeh 樓鑰 (1137–1213). TSCC ed.

Kung-yang chuan 公羊傳. 28 ch. Shih-san ching chu-shu ed.

Kuo-li chung-yang t'u-shu kuan shan-pen shu-mu 國立中央圖書館善本書目. Taipei: Chung-hua ts'ung-shu wei-yüan hui, 1957.

Kuo-yü 國語. 21 ch. Shanghai: Shanghai ku-chi ch'u-pan-she, 1988 ed.

Kyoto daigaku bungakubu Kanseki bunrui mokuroku 京都大學文學部漢籍分類目錄. Vol. 1. Kyoto: Kyoto University Bungakubu, 1959.

Kyoto daigaku jimbun kagaku kenkyūjo Kanseki mokuroku 京都大學人文科學研究所漢籍目錄. Kyoto: Dōhōsha, 1981.

Le-ch'ing hsien-chih 樂清縣志. 16 ch. Edited by Lu Lü-hsiang 路履祥 et al. 1901 ed.

Le-ch'üan chi 樂全集. 40 ch. + 1. By Chang Fang-p'ing 張方平 (1007–1091). SKCS ed.

Li-chi 禮記. 63 ch. Shih-san ching chu-shu ed.

Li Kou chi 李覯集. By Li Kou 李覯 (1009–1059). Taipei: Han-ching, 1983 ed.

Li Shu-ku hsien-shen nien-p'u 李恕谷先生年譜. 5 ch. By Feng Ch'en 馮辰 and Liu

T'iao-tsan 劉調贊. Chin-tai Chung-kuo shih-liao ts'ung-k'an hsü-pien reprint of 1736 ed. Taipei: Wen-hai ch'u-pan-she, 1983.

Liang-hsi wen-chi 兩谿文集. 24 ch. By Liu Ch'iu 劉球 (1392–1443). SKCS ed.

Liu Chiang-tung chia-ts'ang shan-pen Tsang-shu 劉江東家藏善本葬書. 1 ch. Attributed to Kuo P'u 郭璞 (267–324). Pai-pu ts'ung-shu chi-ch'eng ed.

Lu Fang-weng ch'üan-chi 陸放翁全集. 186 ch. By Lu Yu 陸游 (1125–1210). Hong Kong: Kuang-chih shu-chü ed.

Lu-kung wen-chi 潞公文集. 40 ch. By Wen Yen-po 文彥博 (1006–1097). SKCS ed.

Lü-te chi 慮得集. 4 ch. By Hua Tsung-hsüeh 華悰韡 (1341–1397). Ming printed ed.

Lü-t'ing chih-chien ch'uan-pen shu-mu 邵亭知見傳本書目. 16 ch. By Mo Yu-chih 莫友芝 (1811–1871). Shu-mu wu-pien ed. Taipei: Kuang-wen shu-chü, 1972.

Lun-heng 論衡. 30 ch. By Wang Ch'ung 王充 (27–ca. 97). Shanghai: Shanghai jen-min ch'u-pan-she, 1974.

Lun-hsüeh 論學. 2 ch. By Li Kung 李塨 (1659–1733). Pai-pu ts'ung-shu chi-ch'eng ed.

Lun-yü 論語. 20 ch. Shih-san ching chu-shu ed.

Mei-kuo kuo-hui t'u-shu kuan ts'ang Chung-kuo shan-pen shu-mu 美國國會圖書館藏中國善本書目. Edited by Wang Chung-min 王重民. Taipei: Wen-hai ch'u-pan-she, 1972 reprint.

Meng-liang lu 夢粱錄. 20 ch. (1274). By Wu Tzu-mu 吳自牧 (ca. 1256–1334+). In *Tung-ching Meng-hua lu wai ssu chung* 東京夢華錄外四種. Shanghai: Chung-hua shu-chü, 1962.

Meng tzu 孟子. 14 ch. Shih-san ching chu-shu ed.

Mien-chai chi 勉齋集. 40 ch. By Huang Kan 黃榦 (1152–1221). SKCS ed.

Min-chung li-hsüeh yüan-yüan k'ao 閩中理學淵源考. 92 ch. By Li Ch'ing-fu 李清馥 (eighteenth century). SKCS ed.

Ming chi-li 明集禮. 53 ch. Edited by Hsü I-k'uei 徐一夔 (1318–ca. 1400) et al. SKCS ed.

Ming-i tai-fang lu 明夷待訪錄. 1 ch. By Huang Tsung-hsi 黃宗羲 (1610–1695). Taipei: Kuo-hsüeh chi-pen ts'ung-shu ed.

Ming shih 明史. 332 ch. Edited by Chang T'ing-yü 張廷玉 (1672–1775). Peking: Chung-hua shu-chü, 1974.

Mo tzu hsien-ku 墨子閒詁. 15 ch. By Mo Tzu 墨子 (ca. 420 B.C.). *Hsien-ku* by Sun I-jang 孫詒讓 (1848–1908). Taipei: Shih-chieh shu-chü reprint.

Mu-an chi 牧庵集. 36 ch. By Yao Sui 姚燧 (1238–1314). TSCC ed.

Naikaku bunko Kanseki bunrui mokuroku 內閣文庫漢籍分類目錄. Tokyo: Naikaku bunko, 1956.

Nan-hsüan chi 南軒集. 44 ch. By Chang Shih 張栻 (1133–1180). SKCS ed.

Ou-yang Hsiu ch'üan-chi 歐陽修全集. 157 ch. By Ou-yang Hsiu 歐陽修 (1007–1072). Taipei: Shih-chieh shu-chü, 1961.

Pa-ch'ien chüan lou shu-mu 八千卷樓書目. 20 ch. By Ting Ping 丁丙 (1832–1899). Shu-mu ssu-pien ed. Taipei: Kuang-wen shu-chü, 1970.

Pei-ching t'u-shu kuan shan-pen shu-mu 北京圖書館善本書目. Peking: Chung-hua shu-chü, 1959.

Pei-hsi ta-ch'üan-chi 北溪大全集. 50 ch. By Ch'en Ch'un 陳淳 (1159–1223). SKCS ed.

P'ing-chou k'o-t'an 萍州可談. 3 ch. By Chu Yü 朱彧 (ca. 1075–1119). TSCC ed.

Po-hu t'ung 白虎通. 4 ch. Edited by Pan Ku 班固 (32–92). TSCC ed.

Po-t'ien ts'ao-t'ang ts'un-kao 白田草堂存稿. 8 ch. By Wang Mao-hung 王懋竑 (1668–1741). In *Kuang-ya shu-chü ts'ung-shu* 廣雅書局叢書. Kuang-hsü ed.

San-shan chih 三山志. 42 ch. By Liang K'o-chia 梁克家 (1128–1187). Sung-Yüan ti-fang chih ts'ung-shu ed. Taipei: Kuo-t'ai wen-hua shih-yeh, 1980 reprint.

Sang-fu tsa-shuo 喪服雜說. 1 ch. By Chang Hua-li 張華理. In *Tu-li ts'ung-ch'ao* 讀禮叢鈔. Edited by Yen Jo-ch'ü 閻若璩 (1636–1704) et al. Taipei: Wen-hai ch'u-pan-she's Kuo-hsüeh chi yao, 1967 reprint (facsimile of 1891 ed.).

Seikadō bunko Kanseki bunrui mokuroku 靜嘉堂文庫漢籍分類目錄. Taipei: Chin-hsüeh shu-chü, 1969 reprint of 1930 ed.

Shan-yu shih-k'o ts'ung-pien 山右石刻叢編. 40 ch. By Hu P'ing-chih 胡聘之. In *Shih-k'o shih-liao hsin-pien* 石刻史料新編. Taipei: Hsin wen-feng, 1977.

Shang-hai t'u-shu kuan shan-pen shu-mu 上海圖書館善本書目. 5 ch. Shanghai: Shanghai Library, 1957.

Shang-shu 尚書. 20 ch. Shih-san ching chu-shu ed.

Shao-shih wen-chien lu 邵氏聞見錄. 20 ch. By Shao Po-wen 邵伯溫 (1056–1134). Peking: Chung-hua shu-chü, T'ang-Sung shih-liao pi-chi ts'ung k'an, 1983.

Shih-chi 史記. 130 ch. By Ssu-ma Ch'ien 司馬遷 (145?–86? B.C.). Peking: Chung-hua shu-chü, 1962.

Shih ching 詩經. 20 ch. Shih-san ching chu-shu ed.

Shih-lin kuang-chi 事林廣記. Edited by Ch'en Yüan-ching 陳元靚 (ca. 1200–1266). Peking: Chung-hua shu-chü reprint.

Shih-san ching chu-shu 十三經注疏. Taipei: I-wen yin-shu-kuan, 1821 reprint of Sung editions.

Shih-shuo-hsin-yü chiao-chien 世說新語校箋. 36 ch. By Liu I-ch'ing 劉義慶 (403–444). *Chiao-chien* by Yang Yung 楊勇. Hong Kong: Ta-chung shu-chü, 1969.

Shih-wu chi-yüan 事物紀原. 10 ch. By Kao Ch'eng 高承 (eleventh century). TSCC ed.

Shu Chu chih-i 述朱質疑. By Hsia Hsin 夏炘 (1789–1871). In *Ching-tzu t'ang ch'üan-shu* 景紫堂全書. Taipei: I-wen yin-shu-kuan, 1969.

Shu-ku t'ang ts'ang shu-mu 述古堂藏書目. 4 ch. By Ch'ien Tseng 錢曾 (1629–1901). TSCC ed.

Shuang-feng hsien-sheng nei wai fu-chih t'ung-shih 雙峯先生內外服制通釋. 10 ch. By Ch'e Kai 車垓 (d. 1276). In *Chen-pi lou ts'ung-shu* 沈碧樓叢書. 1913 ed.

Ssu-k'u ch'üan-shu tsung-mu 四庫全書總目. 200 ch. Edited by Chi Yün 紀昀 (1724–1805) et al. Peking: Chung-hua shu-chü, 1965 reprint.

Ssu-li ch'u-kao 四禮初稿. By Sung Hsün 宋纁 (d. 1591). Preface 1573.

Ssu-li ch'üeh-i 四禮權疑. 8 ch. By Ku Kuang-yü 顧廣譽 (1800–1867). In *Huai-lu ts'ung-shu* 槐廬叢書. Taipei: I-wen yin-shu-kuan reprint.

Ssu-li ho-ts'an 四禮合參. 15 ch. By Li Ying-ch'ien 李應乾 (eighteenth century). 1739 ed. of Hsin-yüan lou.

Ssu-li i 四禮疑. 5 ch. By Lü K'un 呂坤 (1536–1618). Preface 1614.

Ssu-li i i-lun 四禮疑疑論. 4 ch. By Lu T'ung-shen 路同申. Handwritten copy in the Shanghai Library, preface 1823.

Ssu-li ts'ung-i 四禮從宜. By Jen Jo-hai 任若海. Handwritten copy of 1859 ed. in the Shanghai Library.

Ssu-li ts'ung-i 四禮從宜. 6 ch. By Lin Ch'üan 林荃. 1893 ed. of Shu-chien chai.

Ssu-li ts'ung-i 四禮從宜. 4 ch. By Su Tun-yüan 蘇惇元 (1801–1857). 1844 ed.

Ssu-li yüeh-yen 四禮約言. by Lü Wei-ch'i 呂維祺 (1587–1641). 1763 ed. of Po-ya t'ang.

Ssu-ma shih shu-i 司馬氏書儀. 10 ch. By Ssu-ma Kuang 司馬光 (1019–1086). TSCC ed.

Ssu-ma Wen-cheng kung ch'uan-chia chi 司馬文正公傳家集. 80 ch. (1741). By Ssu-ma Kuang 司馬光 (1019–1086). Taipei: Kuo-hsüeh chi-pen ts'ung-shu ed.

Ssu-ma Wen-kung nien-p'u 司馬溫公年譜. 8 + 1 ch. By Ku Tung-kao 顧棟高 (1679–1759) and Liu Ch'eng-kan 劉承幹 (twentieth century). Honan: Chung-chou ku-chi ch'u-pan-she, 1987.

Ssu-pien lu chi-yao 思辨錄輯要. 35 ch. By Lu Shih-i 陸世儀 (1611–1672). SKCS ed.

Su Shih wen-chi 蘇軾文集. 73 ch. By Su Shih 蘇軾 (1036–1101). Peking: Chung-hua shu-chü, 1986.

Su-shih yen-i 蘇氏演義. 2 ch. By Su O 蘇鶚 (ninth century). TSCC ed.

Su Shun-ch'in chi 蘇舜欽集. 16 + 2 ch. By Su Shun-ch'in 蘇舜欽 (1008–1048). Shanghai: Shanghai ku-chi ch'u-pan-she, 1981.

Sui shu 隋書. 85 ch. By Wei Cheng 魏徵 (580–643) and Ling-hu Te-fen 令狐德棻 (ca. 640). Peking: Chung-hua shu-chü, 1973.

Sung-chiang fu hsü-chih 松江府續志. 40 ch. Edited by Yao Kuang-fa 姚光發 et al. Taipei: Ch'eng-wen ch'u-pan-she, 1974 reprint of 1884 ed.

Sung hsing-t'ung 宋刑統. 30 ch. By Tou I 竇儀 (914–966) et al. Taipei: Wen-hai, 1964 reprint of 1918 ed.

Sung Hsüeh-shih wen-chi 宋學士文集. 75 ch. By Sung Lien 宋濂 (1310–1381). Wan-yu wen-k'u ed.

Sung hui-yao chi-pen 宋會要輯本. 460 ch. Edited by Hsü Sung 徐松 (1781–1848) et al. Taipei: Shih-chieh shu-chü reprint, 1964.

Sung shih 宋史. 496 ch. Edited by T'o T'o 脫脫 (1313–1355) et al. Peking: Chung-hua shu-chü, 1977.

Sung shu 宋書. 100 ch. By Shen Yüeh 沈約 (441–513). Peking: Chung-hua chu-chü, 1974.

Sung ssu-tzu ch'ao shih 宋四子抄釋. 21 ch. Edited by Lü Nan 呂楠 (1479–1542). Taipei: Shih-chieh shu-chü, 1962.

Sung ta-chao-ling chi 宋大詔令集. 196 ch. Peking: Chung-hua shu-chü, 1962.

Sung wen-chien 宋文鑑. 150 ch. By Lü Tsu-ch'ien 呂祖謙 (1137–1181). Taipei: Kuo-hsüeh chi-pen ts'ung-shu ed.

Sung-Yüan hsüeh-an 宋元學案. 100 ch. (1846). By Huang Tsung-hsi 黃宗羲 (1610–1695) et al. Shanghai: Commercial Press, 1928.

Ta Han yüan-ling mi-tsang ching 大漢原陵秘葬經. In *Yung-le ta-tien* 永樂大典 *chüan* 8199. Peking: Chung-hua shu-chü, 1960.

Ta-hsüeh yen-i pu 大學衍義補. 160 ch. By Ch'iu Chün 丘濬 (1421–1495). SKCS ed.

Ta-Ming hui-tien 大明會典. 228 ch. By Shen Shih-hsing 申時行 (1535–1614) et al. Taipei: Tung-nan reprint of 1587 ed.

Ta-Ming ling 大明令. In *Huang-Ming chih-shu* 皇明制書. Tokyo: Koten ken-kyūkai, 1966 reprint (facsimile of Ming ed.).

Ta Tai li-chi chin-chu chin-i 大戴禮記今註今譯. Edited by Kao Ming 高明. Taipei: Commercial Press, 1975.

Ta-T'ang K'ai-yüan li 大唐開元禮. 150 ch. Edited by Hsiao Sung 蕭嵩 (eighth century) et al. SKCS ed.

Ta-Yüan sheng-cheng kuo-ch'ao tien-chang 大元聖政國朝典章. 60 ch. (1307). Facsimile reproduction of Yüan ed.

T'ai-ch'ang yin-ko li 太常因革禮. 100 ch. Edited by Ou-yang Hsiu 歐陽修 (1007–1072) et al. TSCC ed.

T'ai-chou ching-chi chih 台州經籍志. 40 ch. Edited by Hsiang Yüan-hsün 項元勛. Shu-mu san-pien ed. Taipei: Kuang-wen shu-chü, 1969.

T'ai-chou fu-chih 台州府志. 100 ch. Edited by Wang Chou-yao 王舟瑤 (1858–1925) et al. 1926 ed.

T'ang hui-yao 唐會要. 100 ch. By Wang P'u 王溥 (922–982). Taipei: Shih-chieh shu-chü, 1968.

Tao-shan ch'ing-hua 道山清話. 1 ch. Anon. TSCC ed.

Te-an fu-chih 德安府志. 20 ch. Edited by Keng Yin-pu 賡音布. Chung-kuo fang-chih ts'ung-shu ed. Taipei: Ch'eng-wen ch'u-pan-she, 1970 reprint of 1888 ed.

Ti-li hsin-shu 地理新書. 15 ch. Edited by Wang Chu 王洙 (997–1057). Taipei: National Central Library microfilm of 1192 ed.

T'ieh-ch'in t'ung-chien lou ts'ang-shu mu-lu 鐵琴銅劍樓藏書目錄. 24 ch. (1898). By Ch'ü Yung 瞿鏞 (fl. 1857). 1898 ed.

Ts'ai-shih chiu-ju shu 蔡氏九儒書. 9 + 1 ch. Edited by Ts'ai K'un 蔡鵾 (Ming) San-yü shu-hang 1868 ed.

Ts'ao Yüeh-ch'uan chi 曹月川集. 1 ch. By Ts'ao Tuan 曹端 (1376–1434). SKCS ed.

Tso-chuan 左傳. 58 ch. Shih-san ching chu-shu ed.

Tsu-lai Shih hsien-sheng wen-chi 徂徠石先生文集. By Shih Chieh 石介 (1005–1045). Peking: Chung-hua shu-chü, 1984.

Tu-li t'ung-k'ao 讀禮通考. 120 ch. By Hsü Ch'ien-hsüeh 徐乾學 (1631–1694). SKCS ed.

Tun-huang pao-tsang 敦煌寶藏. 140 vols. Edited by Huang Yung-wu 黃永武. Taipei: Hsin-wen-feng, 1981–1986.

Tun-huang to-so 敦煌掇瑣. Edited by Liu Fu 劉復 (1891–1934). Peking: Institute of Archaeology, 1957 reprint of 1925 ed.

Tung-ching meng-hua lu 東京夢華錄. 10 ch. (1147). Attributed to Meng Yüan-lao 孟元老 (fl. 1126–1147). In *Tung-ching meng-hua lu wai ssu chung* 外四種. Shanghai: Chung-hua shu-chü, 1962.

Tung-hu ts'ung-chi 東湖叢記. 6 ch. By Chiang Kuang-hsü 蔣光煦 (1813–1860). Shu-mu ts'ung-pien ed. Taipei: Kuang-wen shu-chü, 1967.

Tung-lai chi 東萊集. 40 ch. By Lü Tsu-ch'ien 呂祖謙 (1137–1181). SKCS ed.

Tung-li hsü-chi 東里續集. 62 ch. By Yang Shih-ch'i 楊士奇 (1365–1444). SKCS ed.

Tung-li wen-chi 東里文集. 25 ch. By Yang Shih-ch'i 楊士奇 (1365–1444). SKCS ed.

T'ung-chih t'iao-ko 通制條格. Anon. 1930 reprint ed.

T'ung-tien 通典. 200 ch. By Tu Yu 杜佑 (735–812). Taipei: Hsin-hsing shu-chü reprint of Shih-t'ung ed.

Tzu-chih t'ung-chien 資治通鑑. 294 ch. By Ssu-ma Kuang 司馬光 (1019–1086). Peking: Chung-hua shu-chü, 1956.

Wang Hsin-chai hsien-sheng ch'üan-chi 王心齋先生全集. 6 + 2 ch. By Wang Ken 王艮 (1483–1541). Ming printed ed.

Wang Lin-ch'uan chi 王臨川集. 100 ch. By Wang An-shih 王安石 (1021–1086). Taipei: Shih-chieh shu-chü, 1966.

Wang-shih chia-ts'ang chi 王氏家藏集. 66 ch. By Wang T'ing-hsiang 王廷相 (1474–1544). Taipei: Wei-wen, 1976 reprint of National Central Library copy.

Wang Yang-ming ch'üan-shu 王陽明全書. By Wang Shou-jen 王守仁 (1472–1529). Taipei: Cheng-chung shu-chü, 1955.

Wei-chai chi 韋齋集. 12 ch. By Chu Sung 朱松 (1097–1143). SKCS ed.

Wei shu 魏書. 114 ch. By Wei Shou 魏收 (506–572). Peking: Chung-hua shu-chü, 1974.

Wen-chou ching-chi chih 溫州經籍志. 33 ch. Edited by Sun I-jang 孫詒讓 (1848–1908). Shu-mu san-pien ed. Taipei: Kuang-wen shu-chü.

Wen-chung chi 文忠集. 200 ch. By Chou Pi-ta 周必大 (1126–1204). SKCS ed.

Wen-hsien t'ung-k'ao 文獻通考. 348 ch. By Ma Tuan-lin 馬端臨 (1254–1324/25). Taipei: Hsin-hsing shu-chü reprint of Shih-t'ung ed.

Wen hsüan 文選. 60 ch. By Hsiao T'ung 蕭統 (501–531). Hong Kong: Commercial Press, 1965 ed.

Wen-i chi 文毅集. 16 ch. By Hsieh Chin 解縉 (1369–1415). SKCS ed.

Wen-kung chia-li 文公家禮. 7 ch. Edited by Chiang Kuo-tso 蔣國祚 et al. 1602 ed.

Wen-kung chia-li hui-ch'eng 文公家禮會成. 8 ch. By Wei T'ang 魏堂. Preface 1557.

Wen-kuo chai chi (Wu Ch'ao-tsung hsien-sheng) 聞過齋集(吳朝宗先生). By Wu Hai 吳海 (fourteenth century). TSCC ed.

Wen-lu t'ang fang-shu chi 文祿堂訪書記. 5 ch. By Wang Wen-chin 王文進 (b. 1894). Shu-mu ts'ung-pien ed. Taipei: Kuang-wen shu-chü, 1967.

Wen-ting chi 文定集. 24 ch. By Wang Ying-ch'en 汪應辰 (1118–1176). TSCC ed.

Weng T'ai-shih pu-hsüan Wen-kung chia-li 翁太史補選文公家禮. 8 ch. By Weng Cheng-ch'un 翁正春 (1553–1627). Chien-i shu-lin Ming ed.

Wu-li t'ung-k'ao 五禮通考. 262 ch. By Ch'in Hui-t'ien 秦蕙田 (1702–1764). SKCS ed.

Wu-tai hui-yao 五代會要. 30 ch. By Wang P'u 王溥 (922–982). Taipei: Shih-chieh shu-chü, 1960.

Wu Wen-cheng chi 吳文正集. 98 ch. By Wu Ch'eng 吳澄 (1247–1331). SKCS ed.

Yen-i i-mou lu 燕翼詒謀錄. 5 ch. By Wang Yung 王栐 (d. 1227+). Peking: Chung-hua shu-chü, T'ang-Sung shih-liao pi-chi ts'ung-k'an, 1981.

Yen-shih chia-hsün 顏氏家訓. 7 ch. By Yen Chih-t'ui 顏之推 (531–591+). In *Yen-shih chia-hsün chi-chieh* 集解. *Chi-chieh* by Wang Li-ch'i 王利器. Taipei: Ming-wen shu-chü, 1982.

Yen-t'ieh lun chiao-chu 鹽鐵論校注. 10 ch. By Huan K'uan 桓寬 (first century B.C.). *Chiao-chu* by Wang Li-ch'i 王利器. Taipei: Shih-chieh shu-chü ed.

Ying-shu yü-lu 楹書隅錄. 5 ch. By Yang Shao-ho 楊紹和 (1830–1875). Shu-mu ts'ung-pien ed. Taipei: Kuang-wen shu-chü, 1967.

Yu-hui t'an-ts'ung 友會談叢. 1 ch. By Shang-kuan Jung 上官融. Pai-pu ts'ung-shu chi-ch'eng ed.

Yü-han shan-fang chi i-shu 玉函山房輯佚書. Edited by Ma Kuo-han 馬國翰 (1794–1857). Taipei: Wen-hai reprint.

Yün-ku tsa-chi 雲谷雜記. By Chang Hao 張淏 (fl. 1216). Pai-pu ts'ung-shu chi-ch'eng ed.

SECONDARY SOURCES

Addison, James Thayer. *Chinese Ancestor Worship: A Study of Its Meanings and Its Relations with Christianity*. Shanghai: Chung Hua Sheng Kung Hui, 1925.

Ahern, Emily M. "Affines and the Rituals of Kinship." In *Religion and Ritual in Chinese Society*, edited by Arthur P. Wolf. Stanford: Stanford University Press, 1974.

———. *The Cult of the Dead in a Chinese Village*. Stanford: Stanford University Press, 1973. (*See also* Emily Martin.)

Ariès, Philippe. *The Hour of Our Death*. New York: Vintage, 1981.

Bell, Catherine. "Religion and Chinese Culture: Toward an Assessment of 'Popular Religion.'" *History of Religions* 29.1 (1989): 35–57.

Bilsky, Lester James. *The State Religion of Ancient China*. 2 vols. Taipei: Chinese Association for Folklore, 1975.

Bloch, Maurice. *From Blessing to Violence: History and Ideology in the Circumcision Ritual of the Merina of Madagascar*. Cambridge: Cambridge University Press, 1986.

———. *Ritual, History and Power: Selected Papers in Anthropology*. London: Athlone, 1989.

Bloom, Irene. "On the Matter of the Mind: The Metaphysical Basis of the Expanded Self." In *Individualism and Holism: Studies in Confucian and Taoist Values*, edited by Donald J. Munro. Ann Arbor: Center for Chinese Studies, University of Michigan, 1985.

Bodde, Derk. *Essays on Chinese Civilization*, edited by Charles Le Blanc and Dorothy Borei. Princeton: Princeton University Press, 1981.

———. *Festivals in Classical China: New Year and Other Annual Observances During the Han Dynasty 206 B.C.–A.D. 220*. Princeton: Princeton University Press, 1975.

Bol, Peter K. "Chu Hsi's Redefinition of Literati Learning." In *Neo-Confucian Education: The Formative Stage*, edited by Wm. Theodore de Bary and John W. Chaffee. Berkeley: University of California Press, 1989.

———. "Ch'eng Yi and the Cultural Tradition." In *The Power of Culture: Studies in Chinese Cultural History*, edited by Andrew H. Plaks and Willard J. Peterson. Hong Kong: University of Hong Kong Press, forthcoming.

———. *This Culture of Ours: Intellectual Transitions in T'ang and Sung China*. Stanford: Stanford University Press, forthcoming.

———. "Rulership and Sagehood, Bureaucracy and Society: A Historical Inquiry into the Political Visions of Ssu-ma Kuang (1019–1086) and Wang An-shih (1021–1086)." Paper presented at the conference on Sung Statescraft, 1986.

Brook, Timothy. "Funerary Ritual and the Building of Lineages in Late Imperial China." *Harvard Journal of Asiatic Studies* 49 (1989): 465–99.

Brook, Timothy. "Gentry Dominance in Chinese Society: Monasteries and Lineages in the Structuring of Local Society." Ph.D. diss., Harvard University, 1984.

Brown, Elizabeth A. R. "Death and the Human Body in the Later Middle Ages: The Legislation of Boniface VIII on the Division of the Corpse." *Viator* 12 (1981): 221–70.

Burke, Peter. *Popular Culture in Early Modern Europe*. New York: New York University Press, 1978.

Burkhardt, V. R. *Chinese Creeds and Customs*. Hong Kong: South China Morning Post, 1982.

Chaffee, John W. *The Thorny Gates of Learning in Sung China: A Social History of Examinations*. Cambridge: Cambridge University Press, 1985.

Chan, Wing-tsit [Ch'en Jung-chieh 陳榮捷]. "The Ch'eng-Chu School of Early Ming." In *Self and Society in Ming Thought*, edited by Wm. Theodore de Bary. New York: Columbia University Press, 1970.

———, ed. *Chu Hsi and Neo-Confucianism*. Honolulu: University of Hawaii Press, 1986.

———. "Chu Hsi and Yüan Confucianism." In *Yüan Thought: Chinese Thought and Religion under the Mongols*, edited by Hok-lam Chan and Wm. Theodore de Bary. New York: Columbia University Press, 1982.

———. "Chu Hsi's Completion of Neo-Confucianism." *Études Song, In Memoriam Étienne Balazs* 2 (1973): 59–70.

———. *Chu Tzu hsin t'an-so* 朱子新探索. Taipei: Hsüeh-sheng shu-chü, 1988.

———. *Chu Tzu men-jen* 朱子門人. Taipei: Hsüeh-sheng shu-chü, 1982.

———. "The *Hsing-li ching-i* and the Ch'eng-Chu School of the Seventeenth Century." In *The Unfolding of Neo-Confucianism*, edited by Wm. Theodore de Bary. New York: Columbia University Press, 1975.

———, trans. *Instructions for Practical Living and Other Neo-Confucian Writings by Wang Yang-ming*. New York: Columbia University Press, 1963.

Chang, K. C. *Art, Myth, and Ritual: The Path to Political Authority in Ancient China*. Cambridge: Harvard University Press, 1983.

Chang Liwen. "An Analysis of Chu Hsi's System of Thought of *I*." In *Chu Hsi and Neo-Confucianism*, edited by Wing-tsit Chan. Honolulu: University of Hawaii Press, 1986.

Chard, Robert L. "The New Year Stove Rituals and the Stove God Scriptures in Domestic Popular Religion." Paper presented at the conference on Rituals and Scriptures in Chinese Popular Religion, Bodega Bay, January 1990.

Ch'en Cheng-fu 陳正夫 and Ho Chih-ching 何植靖. *Chu Hsi p'ing-chuan* 朱熹評傳. Nanchang: Kiangshi jen-min ch'u-pan-she, 1984.

Ch'en Lai 陳來. "Chu Tzu 'Chia-li' chen-wei k'ao-i" 朱子《家禮》真偽考議. *Pei-ching ta-hsüeh hsüeh-pao* 1989.3: 115–22.

———. *Chu Tzu shu-hsin pien-nien k'ao-cheng* 朱子書信編年考證. Shanghai: Shanghai jen-min ch'u-pan-she, 1989.

Ch'en Yin-k'o 陳寅恪. *T'ang-tai cheng-chih shih shu-lun kao* 唐代政治史述論稿. Taipei: Commercial Press, 1966 reprint of 1943 original.

Chiang Li-ts'ai 蔣勵材. "Ch'un-ju Chang Nan-hsüan ti Hsiang-hsüeh" 醇儒張南軒的湘學. *K'ung-Meng hsüeh-pao* 36 (1978): 169–208.

Ch'ien, Edward T. *Chiao Hung and the Restructuring of Neo-Confucianism in the Late Ming*. New York: Columbia University Press, 1986.

————. "The Neo-Confucian Confrontation with Buddhism: A Structural and Historical Analysis." *Journal of Chinese Philosophy* 9 (1982): 307–28.

Ch'ien Mu 錢穆. *Chu Tzu hsin hsüeh-an* 朱子新學案. 5 vols. Taipei: San-min shu-chü, 1971.

————. "A Historical Perspective on Chu Hsi's Learning." In *Chu Hsi and Neo-Confucianism*, edited by Wing-tsit Chan. Honolulu: University of Hawaii Press, 1986.

————. "Lüeh lun Wei-Chin Nan-pei-ch'ao hsüeh-shu wen-hua yü tang-shih men-ti chih kuan-hsi" 略論魏晉南北朝學術文化與當時門第之關係. *Hsin-ya hsüeh-pao* 5.2 (1963): 23–77.

————. *Sung-Ming li-hsüeh kai-shu* 宋明理學概述. Taipei: Hsüeh-sheng shu-chü, 1977 (first edition 1953).

Chikusa Masaaki 竺沙雅章. *Chūgoku bukkyō shakai shi kenkyū*. (Tōyōshi kenkyū sōkan vol. 34.) Kyoto: Dōhōsha, 1982.

————. "Shiba Kō O Anseki yo bukkyō" 司馬光王安石與佛教. In *Chi-nien Ssu-ma Kuang, Wang An-shih shih-shih chiu-pai chou-nien hsüeh-shu yen-t'ao-hui lun-wen chi* 紀念司馬光王安石逝世九百周年學術研討會論文集. Taipei: Wen-shih-che, 1986.

Ch'ing, Julia. *To Acquire Wisdom: The Way of Wang Yang-ming*. New York: Columbia University Press, 1976.

Chou I-liang 周一良. "Tun-huang hsieh-pen shu-i chung so-chien ti T'ang-tai hun-sang li-su" 敦煌寫本書儀中所見的唐代婚喪禮俗. *Wen-wu* 1985.7: 17–25.

Chow, Kai-wing. "Ritual and Ethics: Classical Scholarship and Lineage Institutions in Late Imperial China, 1600–1830." Ph.D. diss., University of California, Davis, 1988.

Chu Hung-lam. "Ch'iu Chün (1421–1495) and the *Ta-hsüeh yen-i pu*: Statecraft Thought in Fifteenth-Century China." Ph.D. diss., Princeton University, 1983.

Chu, Ron-guey. "Chu Hsi and Public Instruction." In *Neo-Confucian Education: The Formative Stage*, edited by Wm. Theodore de Bary and John W. Chaffee. Berkeley: University of California Press, 1989.

Chun, Allen J. "Conceptions of Kinship and Kingship in Classical Chou China." *T'oung Pao*, forthcoming.

Cohen, Myron L. *House United, House Divided: The Chinese Family in Taiwan*. New York: Columbia University Press, 1976.

Creel, Herrlee Glessner. *The Birth of China: A Study of the Formative Period of Chinese Civilization*. New York: Ungar, 1937.

Dardess, John W. "The Cheng Communal Family: Social Organization and Neo-Confucianism in Yüan and Early Ming China." *Harvard Journal of Asiatic Studies* 34 (1974): 7–52.

————. *Confucianism and Autocracy: Professional Elites in the Founding of the Ming Dynasty*. Berkeley: University of California Press, 1983.

Davis, Natalie Zemon, "Ghosts, Kin, and Progeny: Some Features of Family Life in Early Modern France." *Daedalus* 106 (1977): 87–114.

de Bary, Wm. Theodore. "Human Rites: An Essay on Confucianism and Human Rights." In *Confucianism: The Dynamics of Tradition*, edited by Irene Eber. New York: Macmillan, 1986.

————. "Individualism and Humanitarianism in Late Ming Thought." In *Self and Society in Ming Thought*, edited by Wm. Theodore de Bary. New York: Columbia University Press, 1970.

de Bary, Wm. Theodore. *The Liberal Tradition in China*. Hong Kong: Chinese University Press, 1983.

———. *Neo-Confucian Orthodoxy and the Learning of the Mind-and-Heart*. New York: Columbia University Press, 1981.

———. "A Reappraisal of Neo-Confucianism." In *Studies in Chinese Thought*, edited by Arthur F. Wright. Chicago: University of Chicago Press, 1953.

——— et al. *Sources of Chinese Tradition*. New York: Columbia University Press, 1960.

———, and John W. Chaffee, eds. *Neo-Confucian Education: The Formative Stage*. Berkeley: University of California Press, 1989.

de Groot, J. J. M. "Buddhist Masses for the Dead at Amoy: An Ethnological Essay." In *Actes du Sixieme Congrès International des Orientalistes, Part 4, Section 4*. Leiden: E. J. Brill, 1885.

———. *The Religious System of China*. 6 vols. Leyden: E. J. Brill, 1892–1910.

DeWoskin, Kenneth J. *A Song for One or Two: Music and the Concept of Art in Early China*. Ann Arbor: Center for Chinese Studies, University of Michigan, 1982.

Doolittle, Justus. *Social Life of the Chinese, with some Account of their Religious, Governmental, Educational, and Business Customs and Opinions, with Special but not Exclusive Reference to Fuhchau*. New York: Harper, 1865.

Doré, Henry. *Researches into Chinese Superstitions*. Translated by M. Kennelly. Taipei: Ch'eng-wen ch'u-pan-she, 1966 reprint of 1914 ed.

Duara, Prasenjit. *Culture, Power, and the State: Rural North China, 1900–1942*. Stanford: Stanford University Press, 1988.

Duby, Georges. *The Knight, the Lady and the Priest: The Making of Modern Marriage in Medieval France*. New York: Pantheon, 1983.

Dull, Jack L. "A Historical Introduction to the Apocryphal (Ch'an-Wei) Texts of the Han Dynasty." Ph.D. diss., University of Washington, 1966.

Dunne, George H. *Generation of Giants: The Story of the Jesuits in China in the Last Decades of the Ming Dynasty*. Notre Dame: University of Notre Dame Press, 1962.

Eberhard, Wolfram. *Guilt and Sin in Traditional China*. Berkeley: University of California Press, 1967.

Ebrey, Patricia Buckley. *The Aristocratic Families of Early Imperial China: A Case Study of the Po-ling Ts'ui Family*. Cambridge: Cambridge University Press, 1978.

———, ed. *Chinese Civilization and Society: A Sourcebook*. New York: Free Press, 1981.

———, trans. *Chu Hsi's Family Rituals: A Twelfth-Century Chinese Manual for the Performance of Cappings, Weddings, Funerals, and Ancestral Rites*. Princeton: Princeton University Press, 1991.

———. "Conceptions of the Family in the Sung Dynasty." *Journal of Asian Studies* 43 (1984): 219–45.

———. "Concubines in Sung China." *Journal of Family History* 11 (1986): 1–24.

———. "Cremation in Sung China." *American Historical Review* 95 (1990): 406–28.

———. "The Dynamics of Elite Domination in Sung China." *Harvard Journal of Asiatic Studies* 48 (1988): 493–519.

———. "The Early Stages in the Development of Descent Group Organization." In *Kinship Organization in Late Imperial China, 1000–1940*, edited by Patricia Buckley Ebrey and James L. Watson. Berkeley: University of California Press, 1986.

———. "Education through Ritual: Efforts to Formulate Family Rituals During the Sung Period." In *Neo-Confucian Education: The Formative Stage*, edited by Wm. Theordore de Bary and John W. Chaffee. Berkeley: University of California Press, 1989.

———. *Family and Property in Sung China: Yüan Ts'ai's Precepts for Social Life*. Princeton: Princeton University Press, 1984.

———. "Shifts in Marriage Finance from the Sixth to the Thirteenth Centuries." In *Marriage and Inequality in Chinese Society*, edited by Rubie S. Watson and Patricia Buckley Ebrey. Berkeley: University of California Press, 1991.

———. "Sung Neo-Confucian Attitudes toward Geomancy." Unpublished paper.

———. "T'ang Guides to Verbal Etiquette." *Harvard Journal of Asiatic Studies* 45 (1985): 581–613.

Egan, Ronald C. *The Literary Works of Ou-yang Hsiu (1007–72)*. Cambridge: Cambridge University Press, 1984.

Elman, Benjamin A. *From Philosophy to Philology: Intellectual and Social Aspects of Change in Late Imperial China*. Cambridge: Harvard University Press, 1984.

Eno, Robert. "Masters of the Dance: The Role of T'ien in the Teachings of the Early Juist (Confucian) Community." Ph.D. diss., University of Michigan, 1984.

Farmer, Edward L. "Social Regulations of the First Ming Emperor: Orthodoxy as a Function of Authority." In *Orthodoxy in Imperial China*, edited by Kwang-Ching Liu. Berkeley: University of California Press, 1989.

Fehl, Noah Edward. *Li: Rites and Propriety in Literature and Life, A Perspective for a Cultural History of Ancient China*. Hong Kong: The Chinese University, 1971.

Fei, Hsiao-tung. *Peasant Life in China: A Field Study of Country Life in the Yangtze Valley*. London: Routledge, 1939.

Fielde, Adele M. *A Corner of Cathay: Studies from Life among the Chinese*. New York: Macmillan, 1894.

Fingarette, Herbert. *Confucius—the Secular as Sacred*. New York: Harper and Row, 1972.

Fisher, Carney T. "The Ritual Dispute of Sung Ying-tsung." *Papers on Far Eastern History* 36 (1987): 109–38.

Forke, Alfred, trans. *Lun-Heng*. New York: Paragon Book Gallery 1962 reprint of 1907–1911 ed.

Freedman, Maurice. *Lineage Organization in Southeastern China*. London: Athlone Press, 1958.

———. "Rites and Duties, or Chinese Marriage." In his *The Study of Chinese Society*. Stanford: Stanford University Press, 1979.

———. "Ritual Aspects of Chinese Kinship and Marriage." In his *The Study of Chinese Society*. Stanford: Stanford University Press, 1979.

Fu, Charles Wei-hsun. "Chu Hsi on Buddhism." In *Chu Hsi and Neo-Confucianism*, edited by Wing-tsit Chan. Honolulu: University of Hawaii Press, 1986.

Fung Yu-lan. *A History of Chinese Philosophy*. 2 vols. Translated by Derk Bodde. Princeton: Princeton University Press, 1952.

Gardner, Daniel K. *Chu Hsi and the Ta-hsüeh: Neo-Confucian Reflection on the Confucian Canon*. Cambridge: Harvard University Press, 1986.

Geertz, Clifford. *Local Knowledge: Further Essays in Interpretive Anthropology*. New York: Basic Books, 1983.

Goodrich, L. Carrington, and Chaoying Fang, eds. *Dictionary of Ming Biography, 1368–1644*. New York: Columbia University Press, 1976.

Goody, Jack. *The Logic of Writing and the Organization of Society*. Cambridge: Cambridge University Press, 1986.

Graham, A. C. *Two Chinese Philosophers: Ch'eng Ming-tao and Ch'eng Yi-ch'uan*. London: Lund Humphries, 1958.

Gray, John Henry. *China: A History of the Laws, Manners, and Customs of the People*. London: Macmillan, 1878.

Haeger, John Winthrop. "The Intellectual Context of Neo-Confucian Syncretism." *Journal of Asian Studies* 31.3 (1972): 499–513.

Hall, David L., and Roger T. Ames. *Thinking Through Confucius*. Albany: State University of New York Press, 1987.

Handlin, Johanna F. *Action in Late Ming Thought: The Reorientation of Lü K'un and Other Scholar-Officials*. Berkeley: University of California Press, 1983.

Hansen, Valerie. *Changing Gods in Medieval China, 1127–1276*. Princeton: Princeton University Press, 1990

Harrell, Stevan. *Ploughshare Village: Culture and Context in Taiwan*. Seattle: University of Washington Press, 1982.

Hartman, Charles. *Han Yü and the T'ang Search for Unity*. Princeton: Princeton University Press, 1986.

Hartwell, Robert M. "Demographic, Political, and Social Transformations of China, 750–1550." *Harvard Journal of Asiatic Studies* 42 (1982): 365–442.

———. "Historical Analogism, Public Policy, and Social Science in Eleventh- and Twelfth-Century China." *American Historical Review* 76 (1971): 690–727.

Harvey, Edwin D. *The Mind of China*. New Haven: Yale University Press, 1933.

Hawkes, David, trans. *The Story of the Stone*. 5 vols. New York: Penguin, 1973–77.

Hayes, James. "Specialists and Written Materials in the Village World." In *Popular Culture in Late Imperial China*, edited by David Johnson, Andrew J. Nathan, and Evelyn S. Rawski. Berkeley: University of California Press, 1985.

Hobsbaum, Eric, and Terence Ranger, eds. *The Invention of Tradition*. Cambridge: Cambridge University Press, 1983.

Holzman, Donald. "Filial Piety in Ancient and Early Medieval China: Its Perennity and Its Importance in the Cult of the Emperor." Paper presented at the conference on the Nature of State and Society in Medieval China, Stanford, August 16–18, 1980.

———. *Poetry and Politics: The Life and Works of Juan Chi (A.D. 210–263)*. Cambridge: Cambridge University Press, 1976.

Hsiao, Kung-chuan. *A History of Chinese Political Thought*. Vol. 1, *From the*

Beginning to the Sixth Century A.D. Translated by F. W. Mote. Princeton: Princeton University Press, 1979.

Hsieh, Shan-yüan. *The Life and Thought of Li Kou, 1009–1059.* San Francisco: Chinese Materials Center, 1979.

Hsu, Francis L. K. *Americans and Chinese.* London: Cresset, 1955.

———. *Under the Ancestors' Shadow: Kinship, Personality and Social Mobility in China.* 1948. Revised ed. Stanford: Stanford University Press, 1971.

Hsü Fu-kuan. "A Comparative Study of Chu Hsi and the Ch'eng Brother." In *Chu Hsi and Neo-Confucianism,* edited by Wing-tsit Chan. Honolulu: University of Hawaii Press, 1986.

Hsü P'ing-fang 徐苹芳. "Sung-tai mu-tsang ho chiao-ts'ang ti fa-chüeh" 宋代墓葬和窖藏的發掘. In *Hsin Chung-kuo ti k'ao-ku fa-hsien ho yen-chiu* 新中國的考古發現和研究. Peking: Wen-wu, 1984.

Huang Min-chih 黃敏枝. *Sung-tai fo-chiao she-hui ching-chi shih-lun chi* 宋代佛教社會經濟史論集. Taipei: Hsüeh-sheng shu-chü, 1988.

Huc, M. *The Chinese Empire.* 2 vols. London: Longman, Brown, Green, and Longman, 1855.

Hummel, Arthur W., ed. *Eminent Chinese of the Ch'ing Period.* Washington, D.C.: Government Printing Office, 1943.

Huntington, Richard, and Peter Metcalf. *Celebrations of Death: The Anthropology of Mortuary Ritual.* Cambridge: Cambridge University Press, 1979.

Hymes, Robert P. *Statesmen and Gentlemen: The Elite of Fu-chou, Chiang-hsi in Northern and Southern Sung.* Cambridge: Cambridge University Press, 1986.

Johnson, David. "The City-God Cults of T'ang and Sung China." *Harvard Journal of Asiatic Studies* 45 (1985): 363–457.

———. "Communication, Class, and Consciousness in Late Imperial China." In *Popular Culture in Late Imperial China,* edited by David Johnson, Andrew J. Nathan, and Evelyn S. Rawski. Berkeley: University of California Press, 1985.

———. "The Last Years of a Great Clan: The Li Family of Chao Chün in Late T'ang and Early Sung." *Harvard Journal of Asiatic Studies* 37 (1977): 5–102.

———, ed. *Ritual Opera, Operatic Ritual: "Mu-lien Rescues His Mother" in Chinese Popular Culture.* Berkeley: Chinese Popular Culture Project, 1989.

Johnston, R. F. *Lion and Dragon in Northern China.* New York: Dutton, 1910.

Jordan, David K. *Gods, Ghosts, and Ancestors: The Folk Religion of a Taiwanese Village.* Berkeley: University of California Press, 1972.

Kao Ling-yin 高令印, and Ch'en Ch'i-fang 陳其芳. *Fu-chien Chu Tzu hsüeh* 福建朱子學. Fu-chou: Fu-chien jen-min ch'u-pan-she, 1986.

Kao Ming. "Chu Hsi's Discipline of Propriety." In *Chu Hsi and Neo-Confucianism,* edited by Wing-tsit Chan. Honolulu: University of Hawaii Press, 1986.

——— 高明. *Li-hsüeh hsin-t'an* 禮學新探. Hong Kong: Chung-wen ta-hsüeh, 1963.

Kassoff, Ira E. *The Thought of Chang Tsai, 1020–1077.* Cambridge: Cambridge University Press, 1984.

Keightley, David N. "The Religious Commitment: Shang Theology and the Genesis of Chinese Political Culture." *History of Religions* 17 (1978): 211–25.

———. *Sources of Shang History: The Oracle-Bone Inscriptions of Bronze Age China.* Berkeley: University of California Press, 1978.

Kelleher, M. Theresa. "Back to Basics: Chu Hsi's *Elementary Learning (Hsiao-hsüeh)*." In *Neo-Confucian Education: The Formative State*, edited by Wm. Theodore de Bary and John W. Chaffee. Berkeley: University of California Press, 1989.

Kinugawa Tsuyoshi 衣川強. "Sōdai no meizoku—Kanan Ryoshi no baai" 宋代 の名族—河南呂氏のばあい. *Kobe shōka daigaku jimbun ronshū* 9 (1973): 134–66.

Kitamura, Ryoka 北村辰和. "Mau Kirei no reigaku" 毛奇齢の禮説. *Machikane-yama ronsō: Tetsugakuhen* 11 (1978): 17–34.

Klapisch-Zuber, Christiane. *Women, Family, and Ritual in Renaissance Italy*. Translated by Lydia G. Cochrane. Chicago: University of Chicago Press, 1985.

Kulp, Daniel Harrison. *Country Life in South China: The Sociology of Familism*. New York: Teachers College, 1925.

Kuo Hu-sheng 郭湖生 et al. "Ho-nan Kung-hsien Sung-ling tiao-ch'a" 河南鞏縣 宋陵調查. *K'ao-ku* 1964.11: 564–75.

Langlois, John D., Jr., and Sun K'o-k'uan. "Three Teachings Syncretism and the Thought of Ming T'ai-tsu." *Harvard Journal of Asiatic Studies* 43 (1983): 97–139.

Lears, T. J. Jackson. "The Concept of Cultural Hegemony: Problems and Possibilities." *American Historical Review* 90.3 (1985): 567–93.

Lee, Thomas H. C. *Government Education and Examinations in Sung China*. Hong Kong: Chinese University of Hong Kong Press, 1985.

Legge, James, trans. *The Chinese Classics*. 5 vols. Hong Kong: Hong Kong University Press, 1961 reprint of Oxford, 1865–1895 ed.

————, trans. *Li Chi, Book of Rites*. 2 vols. New York: University Books, 1967 reprint of Oxford 1885 Sacred Books of the East ed.

Levering, Miriam. "Ta-hui and Lay Buddhists: Ch'an Sermons on Death." In *Buddhist and Taoist Practice in Medieval Chinese Society*, edited by David W. Chappell. Buddhist and Taoist Studies II. Honolulu: University of Hawaii Press, 1987.

Levi, Jean. "Les Fonctionnaires et le Divin: Luttes de Pouvoirs entre Divinités et Administrateurs dans les Contes des Six Dynasties et des Tang." *Cahiers d'Extreme-Asie* 2 (1986): 81–108.

Lewis, Gilbert. *Day of Shining Red: An Essay on Understanding Ritual*. Cambridge: Cambridge University Press, 1982.

Lewis, Mark Edward. *Sanctioned Violence in Early China*. Albany: State University of New York, 1990.

Li Wei-jan 李蔚然. "Nan-ching Chung-hua men-wai Sung-mu" 南京中華門外 宋墓. *K'ao-ku* 1963.6: 343, 339.

Liu, Hui-chen Wang. "An Analysis of Chinese Clan Rules: Confucian Theories in Action." In *Confucianism in Action*, edited by David S. Nivison and Arthur F. Wright. Stanford: Stanford University Press, 1959.

————. *The Traditional Chinese Clan Rules*. Locust Valley, N.Y.: J. J. Augustin, 1959.

Liu, James T. C. *China Turning Inward: Intellectual-Political Changes in the Early Twelfth Century*. Cambridge: Harvard University Press, 1988.

———. "How Did a Neo-Confucian School Become the State Orthodoxy?" *Philosophy East and West* 23 (1973): 483–505.

———. *Ou-yang Hsiu: An Eleventh-Century Neo-Confucianist*. Stanford: Stanford University Press, 1967.

Liu Shih-chi 劉仕驥. *Chung-kuo tsang-su sou-ch'i* 中國葬俗搜奇. Hong Kong: Shang-hai shu-chü, 1957.

Lo, Winston W. *An Introduction to the Civil Service of Sung China*. Honolulu: University of Hawaii Press, 1987.

Loewe, Michael. *Chinese Ideas of Life and Death: Faith, Myth and Reason in the Han Period (202 B.C.–A.D. 220)*. London: Allen and Unwin, 1982.

———. *Crisis and Conflict in Han China, 104 B.C. to A.D. 9*. London: Allen and Unwin, 1974.

Makino Tatsumi 牧野巽. *Kinsei Chūgoku sōzoku kenkyū* 近代中國宗族研究. Tokyo: Nikkō, 1949.

———. "Sōshi to sono hattatsu" 宗祠と其の發達. *Tōyō gakuhō (Tokyo)* 9 (1939): 173–250.

Makio Ryōkai 牧尾良海. "Shūshi to fūsui shisō 朱子と風水思想. *Chizan gakuhō* 智山學報 23–24 (1974): 361–77.

Mann, Susan. "Grooming a Daughter for Marriage: Brides and Wives in the Mid Ch'ing Period." In *Marriage and Inequality in Chinese Society*, edited by Rubie S. Watson and Patricia Buckley Ebrey. Berkeley: University of California Press, 1991.

Martin, Emily. "Gender and Ideological Differences in Representations of Life and Death." In *Death Rituals in Late Imperial and Modern China*, edited by James L. Watson and Evelyn S. Rawski. Berkeley: University of California Press, 1988.

Martin, W. A. P. *The Lore of Cathay, or The Intellect of China*. New York: Revell, 1901.

Mather, Richard B., trans. *A New Account of Tales of the World*. Minneapolis: University of Minnesota Press, 1976.

Matsui Shūichi 松井秀一. "Hoku Sō shoki kanryō no ichi tenkei—Seki Kai to sono keifu o chūshin ni" 北宋初期官僚の一典型—石介とその系譜お中心に. *Tōyō gakuhō* 51.1 (1968): 44–92.

Matsumoto Koichi 松本浩一. "Sorei, sairei ni miru Sōdai shūkyōshi no ichi keikō" 葬禮, 祭禮にみる宋代宗教史の一傾向. In *Sōdai no shakai to bunka*, edited by Sōdaishi kenkyūkai. Tokyo: Kyūko, 1983.

McMullen, David. "Bureaucrats and Cosmology: The Ritual Code of T'ang China." In *Rituals of Royalty: Power and Ceremonial in Traditional Societies*, edited by David Cannadine and Simon Price. Cambridge: Cambridge University Press, 1987.

———. *State and Scholars in T'ang China*. Cambrige: Cambridge University Press, 1988.

Miyakawa, Hisayuki. "The Confucianization of South China." In *The Confucian Persuasion*, edited by Arthur F. Wright. Stanford: Stanford University Press, 1960.

Miyazaki Ichisada 宮崎市定. *Ajiashi kenkyū II* アジア史研究. Kyoto: Tōyōshi kenkyūkai, 1957.

Moore, Sally F., and Barbara G. Meyerhoff, eds. *Secular Ritual*. Amsterdam: Van Gorcum, 1977.

Morita Kenji 森田憲司. "Sō Gen jidai ni okeru shūfu" 宋元時代にける修譜. *Tōyōshi kenkyū* 37 (1979): 509–35.

Moule, Arthur E. *New China and Old: Personal Recollections and Observations of Thirty Years*. London: Seeley, 1902.

Munro, Donald J. *Images of Human Nature: A Sung Portrait*. Princeton: Princeton University Press, 1988.

Naquin, Susan. "Funerals in North China: Uniformity and Variation." In *Death Ritual in Late Imperial and Modern China*, edited by James L. Watson and Evelyn S. Rawski. Berkeley: University of California Press, 1988.

———. "Marriage in North China: The Role of Ritual." Paper presented at the conference on Marriage and Inequality in Chinese Society, 1988.

Niida Noboru 仁井田陞. *Shina mibunhō shi* 支那身分法史. Tokyo: Zayūhō kankōkai, 1937.

Ocko, Jonathan K. "Women, Property, and the Law in the PRC." In *Marriage and Inequality in Chinese Society*, edited by Rubie S. Watson and Patricia Buckely Ebrey. Berkeley: University of California Press, 1991.

Ortner, Sherry B. "Theory in Anthropology since the Sixties." *Comparative Studies in Society and History* 26 (1984): 126–66.

Overmyer, Daniel L. "Values in Chinese Sectarian Literature: Ming and Ch'ing Pao-chüan." In *Popular Culture in Late Imperial China*, edited by David Johnson, Andrew J. Nathan, and Evelyn S. Rawski. Berkeley: University of California Press, 1985.

P'an, Fu-en 潘富恩, and Hsü Yü-ch'ing 徐余慶. *Lü Tsu-ch'ien ssu-hsiang ch'u-t'an* 呂祖謙思想初探. Hangchow: Che-chiang jen-min ch'u-pan-she, 1984.

Powers, Martin J. "Pictorial Art and Its Public in Early Imperial China." *Art History* 7.2 (1984): 135–63.

Pulleyblank, E. G. "Chinese Historical Criticism: Liu Chih-chi and Ssu-ma Kuang." In *Historians of China and Japan*, edited by W. G. Beasley and E. G. Pulleyblank. London: Oxford University Press, 1961.

———. "Neo-Confucianism and Neo-Legalism in T'ang Intellectual Life, 755–805." In *The Confucian Persuasion*, edited by Arthur F. Wright. Stanford: Stanford University Press, 1960.

Rawski, Evelyn S. "Economic and Social Foundations of Late Imperial Culture." In *Popular Culture in Late Imperial China*, edited by David Johnson, Andrew J. Nathan, and Evelyn S. Rawski. Berkeley: University of California Press, 1985.

Rossabi, Morris, ed. *China among Equals: The Middle Kingdom and Its Neighbors, 10th–14th Centuries*. Berkeley: University of California Press, 1983.

Rowbotham, Arnold H. *Missionary and Mandarin: The Jesuits at the Court of China*. Berkeley: University of California Press, 1942.

Sariti, Anthony. "Monarchy, Bureaucracy, and Absolutism in the Political Thought of Ssu-ma Kuang." *Journal of Asian Studies* 31.1 (1972): 53–76.

Schirokauer, Conrad. "Chu Hsi and Hu Hung." In *Chu Hsi and Neo-Confucianism*, edited by Wing-tsit Chan. Honolulu: University of Hawaii Press, 1986.

———. "Chu Hsi as an Administrator: A Preliminary Study." In *Études Song, In*

Memoriam Étienne Balazs, Série I, Histoire et Institutions 3, edited by Françoise Aubin. Paris: Mouton, 1976.

———. "Chu Hsi's Political Career: A Study in Ambivalence." In *Confucian Personalities*, edited by Arthur F. Wright and Denis Twitchett. Stanford: Stanford University Press, 1962.

———. "Neo-Confucians under Attack: The Condemnation of *Wei-hsüeh*." In *Crisis and Prosperity in Sung China*, edited by John Winthrop Haeger. Tucson: University of Arizona Press, 1975.

Schopen, Gregory. "Burial 'Ad Sanctos' and the Physical Presence of the Buddha in Early Indian Buddhism." *Religion* 17 (1987): 193–225.

Schwartz, Benjamin I. *The World of Thought in Ancient China*. Cambridge: Harvard University Press, 1985.

Seidel, Anna. "Traces of Han Religion in Funeral Texts Found in Tombs." In *Dōkyō to shūkyō bunka*. Tokyo: Heibonsha, 1987.

Shapiro, Sidney, trans. *The Family* (by Pa Chin). Peking: Foreign Languages Press, 1958.

Ssu-ch'uan sheng po-wu-kuan 四川省博物館 et al. "Ssu-ch'uan Kuang-yüan shih-k'o Sung-mu ch'ing-li chien-pao" 四川官原石刻宋墓清理簡報. *Wen-wu* 1982.6: 53–61.

Steele, John, trans. *The I-li, or Book of Etiquette and Ceremonial*. London: Probsthain, 1917.

Stein, Rolf A. "Religious Taoism and Popular Religion from the Second to the Seventh Centuries." In *Facts of Taoism*, edited by Holmes Welch and Anna Seidel. New Haven: Yale University Press, 1979.

Stock, Brian. *The Implications of Literacy: Written Language and Models of Interpretation in the Eleventh and Twelfth Centuries*. Princeton: Princeton University Press, 1983.

Su Pai 宿白. *Pai-sha Sung-mu* 白沙宋墓. Peking: Wen-wu, 1957.

Taga Akigoro 多賀秋五郎. *Chūgoku sōfu no kenkyū* 中國宗譜の研究. Tokyo: Nihon gakushutsu shinkōkai, 1981.

———. *Sōfu no kenkyū* 宗譜の研究. Tokyo: Tōyō bunko, 1960.

T'ai-yüan shih wen-wu kuan-li wei-yüan hui 太原市文物管理委員會. "T'ai-yüan shih Nan-p'ing-t'ou Sung-mu ch'ing-li chien-pao" 太原市南坪頭宋墓清理簡報. *Wen-wu ts'an-k'ao tzu-liao* 1956.3: 41–44.

Takeda Ryūji 竹田龍兒. "Tōdai shizoku no kahō ni tsuite" 唐代士族の家法につ いて. *Shigaku* 28.1 (1955): 84–105.

Tambiah, Stanley Jeyeraja. *Culture, Thought, and Social Action*. Cambridge: Harvard University Press, 1985.

T'ang Chang-ju 唐長孺. *Wen-Chin Nan-pei-ch'ao shih-lun ts'ung* 魏晉南北朝史論叢. Peking: Hsin-hua shu-chü, 1955.

Tao, Jing-shen. "Barbarians or Northerners: Northern Sung Images of the Khitan." In *China among Equals*, edited by Morris Rossabi. Berkeley: University of California Press, 1983.

Teiser, Stephen F. *The Ghost Festival in Medieval China*. Princeton: Princeton University Press, 1988.

Teng Ssu-yü, trans. *Family Instructions for the Yen Clan by Yen Chih-t'ui*. Leiden: E. J. Brill, 1968.

Thompson, Stuart E. "Death, Food, and Fertility." In *Death Rituals in Late Imperial and Modern China*, edited by James L. Watson and Evelyn S. Rawski. Berkeley: University of California Press, 1988.

Tjan, Tjoe Som, trans. *Po Hu T'ung: The Comprehensive Discussions in the White Tiger Hall*. Leiden: E. J. Brill, 1952.

Toews, John E. "Intellectual History after the Linguistic Turn: The Autonomy of Meaning and the Irreducibility of Experience." *American Historical Review* 92.4 (1987): 879–907.

Tso Yün-p'eng 左云鵬. "Tz'u-t'ang tsu-chang tsu-ch'üan ti hsing-ch'eng chi ch'i tso-yung shih-shuo" 祠堂族長族權的形成及其作用試說. *Li-shih yen-chiu* 1964.5–6: 97–116.

Tu Wei-ming. *Centrality and Commonality: An Essay on Chung-yung*. Honolulu: University of Hawaii Press, 1976.

———. "*Li* as a Process of Humanization." *Philosophy East and West* 22 (1972): 187–201.

———. *Neo-Confucian Thought in Action: Wang Yang-ming's Youth (1472–1529)*. Berkeley: University of California Press, 1976.

———. "Yen Yüan: From Inner Experience to Lived Concreteness." In *The Unfolding of Neo-Confucianism*, edited by Wm. Theodore de Bary. New York: Columbia University Press, 1975.

Twitchett, Denis. "The Composition of the T'ang Ruling Class: New Evidence from Tun-huang." In *Perspectives on the T'ang*, edited by Arthur F. Wright and Denis Twitchett. New Haven: Yale University Press, 1973.

———. "The Fan Clan's Charitable Estate, 1050–1760." In *Confucianism in Action*, edited by David S. Nivison and Arthur F. Wright. Stanford: Stanford University Press, 1959.

Übelhör, Monika. "The Community Compact (*Hsiang-yüeh*) of the Sung and Its Educational Significance." In *Neo-Confucian Education: The Formative Stage*, edited by Wm. Theodore de Bary and John W. Chaffee. Berkeley: University of California Press, 1989.

Ueyama Shumpei 上山春平. "Shushi no 'Karei' to 'Girei kyōden tsūkai'" 朱子 の［家禮］と［儀禮經傳通解］. *Tōyō gakuhō* 54 (1982): 173–256.

Umehara, Kaoru 梅原郁. *Sōdai kanryō seido kenkyū*. Kyoto: Dōhōsha, 1985.

Waley, Arthur, trans. *The Analects of Confucius*. New York: Vintage, 1938.

———, trans. *The Book of Songs*. London: Allen, 1937.

Walshe, W. Gilbert. "Some Chinese Funeral Customs." *Journal of the Royal Asiatic Society, North China Branch* 35 (1903–1904): 26–64.

Waltner, Ann. "The Moral Status of the Child in Late Imperial China: Childhood in Ritual and in Law." *Social Research* 53 (1986): 667–87.

Wang, Zhongshu. *Han Civilization*. New Haven: Yale University Press, 1982.

Watson, Burton, trans. *Basic Writings of Mo Tzu, Hsün Tzu, and Han Fei Tzu*. New York: Columbia University Press, 1967.

Watson, James L. "Funeral Specialists in Cantonese Society: Pollution, Performance, and Social Hierarchy." In *Death Ritual in Late Imperial and Modern China*, edited by James L. Watson and Evelyn S. Rawski. Berkeley: University of California Press, 1988.

————, and Evelyn S. Rawski, eds. *Death Ritual in Late Imperial and Modern China*. Berkeley: University of California Press, 1988.

Watson, Rubie S. "Class Differences and Affinal Relations in South China." *Man* 16 (1981): 593–615.

————. "Remembering the Dead: Graves and Politics in Southeastern China." In *Death Ritual in Late Imperial and Modern China*, edited by James L. Watson and Evelyn S. Rawski. Berkeley: University of California Press, 1988.

————. "Wives, Concubines, and Maids: Servitude and Kinship in the Hong Kong Region, 1900–1940." In *Marriage and Inequality in Chinese Society*, edited by Rubie S. Watson and Patricia Buckley Ebrey. Berkeley: University of California Press, 1991.

Wechsler, Howard J. *Offerings of Jade and Silk: Ritual and Symbol in the Legitimation of the T'ang Dynasty*. New Haven: Yale University Press, 1985.

Weinstein, Stanley. *Buddhism under the T'ang*. Cambridge: Cambridge University Press, 1987.

Weller, Robert P. *Unities and Diversities in Chinese Religion*. Seattle: University of Washington Press, 1987.

Williams, S. W. "The Worship of Ancestors among the Chinese." *China Repository* 18 (1849): 363–84.

Wolf, Arthur P., and Chieh-shan Huang. *Marriage and Adoption in China, 1845–1945*. Stanford: Stanford University Press, 1980.

Wolf, Margery. *Women and the Family in Rural Taiwan*. Stanford: Stanford University Press, 1972.

Wu Hung. "From Temple to Tomb: Ancient Chinese Art and Religion in Transition." *Early China* 14 (1989): 78–115.

Yamane Mitsuyoshi 山根三芳. "Chōshi reisetsu kō" 張子禮說考. *Nihon Chūgoku gakkaihō* 22 (1970): 72–92.

————. "Ni-Teishi reisetsu kō" 二程子禮說考. In *Yoshioka hakushi kanreki kinen Dōkyō kenkyū ronshū*. Tokyo: Kokusho kankōkai, 1977.

————. "Shiba Kō reisetsu kō" 司馬光禮說考. In *Mori Mikisaburō hakushi kōshō kinen Tōyō gaku ronshū*. Tokyo: Hōyū shoten, 1979.

Yang, C. K. *Religion in Chinese Society*. Berkeley: University of California Press, 1961.

Yang Shu-ta 楊樹達. *Han-tai hun-sang li-su k'ao* 漢代婚喪禮俗考. Taipei: Hua-shih ch'u-pan-she, 1976.

Yao Ming-ta 姚名達. *Ch'eng I-ch'uan nien-p'u* 程伊川年譜. Shanghai: Commercial Press, 1937.

Yü Ying-shih 余英時. *Chung-kuo chih-shih chieh-ts'eng shih lun* 中國知識階層史論. Taipei: Lien-ching, 1980.

————. "Individualism and the Neo-Taoist Movement in Wei-Chin China." In *Individualism and Holism: Studies in Confucian and Taoist Values*, edited by Donald J. Munro. Ann Arbor: Center for Chinese Studies, University of Michigan, 1985.

————. "Morality and Knowledge in Chu Hsi's Philosophical System." In *Chu Hsi and Neo-Confucianism*, edited by Wing-tsit Chan. Honolulu: University of Hawaii Press, 1986.

Yü Ying-shih. ''O Soul, Come Back—A Study in the Changing Conceptions of the Soul and Afterlife in Pre-Buddhist China.'' *Harvard Journal of Asiatic Studies* 47 (1987): 363–95.

Zito, A. R. "City Gods, Filiality, and Hegemony in Late Imperial China." *Modern China* 13.3 (1987): 333–71.

———. "Re-presenting Sacrifice: Cosmology and the Editing of Texts." *Ch'ing-shih wen-t'i* 5.2 (1984): 47–78.

INDEX

Addison, James, 3
adoption, 210–11
Analects, 16, 18
ancestors, 16, 22–23, 81; in Chinese civilization, 3; early, 63, 127; early ideas of, 15–
  16; number of generations served, 61, 105–
  6, 152; reports to, 82. *See also* ancestral
  rites; ancestral tablets
ancestral portraits, 62, 105, 184
ancestral rites, 21–23, 26–27, 46–67, 127,
  133, 151, 183–85; Chu Hsi on, 123–29;
  dates for, 62, 105, 128–29, 183, 210; by
  descent groups, 158–65; endowing, 106,
  159; in the *Family Rituals*, 106, 107–9;
  gradations by rank, 47, 53, 61; at graves,
  63–64, 124, 127–29; presiding at, 56–60.
  See also ancestors; ancestral tablets; offering halls
ancestral tablets, 62–63, 97; arrangement of,
  106, 150, 183; associating, 98, 106, 138,
  210–11; made of paper, 183; for wives, 125
ancestral temples, 22, 30, 53–56, 160–61,
  193. *See also* family shrines; offering halls
aristocratic families, 37–39
astrologers, 8

Book of Burials, 72, 94
Book of Documents, 15, 16
Book of Poetry, 15, 16
bowing, 82
Buddhism, 36, 41, 85, 89, 131; Confucian
  opposition to, 77–79, 88–89, 127, 134,
  153; and cremation, 95
Buddhist monks, 8, 42, 43, 73, 88, 97; as funeral experts, 214
Buddhist nuns, 76
Buddhist services, 76, 88–89, 119, 138, 154,
  182, 212–15
Buddhist temples, 73, 95; leaving coffins in,
  94
burial, 23, 36, 68, 72; archaeological evidence for, 90–91; delay of, 94; in Han period, 32; moving bodies for, 93; Sung customs for, 89–98; technology of, 90–92. *See
  also* geomancy

capping, 19–20, 22, 80n, 131
catafalques, 96
censorship, 200
Chang Chia-ling, 189
Chang Chün, 120, 121
Chang Shih, 109–11, 119–20, 122, 125, 132–
  33, 138, 173, 222; on ancestral rites, 127,
  129; book on family rituals, 131, 173; on
  reforming customs, 132
Chang Te-hsiang, 94
Chang Tsai, 48, 87n, 135, 178, 199, 222–23;
  on ancestral rites, 62, 64, 104, 133; cited
  by Chang Shih, 131; cited by Lü Tsu-
  ch'ien, 123; cited by Yang Fu, 147; on de-
  scent-line system, 57–62; discussed by Chu
  Hsi, 111, 125, 135–36; family of, 59; theo-
  ries of ritual, 50–52
Chang Tuan-i, 75
Chao Chü-hsin, 159–60, 172n
chao-mu, 72, 93, 105, 159
Chao Shih-shu, 146
Ch'e Kai, 147n
Chen Te-hsiu, 141, 172n
Ch'en Ch'üeh, 160, 189
Ch'en Ch'un, 110–12, 146–47, 159, 199; on
  geomancy, 147, 199; on tombs, 147
Ch'en Lai, 103n
Ch'en Liang, 138
Ch'en Tan, 119, 125–26
Cheng Chung, 39
Cheng communal family, 149–50, 183
Cheng Family Ceremonies, 149–50, 179
Cheng-ho wu-li hsin-i, 102, 105–7, 117, 119,
  151, 190, 223; cited by Chu Hsi, 116, 130;
  cited by Lü Tzu-ch'ien, 123
Cheng Hsüan, 19, 22n, 29
Cheng Pi-cho, 180
Cheng Po-hsiung, 130
Cheng Yü-ch'ing, 39
Cheng Yüan-ch'ing, 190
Cheng Yung, 150
Ch'eng brothers, 102, 135–36
Ch'eng Fan, 76
Ch'eng Hao, 48, 51, 63, 67